JON BALSERAK
SENT FOR REVIEW IN RRR
REC. ON SEPT 28 2009 ON THE
DAY I RETURNED TO ⟩ BRISTOL FROM PHILLY

THE THEOLOGY

of the

CZECH BRETHREN

from

HUS TO COMENIUS

The Theology
of the
Czech Brethren
from
Hus to Comenius

✠

Craig D. Atwood

THE PENNSYLVANIA STATE UNIVERSITY PRESS

UNIVERSITY PARK, PENNSYLVANIA

Library of Congress Cataloging-in-Publication Data

Atwood, Craig D.
The theology of the Czech Brethren from Hus to Comenius / Craig D. Atwood.
p.   cm.
Summary: "Examines the history and development of Moravian theology, from
its origins in the Hussite movement to the work of Comenius. Explores the
theology of the Unity of the Brethren within the context of the Protestant
Reformation"—Provided by publisher.
Includes bibliographical references (p.   ) and index.
ISBN 978-0-271-03532-1 (cloth : alk. paper)
1. Bohemian Brethren—Doctrines—History.
I. Title.

BX4923.A88 2009
230.46—dc22
2009001845

To My Bride, My other Self,
Grace, Faith, Elizabeth, and Hope,
Creed and Home,
Friends and Saints here and above,
Creator, Savior, and One who Blesses
One in love,
Unity

What does the Lord require of you but to do justice, and to love kindness,
and to walk humbly with your God?
—MICAH THE PROPHET

Faith without works is dead.
—JAMES THE JUST

Now faith, hope, and love abide, these three; and the greatest of these is love.
—PAUL OF TARSUS

Truth conquers all.
—JAN HUS

But since we believe that Christ won us from the Devil's power through the weakness
and humbleness of his Cross, we cannot agree that he causes our perfection in the faith
through secular power, as though power were more beneficial to us than faith.
—PETER CHELČICKÝ

We are people who have decided once and for all to be guided only by the gospel
and example of our Lord Jesus Christ and his holy apostles in gentleness, humility,
patience, and love for our enemies. By this we may do good to our enemies,
wish them well, and pray for them.
—GREGORY THE PATRIARCH

Why did God make you?
That I should know, worship, and love him,
and having his love, that I should be blissful.
—LUKE OF PRAGUE

Let everything flow of its own accord, let violence be absent from the process.
—JOHN AMOS COMENIUS

If we believe so with all our heart, let us follow after the things which make for peace.
—JOHN AMOS COMENIUS

The time will come, Comenius, when hosts of noble minded men will honour
what thou hast done, honouring as well the dreams of thy hopes.
—GOTTFRIED LEIBNIZ

Contents

✠

Illustrations

✝

Preface

✝

This book is a work of historical theology, but it may also be considered a work of cultural history. Its major purpose is to learn from the past by looking closely at the intersection of ideas and history. Rather than focus on dominant institutions, it examines how the Unity of the Brethren, a small free church in the Reformation era, approached the fundamental questions of life and faith. In doing so we may gain insights about religious faith and society today, but it is important to remember that learning from the past is different from being confined by the past. Entering into dialogue with those who have gone before is different from letting the dead answer the questions and longings of the living. Historical theology is the process of finding words and concepts that express the living faith of a community that extends through time and space.

The Unity of the Brethren was one fruit of the Czech Reformation's attempt to restore the Christian Church to its apostolic character as a community of the followers of Christ. It was the smallest of the three Hussite churches (Utraquist, Táborite, Brethren) that broke away from Rome decades before Martin Luther began questioning the sale of indulgences. Though the Unity has often been overlooked by western European and American historians, it was an important counterforce in the age of confessionalism and religious wars. Forged in the crucible of religious oppression and virtually destroyed by religious prejudice, the Unity persistently opposed the alliance of church and state while remaining an active participant in social and political reform. Highly disciplined and yet remarkably humanistic, the Brethren were pioneers in Protestant moral thought.

The Brethren's theology was profoundly simple: the essence of Christianity is faith, love, and hope. They turned away from elaborate ritual and metaphysical speculation and sought to return to the message of Christianity as given by Jesus in the Sermon on the Mount. More important, they structured their social and religious lives accordingly. This small community of faith consistently offered the voice of reason, toleration, and reconciliation in the face of war, persecution, and torture. Their story shows us that it is possible to live in faith, love, and hope despite the efforts of fanatics and demagogues to foment fear and violence. It is not clear how Christianity and world civilization will be transformed in the twenty-first century, but we have an opportunity to build a more just and benevolent social order if we choose.

Naturally, this work will have special relevance for anyone interested in the Unity of the Brethren, the Czech Reformation, or John Amos Comenius, but it is intended to be a resource for a broader audience as well. Historians of the early modern period should pay attention to the distinctive theology of the Unity of the Brethren as an independent voice among the louder and better-known Lutheran and Calvinist voices. The Unity demonstrates that the Protestant Reformation could have developed in a variety of ways. Those interested in the Radical Reformation and the history of pacifism should also pay attention to the first peace church to establish its own priesthood, write catechisms, and debate government officials.[1] Those interested in dissenter movements in Christianity will also find much of interest in the theology of the Czech Brethren.

Part of what complicates and confuses the history of the Unity of the Brethren is that the modern Moravian Church (Brüdergemeine in Germany) claims to be the direct descendent of the old Bohemian and Moravian or Czech Brethren. One of the last active bishops of the Unity, Daniel Ernst Jablonsky, recognized the Herrnhuters as Brethren when he laid hands on David Nitschmann and Nicholas von Zinzendorf as bishops of the Unitas Fratrum in the 1730s.[2] The period between the decree of expulsion from Bohemia and Moravia in 1627 and the arrival of Moravian refugees on Count Zinzendorf's estate is called the time of the Hidden Seed in the official historiography of the Moravian Church.[3]

---

1. David Martin, *Pacifism* (Boston: Routledge, 1998), 42.

2. J. Taylor Hamilton and Kenneth G. Hamilton, *History of the Moravian Church: The Renewed Unitas Fratrum, 1722–1957* (Bethlehem, Pa.: Moravian Church in America, 1967), 62–67; Friedrich Ludwig Kölbing, *Nachricht von dem Angange der bischöflichen Ordination in der erneuerten evangelischen Brüderkirche* (Gnadau, 1835); Joseph Müller, *Das Bischoftum der Brüder Unität* (Herrnhut, 1899).

3. Theodor Gill, "Zinzendorf und die Mähren," in *Graf ohne Grenzen: Leben und Werk von Nikolaus Ludwig Graf von Zinzendorf*, ed. Dieter Meyer and Paul Peucker (Herrnhut: Unitäts-archiv-Comeniusbuchhandlung, 2000), 37–42; Hamilton and Hamilton, *History of the Moravian Church*, 13–14.

The Brüdergemeine's ambitious mission to indigenous and enslaved peoples took them to the Caribbean, Pennsylvania, North Carolina, Surinam, and South Africa. In English-speaking lands they eventually adopted the name Moravian Church in honor of their roots in the church of Comenius. Thus the names of Hus and Comenius are known today in remote corners of the world, such as the Meskito Coast. Although Moravian Church historians continue to stress the connection between the Hussites and Zinzendorf's movement, there are reasons to doubt that the Moravian refugees had preserved their old church as a "Hidden Seed" or that it was revived by Zinzendorf.[4] Several Czech religious bodies that emerged in the nineteenth and twentieth centuries also lay claim to the heritage of the Unity and the Hussites but are not part of the Brüdergemeine. The purpose of this book is not to adjudicate competing claims to the heritage of the Brethren but to offer resources for all who wish to learn from their legacy.

This book examines the Unity of the Brethren as an independent church in its own right rather than as a forerunner to the Brüdergemeine. This approach allows the unique voice of the Brethren to speak to the wider world, but it may also challenge the Moravian Church's understanding of its origin and development. Normative stories serve to establish an institution's identity and provide for its continuation. People look for a "usable past" that justifies the present and lays a foundation for the future by creating a sense of belonging and identity. These stories are more than history; they function almost as myths, as grand narratives that establish meaning and sanctify current existence. This book corrects some aspects of the normative story of the Unity of the Brethren, such as their connection to the Waldensians. It has been easier and safer for generations of Moravians to repeat in ever simpler forms their traditional story rather than to probe the past and ponder the theological

---

4. W. R. Ward, "The Renewed Unity of the Brethren: Ancient Church, New Sect, or Interconfessional Movement?" *Bulletin of the John Rylands Library* 70 (1988): lxvii–xcii. In "Mährische Brüder, böhmische Brüder, und die Brüdergemeine," *Unitas Fratrum* 48 (2001): 106–14, Edita Sterik discusses the differences, for Zinzendorf, between the Moravian and the Bohemian Brethren. In "The Pious Fraud of Count Zinzendorf," *Iliff Review* 11 (1954): 29–38, Enrico Molnár accuses Zinzendorf of intentionally and systematically deceiving the Moravian emigrants into believing that he was renewing the church of their ancestors. For the Moravian Church's understanding of the relationship, see David Schattschneider, "The Unitas Fratrum and the 'Renewed' Moravian Church: Continuity and Change" (paper given at the Conference of the Czechoslovak Society of Arts and Sciences, Bethlehem, Pa., October 1989).

concerns that motivated their ancestors in the faith.[5] This book is written in the conviction that it is important for every generation to challenge the tale it has inherited and examine the actual history with fresh eyes and new insights provided by new perspectives. We can learn from the past only when we approach it directly and honestly.

One of the towering figures in this study is Jan Hus, who bequeathed to the Unity an unshakable conviction that ethics is part of doctrine. He used the pulpit and pen to oppose corruption and the oppression of the poor by the powerful. He defended the rights of the weak and urged priests to care for all of the needs of their flock. As he showed by his own example, servants of Christ are called to fulfill their duty even at the cost of their livelihoods and lives. Hus became the symbol of the Czech Reformation and remains an important figure to many Christians. Perhaps the best legacy of Hus is his motto "Truth will conquer." Truth is not a matter of repeating familiar clichés more loudly or frequently; it is a process of discernment in a way that makes sense in every generation. This, more than the specific problems Hus addressed or the theological ideas he promoted, remains his enduring legacy.

The Unity of the Brethren embraced the idea that while God is eternal, all things on this earth, including doctrine, are part of the process of history and change. Theology is an imperfect human effort to make sense of the reality of God and the work of God in the world in a particular time and place. This does not mean that there are no lasting truths or normative teachings for followers of Christ, but it does mean that the study of scripture, theology, and care of souls must take seriously the historical and cultural context of everything that has been expressed in human language. Failure to do so ensures the misunderstanding of both the past and the present. A misreading of the past limits our ability to face the future with hope and courage.

Paul Oskar Kristellar once wrote, "the record of the past in which all battles are decided and many pains forgotten, whereas the most distinguished characters, actions, and works stand out more clearly and in more final form

5. Truman Dunn, "Preserving the Unity: Community and Conflict in Moravian Church History" (Ph.D. diss., Union Theological Seminary, 1989), points to the fear of critical self-examination in the Moravian Church, but he identifies it as a pathological fear of conflict itself. "Throughout its history, the Moravian Church has sought to avoid or submerge conflict as a means of preserving the unity of the community." Dunn overstates the case here; in fact, the Brethren were frequently at odds with Catholics, Utraquists, Lutherans, Reformed, and Anabaptists.

than they did in their own time, may lull us into a false security and indolence in view of the pains we have to suffer, the decisions we have to make, the actions and works we have to accomplish, without yet knowing the outcome, or the value they may have if and when they appear in turn as a settled and hardened past to a future observer."[6] In the pages that follow, I try to recapture the significance of those old debates and show how they helped shape our contemporary world. We will see that the Unity of the Brethren pursued a different path from other religious groups, a path that holds promise for today.

By 1992 it looked like the Brethren's vision of a just and peaceful world was becoming a reality. After two world wars, humankind had indeed become weary of war, as Comenius predicted. It looked like humane values would triumph. The ecumenical movement made great progress in overcoming the divisions among Christians. Interfaith dialogue with other religions was becoming normal. The cold war ended without a nuclear exchange, and Eastern Europe was freed from Soviet totalitarianism. Comenius's vision of an institution where the leaders of the world could discuss ways to solve problems was realized in the United Nations. There was hope for a better future. But, as I write these words in 2008, the historical setting has changed. Religious fanaticism fuels murderous conflict and genocide around the world. American churches are riven by conflict over sexuality, and Christian nationalists promote the type of dominion rejected by the Brethren. The temperature of the oceans continues to rise, and deserts are expanding. The worst pandemic since the Black Death ravages Africa, while the rest of the world looks away. The struggle for peace, justice, freedom, decency, and truth continues. I believe that the witness of the Unity of the Brethren and Comenius is particularly relevant for these times. Faith, hope, and love are essential, particularly in the darkest times.

6. Paul Oskar Kristellar, *Renaissance Thought: The Classic, Scholastic, and Humanist Strains* (New York: Harper Torchbooks, 1961), 90.

Acknowledgments

✝

As a student at the Moravian Theological Seminary, I found that much of the discussion of Moravian theology was based on oral tradition and received assumptions rather than rigorous theological and historical study. I have felt for more than twenty years that there was a need for a book like this one, but I did not expect that I would be the one to write it, as my expertise is actually on Zinzendorf and the Brüdergemeine. I do not know Czech, so I have had to "stand on the back of giants," relying heavily on the publications of others. Among the most important scholars upon whose work I depended are Howard Kaminsky, Joseph Müller, Matthew Spinka, Amedeo Molnár, Rudolf Říčan, A. M. O. Dobbie, Jaroslav Pelikan, Murray Wagner, Peter Brock, Thomas Fudge, and David Holeton. Although I do not personally know any of these scholars, some of whom have died, I wish to express my gratitude to them all for their contributions to my knowledge of the Hussite tradition.

I owe personal words of gratitude to many friends and colleagues. First is C. Daniel Crews, archivist of the Moravian Church, Southern Province. Not only did I draw upon Daniel's research on Hus, Luke of Prague, and the history of the Unity, he read the entire manuscript when it was still a very rough draft. It benefited from his critique. My first in-depth exposure to the Unity and its rich heritage came when I was a student at the Moravian Theological Seminary, where David Schattschneider shared his vast knowledge of this rather obscure church. I wish to acknowledge David's contribution at the outset, since his name rarely appears in the footnotes. In addition to his oral history of the Unity, David supplied me with copies of many articles that are difficult to find. I also learned much from Anthony Grafton, who allowed me to participate in his seminar on early modern Europe at Princeton University. This helped me place the Unity in a wider historical context and allowed for an in-depth study of Comenius. Our discussions of Comenius in that seminar inspired Howard Louthan and Andrea Sterk to translate *The Labyrinth of the World,* for which many people are grateful. Another professor who deserves my gratitude is Peter Kaufman, who has supported me both professionally and intellectually. Some of the ideas in this book were formulated during a yearlong colloquium on religion and history led by Peter. Finally, it was Keith Stanley who provided an authoritative translation of Comenius's motto, *omnia sponte fluant, absit violentia rebus.* I also appreciate Keith's support for "Moravian common sense in doctrine."

I had hoped that Daniel Crews, David Schattschneider, or another Moravian historian would write an extensive study of the Unity, but the task fell to me owing to an unexpected series of events, the most important of which was being asked by Home Moravian Church to serve as their theologian in residence. I am deeply grateful to Home Church for making me part of their community of faith and providing the resources I needed for this project. Pastor Gerry Harris was the driving force behind this book and a valuable conversation partner during the writing of it. I am humbled now to hold the title of John Comenius Visiting Professor of Moravian Studies at Wake Forest University, a position established through Gerry's efforts. In this regard, Gene and Carol Ann Adcock also deserve special recognition. Other members of Home Church played valuable roles in this book, most notably Gil Frank, who proofread the entire manuscript, and Jonathan Hancock, who took time away from his studies at Dartmouth to read the manuscript and make sure that college students could understand it. My students in a seminar titled Heretics, Pacifists, and Teachers: Theology from Hus to Comenius also deserve credit for reading and responding to the manuscript.

Kathy Barnes, Jane Shore, Katrina Bodford, and Bonnie Dills provided various types of administrative support. Some three dozen members of Home Church endured a year of lectures on the Unity. Many of them also accompanied me on a trip to the Czech Republic, where I could lecture more on Táborites, defenestration, and exile while taking the photos for this book. I am grateful to another Moravian congregation, Hope Church, for their role in raising me in the faith, teaching me the love of Christ, and allowing me to ask questions. I cannot imagine my life without having that community of faith in my formative years. The year 2005 marked the 225th anniversary of that congregation and its gentle witness in the world. Hope provided the name of my eldest daughter and the final word in this book.

My four daughters remind me that it is unwise to live in the past without enjoying the possibilities of the future and the laughter of the present. They are present in subtle ways in this volume. It is encouraging that one of the greatest scholars of all time, Comenius, wrote many of his works out of his love for children. My deepest gratitude goes to my wife, Julie, the future Dr. Atwood, who endured long discussions about dead bishops, church disputes, pedagogy, theology, and faith, not to mention my many sleepless nights and distracted days over the past three years. She has helped me see many things more clearly and is a witness to the power of faith, love, and hope.

This book does not pretend to be the complete and final statement on the development of the Brethren's theology. It has weaknesses, but there are times when it is better to do something imperfectly than to do nothing perfectly. Mistakes can be corrected, but it is hard to overcome trivialization. This book is published in the hope that future scholars will correct its errors, refine its picture, and offer new and better insights. If it inspires a bright scholar to probe more deeply into the Brethren's theological heritage, even if his or her goal is to refute what is written here, then my labors will have been worthwhile.

Winston-Salem, North Carolina, 2008

INTRODUCTION

For more than two centuries, the Unity of the Brethren (in Latin, Unitas Fratrum) was a distinctive church with a supple theological tradition that allowed it to work for peace, justice, and reconciliation even in the midst of persecution. The Brethren developed new understandings of the Bible, sacraments, and church discipline that influenced the Protestant reformers of the sixteenth century. The Unity's writings were read with approval by reformers like Erasmus, Luther, Calvin, Melanchthon, Zell, and Bucer. In addition, the Unity published the first Protestant hymnals, and many of their hymns became part of the Protestant corpus. With their conviction that obedience to Jesus' ethical teaching is as important as doctrine, the Unity anticipated some of the themes and issues of the Radical Reformation and charted the path followed by the eighteenth-century Pietists and Methodists.[1] Throughout their history, the Brethren maintained a strict discipline with clear boundaries of membership, but they were also intentionally ecumenical. Their confessions of faith rejected rigid confessionalism and sought common ground with other churches on the essentials of the faith. Their doctrine insisted that faith must be completed in love, and their schools were based on the conviction that love rather than fear is the proper basis for learning.

---

1. Craig D. Atwood, "Separatism, Ecumenism, and Pacifism: The Bohemian and Moravian Brethren in the Confessional Age," in *Confessionalism and Pietism: Religious Reform in Early Modern Europe*, ed. Fred van Lieburg (Mainz: Verlag Philipp von Zabern, 2006), 71–90.

The first generation of Brethren formed a believers' church that separated itself from the secular world by refusing to swear oaths or participate in state-sanctioned violence. The second generation, acting from internal motivations rather than outside pressure, adopted a more positive stance toward society. This was one of the more remarkable transformations of a community of faith in the history of Christianity. Under the leadership of Luke of Prague, they transformed the Unity into a voluntary church that practiced infant baptism while repudiating the notion of a state church. The Unity can legitimately be considered the first voluntary church in Western history. As such, their understanding of the church as a community of faith within society set the pattern for many modern churches.

Throughout the Reformation era the Unity maintained its existence as a separate church while maintaining good relationships with other Protestant bodies, particularly the Reformed Church. Often subjected to persecution in their homeland, the Brethren were eventually driven into exile in Poland, where they dwindled into obscurity after 1648. Despite exile and the destruction of their institutional life, the Brethren had a lasting impact on Western civilization through the work of Bishop John Amos Comenius (1592–1670). Comenius produced some of the most important works ever written in the areas of education, social reform, and peacemaking. Comenius used the heritage of the Unity in his proposals for universal reform. Aware that the Unity he served was dying, he labored to preserve its distinctive theological heritage for the future. His works had a great impact beyond the confines of the Unity, and they continue to speak to reformers in the twenty-first century.

THE CZECH REFORMATION AND THE UNITY IN
HISTORICAL RESEARCH

This is the first book to focus on the theology of the Unity of the Brethren ever written in English. Despite the importance of the Unity of the Brethren and the Moravian Church to the development of Christianity and Western society, little attention has been given to their history and theology, especially among American scholars. Edmund de Schweinitz was the only American scholar to publish a history of the Unity (in 1885), which continued to be the standard text until the 1960s. Knowledge of the Hussite period and Comenius has progressed a great deal since de Schweinitz's day. In the 1990s C. Daniel Crews published his translation of Rudolf Říčan's 1957 history of the Unity, which had earlier appeared in German translation, but it deals only in cursory fashion with the theology of the Brethren.[2] In honor of the 550th anniversary of the founding of the Unity, Crews wrote a popular history of the church in 2007.[3]

Many factors contribute to historians' relative lack of attention to the Unity and its theology. First of all, the Unity's history does not fit neatly into the chronology generally employed in Western historiography: the patristic period of the church followed by the Middle Ages, the Protestant Reformation of the sixteenth century, and then the modern period. The Unity had roots in medieval reform movements that called the church to live in apostolic poverty. Many of these reform groups, such as the Waldensians, were condemned by the papacy as heretics.[4] Historians often discuss the Unity as a medieval heresy rather than an early Protestant church. It is interesting that few scholars would use the word "heresy" to discuss various Christian groups after the time of Luther but have no problem employing it for pre-sixteenth-century religious movements, such as the Unity.[5] By using the language of the dominant institution,

2. Edmund de Schweinitz, *The History of the Church Known as the Unitas Fratrum or The Unity of the Brethren, Founded by the followers of John Hus, the Bohemian Reformer and Martyr*, 2d ed. (Bethlehem, Pa.: Moravian Publications Office, 1901); Rudolf Říčan, *The History of the Unity of the Brethren: A Protestant Hussite Church in Bohemia and Moravia*, trans. C. Daniel Crews (Bethlehem, Pa.: Moravian Church in America, 1992).

3. C. Daniel Crews, *Faith, Love, and Hope: A History of the Unitas Fratrum* (Winston-Salem: Moravian Archives, 2008).

4. In his *Western Society and the Church in the Middle Ages*, vol. 2 of *The Penguin History of the Church*, ed. Owen Chadwick (London: Penguin Books, 1970), R. W. Southern manages to ignore the Hussites entirely. The Cathars and Lollards have attracted the most interest among medievalists, but two works in English highlight the history of the Unity within the context of late medieval "heretical" movements: Malcolm Lambert, *Medieval Heresy: Popular Movements from the Gregorian Reform to the Reformation*, 3d ed. (Oxford: Blackwell, 1992), and Gordon Leff, *Heresy in the Later Middle Ages: The Relation of Heterodoxy to Dissent, c. 1250–c. 1450*, 2 vols. (Manchester: Manchester University Press, 1967). Peter Biller, *The Waldenses, 1170–1530: Between a Religious Order and a Church* (Aldershot: Ashgate, 2001), gives a good critical examination of the historiography of medieval dissenter groups, particularly in British and American scholarship

5. Zdeněk V. David, *Finding the Middle Way: The Utraquists' Liberal Challenge to Rome and Luther* (Baltimore: Johns Hopkins University Press, 2003), 3–7, discusses how religious bias has influenced both Catholic and Protestant perceptions of the churches of the Czech Reformation as heretical. "The Czechs were considered a 'nation of heretics' par excellence, while no similar stigmatization seemed to be collectively inflicted on any nation producing or following the teachings of Luther, Zwingli, or Calvin" (5).

historians have contributed to the marginalization and silencing of dissenters such as the Brethren and the Waldensians.

Since it began before Luther's reform, the Czech Reformation is often ignored by Reformation historians, even though it anticipated many of the themes of the sixteenth-century reformations. The only question that has attracted significant attention by Reformation historians through the years has been whether the Hussites had any influence on Martin Luther.[6] There has been little interest in the Brethren and their continuing existence for their own sake outside of central Europe, but this is changing. Increasingly, historians have noted that not a single reformation began with Luther's posting of the Ninety-five Theses in 1517.[7] Luther's work was a dramatic episode in a two-hundred-year period of reformation and division in the Western church. Many scholars today refer to an "age of reform" to indicate that there was more than one reformation.

Czech historians and theologians in the mid-twentieth century introduced the term "First Reformation" to describe the variety of late medieval and early modern reform movements, such as the Franciscans, Waldensians, Beghards, Beguines, *devotio moderna*, Hussites, and Anabaptists, who advocated a praxis approach to reform rather than the doctrinal approach of magisterial reformers like Luther and Calvin.[8] Historians in general have not adopted the term "First Reformation" for several good reasons. For one thing, it is hard to establish historical connections between these diverse groups, some of which promoted Catholic doctrine and some of which rejected the papacy as the Antichrist. Plus, the so-called First Reformation did not include the sweeping social, economic, cultural, artistic, and political changes associated with the reformations of the sixteenth century that are of interest to most historians.[9] There is also

6. Jarold Knox Zeman, *The Hussite Movement and the Reformation in Bohemia, Moravia, and Slovakia, 1350–1650: A Bibliographical Study Guide* (Ann Arbor: Center for Reformation Research, 1977), 232–38.

7. Hans J. Hillerbrand, "Was There a Reformation in the Sixteenth Century?" *Church History* 72 (2003): 525–52, provides a useful overview of the historiography of the Reformation. In *Reformation of Church and Dogma (1300–1700)*, the fourth volume of his magisterial history of Christian doctrine, *The Christian Tradition: A History of the Development of Doctrine*, 5 vols. (Chicago: University of Chicago Press, 1971–89), Jaroslav Pelikan takes a broader view of the Reformation, treating Hussites, Catholic reformers, and Protestants in a single volume in order to demonstrate their interdependence.

8. For a brief discussion of this idea, see Amedeo Molnár, "The Brethren's Theology," in Říčan, *History of the Unity*, 390–92. For a longer discussion, see Jan Milíč Lochman, *Living Roots of the Reformation* (Minneapolis: Augsburg, 1979), 71–96.

9. A tremendous amount of research has been done on the religious, social, and political aspects of

the fact that terms such as "first" and "second" merely increase divisions between such movements rather than move toward a more accurate analysis of the complexities of the early modern period.

Perhaps it is best to use the term "Czech Reformation" to distinguish the history of religious and political conflict in Bohemia and Moravia in the fifteenth century from the German, Swiss, Scottish, and English reformations that took place in the next century.[10] One can also use the term "Hussite Reformation" because of the prominent role played by the martyr Jan Hus as the key figure of the Czech Reformation, just as one may speak of the Lutheran Reformation. In using the word "Hussite," though, it is important to keep in mind that the reform effort in Bohemia had been active years before Hus began preaching in the city of Prague.

Another factor in the relative lack of interest in the history of the Brethren and their theology is the problem of language. Most of the source materials and secondary scholarship for the Unity is in Czech, often in hard-to-obtain sources.[11] The language barrier has prevented most English-speaking scholars, including scholars of the Moravian Church, from examining the Unity. It is possible, however, to study the theology of the Unity through the sources that have been translated by Czech and German scholars, which is what I have done. There are works of superior scholarship on the Hussite heritage, such as Josef Müller's monumental history of the Unity, grounded firmly in the records of the Unity itself, but more extensive translation of original and secondary sources is needed.

HISTORICAL OVERVIEW OF THE CZECH REFORMATION

Because most people are unfamiliar with the history of the Czech Reformation and the Unity of the Brethren, a timeline is provided in the Appendix to

the sixteenth-century reformations. A good place to begin is Steven E. Ozment, ed., *Reformation Europe: A Guide to Research* (St. Louis: Center for Reformation Research, 1982). Very little on the Hussites, other than Hus himself, is given.

10. For example, see Robert Scribner, Roy Porter, and Mikuláš Teich, eds., *The Reformation in National Context* (Cambridge: University of Cambridge Press, 1994), which includes a chapter on Bohemia and Moravia.

11. Though dated, Zeman's *Hussite Movement* provides a valuable list of sources on the Hussite movement available in North American libraries.

help orient the reader. The primary goal of this book is to introduce English-speaking audiences to the richness of the Brethren's theological heritage, so I have used the anglicized version of many names of persons and places. This is especially true of first names: Matěj becomes Matthew; Řehoř, Gregory; Jiří, George; Vaclav, Wenceslas; Lukáš, Luke; Mikulás, Nicholas; Petr, Peter; and Tůma, Thomas. I hope this makes the book easier to read without causing confusion, but when quoting other scholars I have left the names as they wrote them.

Before examining the theology of the Unity in detail, a brief overview of the Czech Reformation may be helpful. At the end of fourteenth century there was an effort to reform the Catholic Church in the kingdoms of Bohemia and Moravia (the modern Czech Republic) in the face of numerous abuses. Jan Hus (1369–1415), the rector of the University of Prague and a Catholic theologian, emerged as the leader of this Czech reform. He was popular with the laity because he called for priests to remember their vows of poverty and to serve as shepherds rather than lords. Hus was burned at the stake as a heretic by the Council of Constance in 1415 because of his insistence that the church of his day was in error and had erred in the past. He also asserted that the Bible and plain reason, not canon law, are the final authority in the church. Some of Hus's most important ideas became part of general Protestant teaching during the sixteenth century.

After Hus's execution the kingdom of Bohemia openly rebelled against the Holy Roman emperor and the pope. The Czech Reformation developed into one of the first genuine political revolutions in Europe in 1419.[12] Invoking the name of "Saint Jan Hus," the people of Bohemia rose up against their monarch, established new political orders, and created two churches that were formally separated from the papacy. Though rarely mentioned in histories of Christianity, these were the first enduring non-Catholic Western churches that endorsed the ancient confessions of faith (the Nicene and Apostles' Creeds).

---

12. Howard Kaminsky, *A History of the Hussite Revolution* (Berkeley and Los Angeles: University of California Press, 1967); František Šmahel, "The Hussite Movement: An Anomaly of European History?" in *Bohemia in History*, ed. Mikulás Teich (Cambridge: Cambridge University Press, 1988), 79–97; Josef Macek, *The Hussite Movement in Bohemia*, trans. Vilèm Fried and Ian Milner (Prague: Orbis, 1965); František M. Bartoš, *The Hussite Revolution, 1424–1437*, trans. and ed. John M. Klassen (New York: Columbia University Press, 1986); Frederick G. Heymann, *Jan Žižka and the Hussite Revolution* (Princeton: Princeton University Press, 1955). Marxist historians in eastern Europe obviously emphasized the political and revolutionary aspects of the Hussite movement.

FIG. 1   Statue of Jan Hus in the Old Town Square in Prague.

Hus's followers took the radical step of giving the laity permission to drink from the chalice during Holy Communion, in direct violation of church law. The chalice became the symbol of resistance to the papacy among all the Hussite parties. Five crusades were launched against the Hussites in the fifteenth century, but none of them was successful.[13] Hussite soldiers used the chalice as their coat of arms as they defended the right of all people to be included in the full communion of the church. The more moderate Hussites were called Utraquists, from the Latin phrase for "communion in both kinds," that is, bread and wine. In the sixteenth century the monarchs of England and Sweden established national ecclesiastical bodies, the Church of England and the Church of Sweden, but by that time the Bohemian Church was more than a century old.[14] For much of its history, the Utraquist consistory hoped for reconciliation with Rome, but this never happened. Throughout its history the Utraquist Church relied on Catholic bishops outside Bohemia to ordain its priests.[15]

The most radical of the Hussite groups, the Táborites, were inspired by apocalyptic prophecies about the end of the reign of the Antichrist and the coming of the New Jerusalem.[16] Inspired by apocalyptic zeal, they formed the most effective portion of the Hussite army, and they used force of arms to promote a more complete reform of the church. Though they frequently fought each other with words as well as swords, the Utraquists and Táborites managed to agree on the famous Four Articles of Prague as a basis for church reform.[17] The articles demanded that (1) the Word of God should be preached everywhere, freely; (2) all believers should receive both the body and the blood of Christ reverently from baptism until death; (3) the clerical order must be

13. Frederick G. Heymann, "The Crusades Against the Hussites," in *The Fourteenth and Fifteenth Centuries*, ed. Harry W. Hazard, 586–648, vol. 3 of *A History of the Crusades*, ed. Kenneth M. Sutton (Madison: University of Wisconsin Press, 1975), 27–41.

14. See David, *Finding the Middle Way*, for a detailed study of the Bohemian national church.

15. Ibid. The Utraquists' desire to reconcile with Rome has been a source of confusion for both Protestant and Catholic historians through the centuries.

16. Craig D. Atwood, *Always Reforming: A History of Christianity Since 1300* (Macon: Mercer University Press, 2001), 48–54. A good brief introduction to the Táborites in the context of other millennialist movements in medieval Europe can be found in Norman Cohn, *The Pursuit of the Millennium*, 2d ed. (New York: Oxford University Press, 1970). Unfortunately, Cohn undervalues the sophistication of the Táborite Church and its importance for Protestant history.

17. The full text of the Four Articles is found in Jaroslav Pelikan and Valerie Hotchkiss, eds., *Creeds and Confessions of Faith in the Christian Tradition*, 3 vols. (New Haven: Yale University Press, 2003), 1:793–95.

reformed and simony abolished; and (4) sin, including sins of the clergy and rulers, should be punished and destroyed.

The Council of Basel, which met from 1431 to 1449, was called by Pope Martin V after the shocking defeat of the imperial army at the Battle of Domažlice in August 1431 by Prokop Holý's Hussite army. It had become evident that the Hussites could not be forced to submit to the papacy by force of arms; therefore the Catholic Church tried to come to an agreement with them. Utraquist, Táborite, and Catholic representatives agreed on terms for negotiation, called the Judge of Cheb (for the town in which it was signed), and the Hussites defended the Four Articles of Prague at the Council. The Utraquists compromised and signed an agreement with the Catholics called the Compacta. They made a military alliance with the Catholics against the Táborites, and Holý's forces were for the first time defeated in battle, at Lipany in 1434. The last stronghold, the city of Tábor, surrendered to the king in 1452 and accepted the authority of the Utraquist bishop of Prague, Jan Rokycana.

Around the time that the city of Tábor was preparing to surrender to the king, Rokycana's nephew, a young man of the lesser nobility named Gregory (Řehoř) (c. 1425–1474) became interested in the radical side of the Hussite movement. He read the works of the most original Hussite thinker, Peter Chelčický (c. 1380–c. 1458), who had distanced himself from the violence of the Hussite revolution. Using Chelčický's theology as a guide, Gregory and a small band of friends who were dissatisfied with the worldliness of the Utraquist Church formed a small Christian community in the winter of 1457–58 in Kunwald in eastern Bohemia.[18] They called themselves the Unity of the Brethren, and their theology stressed humility, discipline, peacefulness, and simplicity in worship and life. In 1467 the Brethren established their own priesthood and episcopacy, marking the real founding of the church.

As the first generation of Brethren died off, there was dissension over the elders' strict application of biblical teaching. This dissension led to open schism around 1495. The Minor Party wanted to keep strictly to the writings of Gregory, while the Major Party, led by Luke (Lukáš) of Prague (c. 1460–1528), opted for more engagement with the world. The Minor Party, for the most

---

18. The best history of the Unity of the Brethren available in English is Říčan's *History of the Unity.* The most comprehensive history is Joseph Müller, *Geschichte der böhmischen Brüder,* 3 vols. (Herrnhut: Verlag der Missionsbuchhandlung, 1922–31).

part, joined with the Anabaptists in Moravia. Luke led the main branch of the Unity for decades and was instrumental in establishing much of the doctrine and practice of the Unity. As such, he is a major focus of study in this book.

Luke also had direct contact with Martin Luther, and he criticized the German reformer's idea of justification by faith alone. As early as the Leipzig Disputation in 1419, Luther recognized many similarities between his critique of Catholic doctrine and the thought of Hus. After the death of the conservative and scholastic Luke, the Unity embraced key Protestant doctrines, most notably that there are only two sacraments, and the Brethren established close connections with the reformers Phillip Melanchthon and Martin Bucer. Many Unity pastors and theologians studied at Wittenberg, Geneva, Herborn, and Heidelberg, where they learned Lutheran and Reformed theology while introducing the doctrine and practice of the Unity to key figures in Protestantism. The Unity suffered from periods of persecution in Bohemia throughout the sixteenth century, and their principal bishop, Jan Augusta (1500–1572), was imprisoned for sixteen years at midcentury. Thanks in part to persecution, the Unity spread to Poland and Hungary, where it had close ties to the Reformed Church.

In the early seventeenth century, when the Habsburg emperor Ferdinand II threatened to extinguish all religious dissent in his realm, the Brethren in Bohemia joined with other Czech Protestants in rebellion. With the support of the Utraquists and Unity, the nobility crowned Frederick V, the elector of the Palatinate, rather than Emperor Ferdinand, king of Bohemia. This began the Thirty Years' War (1618–48), which led to the destruction of the Unity. After the defeat of the Protestants at the Battle of White Mountain in 1620, the Habsburgs set out to re-Catholicize Bohemia and Moravia. Many of the Brethren fled into exile, especially to Poland, where they had already established congregations. The Unity was left out of the Peace of Westphalia in 1648, which granted toleration to the Reformed churches, and the fate of the church was sealed. Recognizing that his church was dying, Bishop Comenius wrote several works to preserve its witness. Though scattered remnants of the Brethren survived at least until the nineteenth century in Poland, Hungary, and Prussia, the Unity itself largely died out in the seventeenth century.

In his last years Comenius published a variety of resources to preserve the heritage of the Unity of the Brethren, including an account of the Unity's doctrine and order, called the *Ratio disciplinae*.[19] This last work in particular helped pass on the heritage of the Brethren to the emerging Pietist movement of the eighteenth century. In 1702 August Hermann Francke, head of the famous Pietist institutions in Halle, published Comenius's *Panegersia, or Universal Awakening*, the introduction to his ambitious plans for the reformation of church and society.[20] Another Halle professor, Johann Franz Buddeus, republished Comenius's *Ratio disciplinae*.[21] The Pietists sought to renew the spiritual life of the church in Germany and the Netherlands. Much like the Brethren, they emphasized the idea of spiritual rebirth, formation of Christian communities, and social ministry.[22] John Wesley, the founder of the Methodists, was profoundly influenced by the Pietists. In the judgment of one early Pietist leader, "The Bohemian community had apparently come very near to being the ideal community of the New Testament in terms of church order, discipline, and moral life."[23]

Remnants of the Brethren in Moravia found refuge on the estate of Count Nicholas von Zinzendorf in Upper Lusatia in the 1720s. There they formed the core of a new Pietist church called the Brüdergemeine (Community of the Brethren).[24] In 1727, Zinzendorf, who had studied with Francke, used the

19. An English translation of the *Ratio* is available at http://www.moravianarchives.org/images/pdfs/Ratio.pdf.

20. Karel Rýdl, "John Amos Comenius in the Development of European Pedagogical and Philosophical Thinking in the Eighteenth Century," in *Homage to J. A. Comenius*, ed. Jaroslava Pešková, Josef Cach, and Michal Svatoš, trans. Vladimír Kosina, Zdenka Marečková, Paula Novotná-Tipton, and Peter Svobodný (Prague: Karolinum, 1991), 171–79.

21. These were translated into German and published in 1739. Comenius, *Kurtzgefaßte Kirchenhistorie der böhmischen Brüder* (Schwabach, 1739), reprinted in *Quellen zur Geschichtsschreibung der böhmischen Brüder*, vol. 4 of *Nicholas Ludwig von Zinzendorf: Materialien und Dokumente*, ed. Erich Beyreuther, Gerhard Meyer, and Amedeo Molnár (Hildesheim: Georg Olms, 1980).

22. W. R. Ward, *The Protestant Evangelical Awakening* (Cambridge: Cambridge University Press, 1992); Ted Campbell, *Religion of the Heart: A Study of European Religious Life in the Seventeenth and Eighteenth Centuries* (Columbia: University of South Carolina Press, 1991); F. Ernest Stoeffler, *The Rise of Evangelical Pietism* (Leiden: E. J. Brill, 1965); and Stoeffler, *German Pietism During the Eighteenth Century* (Leiden: E. J. Brill, 1973).

23. Leendert F. Groenendijk and Johan C. Sturm, "Das Exempel Böhmens in den Niederlanden: Comenius' Bedeutung für die familienpädagogische Offensive der pietischen Reformation," *Zeitschrift für Pädagogik* 38 (1992): 168.

24. David Cranz, *The Ancient and Modern History of the Brethren*, trans. and rev. Benjamin LaTrobe (London, 1780); Joseph Müller, *Zinzendorf als Erneuerer der alten Brüderkirche* (Leipzig, 1900); J. Taylor Hamilton, *The Recognition of the Unitas Fratrum as an Old Protestant Episcopal Church by the Parliament of Great Britain in 1749* (Nazareth, Pa.: Moravian Historical Society, 1925); Hamilton and Hamilton, *History of the Moravian Church*, 23–33; Colin Podmore, *The Moravian Church in England, 1728–1760* (Oxford: Clarendon Press, 1998), 160–67.

Ratio disciplinae and Buddeus's account of the Brethren as one of the resources in the formation of the Herrnhut community. Comenius's grandson, Daniel Ernst Jablonsky, recognized the Herrnhuters as Brethren when he laid hands on David Nitschmann and Nicholas von Zinzendorf, making them bishops of the Unity of the Brethren.[25] In America the Brüdergemeine adopted the name Moravian Church in the nineteenth century to emphasize its connection to Hus and the Czech Brethren, but the original Unity died in the seventeenth century.

THE EUCHARIST, HERESY, AND REVOLUTION

One of the difficulties of dealing adequately with the past is that so many issues for which people were once willing to die are now so commonplace that we can hardly imagine why there was a controversy to begin with. Many theological issues that once gave life to a community of faith today seem quaint or even disturbing. Much of what vexes and inspires us today will likewise be confusing or irrelevant to future generations. One of these issues from Christian history is the lay chalice, which was the unifying symbol for the Hussites. In order to make sense of the Czech Reformation, it will be helpful to look briefly at the history of the Eucharist in Western Christianity and its connection to political life.

The Eucharist, or Holy Communion, is the central ritual of Christianity.[26] It is a simple meal of bread and wine taken in worship as a way to participate in the life, sufferings, and death of Jesus Christ. It is a visible and tangible "means of grace," or a mode of spiritual blessing. It also provides worshippers with a connection to previous generations of Christians and symbolizes the unity of the church. In short, the Eucharist is a meal that helps define the nature of a Christian community. Those who are allowed to take Holy Communion are in the church. Unbelievers, infidels, heretics, and others deemed

25. Hamilton and Hamilton, *History of the Moravian Church*, 62–67; Kölbing, *Nachricht von dem Angange*; Müller, *Bischoftum der Brüder Unität*.
26. For an introduction to the historical development of the eucharistic rite from the New Testament to the present, see Cheslyn Jones, Geoffrey Wainwright, and Edward Yarnold, eds., *The Study of Liturgy* (New York: Oxford University Press, 1978), 147–288.

unworthy may not share the meal. Over the centuries, the Eucharist became a powerful tool for discipline and control in the church, and as the church expanded and exerted more influence in society, the Eucharist became a political tool of social control as well.

Miri Rubin sums up the complex relationship between the church's claims to universal authority in the Middle Ages and the development of the Catholic Mass or Eucharist: "Out of a wide range of religious practices and diverse understandings of the place of priests in communities, a new blueprint was carefully drawn, one which could bring together disparate regions and peoples through adherence to a single ritual practice and a shared ethical and mythical framework. . . . Within the cultural system of this world and the language of sacramental religion which communicated so many of its meanings, the Eucharist offered access to the supernatural, grace, hope for salvation, and a framework for meaning in human relations."[27] In other words, as the Roman Catholic Church was attempting to create a Christian society obedient to its teachings, what we call Christendom, the Eucharist became a primary means to compel conformity and universality. Since it had become a central focus of meaning and unity of church and society, it is not surprising that this ritual would be a focus of controversy during periods of social and political strife.

A key component of the history of the Eucharist is the development of the doctrine of transubstantiation in the Catholic Church. For centuries Christians had taken Jesus' words in the Gospels ("this is my body") more or less literally, but theologians were content to view the body and blood of Christ in the Eucharist as a mystery. During the Middle Ages there was a lively debate among scholar-monks over the nature of this mystery, and the papacy felt a need for greater definition of the Eucharist. In the thirteenth century, Scholastic theologians used Aristotelian philosophy to give intellectual respectability to the claim that a miracle occurs each time the Mass is celebrated. The outward appearance (or accidents) of the bread and wine remains unchanged, but the priest transforms the *essence* or substance of the bread and wine completely into the body and blood of Christ. This doctrine, called transubstantiation, was decreed the official dogma of the Roman Catholic Church by the

---

27. Miri Rubin, *Corpus Christi: The Eucharist in Late Medieval Culture* (Cambridge: Cambridge University Press, 1991), 12–13.

Fourth Lateran Council in 1215.[28] It became heresy to teach any other view or even to question the official dogma, and in the fourteenth century "the doctrine of transubstantiation comes to be more a question of the authority of the post-apostolic Church than of the understanding of the Eucharist."[29]

For most of Christian history, the laity drank the blood of Christ from the cup, just like the priest, during communion. When the Catholic Church developed the doctrine of transubstantiation, though, eucharistic practices changed. As the Mass became a regularly repeated miracle performed by the priest, there was a growing fear that the unwashed masses would profane the sacred. This fear that the laity would spill Christ's blood was closely connected to the growing power of the church and its clergy as a separate order of society. "As the church came to be the articulator of hegemonic culture, of the symbolic order of the world," Rubin explains, "the place and role, education and privilege of the clergy, were reconsidered. . . . Priests were seen as teachers but above all as ritual performers of sacramental acts, those acts which tie the Christian world to God through repeated, and reiterated procedures that only the priest could perform."[30] There was a clear division between the priests and the laity that was symbolized by who could drink the blood of Christ.[31]

Communion in one kind, that is, with bread alone, became the normal practice of the Catholic Church and was officially proclaimed dogma by the Fourth Lateran Council in 1215.[32] Only ordained priests could commune "in both kinds." Gradually theologians adopted the idea of "concomitance" to justify the denial of the cup to the laity. Concomitance meant that when the wafer, or host, was consecrated by the priest with the words "this is my body," it became the full body of Christ, complete with blood. Since the laity, theoretically, received the blood along with the body, there was no longer any reason for them to drink from the cup. Reports of miracles associated with the host,

---

28. Ibid., 14–32; Jaroslav Pelikan, *Christian Tradition*, vol. 3, *The Growth of Medieval Theology (600– 1300)* (Chicago: University of Chicago Press, 1978), 74–80, 202–4.

29. Pelikan, *Christian Tradition*, 4:56.

30. Rubin, *Corpus Christi*, 49–50.

31. It should be noted that this was the case only in the Roman Catholic Church. The laity continued to receive both bread and wine in the Eastern Orthodox churches, but in those churches the division between clergy and laity was symbolized by the iconostasis, which screened the altar from the worshippers.

32. Rubin, *Corpus Christi*, 72. There is a thirteenth-century picture of a priest serving the chalice to laypersons who are drinking through a straw, presumably to avoid spilling the blood.

especially visions of a bleeding host, proliferated in the fourteenth and fifteenth centuries and were used as evidence of concomitance.[33]

Because of the miracle of transubstantiation, the laity could adore the actual body of Christ in their local church. The consecrated host was often kept in a pyx or monstrance on the altar, and the faithful were instructed to revere the host just as they would Jesus. When a priest took communion to those too sick to attend services, he was instructed to carry the host in a solemn procession with bells and candles. Gradually this procession of the host through the streets developed into a new Corpus Christi (Body of Christ) festival of the church, introduced in the thirteenth century.[34] The adoration of the host quickly became an important part of lay devotion throughout Europe.

There is little evidence that the laity expressed concern over being denied the cup or that theologians objected to the doctrine of concomitance before 1400. In fact, there seems to have been little interest among the laity in the fifteenth century in taking communion at all. Most were content to adore the consecrated host. The various dissenting movements in the late Middle Ages, such as the Waldensians, did not make the lay chalice an issue, although some dissenters objected to the pomp of Catholic worship.[35] It appears that the Hussite priest Jakoubek of Stříbro was the first priest in western Europe publicly to offer the chalice to laypersons in defiance of Catholic teaching.

For centuries it was the lay chalice that kept all of the Hussite churches separated from Rome. The papacy's refusal to tolerate the practice of the lay chalice indicates that there were more substantive issues involved than fear of spilling the blood of Christ. Advocates and critics alike saw clearly that access to the chalice was symbolic of all the other issues of the Czech Reformation, especially the political power of the church. In the 1960s, reforming cardinals and theologians at the Second Vatican Council approved giving the cup to the laity and even allowed laypersons to assist in serving communion. This step was connected to the new official definition of the church as the "people of God," which had been central to the Czech Reformation.[36] It took only 550 years for

33. Ibid., 71, 108–29.

34. Ibid., 74–82.

35. Euan Cameron, *Waldenses: Rejections of Holy Church in Medieval Europe* (Oxford: Blackwell, 2000), 149.

36. Pelikan, *Christian Tradition*, vol. 5, *Christian Doctrine and Modern Culture (Since 1700)* (Chicago: University of Chicago Press, 1989), 326–36. For more information on Vatican II, see the *Doctrinal Decrees*

the Hussite reform to transform the entire Christian world. Today almost all Christians are able to drink from the chalice during Holy Communion.

THEOLOGY OF THE UNITY

The Unity of the Brethren represented a type of "third way" in Protestantism in the early modern period. Though closely aligned with the Lutheran and Reformed churches, many aspects of the Brethren's doctrine and practice were similar to the Anabaptists. For instance, the Unity advocated separation of church and state, and the Brethren's ethics was based on the Sermon on the Mount. In dealing with other churches and changing social circumstances, the Unity adapted its doctrine, but we will see that the Unity of the Brethren had a clear and consistent theological tradition that was supple enough to adapt to changing historical situations. From Gregory to Comenius that tradition was expressed in ever more sophisticated ways, but it was based on several core convictions. Seven of these are identified and discussed in detail at the end of the book, but it may help to discuss them briefly at the beginning as well.

1. The continual search for sound doctrine was a theological principle for the Unity. The Brethren rejected the notion that a church can write an authoritative statement of faith for all time. This approach allowed the Brethren to be flexible as society changed. The Unity understood that doctrine is simply a way to learn from the insights of the past in order to live faithfully in the present while wisely preparing for the future.[37] Without a rich and supple doctrinal tradition, there is nothing to unite the community of faith other than bureaucracy, inertia, habit, and class consciousness. As a community changes as part of the flow of history and the gaining of new insights, its teachings will change. Thus it is not surprising that the doctrine of the Unity changed over time.

2. The Unity taught that the church must distinguish between those things that are essential to salvation and those that minister to salvation. The essentials

---

of the Second Vatican Council, in Pelikan and Hotchkiss, *Creeds and Confessions*, 3:540–673. The most important statement of the council is *Lumen gentium*, which defines the church as the "people of God."

37. This idea is explored in more depth and greater nuance by Douglas John Hall, *Professing the Faith*, vol. 2 of Hall, *Christian Theology in a North American Context*, 3 vols. (Minneapolis: Fortress Press, 1996), 1–21.

for the Brethren were the work of God the Father, Son, and Holy Spirit in creation, redemption, and sanctification; and, second, that humans must respond to God in faith, love, and hope. God provides the priesthood, sacraments, vestments, and even the scriptures to lead people to the essential matters. This may have been the Brethren's most important contribution to Christian theology in general. It was the foundation for their ecumenical activity and the means by which they were able to adapt to changing circumstances.

3. The Brethren created the first truly voluntary church in Western history. They associated the state church with the emperor Constantine, who they believed brought the oppression and violence of the Roman Empire into the church. If the church wanted to follow the teachings of Jesus rather than Caesar, then it would have to reject political authority. Despite pressure from the magisterial reformers in Wittenberg and Geneva, the Unity never abandoned this foundation of its faith. The Brethren also taught that there is no true Christianity without a visible community of love. Their understanding of Christian community was inspired by the example of the early church of the apostles.

4. One of the fundamental impulses of the Czech Reformation was the effort to provide scripture in the language of the people and to make scripture the law of the church. It was the Brethren who provided the definitive translation of the Bible in Czech. They made a clear distinction between the Gospels, which were binding on the followers of Christ, and the Old Testament, which was not. The Eucharist was also vital to the life of the Unity, and the chalice was one of the symbols of the church. The Brethren taught that Christ was truly spiritually present in the Eucharist. It was a communion with Christ.

5. The Brethren placed greater emphasis on orthopraxy (right action) than on orthodoxy (right belief). Christianity was not a theoretical science for the Brethren; it was the art of following Christ in the real world. This meant that social ethics (based on the Sermon on the Mount) was a part of the Brethren's theology in a more intense way than it was for other Protestants. The Brethren disagreed with Luther over the importance of the Epistle of James for Christian teaching. They based their theology and praxis on the Epistle of James, which asserts that without works, faith is dead. The Unity's moral teaching may be understood as an interesting blend of Anabaptist and Reformed ethics, but its doctrine predated both of those Christian traditions and was more Christocentric in its development of ethics. The Brethren called themselves

Brethren of the Law of Christ, and they maintained this identity despite the criticism of Protestants and Catholics alike.

6. Education was central to the doctrine of the Unity. The Brethren believed that people grow in faith, understanding, and ability to follow Christ. They published the first Protestant catechisms and helped define the Protestant understanding of confirmation as a rite of personal profession of faith for those baptized as children. It was this idea of pedagogy and growth in love that connected the Unity to the sixteenth-century humanists, although the Brethren were not sophisticated scholars. Comenius is the most famous proponent of the Brethren's pedagogical view of religious faith.

7. Throughout their history, the Brethren witnessed to Christ as the Prince of Peace who calls his followers to love even their enemies. The Brethren taught that Christian love is by its nature nonviolent and not coercive. This applies to education, home life, economics, and politics. The Unity was not always dogmatically pacifist, but its members avoided violence as inconsistent with the ethic of love. They simply could not understand how people could love their neighbors while torturing or killing them.

The Unity was a product of the Czech Reformation and shared many of the convictions of that fifteenth-century movement, and the encounter with the Protestant Reformation of the sixteenth century brought changes to the Unity, but the Brethren also brought the convictions of the Czech Reformation into the discussions of the sixteenth century. The writings of the Brethren lack the grandeur of Luther's works or the systematic rigor of Calvin, but the Brethren made distinctive and important contributions to Western Christianity. Ernst Troeltsch noted that the historic influence of the Hussite movement was "both extensive and profound," particularly in the area of social doctrine.[38]

---

38. Ernst Troeltsch, *The Social Teachings of the Christian Churches*, trans. Olive Wyon, 2 vols. (New York: Macmillan, 1931), 1:368.

Part One

THE CZECH REFORMATION

One

PRAGUE AND OXFORD

The Unity of the Brethren was organized sometime in 1457 or 1458 in Kunwald in northeast Bohemia, but its roots go back to the Czech Reformation. While a book on theology cannot do justice to the fascinating history of the Czech Reformation and the ensuing Hussite Wars, it is necessary to have some understanding of the roots of the Unity if we are to make sense of the distinctive emphases of the Unity's theology. The story of the Brethren's theology begins in the middle of the fourteenth century, when the Holy Roman emperor Charles IV (1316–1378, emperor 1355–78) made Prague the capital of the empire.

PRAGUE AND CHARLES IV

Charles IV was one of the most effective medieval rulers. His Golden Bull of 1356 stabilized imperial elections for centuries, and he tried to create a centralized state in Bohemia.[1] He was fluent in German, Spanish, French, Latin, and even Czech. His father, John of Luxemburg, had given Charles authority over the strategically important kingdom of Bohemia, and when Charles became

---

1. František Kavka, "Politics and Culture Under Charles IV," in Tiech, *Bohemia in History*, 59–77; Thomas Fudge, *The Magnificent Ride: The First Reformation in Hussite Bohemia* (Aldershot: Ashgate, 1998), 5–15. For more on Charles, see Ferdinand Seibt, ed., *Kaiser Karl IV: Staatsmann und Mäzen* (Munich: Adalbert-Stifter-Verein, 1978).

king and Roman emperor (elected 1346, crowned 1355), he made Prague his capital. Unlike many medieval rulers, Charles was more interested in the prosperity and health of his realm than in pursuing chivalric dreams of battlefield glory. He built the beautiful stone bridge across the Vltava River in Prague that unites the Lesser Town with the Old Town, whose main public square is in front of the Týn Church. Lesser Town is the site of Hradčany Castle, the seat of government, and Saint Vitus Cathedral, the seat of the bishop.

Perhaps Charles IV's most important achievement was the establishment of a university in 1356 in the Old Town. Now known as Charles University, this was the first university in central Europe. Many of the faculty came from Germany, but Charles encouraged the development of a native Czech faculty. Many of the key figures in the Czech reform movement, including Jan Hus, were masters of philosophy in the arts faculty. The first great conflict of the Reformation was fought between the Germans in the theology faculty and the Czechs in the philosophy faculty.

FIG. 2   Modern view of Charles Bridge and the Vltava River in Prague.

Charles also established the New Town adjacent to the Old Town, and it quickly swelled with people of the lower estates fleeing the hardships of peasant life. During the Hussite Revolution, the three sections of Prague (Lesser Town, Old Town, and New Town) represented three distinct populations and approaches to religion. At times they were at war with one another. The Lesser Town, with the royal castle and Saint Vitus Cathedral, remained monarchal, with a large Catholic influence. The Old Town, especially the university, was the center of moderate Hussitism (Utraquism). The New Town was one of the centers of radical Hussitism.

Like many monarchs of the day, Charles preferred to use clerics in his administration rather than secular lords because they had fewer feudal obligations and kinship ties that created competing loyalties.[2] Clerics also tended to be better educated and less rebellious than landed nobles. Charles was convinced that the church could be a major force for social improvement, which would in turn increase the peace, prosperity, and power of his kingdom. Therefore he was a patron of the church, building sanctuaries, endowing monasteries, and advocating higher standards of education and morality for the clergy. Charles succeeded in making Prague an archbishopric, elevating its status greatly in the church. Charles aligned himself with the papacy to such a degree that William of Ockham referred to him derisively as the pope's emperor, the Pfaffenkaiser.[3]

AVIGNON PAPACY AND THE CHURCH IN BOHEMIA

The most immediate effect of Charles's patronage of the church was an increase in the percentage of the population who served in holy orders (priests, monks, friars, deacons, and lesser orders) and the spread of basic education through the church. By 1400 Prague was one of the most clerical cities in Europe, having one priest per two hundred people. Records indicate that between 1395 and 1416 more than thirteen thousand men were ordained into the lowest level of priesthood, an average of more than six hundred per year.[4]

2. Lambert, *Medieval Heresy*, 307–10, gives a good summary of Charles's use of clerics.
3. Fudge, *Magnificent Ride*, 15; Matthew Spinka, *John Hus: A Biography* (Princeton: Princeton University Press, 1968), 7.
4. František Šmahel, "Literacy and Heresy in Hussite Bohemia," in *Heresy and Literacy, 1000–1530,* ed. Peter Biller and Anne Hudson (Cambridge: Cambridge University Press, 1994), 240.

There were also twenty-eight lower and middle schools, primarily for preparing people for careers in the church or government. This entailed a significant financial burden on the populace, but it also meant that the capital had a sizeable educated class. These men (and some prominent women) made up most of the intelligentsia, a "clerical proletariat" that became the backbone of the Czech Reformation.[5]

Though the power of the papacy may have peaked with the rule of Innocent III at the beginning of the thirteenth century, the Catholic Church maintained great institutional power in Europe in the era of Charles IV. This was the period of the early Renaissance in Italy, with its magnificent art and architecture and its fratricidal politics. Under Pope Clement V, in 1309 the papacy had moved its headquarters from the Vatican palace in Rome to Avignon, France, where it was less subject to Italian politics.[6] In Avignon the popes lived as Renaissance lords in pomp and splendor, but, more important, they were secure in a beautiful fortress from which they administered a rapidly growing bureaucracy. Security, opulence, and bureaucracy were expensive, and many of the Avignon popes were more skillful as administrators and financiers than as spiritual leaders. By the mid-fourteenth century the papacy controlled one of the most efficient systems of finance in Europe and had the ability to levy taxes (the tithe) on those who worked the land and did business in the cities.[7]

Many church offices throughout Europe possessed political power at the local, national, and international levels. To an ambitious individual the church offered opportunities and benefits not available in secular society. Income-producing offices in the church were called benefices, and the income usually came through an endowment. In many cases only a portion of the income actually went to the individual holding office; some went to support the church hierarchy. Increasingly in the fourteenth century, church or canon law allowed the papal administration greater say in the granting of benefices. The papacy also granted itself rights to more of the income produced by endowments.

Some priests were willing to pay bishops and the papacy for the wealthier

5. Ibid., 242–53; Lambert, *Medieval Heresy*, 310.

6. Francis Oakley, *The Western Church in the Later Middle Ages* (Ithaca: Cornell University Press, 1979), 25–54, gives a nuanced and well-informed discussion of the difficulties the papacy faced in the fourteenth century and the reasons for removing the papacy from the complexities of Italian politics.

7. Ibid., 48–50.

benefices.[8] This practice of buying and selling benefices, and of charging fees for basic religious services such as hearing confession and administering last rites, was condemned by reformers as "simony." The name comes from the story of Simon Magus, who offered the apostles money to teach him how to do miracles in the name of Jesus (Acts 8:18). Church reformers throughout the Middle Ages, including reforming popes like Gregory VII, had tried to abolish simony. Such reform efforts often led to bitter conflict with secular rulers, most notably the famous investiture struggle, but by the late fourteenth century simony was such a common practice that papal bureaucrats kept lists of the sale price of various offices.[9]

Elevating Prague to archiepiscopal status meant money and power for the city, but this also became a source of contention that contributed to the Czech Reformation. Not only did the church own at least 25 percent of the land in Bohemia,[10] it also levied heavy taxes on the common people. The clergy, by contrast, had little tax obligation to the state. Many people in the kingdom saw the church, staffed primarily by Germans, as a foreign institution mainly interested in raising money and increasing its political power. Simony became a major theological issue in the Czech Reformation. Moreover, a struggle took place over the control of the archiepiscopal see throughout the Hussite period. If the archbishop of Prague had approved, the Czech reform would have had the potential to transform all of central Europe. That was the dream of the reformers and the nightmare of their powerful opponents. Prague became a strategic battlefield in the war over reform.

EARLY REFORM EFFORTS IN PRAGUE

Modern research confirms Charles's own assessment that fourteenth-century Bohemia was only nominally Christianized. Based on sources such as the

8. Ibid., 50–54, 213–19; Southern, *Western Society and the Church*, 151–69.

9. Euan Cameron, *The European Reformation* (Oxford: Clarendon Press, 1991), 20–47, provides a succinct account of financial corruption in the late medieval church and the numerous failed efforts to address the problems in the fifteenth century. Much of what he says describes the situation in Bohemia before Hus.

10. The exact percentage is impossible to determine. Modern historians have speculated that it may have been as high as 50 percent. See Fudge, *Magnificent Ride*, 15–16; cf. Heymann, *Jan Žižka*, 39.

visitation protocol of Archdeacon Pavel of Janovice in 1378–82, it appears that among the common people in Prague and in rural villages, "knowledge of Church doctrine was limited to the barest essentials, in most cases to familiarity with the *Credo*, prayer, and the Ten Commandments."[11] (In all fairness, it should be noted that the same can be said of many Christian congregations in modern America.) To redress this situation, Charles encouraged a humanistic form of piety similar to the *devotio moderna* (modern or new devotion) in the Netherlands, which was associated with the work of Thomas à Kempis. The *devotio moderna* was an informal movement that encouraged frequent communion, the reading of devotional books (especially Augustine), and personal imitation of Christ among the laity.[12] Portions of the Bible were translated into Czech for wealthy laypersons who wanted to live more devoutly. In Malcolm Lambert's judgment, "the *devotio moderna* of Bohemia helped to create in some influential circles the atmosphere of moral earnestness and a certain caution towards the formal and external machinery of traditional religious life that made a propitious climate of opinion for Hussitism."[13]

Although Charles IV did little to change the basic structure of the church and its relationship to secular authority, he assisted in the careers of two early reformers in Prague. One was an Austrian named Konrad Waldhauser (d. 1369), an Augustinian canon who accepted Charles's invitation to help root out corruption in the church. Kaminsky describes Konrad's efforts thus: "soon Prague's upper-class Germans were treated to sermons in their own language, criticizing their luxuries, their avarice, their pride, and their tepidity in religion. Rich people often like to hear such things."[14] Konrad went beyond goading wealthy people to be more charitable; he also railed against the mendicant orders (Dominicans and Franciscans) for their ambition and greed. He called on the clergy to return to their primary duties of caring for the souls of their flock rather than enriching their religious orders and seeking worldly security.

One priest Waldhauser converted was Milíč of Kroměříž, a bright young

---

11. Šmahel, "Literacy and Heresy," 242; Fudge, *Magnificent Ride*, 30–31. The situation was not much different in German-speaking lands, even after the Reformation. See Gerald Strauss, *Luther's House of Learning: Indoctrination of the Young in the German Reformation* (Baltimore: Johns Hopkins University Press, 1979).

12. Oakley, *Western Church*, 100–113.

13. Lambert, *Medieval Heresy*, 310.

14. Kaminsky, *Hussite Revolution*, 8.

man from Moravia who served in Charles's chancery.[15] Milíč was an active member of the intelligentsia in the capital and was well acquainted with many skillful and powerful people in the government. Intelligent, sophisticated, and knowledgeable about international affairs, he quickly became prominent in the court. True to the custom of the day, he was given a benefice as a canon of Saint Vitus Cathedral, which came with a handsome income. Unexpectedly, though, he did not follow the normal procedure of keeping the income and hiring a poorly paid priest as his vicar. He actually devoted himself to his duties after he was ordained.[16]

Milíč continued Waldhauser's reforming efforts in the capital through his vigorous preaching, writing, and agitation within the government, but unlike his mentor, Milíč preached in Czech to common people. This was an age of speculation about the apocalypse in the wake of the Black Death, and Milíč employed eschatology in the interest of church and social reform. He was convinced that the Antichrist was actively working in Europe against the true church of Christ. According to medieval theology, the Antichrist would be a human being with great political and spiritual authority who would lead the people astray and oppress them in many ways.[17] Although he was a royal official, Milíč publicly proclaimed in 1366 that the emperor Charles was none other than the Antichrist waging war on Christ's faithful.[18]

Not surprisingly, Milíč was arrested by the archbishop, but he was shown mercy by the "Antichrist" himself. The following year Milíč went to Rome to share his views on the apocalypse with Pope Urban V, but the pope was still in Avignon. When Milíč took his message to the streets of Rome, he was arrested by the Roman Inquisition. Thanks to the intervention of Charles and Urban, Milíč was released and soon was preaching again in Prague, although

15. One of the few English-language studies of Milíč is Peter C. A. Morée, *Preaching in Fourteenth-Century Bohemia: The Life and Ideas of Milicius de Chremsir and His Significance in the Historiography of Bohemia* (Slavkov: Eman, 1999).

16. Kaminsky, *Hussite Revolution*, 9–10; Fudge, *Magnificent Ride*, 48.

17. "Totally evil, destined to appear in the in the Last Days to wage war on Christ, the Antichrist represented not merely this or that lapse from the Christian norm but the union of all the forces of perdition, including those in high place who were supposed to guard the Christian order but did not do so." Kaminsky, *Hussite Revolution*, 10. See also Fudge, *Magnificent Ride*, 49. On the growth of speculation about the appearance of the Antichrist, see Bernard McGinn, *Antichrist: Two Thousand Years of the Human Fascination with Evil* (San Francisco: HarperSanFrancisco, 1994), esp. 143–87.

18. Kaminsky, *Hussite Revolution*, 10.

he was more cautious in identifying the Antichrist by name. Milíč's sermons were unusually well attended, and he preached several times each Sunday and often during the week. Even more important for the spread of reform was his team of young clerics, who transcribed his sermons and made multiple copies for distribution, sometimes within twenty-four hours.[19] Milíč did not have the advantage of the printing press, which Luther used so effectively 150 years later.

Milíč did not lose his zeal for reforming the church after his encounter with the pope, and his verbal assaults on high church officials in Bohemia were relentless. He was convinced that the worst ills of society could be addressed if prelates, priests, and monks were forced to live according to their vows of poverty, chastity, and obedience to the teachings of Christ. His most ambitious effort at social reform involved the reclamation of women from prostitution. Unlike most theologians of the day, he recognized that women did not choose a life of prostitution because of moral failings or lust but because of poverty and hopelessness. The worst "red light district" in Prague was nicknamed Venice, and some of the brothels there were actually owned by the church. According to many Catholic sources, it seems evident that many priests and monks indulged the temptations of the flesh by frequenting the brothels of Venice, a strategy hardly consistent with clerical celibacy.[20] Milíč persuaded Charles IV to let him transform one of the brothels into a home for prostitutes converted to a religious life by his preaching. He renamed it Jerusalem. It was similar to the Beguine houses of the Netherlands, semimonastic homes for women who dedicated themselves to chastity, prayer, and acts of mercy.[21]

The name Jerusalem has eschatological overtones, anticipating as it does the New Jerusalem of the book of Revelation. As David Holeton puts it, "'Jerusalem' came to be seen as a sign of eschatological intervention in a world which was believed to be mortally ill, scarred by the signs of the end of time. The marks of the kingdom were present: lives were changed and people from all social classes lived together in peace, filled with a spirit of ecumenical charity."[22] One of the unique features of life in Milíč's Jerusalem was the daily celebration of the Eucharist. Milíč believed that the moral transformation evident in this

---

19. Šmahel, "Literacy and Heresy," 239.
20. Fudge, *Magnificent Ride*, 49–50.
21. Oakley, *Western Church*, 92–94.
22. David Holeton, "The Communion of Infants and Hussitism," *Communio Viatorum* 27 (1984): 208.

community was a direct result of frequent lay communion. In the Eucharist believers were brought into the immediate presence of the Christ who conquered sin and reigns with God; therefore the Eucharist itself was an entry into the Kingdom of God on earth. In Thomas Fudge's words, "The signs of the kingdom were present in Prague: the transformation of lives, people of different social classes living together in harmony and a prevailing attitude of peace and charity. The only innovation was the practice of frequent lay communion."[23]

Jerusalem was also home to a group of reform-minded followers of Milíč who preached to the common people and organized various types of social programs for the poor. As with the Beguine houses, all of this took place outside of the normal parish structure, so people from all over the city were welcome to attend the sermons and receive the sacraments. Both clergy and laity were attracted by Milíč's piety and began to view him as a saint, but his work angered the powerful church officials who were often the objects of his criticism. In 1373 his opponents took steps to stop his preaching, end his reform, and close Jerusalem. They accused Milíč of several counts of heresy and of violating the moral teachings of the church, and he was forced to travel to Avignon to defend himself. Although he was exonerated by Pope Gregory XI, Milíč died on the return journey. Jerusalem was closed and given to the Cistercian order for its students at the university. The priests who were loyal to Milíč lost their positions, but this only confirmed in them the desire for reform.[24]

Milíč may be considered the originator of the Czech Reformation, and some of his principles were central to the Unity of the Brethren, especially the idea that eschatology provides the vision for the true Christian community on earth. Milíč's Jerusalem was an early first step toward the Brethren's emphasis on the church as a community of faith that lives in love and looks with hope to the in-breaking Kingdom of God on earth. Eschatology, for the Brethren, was more concerned with creating a community patterned on the biblical vision of the Kingdom of God than speculating about the return of Christ. They saw the Eucharist as a foretaste of that kingdom.

Milíč was less interested in philosophical debates than in the concrete care

---

23. Fudge, *Magnificent Ride*, 50.
24. Kaminsky, *Hussite Revolution*, 13–14.

of souls and reform of the society in which he lived. The imperative of the Gospels was not to comfort the wealthy and powerful in their luxury and privilege; it was to liberate people from the oppression of sin and an unjust social order. There is a direct connection between Milíč's interest in practical theology and the development of the Unity's praxis-oriented doctrine. Equally important, Milíč taught that the church did not exist for its own sake but only to serve God's people. The clergy were servants and shepherds, not lords and masters. They were to live what they preached and be content with the blessings of a simple life. This view of pastors as faithful shepherds of the flock rather than lords shaped the Unity's doctrine and practice profoundly.

ANXIETY

Milíč's apocalyptic view of the world was an expression of the anxieties prevalent in the late fourteenth century, which grew worse in the years following his death. Of critical importance for understanding the history of the Czech Reformation was the papal schism (the Great Schism) that divided Western Christianity from 1378 to 1414.[25] It began soon after the college of cardinals elected Pope Urban VI in 1378 while meeting in Rome. There was a great deal of anger among the citizens of Rome over the transfer of the papal residence to Avignon almost seventy years earlier. The people made it clear through rioting and threats of violence that they wanted a Roman pontiff who would live and serve in Rome. The cardinals obliged, but soon regretted their decision when Pope Urban VI attempted to remove some of the cardinals' traditional privileges. The cardinals reassembled outside Rome and declared that the election had been invalid on the grounds that they had been intimated by the mob. They deposed Urban and elected a new pope, Clement VII, but Urban refused to relinquish the papal chair. He simply excommunicated the cardinals, appointed new ones, and established his own curia in Rome. Clement set up a rival papal administration in Avignon, with a separate curia and college of cardinals.

Thus Western Christendom was divided between two popes, each with loyal

25. The Great Schism is discussed in most histories of Western Christianity. One of the more useful is Oakley, *Western Church*, 55–66.

cardinals, curia, and financial structure. Each pope excommunicated the follow-ers of the other, and each vied for the loyalty of the various rulers and prelates of Europe, using bribery when necessary. For those who cared deeply about the church, the sacraments, and the well-being of society, the papal schism was traumatic. Despite the insidious corruption that had tarnished papal author-ity in the late Middle Ages, there was still a strong sense that only the pope had the potential to bring peace and establish a just social order. For centuries the church had been the only institution that offered a sense of European unity. Kings, dukes, princes, and barons might be at war with one another and com-pete over strategic territories, but they all belonged to one church ruled by a single pontiff.

Though there had been disputes and even the appointment of "antipopes" by emperors through the years, never had cardinals themselves elected two popes.[26] The schism undermined, challenged, and eventually shattered the illu-sion that the papacy could unify society, as successive popes in Avignon and Rome fought to gain the loyalty of the various political units of Europe. Rival rulers could choose rival popes who obligingly excommunicated those who gave allegiance to the other side. Though most people in Europe, especially in the countryside, may have had little understanding of Christian doctrine or knowledge of church politics, the papal schism affected them in several ways.

Medieval society had faced many upheavals and economic changes through the centuries. Even the most secure classes lived in a threatening and uncer-tain world where famine, plague, war, and rioting could suddenly cause loss of life and property. Most people were able to deal with the normal tragedies of life with courage and resilience, in part because of the strength of the medie-val Catholic Church's sacramental system.[27] Few people knew or even cared about the official teachings of the church, let alone the subtleties of Scholas-tic theology, but they did know the value of baptism, penance, processions, holy water, priestly blessings, masses for the dead, and the intercession of the saints. The rites of the church offered hope and stability in a world filled with terror and uncertainty.

---

26. Ibid., 157–74; Pelikan, *Christian Tradition*, 4:69–85.

27. František Graus, "The Crisis of the Middle Ages and the Hussites," trans. James J. Heaney, in *The Reformation in Medieval Perspective*, ed. Steven E. Ozment (Chicago: University of Chicago Press, 1971), 76–103.

The papal schism called all of this into question, first for the intellectuals and then for the common believers. František Graus has concluded that this was the great crisis of the late Middle Ages: "something had indeed happened to the church, and the reverberations were felt throughout all of Catholic Europe, though with different power and intensity. But *no part* of Europe escaped the shock of the so-called Papal Schism in 1378."[28] In a situation where every person in Christendom, even every priest, had been excommunicated by at least one of the popes, the salvation of every person was called into question. Corruption in the church merely added fuel to the fire.[29]

The papal schism formed the backdrop for the Hussite Revolution because it was the reason that the Council of Constance was called in 1414. In addition to deposing three popes and consecrating a new pope, Martin V, in 1417, the council also executed the leader of the Czech Reformation, Jan Hus. It was also because of the papal schism that the kingdoms of England and Bohemia came into closer contact with each other, for they both supported the pope in Rome rather than the one in Avignon. The new ties between the kingdoms were solemnized by the marriage of Anne of Bohemia, sister of King Wenceslas, to King Richard II of England, in 1382.[30]

Apocalyptic anxieties were fueled by the rapid social and economic changes taking place in Bohemia at the time. Aside from the personal and social turmoil caused by plagues and wars, the dramatic reduction of the workforce after the Black Death destabilized the economy, hastening the development of early capitalism. Peasants initially saw their status increase as their work became more valuable, but life in the countryside soon became more restrictive, as lords established laws to tie the serfs to their estates.[31] As the population rose, thousands fled the countryside and settled in the burgeoning cities of Europe. Prague was one of the fastest-growing cities and, like all cities, it had a high percentage of poor workers. Late medieval cities were the center of much social unrest because of the critical mass of disaffected people.[32]

In Bohemia the situation was worse than in many places in Europe,

28. Ibid., 88.

29. Pelikan, *Christian Tradition*, 4:85–98, discusses how the schism and widespread corruption reinvigorated the ancient debates on Donatism and the efficacy of the sacraments in the fifteenth century.

30. Oakley, *Western Church*, 195; Kaminsky, *Hussite Revolution*, 24.

31. Fudge, *Magnificent Ride*, 18–29, discusses these economic and social issues in detail.

32. Graus, "Crisis of the Middle Ages," 86–88.

because the man who succeeded Charles as king lacked his father's strength, wisdom, and skill in ruling. According to even friendly accounts, Wenceslas (Vaclav) IV, who ruled from 1363 to 1419, was a weak and ineffective monarch who preferred hunting and drinking to the dour disciplines of economics and jurisprudence. Twice he was imprisoned by rivals (1394, 1402), and though he regained his freedom, he lost his ability to govern effectively.[33] With economic conditions worsening for most people in the kingdom, the capital city growing in size and instability, a weak king, and a church with two rival pontiffs, it is no wonder that apocalyptic speculation and cries for radical reform found attentive listeners among the intellectuals and the masses.

MATTHEW OF JANOV

To the minds of many residents of Prague, the papal schism and the general corruption in the Bohemian church and monarchy confirmed Milíč's warnings. One of them was a theological student named Matthew (Matěj) of Janov. Matthew left Prague to study at the University of Paris in the 1370s, where he wrote a Milíč-inspired apocalyptic treatise, *Regulae veteris et novi testamenti* (Rules of the Old and New Testaments). In it, he attacked the mendicant orders as examples of the Antichrist in action. Much of the treatise was borrowed from the work of William of Saint Amour, whose radical theology found its way into Bohemia via Matthew.[34]

Although he was a sincere follower of Milíč, Matthew spent much of his time abroad trying to secure a lucrative and prestigious benefice during the papal schism. "The wealth, prestige, and worldly abundance that Milíč had voluntarily renounced were for Matthew the unattainable goals of a lifetime of inept careerism," according to Kaminsky.[35] Matthew's bitterness at not obtaining a living may have added venom to his reformist theology, but his ideas inspired many later reformers. Having repented of his own attempts to secure a comfortable living, he called upon the church to return to the ideal of apostolic poverty seen in the New Testament. Increasingly he came to identify the

---

33. Ibid., 96; Spinka, *John Hus*, 8–12; Fudge, *Magnificent Ride*, 9–11; Lambert, *Medieval Heresy*, 313.
34. Kaminsky, *Hussite Revolution*, 14; Lambert, *Medieval Heresy*, 312–14.
35. Kaminsky, *Hussite Revolution*, 16.

church, or at least elements within the church, as the Antichrist. He felt freer to attack the papacy directly than Milíč had because the schism that divided the "one holy catholic and apostolic church" meant that at least one of the popes must be false.

In addition to apocalyptic fervor, Matthew offered a pastoral solution to the anxiety of the age. Drawing on the writings of the early church father Irenaeus, Matthew argued that the Eucharist was medicine and nourishment for the soul. Those who sought strength to face the looming apocalyptic struggle or who simply wanted assurance of salvation in the face of death should take the sacrament reverently and often. Contrary to traditional practice in most of Europe, where the laity communed once a year at most, Matthew preached the necessity of frequent communion.[36] It was not enough to adore the consecrated host as the priest held it high behind the altar or as it was carried in a monstrance during processions; believers had to eat the body of Christ. As a result, crowds of ordinary people in Prague began to commune weekly. Some individuals took communion on a daily basis, the way monks and nuns did.

This fervent sharing in the Eucharist by the laity was something that had not been seen in the Catholic Church for centuries. That alone would have concerned officials, particularly in light of the social unrest already evident in Prague, but Matthew also kept up a very public attack on the abuses of the church. Although not as confrontational as Milíč, he made clear who were of the party of the Antichrist. The Antichrist was whatever (or whoever) opposed Christ and his church. The work of the Antichrist included the abuse of the scriptures, neglect of the sacraments, and disunity in the church.[37]

The reform effort of Milíč and Matthew found institutional expression in the establishment of Bethlehem Chapel in 1391 in the Old Town of Prague. It was a preaching place open to all people, and the sermons were normally given in Czech. The call for reform of the church, especially reform of the hierarchy, and concern for the poor were common themes in the sermons of Bethlehem Chapel. The chapel was under the authority of the university, and the preachers were teachers (masters) at the university who were beginning to digest

---

36. Rubin, *Corpus Christi.*
37. Erhard Peschke, *Kirche und Welt in der Theologie der böhmischen Brüder vom Mittelalter zur Reformation* (Berlin: Evangelische Verlagsanstalt, 1981), 9.

FIG. 3   Bethlehem Chapel (reconstructed), Prague.

the works of the Oxford philosophy theologian John Wyclif (c. 1330–1384).[38] Wyclif's ideas helped pushed the Czech Reformation in more revolutionary directions.

WYCLIF

Wyclif's ideas transformed the native and in many ways naïve reform efforts of Milíč and Matthew into a potent intellectual force.[39] Wyclif's works came

38. Though some of his philosophical works have been translated in recent years, Wyclif's radical theology remains of most historical interest, particularly for those studying the Czech Reformation. See A. Hudson, *The Premature Reformation: Wycliffite Texts and Lollard History* (Oxford: Clarendon Press, 1988); John Wyclif, *On Universals*, trans. Anthony Kenny (Oxford: Clarendon Press, 1985).

39. For more information on Wyclif, see Anthony Kenny, ed., *Wyclif in His Times* (Oxford: Clarendon Press, 1986).

to Prague from Oxford because of the connections between Bohemia and England established in 1382 by the marriage of Anne of Bohemia and Richard II. In part because of Queen Anne's patronage and encouragement, a scholarship was established to support Czech students at Oxford University. By the 1390s Czech students, most notably Jerome of Prague, had taken Wyclif's philosophical and theological works to Prague, where they were enthusiastically embraced by the Czech philosophy masters. Stephen Páleč and Stanislav of Znojmo followed Wyclif's thoughts so closely that some of their works were mistaken for Wyclif texts in the nineteenth century.[40]

That Wyclif himself had been declared a heretic by the Dominicans in Oxford in 1382 did not dampen the enthusiasm of the Prague scholars, but Wyclif's writings soon became part of a larger struggle between the Czechs on the faculty and the Germans.[41] The German professors attempted to have all of Wyclif's works, including his philosophical writings, declared heretical in order to intimidate their rivals in the university. In 1408 the archbishop of Prague, Zbyněk, was persuaded to condemn forty-five articles taken from Wyclif's philosophical writings.[42] Since Wyclif's philosophy (unlike his theology) had never been suspected of heresy, many people felt that this condemnation went too far.

The Czech scholars, led by Stephen Páleč, protested to the king. At that time Wenceslas was looking for support for his decision to end his allegiance to the Roman pope against the wishes of Archbishop Zbyněk. The king looked to the university to support his policy of endorsing the Avignon pope, but the German faculty supported the archbishop and the Roman pope. So Wenceslas issued the Decree of Kutná Hora in 1409, which changed the charter of the university and gave the Czechs a majority vote in university affairs. All of the Germans at the university resigned in protest.[43] Most went to the new University of Leipzig; others moved to the University of Vienna, where they continued to agitate against Wyclif and his followers in Prague.[44]

40. Lambert, *Medieval Heresy*, 321.
41. Spinka, *John Hus*, 34–37, 62–65; Lambert, *Medieval Heresy*, 320–22.
42. Spinka, *John Hus' Concept of the Church* (Princeton: Princeton University Press, 1966), 397–400.
43. Kaminsky, *Hussite Revolution*, 56–75; Ferdinand Seibt, "Johannes Hus und der Abzug der deutschen Studenten aus Prag 1409," in *Hussitenstudien: Personen, Ereignisse, Ideen einer frühen Revolution*, ed. Ferdinand Seibt (Munich: R. Oldenbourg Verlag, 1987), 1–16; Lambert, *Medieval Heresy*, 323–25. For a good description of the nature of the "four nations" at the university, see Spinka, *John Hus*, 25–27.
44. Paul P. Bernard, "Jerome of Prague, Austria, and the Hussites," *Church History* 27 (1958): 3–22.

The intellectual aspect of the debate over Wyclif involved the dispute over the *via moderna* (the modern or new way) associated with William of Ockham, which is sometimes called nominalism.[45] Wyclif endorsed the opposing view, called realism or idealism, which claims that the world is composed of universal concepts that appear in concrete form as individuals. These universals, or ideas, are the essence of things. For the realists, universals actually exist invisibly and in fact are more real than the visible objects.[46] Wyclif went so far as to state that "intellectual and emotional error about universals is the cause of all the sin that reigns in the world."[47] The philosophical debate over universals was an old one, and Wyclif's ideas would not have been condemned had he not pushed them beyond the bounds of church dogma in his book *On the Church*, in which he argued that there is a real or ideal church that is invisible and perfect.[48] This is the only true church: "In fact the sole body that can support the predicates of perfection, infallibility, immutability, and unfailing existence is the collectivity of the predestined, past, present, and future, and this group alone can be called the mystical body of Christ. It has only one head, Christ, and as a community it is based on observance of one law, the Law of Christ."[49] For a radical realist like Wyclif, "the holy Catholic Church" identified in the Apostles' Creed could only be the mystical body of Christ, not the Roman Church. Like all ideals, it exists outside of the corruption of time and history.

Wyclif believed that the real or ideal church truly exists but that its membership is known only to God. The visible church is only an imperfect reflection of the real church. Drawing upon the writings of the Apostle Paul and Augustine, Wyclif defined the real church as the totality of those whom God has predestined to salvation. The predestined are part of the true, invisible

---

45. A. Hudson and M. Wilks, eds., *From Ockham to Wyclif* (Oxford: Blackwell, 1987); David Knowles, *The Evolution of Medieval Thought* (New York: Vintage Books, 1962), 1–8, 107–15, 301–40.

46. Anthony Kenny, "The Realism of the *de Universalibus*," in Kenny, *Wyclif in His Times*, 17–30; Wyclif, *On Universals*; Gordon Leff, "Wyclif and Hus: A Doctrinal Comparison," in Kenny, *Wyclif in his Times*, 106. Leff gives a detailed account of Wyclif's teachings and activity in *Heresy in the Later Middle Ages*, 2:500–558.

47. Kenny, "Realism of the *de Universalibus*," 29. For a nice summary of Wyclif's thought, see Lambert, *Medieval Heresy*, 250–57, or Oakley, *Western Church*, 190–200.

48. William R. Cook, "John Wyclif and Hussite Theology, 1415–1436," *Church History* 42 (1973): 335–49.

49. Howard Kaminsky, "Wyclifism as Ideology of Revolution," *Church History* 32 (1963): 61.

church; those whose damnation is foreknown by God are not. Thus even popes might not be among the elect. Certainly no church official can determine who is predestined and who is among the foreknown, since only God knows this. Therefore no church official knows who is truly in the real church, an idea that undermined the papal weapon of excommunication.[50] The pope could excommunicate someone from the Catholic Church, but that had no bearing on a person's membership in the true, invisible church.

Wyclif, following medieval precedent, divided the church into three parts: the church triumphant in heaven, where the ideal is visible and lasts for eternity; the church dormant (or sleeping), made up of those who have died and are in purgatory, and the church militant, which is the imperfect expression of the true church here on earth. The predestined are of the church militant, but the foreknown are merely in it. The church militant includes the entire society, but it can be divided into three parts: clergy, nobility, and commoners, each of which has its role to play.[51] Although the church militant is imperfect and includes those who are not elect, the visible church on earth can and should conform to the ideal as closely as possible by following the law of God given in the Bible. Wyclif contrasted the poverty and humility of the true church of Christ to the pride and power of the medieval church.

Wyclif's importance for the history of the Unity of the Brethren lies in his theological and political works, which helped radicalize the Czech Reformation.[52] Wyclif's concept of the church as the body of the predestined was revolutionary because it held that even the pope might fall outside the true church. "Such an attitude," writes Gordon Leff, "was utterly disruptive of ecclesiastical authority; for if only those chosen by God were of the Church, and they could not be known, there was no reason for accepting any visible priestly authority."[53] Wyclif believed that the papal schism validated his philosophy. The true bride

---

50. Ibid., 59.
51. Ibid., 62; Leff, *Heresy in the Later Middle Ages*, 2:516–46.
52. "Had his death occurred in 1374 or even as much as a year or two later Wycliffe would be remembered only by specialist historians as one of the lesser ornaments of medieval Oxford. They would know him as the author of a number of philosophical works of no particular brilliance though of sustained competence, several of which, despite his enormous reputation, have not yet been found worthy of print." K. B. MacFarlane, *John Wycliffe and the Beginnings of English Nonconformity* (London: English Universities Press, 1952), 1.
53. Leff, "Wyclif and Hus," 112.

of Christ could not be divided between rival popes; therefore the Roman Catholic Church could not be the true church.[54]

Wyclif was writing at the time that the British Crown was engaged in a dispute with the papacy over taxation issues, and he supported the civil authority in his works *On Civil Dominion* and *On the Power of the Pope*.[55] Although he accepted the medieval theory of the three estates (clergy, nobility, commoners), Wyclif severely undermined the medieval church's justification for exercising political and economic power. Each portion of the church militant must fulfill the duties that God had assigned to that estate. All dominion, he argued, comes from God, who appointed secular rulers to wield the sword and punish sinners. A true reformation of the church militant would require that the church renounce civil authority. Clergy, including bishops and cardinals, should be "freed" from the distractions of property, governance, and involvement in secular affairs so they could better devote their time and energy to preaching of the Word of God in the world at large. Instead of being involved in politics, Wyclif argued, the clergy are required by their ordination to follow the example of the apostles by humbly teaching the law of Christ through word and example.

Since the nobility bear the responsibility of governing society, in Wyclif's view, they should use the sword when necessary to enforce the law of Christ as well as to protect the other two estates. The common people must obey the law of Christ and serve the other two estates willingly. Wyclif went beyond the medieval tradition in his emphasis on the responsibility of the secular power to destroy all that opposes the law of Christ. Like King David, the king was ordained by God to be "priest and pontiff of his realm," and he had a sacred obligation to move the church militant closer to the ideal, by force if necessary.[56] But, Wyclif argued, those in mortal sin lose their right to exercise dominion over others. The Hussites used this argument to justify their rebellion against the pope and emperor.

By 1378 Wyclif's views were attracting opposition from Scholastic theologians and the Roman curia, and increasingly he turned directly to scripture for

54. Ibid., 113.
55. See MacFarlane, *John Wycliffe*, 25–75, for a full discussion of Wyclif's involvement in contemporary politics.
56. Kaminsky, "Wyclifism as Ideology," 64.

support. His understanding of the Bible was spelled out in the treatise *De veritate sacrae scripturae* (On the Truth of Holy Scripture).[57] In Wyclif's hands the Bible became a revolutionary text, and he set scripture against the church hierarchy in a way that influenced Hus.[58] God's Word, for Wyclif, existed eternally and was unchanging as an ideal. The written word of the Bible reflected in physical form this eternal Word of God; therefore it gave the reader insight into the mind of God.[59] Though Wyclif often advocated a literal reading of scripture, his approach was actually more nuanced. He "recognized an implicit as well as an explicit meaning" in the text, and he relied on the aid of previous "divinely inspired" interpreters such as Augustine, Bernard of Clairvaux, and the Victorines in interpretation. "His novelty," according to Gordon Leff, "lay in the combination of an historical and metaphysical treatment of the Bible to discount the authority of the contemporary hierarchy."[60]

In addition to his distrust of the church as an institution, Wyclif set up an opposition between scripture and the church hierarchy that meant that the laity should have access to the Bible in order to judge church teaching. This perspective led Wyclif to call for and to produce translations of scripture into English. This is one instance where the Czech Reformation had a direct impact on Wyclif, for he pointed to the example of translations of the Bible into Czech to support his cause. If Queen Anne, a Bohemian, could read scripture in her native tongue, he asked, why shouldn't Englishmen have the same privilege?[61]

Maurice Keen makes a strong case for the impact of Wyclif's scriptural and historical studies in the late 1370s on his understanding of the Eucharist and his opposition to the dogmas of the Fourth Lateran Council.[62] Wyclif had written *On the Truth of Sacred Scripture* and had apparently completed his commentary on the entire Bible before he wrote *De Eucharistia*. In the process, he discovered that the words of institution ("this is my body") appear in different ways in different passages of scripture, and, more important, that the Catholic

---

57. Kantik Ghosh, *The Wycliffite Heresy: Authority and Interpretation of Texts* (Cambridge: Cambridge University Press, 2002), 22.

58. Leff, "Wyclif and Hus," 110–11.

59. Ghosh, *Wycliffite Heresy*, 23.

60. Leff, "Wyclif and Hus," 111.

61. Lambert, *Medieval Heresy*, 263. For more on the issue of vernacular versions, see Ghosh, *Wycliffite Heresy*, 87–111.

62. Maurice Keen, "Wyclif, the Bible, Transubstantiation," in Kenny, *Wyclif in His Times*, 12–15.

Church had not taught transubstantiation consistently until the thirteenth century. Transubstantiation was thus a recent innovation rather than a divine command. In fact, it represented priestly power over the laity more than devotion to the incarnate Word of God.

Wyclif also challenged Catholic teaching on the Eucharist from the perspective of realist metaphysics. He did not deny that the bread and wine were transformed through an ever repeated divine miracle, but he did assert that it was impossible for the *essential* nature of the bread and wine to be replaced by a different essence.[63] In other words, he argued forcefully that the bread and wine of the Eucharist remain bread and wine, even though the act of consecration *adds* to them the body and blood of Christ. This view, similar to Luther's, is commonly called *remanence* and is to be distinguished from the idea that the Eucharist is merely a symbol of the body and blood. As Luther would do later, Wyclif taught that Christ was really present within or under the bread and wine.[64]

Wyclif proclaimed that new types of eucharistic piety, especially the Corpus Christi festival, were simply idolatrous.[65] "What horrified Wyclif most of all about the doctrine of transubstantiation was just this, its carnality," writes Maurice Keen. "The priests who followed that teaching sold the host, which the eye can perceive is bread, as the corporeal body of God: they taught men to bow before what was material and corruptible, the very essence of idolatry; and they taught men to believe that they bit the body of Christ and were nourished bodily thereby, which was blasphemy."[66] Though Hus rejected Wyclif's arguments against transubstantiation, Wyclif's ideas influenced the radical Hussites, including the Brethren. A commission of twelve Oxford scholars, all from the Dominican order, was appointed to review Wyclif's writings on the Eucharist, and they determined that his denial of transubstantiation was indeed heresy. When asked to correct his views, Wyclif published a confession, against the wishes of his most important patron and protector, John of Gaunt, in which he defended the condemned statements.[67] Wyclif was forced out of Oxford,

63. Ibid., 5–10; Leff, "Wyclif and Hus," 117–18.
64. This concept is similar to the Lutheran notion that Christ is physically present with and under the bread and wine. Pelikan, *Christian Tradition*, 4:158–61, 200–201.
65. Leff, "Wyclif and Hus," 118; Lambert, *Medieval Heresy*, 256–57.
66. Keen, "Wyclif, the Bible, Transubstantiation," 14.
67. MacFarlane, *John Wycliffe*, 80–86; Lambert, *Medieval Heresy*, 257.

and he moved to Lutterworth, where he served as rector. Unlike Hus, Wyclif died at home in bed.

REBELS AND LOLLARDS

Although the English Peasants' Revolt of 1381 was not directly tied to the work of Wyclif and his supporters, his ideas were blamed for inspiring the uprising. The revolt was led by a priest named John Bull, who proclaimed the right of the peasants to demand and enforce justice. The rebels took control of London and murdered the archbishop and royal treasurer, but the rebellion ultimately failed, and the participants were brutally destroyed. It is intriguing that the uprising began with riots during the feast of Corpus Christi, which Wyclif had criticized in his writings.[68] Though not directly responsible for the Peasants' Revolt, Wyclif was blamed for it.

Though officially declared a heretic and isolated from the political scene and university life, Wyclif's ideas continued to influence English reformers in the fifteenth century. Some of his students, including a number of prominent knights, became leaders of a reform movement in England.[69] They promoted the use of vernacular translations of scripture and called for thorough reform of church and state, including the seizure of church property by the state. Derisively called Lollards, the Wyclifites published tracts, translations of scripture, and calls for reform that frightened the secular authorities. If the people had the right to punish sinful priests, might they not claim a similar right in regard to the nobility? Would not the Lollards inspire another peasant revolt?

King Henry V introduced the practice of burning heretics in England in 1401 as a way to deal with Lollards, but the movement grew. In 1413 one of the most prominent Lollards, Sir John Oldcastle, was arrested for denying the truth of transubstantiation. After he was rescued from the Tower of London, he gathered supporters for a "wild scheme" to force Lollard reform on England. Oldcastle's Revolt failed and the participants were hanged. The bodies of those accused of heresy as well as the rebels were burned.[70] In 1428 Wyclif's body was exhumed and burned.

68. Cohn, *Pursuit of the Millennium*, 198–204; Lambert, *Medieval Heresy*, 260.
69. MacFarlane, *John Wycliffe*, 87–143; Lambert, *Medieval Heresy*, 266–85.
70. MacFarlane, *John Wycliffe*, 144–68; Lambert, *Medieval Heresy*, 284–85.

The story of Wyclif and the Lollards is closely connected to the history of the Czech Reformation. For one thing, it fixed in the minds of church and government officials throughout Europe the connection between reform, translation of the Bible, heresy, and rebellion. At least one Lollard, Peter Payne, fled England and made his way to Prague, where he became a prominent figure in the Hussite Revolution.[71] By 1406 virtually all of Wyclif's writings were in circulation in Prague, including works declared heretical. The impact of these writings was much more explosive in Bohemia than it had been in England because the Czech Reformation was already well advanced among nobles and commoners. Lambert concludes, "At the moment when Henry V's soldiers were hunting down Oldcastle's conspirators, many of the Bohemian nobles were displaying their solidarity with the cause of their native reform leader, Jan Hus. Four or five years later, when Lollardy was reduced to a few of the clergy and some hardy artisan circles in England, its basis in the nobility and merchant classes almost wholly vanished, Hussite supporters were intimidating their opponents and preparing to do battle for their beliefs."[72]

WALDENSIANS

The Lollards were not the only medieval reform movement to promote reading scripture in the vernacular. The Waldensians, or Waldenses, "the last and most tenacious of the twelfth-century wandering-preacher movements,"[73] figured prominently in the history of the Czech Reformation and had direct contact with the Unity of the Brethren. Some scholars deny that the Waldensians played any role in the Czech Reformation, but the records of the permanent inquisitorial office in Bohemia indicate that of forty-four hundred people investigated for false belief between 1335 and 1355, more than half professed Waldensian ideas.[74] Most of the people questioned by the Inquisition lived in

---

71. There are few works on Peter Payne. See William R. Cook, "Peter Payne, Theologian and Diplomat of the Hussite Revolution" (Ph.D. diss., Cornell University, 1971), and Cook, "Peter Payne and the Waldensians," *Bolletino della Societa di Studi Valdesi* 175 (1975): 3–13. See also Josef V. Polišensky, ed., *Addresses and Essays in Commemoration of the Life and Works of the English Hussite Peter Payne-Englis, 1456–1956* (Prague: Charles University, 1957).

72. Lambert, *Medieval Heresy*, 306.

73. Ibid., 70.

74. Cameron, *Waldenses*, 144–46.

southern and western Bohemia, the regions where religious radicalism took firmest root in the fifteenth century. The town of Písek, for instance, was a noted center of Waldensian activity that became one of the centers of Hussite radicalism.[75] It is reasonable to assume that Hus's reform found fertile soil among people already inclined toward Waldensian beliefs and that some of the Waldensians' ideas influenced the theology of the radical Hussites.

The history of the Waldensians is somewhat obscure, but their origin was similar to that of the Franciscans. Around 1173 a wealthy merchant in Lyons named Valdes (his followers later added the name Peter) experienced a religious conversion and took up a life of apostolic poverty. Learning that Jesus had instructed a rich young ruler to give up his possessions in order to perfect himself (Matt. 19:21), Valdes divided his property with his wife, placed his daughters in a convent, and gave the rest of his money away.[76] He gathered followers who joined him in his effort to live according to the example of the seventy apostles that Jesus sent out without purse or bag to spread his word (Luke 10). They called themselves the *pauperes spiritu* (poor in spirit) and challenged the local priests and monks to observe their vows of chastity, obedience, and poverty.[77]

The call to poverty in the Middle Ages was always a critique of the power of the church, and the hierarchy was well aware of this. In the fourteenth century Pope John XXII went so far as to declare it heretical to teach that Jesus had not owned property.[78] Valdes, like Francis after him, sought papal approval for his group of poor preachers, but the Third Lateran Council in 1179 was not impressed with him or his followers.[79] The archbishop of Lyons condemned Valdes's followers, expelled them from Lyons, and persuaded Pope Lucius III to condemn the movement officially in 1184.[80] By that time the Waldensians had already spread to Lombardy, where they absorbed a number of lay ascetics

75. Šmahel, "Literacy and Heresy," 237–38. See also Murray L. Wagner, *Petr Chelčický: A Radical Separatist in Hussite Bohemia* (Scottsdale, Pa.: Herald Press, 1983), 49.

76. Cameron, *Waldenses*, 11–15. For more on the history of the Waldensians up to the twenty-first century, see Giorgio Tourn, Roger Geymonet, et al., *You Are My Witnesses: The Waldensians Across Eight Centuries* (Cincinnati: Claudiana Press, 1989).

77. Lambert, *Medieval Heresy*, 70–71.

78. For a detailed discussion on John XXII's conflict with the Franciscan order over the issue of poverty, see Lambert, *Medieval Heresy*, 208–35.

79. Cameron, *Waldenses*, 16–17.

80. Ibid., 21; Lambert, *Medieval Heresy*, 74–76.

known as the *humilati*.[81] The Waldensians spread throughout the Alps and established a strong presence in Austria in the second half of the thirteenth century, where they appear "to have been almost on the threshold of a public revolt like that mounted by the Hussites over a century later."[82] From Austria the movement spread to Bohemia and Moravia.

Unlike other condemned groups, such as the Cathars, the followers of Valdes did not object to the basic theology or doctrines of Christianity established in the patristic period.[83] For example, they did not deny the goodness of creation, the Trinity, or the divinity and humanity of Christ. Their preaching focused on the need to repent of pride, luxury, and lust, but some of the Waldensians grew more radical after they were condemned by the church hierarchy. They claimed that the Gospels, rather than the church, were their only authority, and they used vernacular versions of the New Testament in their teaching and preaching. "They stressed the literal understanding of the text," according to Lambert, "and the direct fulfillment in their own lives of Christ's demands."[84] In response to Waldensian preaching, many Catholic bishops made it illegal to own a New Testament translated into the vernacular.

Most of what we know about the medieval Waldensians comes from the records of the Inquisition, which attempted to stamp out this "heresy." In the 1390s inquisitors in central Europe compiled a list of heretical Waldensian ideas that provide a useful summary of their teaching in Bohemia at the time of Hus.[85] For the most part they rejected key elements of popular piety in the Catholic Church, such as the intercessions of the saints, adoration of the images of saints, and the use of "sacramentals" such as bells, holy water, candles, ashes, and other consecrated items. They also rejected the concept of purgatory, masses for the dead, and the use of indulgences.[86] Some Waldensian preachers called for the faithful to follow the "six smaller commandments" that Jesus set forth in the Sermon on the Mount: do not respond to violence with violence, do not

---

81. Lambert, *Medieval Heresy*, 85–88; Cameron, *Waldenses*, 36–48, 160–93.

82. Cameron, *Waldenses*, 102.

83. For Valdes's confession of faith, see ibid., 17–19. For more on the Cathars, see Lambert, *Medieval Heresy*, 115–57; Malcolm Barber, *The Cathars: Dualist Heretics in Languedoc in the High Middle Ages* (Aldershot: Ashgate, 2000).

84. Lambert, *Medieval Heresy*, 82.

85. Cameron, *Waldenses*, 112–18.

86. Lambert, *Medieval Heresy*, 174–77.

divorce your spouse, do not swear oaths, do not be angry without cause, do not look lustfully at someone, and love your enemies.[87] The refusal to swear any oath became the test inquisitors used to determine whether someone was Waldensian.

The Waldensians accused the Catholic clergy of being ignorant, indolent, lascivious, and abusive to the people. Their preachers, by contrast, called *barbes* (brothers), were poor itinerants, like the original apostles. *Barbes* lived on the gifts of friends and were not allowed secular employment or endowments. The intensity of the persecution against the Waldensians made it impossible for them to form a church until the sixteenth century. According to the historian Euan Cameron, "the Waldensians did not offer a comprehensive religious service, nor did they absent themselves from Catholic worship. They attended church, made offerings, confessed their sins to priests, took communion and attended sermons." Some Waldensian preachers allowed their followers to worship in the local Catholic church, but the more radical groups taught that the sacraments of the church were meaningless at best and idolatrous at worst.[88] The faithful should avoid them if at all possible and rely only on the ministration of Waldensian *barbes*.[89]

Unlike the Franciscans and Dominicans, who also endorsed apostolic poverty but had papal approval, the Waldensians attracted few scholars, primarily because they were an illegal movement.[90] It is not surprising, therefore, that there was a certain amount of confusion among the Waldensians about their history. It was easy, in Peter Biller's words, for this history to "be simplified and conflated through the passage of time and tricks of the memory."[91] Thus a myth arose among the Waldensians that their "church" had been founded by a bishop in the fourth century rather than by a merchant named Valdes in the twelfth.

To fully appreciate the Waldensian myth, it is necessary first to look at the Roman Catholic myth of the "Donation of Constantine." This document, written in the eighth century, purported to be a fourth-century statement from the emperor Constantine to Pope Sylvester granting the bishop of Rome

---

87. Ibid., 80–85, 159–61, and 170–76; Říčan, *History of the Unity*, 9.
88. Cameron, *Waldenses*, 211–31, 109, 92–95.
89. Lambert, *Medieval Heresy*, 163, 174.
90. Cameron, *Waldenses*, 82.
91. Biller, *Waldenses*, 204.

authority over the western half of the Roman Empire. Lorenzo Valla proved conclusively in the fifteenth century that the document was in fact an eighth-century forgery, but it was generally accepted as authentic in the Middle Ages and was often used to buttress papal supremacy over secular authorities.[92]

The Waldensians developed a bold countermyth to this Catholic myth. As history, of course, the Waldensian myth has no more validity than the papacy's forged "Donation of Constantine." But it expressed in narrative form a powerful theological perspective that influenced many radical Christian groups, including the Unity of the Brethren and the sixteenth-century Anabaptists.[93] According to the fourteenth-century Waldensian text *Liber electorum* (Book of the Elect), when Constantine converted to Christianity, a faithful priest named Peter recognized this as a threat to true Christianity. He left the Catholic Church in order to preserve the apostolic church. Eight centuries later Valdes became the head of this true church, but in another variation on the myth, Peter Valdes became the faithful priest of the fourth century![94] He, rather than Pope Sylvester, was the true successor of Saint Peter, and the Waldensians were the true apostolic church.

This myth was more than an attempt to establish the legitimacy of the Waldensians; it was a potent interpretation of Christian history.[95] The primitive church of the apostles and church fathers was the true church. After Constantine, the church became part of the Roman Empire's system of oppression and injustice. The church's involvement in secular politics ensured its downfall,

92. Henry Bettenson and Christ Maunder, eds., *Documents of the Christian Church*, 3d ed. (New York: Oxford University Press, 1999), 107–10.

93. The more radical Protestant churches have a completely different perspective on the development of Christian theology from Catholic, Orthodox, and "magisterial" Protestant churches because of their different understanding of Constantine's role. The Faith and Order Commission of the National Council of Churches held a special consultation on this subject in the 1980s: see Mark S. Heim, ed., *Faith to Creed: Toward a Common Historical Approach to the Affirmation of the Apostolic Faith in the Fourth Century* (Grand Rapids: William B. Eerdmans, 1991).

94. Biller, "Medieval Waldensians' Construction of the Past," in *Waldenses*, 191–206, and "The *Liber electorum*," ibid., 207–24; Lambert, *Medieval Heresy*, 170–71; Cameron, *Waldenses*, 119–22. This Waldensian myth is the origin of the Protestant idea of "witnesses of the truth," who remained faithful to the Gospel without being corrupted by the Catholic Church.

95. A more credible version of the myth of the "Constantinian fall" of the church argues that Constantine created an oppressive state church that corrupted Christianity. See, for example, James Carroll, *Constantine's Sword: The Church and the Jews* (New York: Houghton Mifflin, 2001), 165–207. Dan Brown's popular novel, *The DaVinci Code* (New York: Doubleday, 2003), promotes an extreme version of the myth, claiming that Constantine imposed the divinity of Christ on the church and closed the canon of scripture.

and the history of persecution and crusades since the time of Constantine provided ample evidence that the union of church and state was dangerous and heretical. The more radical Hussites, especially the Brethren, adopted this Waldensian attitude toward the Constantinian church.[96] Some modern theologians have likewise rejected the "Constantinian church" and called for the end of Christendom.[97] It may be helpful to recognize that *theologically* the Unity of the Brethren was never a Constantinian church. The price of that knowledge for Moravians, however, is the recognition that the Moravian Church's claim to apostolic episcopal succession rests on the myth of Bishop Peter Valdes.

The Waldensians' radical critique of the Constantinian church, and their rejection of many aspects of medieval piety, added to the growing radicalism of the Czech Reformation, especially in southern Bohemia. By 1400 the Czech Reformation had become an explosive mixture of Milíčian apocalypticism, social unrest, Waldensian anticlericalism, and Wyclifite theology. All that was needed to push reform into revolution was a charismatic leader and a unifying symbol. Jan Hus was both.

96. Šmahel, "Literacy and Heresy," 237–38.
97. For example, Hall, *Thinking the Faith*, vol. 1 of Hall, *Christian Theology in a North American Context*, 200–204. Though his historical presentation is weak, Hall's theological point is sound.

HUS

From 1402 until his death in 1415, Jan Hus was the popular leader of the Czech Reformation. Hus united the social critique of Milíč and the theological work of Wyclif into a potent political synthesis. He was not as original as Wyclif, but his leadership was more effective. As Gordon Leff points out, "Wyclif's main influence was theoretical—in his teachings; that of Hus was predominantly practical, through his preaching and his martyrdom. They met in their common revulsion against the abuses within the Church, above all amongst its hierarchy and religious orders."[1] The old charge that Hus merely plagiarized Wyclif's work has been disproved. Hus drew what he needed from Wyclif to advance the Czech Reformation, but he did so carefully and intelligently.[2] Hus's courageous and consistent call for reform and his martyrdom made him a symbol for the Czech Reformation and encouraged his successors to become even bolder in their opposition to the Roman Church.

Jan Hus was born in the small village of Husinec ("Goosetown") in southern Bohemia sometime around 1372.[3] Little is known about his childhood, but we do know that his intellectual abilities were noticed, and it was arranged

1. Leff, "Wyclif and Hus," 105.

2. Lambert, *Medieval Heresy*, 329; Kaminsky, *Hussite Revolution*, 36–37. J. Loserth made the argument for plagiarism in *Huss und Wiclif* (1884). C. Daniel Crews provides an excellent summary of the scholarly debate generated by Loserth's book in "The Theology of John Hus, with Special Reference to His Concepts of Salvation" (Ph.D. diss., University of Manchester, 1975), 126–35. Leff gives a detailed analysis of Hus's use of Wyclif in *Heresy in the Later Middle Ages*, 2:606–85.

3. For biographical information about Hus I have relied on Spinka's biography, *John Hus*. For his early life, see pp. 21–23. For pictures, see Jiří Kejř, *The Hussite Revolution* (Prague: Orbis, 1988), 46–63.

that he would receive a rudimentary education in Latin and church music. In 1390 he enrolled at the University of Prague in preparation for the priesthood, a common path to a secure living and possible advancement for a bright young commoner from a small town. "When I was a young student," Hus recalled later in life, "I confess to have entertained an evil desire, for I had thought to become a priest quickly in order to secure a good livelihood and dress well and to be held in esteem of man."[4] He lived the typical life of a student but did well in his studies. After receiving his bachelor of arts degree, he stayed on to study philosophy, becoming a master in 1396.

Hus was also acquainted with the works of Matthew of Janov, which appear to have contributed to the "radical and fundamental change which occurred in his religious life prior to his ordination" in 1400, in the words of his biographer Matthew Spinka.[5] Hus later related that he turned away from playing chess, dressing proudly, and other "youthful follies" in order to dedicate himself to the pursuit of truth and service to Christ. He was an active participant in conversations with the reform-minded faculty at the university, and he copied four of Wyclif's philosophical works for his personal use.[6] Among his examiners on the philosophy faculty was Stanislav of Znojmo (d. 1414), an activist in the reform movement and an authority on Wyclif. One of Hus's friends and classmates was Stephen Páleč, who also embraced Wyclif's philosophy and agitated for church reform.[7] In the bitter struggle that ultimately led to Hus's execution, both Stanislav and Páleč eventually turned against Hus and became implacable enemies.[8]

BETHLEHEM CHAPEL

The thirty-year-old philosophy teacher and priest made such an impression on his colleagues that he was chosen to be the rector of Bethlehem Chapel on

4. Quoted in Spinka, *John Hus*, 28.

5. Ibid., 43.

6. In the margins of one of them appears the remark "Wyclif, Wyclif, you will unsettle many a man's mind," but this comment is not in Hus's hand. Oakley, *Western Church*, 196.

7. Maurice Keen, "Influence of Wyclif," in Kenny, *Wyclif in His Times*, 137–40.

8. Spinka, *John Hus*, 34, 160, 180–82. For an extended discussion of the complex philosophical, theological, and political relationships between Stanislav, Páleč, and Hus, see Matthew Spinka, *John Hus at the Council of Constance* (New York: Columbia University Press, 1965), 30–62.

March 14, 1402. This was the beginning of his career as a popular preacher and a thorn in the side of church officials. Over the next twelve years he preached twice each Sunday and feast day, delivering about three thousand sermons in all.[9] The chapel was founded as the successor to Milíč of Korměříž's Jerusalem in 1391 by two of his disciples.[10] One was a royal councilor related to Archbishop Zbyněk, the other, a wealthy merchant. The construction of the chapel was approved by King Wenceslas IV and Jan of Jenštejn, the reforming archbishop of Prague, who may have laid the cornerstone. The name came from the Hebrew etymology of Bethlehem, "house of bread," because the bread of life was to be given to the people through preaching.[11] The chapel was intentionally placed outside the parish system and therefore had greater independence than other institutions. It could hold about three thousand people, most of whom stood throughout the service.

Though he wrote his sermons in Latin, Hus delivered them in Czech, and surviving manuscripts indicate that he extemporized in response to the interest of his listeners.[12] Hus drew large crowds that represented a remarkable cross section of Prague society: burghers, professors, students, merchants, tradesmen, wives, children, servants, and members of the nobility came to hear "God's Little Goose" (a pun on the name Hus). Even Sophie (Žophie) (1376–1428), the queen of Bohemia, attended services regularly, sometimes accompanied by a knight named Jan Žižka (d. 1424), who would play a vital role in the revolution.[13] In 1410 Sophie "wrote to the papacy that Hus' Bethlehem Chapel was exceptionally useful both for her and for her fellow inhabitants of the land for hearing the word of God," writes John Klassen.[14] She was a committed advocate of church reform until the emperor and the pope forced her to submit to church teachings or face the Inquisition and imprisonment.[15]

9. Spinka, *John Hus*, 51–52. Fourteen volumes of his sermons have been published.

10. Thomas Fudge, "*Ansellus Dei* and the Bethlehem Chapel in Prague," *Communio Viatorum* 35 (1993): 127–61. The names of the founders were Vaclav Kříž and Jan of Milheim. On the connections between Jerusalem and Bethlehem, see pp. 131–32. For pictures of the reconstructed Bethlehem Chapel, see Kejř, *Hussite Revolution*, 33–35.

11. Fudge, "*Ansellus Dei*," 128–29. Jenštejn stepped down as archbishop the same year.

12. Spinka, *John Hus*, 52–53; Lambert, *Medieval Heresy*, 319.

13. Fudge, "*Ansellus Dei*," 138.

14. John M. Klassen, *Warring Maidens, Captive Wives, and Hussite Queens: Women and Men at War and Peace in Fifteenth-Century Bohemia* (New York: Columbia University Press, 1999), 232.

15. Ibid., 235–36.

The music at Bethlehem Chapel played an important role in the reformation and the revolution. Music itself was nothing new in worship, of course, but the innovation of Bethlehem Chapel was the translation of the Latin liturgy into the language of the people. Hus and his assistants wrote and reworked several hymns, as well as portions of the Mass itself. While he cautions against seeing Hus as "the harbinger of radical liturgical reform," the historian Thomas Fudge notes that "his role in the development of popular religion and lay piety must in no case be minimized or ignored."[16] The churches that developed out of the Hussite reforms made congregational singing a central part of worship decades before Martin Luther set Protestant doctrine to tavern tunes.

Hus also had the walls of Bethlehem covered with paintings (words and pictures) to instruct the worshippers. A Hussite song instructed people: "If you want to know the Bible / you must go to Bethlehem / and learn it on the walls / as Master Jan of Husinec preached it."[17] In addition to the Decalogue and the Apostles' Creed, translated into Czech, the walls included a summary of Hus's reform program titled *De sex erroribus* (On the Six Errors).[18] These six propositions appeared in Latin and Czech on the northern and southern walls of the chapel and were rediscovered during reconstruction work in 1949.[19]

The first of the "errors" was the boasts of priests who claimed to be able to "create the body of God" when consecrating the elements. Like Wyclif, Hus identified this as pure blasphemy, although he held strongly to the dogma of transubstantiation. What he objected to was the way this was communicated to the people, as an action of the priest rather than as the work of Christ. Second, Hus objected to people's placing their faith in the Virgin Mary or one of the saints rather than in Christ. Though he did not reject the church's teaching on the veneration of the saints per se, Hus insisted that Christians should have faith in God alone because only God is perfect. Third, Hus corrected the

16. Fudge, "*Ansellus Dei*," 144. For a fuller treatment, see Thomas Fudge, "The 'Crown' and the 'Red Gown': Hussite Popular Religion," in *Popular Religion in Germany and Central Europe, 1400–1800*, ed. Robert W. Scribner and Trevor Johnson (London: Macmillan, 1996), 38–57. Much of this material also appears in Fudge, *Magnificent Ride*, 186–216, which includes the texts of many songs written after Hus's execution.

17. Quoted in Fudge, *Magnificent Ride*, 208.

18. Spinka, *Hus and the Council of Constance*, 60–61.

19. Fudge, "*Ansellus Dei*," 135.

FIG. 4 Hussite songs on a wall of Bethlehem Chapel.

misconception that priests and popes can forgive sins. Only God forgives sins; priests merely declare God's forgiveness.

The fourth error was the most important one for the Czech Reformation because it dealt with obedience to authority. Hus rejected the common notion that Christians must be obedient in all things to all authorities (bishops, lords, masters, parents). Instead, he argued, Christians must exercise moral judgment and act according to the law of Christ, even if this means disobeying human authorities. The fifth error pertained to the abuse of ecclesiastical authority. Hus rejected the idea that excommunication in and of itself condemns a person to hell regardless of his or her sinfulness or righteousness. The sixth and final error of the church was simony. On this point in particular Hus was in substantial agreement with many medieval popes and theologians, but the late medieval papacy had endorsed financial practices that had once been condemned. The common element in the six errors was the arrogance of the church in claiming for itself the work of God.

The radical potential of Hus's preaching was given visible form in the work of Nicholas of Dresden, who had fled to Prague to escape the Inquisition in nearby Saxony.[20] Nicholas and his comrades established themselves at the Inn of the Black Rose in the New Town of Prague, where they operated an informal school for reform-minded clerics. Apparently influenced by the Waldensians, the Dresdeners promoted the notion that the contemporary church was a corruption of the original church of Jesus and the apostles. With words and colorful visual images, Nicholas painted a contrast between the ideal model of Jesus and the corruption of the day. He called his treatise *Tabulae veteris et novi coloris* (Tableaux of the Old and New Colors), and some of the images from that work were copied onto the walls of Bethlehem Chapel.[21]

Nicholas's tableaux taught people that Christ rode into Jerusalem in humility on a donkey, but Roman prelates rode like lords on horses. Christ washed the feet of his disciples, but the prelates forced people to kiss their toes. Christ did not have money to pay his taxes, but the prelates took a tenth of the produce of the poorest people. Christ told his disciples not to lord it over one another, but the pope claimed to rule the Roman Empire and be lord over the emperor himself.

Hus used Nicholas's images in Bethlehem Chapel to promote Wyclif's theology. The visible church should conform as closely as possible to the model of the ideal church found in the New Testament and early Christianity. If it failed in this, it should be reformed, by the secular authority if necessary. Although the Dresdeners may have been influenced by the Waldensian idea of the "Constantinian fall of the church," Hus was not so radical. Like Wyclif, he argued that secular government has divine authority to correct abuses in the church, but unlike the later Unity, Hus did not advocate a strict separation of church and state in his quest for church reform.

OPPOSITION

It is impossible to reform a corrupt institution without generating animosity, and the more Hus preached against the sins of the clergy, the more enemies he created. Soon he was swept up in rivalries and conflicts that did not involve him directly but highlighted the corruptions he opposed. In addition to the

20. Spinka, *John Hus*, 48; Kaminsky, *Hussite Revolution*, 83; Fudge, "Ansellus Dei," 133–34.
21. Fudge, *Magnificent Ride*, 226–32, includes pictures of some of the tableaux.

ongoing struggle between the two pontiffs during the papal schism, there was a struggle for control of the archbishop's seat in Prague. Hus was used as a chess piece by powerful political interests because he had such great influence over the populace. As long as Hus was useful to the archbishop or king, he was protected. When he proved too independent for their uses, he was offered up as a sacrifice. This is not the place to catalogue the complex political machinations that led to Hus's excommunication and eventual execution, but a little background is necessary for an understanding of the Czech Reformation and the theology of the Unity.[22]

The early stage of Hus's political difficulties followed the appointment of twenty-six-year-old Zbyněk Zajíc of Hasenburk as archbishop of Prague in 1402, against the wishes of the cathedral chapter.[23] During the ensuing conflict, a doctor of theology at the university, Johannes Hübner, sent a complaint to Rome accusing the Czech masters of teaching Wyclif's heresies. He copied the twenty-four propositions that had been condemned in London in 1382 and added twenty-one he had collected from Wyclif's work on his own (62–63).[24] These forty-five articles formed the core of the heresy accusations in Bohemia for the next decade, and they were the basis of the original charges against Hus at the Council of Constance. Initially Hübner's accusation had little impact, but some of the Czech philosophers, most notably Stanislav Znojmo, Stephan Páleč, and a young scholar named Jakoubek of Stříbro (d. 1429), defended Wyclif's writings, even his condemned eucharistic teaching (65). Though Hus also defended Wyclif, he disagreed with his colleagues on the Eucharist and consistently taught the orthodox doctrine of transubstantiation.[25] It is ironic, then, that Hus, rather than Znojmo and Páleč, was declared a heresiarch.

Somewhat surprisingly, Archbishop Zbyněk initially aligned himself with the reform party at Bethlehem Chapel. He even chose Hus to investigate two reports of "bleeding hosts" (consecrated communion wafers that dripped blood) in Bohemia and accepted Hus's finding that both cases were frauds (67–68).[26] Incidentally, this confirmed Hus's suspicion that priests were using the cult of

---

22. For the full account, consult Spinka, *Hus at the Council of Constance.*
23. Spinka, *John Hus*, 61 (hereafter cited parenthetically).
24. See also Fudge, *Magnificent Ride*, 63–64.
25. Leff, "Wyclif and Hus," 119–20.
26. See also Fudge, *Magnificent Ride*, 65–66.

the saints (relics, pilgrimages, prayers) to deceive people for personal gain, one of the major themes of his preaching at Bethlehem Chapel. But Hübner and the German faculty continued to agitate so aggressively against the reformers that eventually King Wenceslas intervened in support of the Wyclif party. Zbyněk turned against Hus, Bethlehem Chapel, and Wyclif as a result.

In 1408 the papal schism was thirty years old, and there was no solution in sight. A number of cardinals, led by the theologians Francesco Zabarella, Jean Gerson, and Peter d'Ailly, argued that a church council could end the schism, because a council, not the pope, was the highest authority in the church. Wenceslas decided to assist the cardinals in their plan to call a council at Pisa in 1409 to depose both the pope in Rome and the one in Avignon. He was one of the few monarchs officially to ally himself with the new pope elected at Pisa, but he did so against the strong objections of his own archbishop, Zbyněk. The German faculty sided with Zbyněk and the Roman pope, Gregory XII, much to the anger of the king (86–95). Wenceslas responded with the Decree of Kutná Hora in 1409, which gave control of the university to the Czechs.

Hübner's attacks on Wyclif had the unintended effect of solidifying the reform party. As the Czech Reformation spread to the streets of Prague and the Bohemian countryside, his forty-five questionable propositions were used as slogans for reform in songs and on placards. Agitators used Article 10, stating that priests should not own property, to protest tithes, for example.[27] The sight of common people discussing theology and proclaiming condemned propositions in the streets of Prague convinced the archbishop that the Czech Reformation was getting out of hand. He accused Hus of heresy, but this did not prevent Hus from being elected rector of the university (100–103). Stanislav Znojmo and Stephen Páleč were not so lucky. They were imprisoned in Italy, where they had gone to defend their views, and both were forced to repudiate Wyclif's teaching and revoke their own writings. When they returned to Prague, they joined in Zbyněk's campaign against Hus.[28] Páleč was persuaded that peace in the church and obedience to papal authority were more important than truth or conscience, and he was Hus's most remorseless opponent at the Council of Constance.

---

27. Lambert, *Medieval Heresy*, 321.
28. Fudge, *Magnificent Ride*, 68–69.

The struggle between the rival popes inflamed the tense situation in Prague, and Zbyněk moved decisively against the theology of Wyclif and Hus (108–29).[29] He forbade the teaching of the forty-five articles and demanded that students hand over their copies of Wyclif's books. The archbishop supervised the burning of two hundred volumes of Wyclif's writings in July 1410, and he persuaded the pope to ban preaching in "private chapels," a move directed against Bethlehem (108–10). Hus and Jerome of Prague publicly opposed the archbishop, and the public responded enthusiastically, even violently. Fearing for his own life, Zbyněk fled the city and excommunicated Hus for heresy and insubordination (112).[30]

Hus appealed to Pope John XXIII, who had succeeded Alexander V, the pope elected at the Council of Pisa (248).[31] John was opposed to reforms that would reduce papal revenues, and he supported Zbyněk's efforts to silence Hus. When Hus refused to travel to Italy to meet with the curia, the pope issued a second excommunication. The people of Prague responded by taking to the streets, proclaiming that the pope was the Antichrist and Hus a saint. Hus's most passionate disciple, Jerome of Prague, led the rioting and personally assaulted at least one priest.[32]

John XXIII then resorted to the most feared and dangerous weapon in his arsenal: the interdict. This meant that all of the clergy in Prague were forbidden to perform any but the most essential pastoral functions, such as last rites and baptisms. Church bells were to be silenced, weddings postponed, and preaching stopped. Such tactics had worked in other realms in the past, but Hus was a formidable opponent. He was not a rogue priest or angry monk but the rector of the university and a leader with strong popular support. At the time of the interdict, he also had the support of the king and queen. Hus proclaimed that Wenceslas IV rather than Archbishop Zbyněk was the "first prelate" of Bohemia, a position remarkably similar to that of Thomas Cranmer in England a century later. Clearly Hus did not share the Waldensian suspicion

29. See also ibid., 68–76.

30. See also ibid., 73.

31. This John XXIII, obviously, is not to be confused with the Pope John XXIII who called the Second Vatican Council in 1962. The John XXIII who called the Council of Constance is no longer officially recognized as a pope by the Catholic Church. For more on John XXIII, see Oakley, *Western Church*, 64–67.

32. Kaminsky, *Hussite Revolution*, 73; Fudge, *Magnificent Ride*, 74–75.

of secular authorities' influence on the church. Wenceslas ordered the clergy and people to ignore the interdict, and he forced Archbishop Zbyněk to submit and exonerate Hus, but Zbyněk died before the exoneration was made effective (124–29).[33]

With the death of the archbishop in 1411, it looked as if Hus and the reform party would win, thanks to a combination of shrewd politics, convincing theology, and impassioned preaching. There was even hope that a new archbishop could spread the Czech Reformation throughout Europe. As in the case of Wyclif, the secular authorities found Hus's argument that the secular authority could reform the church useful in political struggles against the papacy.[34] As long as Hus's sermons served the interests of the king, he had a margin of protection. But the situation changed rapidly when John XXIII announced a sale of indulgences to finance his war against the kingdom of Naples in May 1412. Emperor Sigismund was promised a share of the proceeds if he allowed preachers to sell indulgences in the empire, and his brother, King Wenceslas, agreed to do the same in Bohemia (132–33).[35]

Anticipating by a century the more famous revolt of Martin Luther against indulgences, Hus and his party publicly opposed their sale. Hus was not as radical or thorough as Luther in his opposition to indulgences, but he did identify them as a symbol of simony and treachery in the church.[36] First the church terrorized people with the fear of purgatory, and then it assured them salvation through the purchase of an indulgence. Hus's student Jakoubek of Stříbro used the pulpit of Bethlehem Chapel to proclaim that indulgences proved that Pope John XXIII was the Antichrist (139).[37]

A university debate on the issue erupted in open rebellion, and people took to the streets. The alliance between the university masters and the secular authorities was broken. The king made it illegal to speak against indulgences. When several young men violated the ban, he had them summarily beheaded. Jerome of Prague had the bodies taken to Bethlehem Chapel, where they were

33. See also Kaminsky, *Hussite Revolution*, 74.
34. Ibid., 94.
35. See also Fudge, *Magnificent Ride*, 76–81.
36. A point made by Crews, *Theology of Hus*, 303–6.
37. For more detail on the Hussite use of the word "Antichrist" in the struggle against the papacy, see Thomas Fudge, "The Night of the Antichrist: Popular Culture, Judgment, and Revolution in Fifteenth-Century Bohemia," *Communio Viatorum* 37 (1995): 33–45.

FIG. 5   Plaque of Hus on the wall of his bedroom in Bethlehem Chapel.

hailed as martyrs and saints.[38] In response, Wenceslas finally enforced the papal interdict. All Christians were forbidden to assist Hus "in food, drink, greeting, discourse, buying and selling, conversation, shelter, or in any other way. In any place where he might seek shelter, all church service and ministrations must be stopped and remain suspended for three days after his departure. Should he die, he must not be buried; or should he be buried, his body must be exhumed" (161).

Hus chose to leave the city and go into voluntary exile in southern Bohemia in 1412 rather than make the people of Prague suffer. During his exile he wrote his most important works, including *De simonia* (On Simony), *De ecclesia* (On the Church), and expositions on the Apostles' Creed, the Lord's Prayer, and the Ten Commandments. These writings, especially *Expositions of the Faith*, became core textbooks for all of the Hussite churches. As we will see, Luke of Prague, the leading theologian of the Brethren, drew on them extensively, though critically, in the elaboration of his own pastoral theology (195–98).

38. Kaminsky, *Hussite Revolution*, 80–83. The worshippers in the chapel sang, "these are the martyrs, these are the holy ones, who for the gospel of God offered their lives and have washed their robes in the blood of the Lamb." Fudge, *Magnificent Ride*, 80.

HUS'S THEOLOGY

In explicating the creed, Hus affirmed the orthodox teaching on the Trinity. The three "persons" of the Father, Son, and Holy Spirit were equal and united. The second person of the Trinity assumed human flesh in the womb of the Virgin Mary. Those with faith in him would be saved and filled with the grace of the Holy Spirit. The incarnate Son of God suffered, died, and was buried. Hus affirmed that Christ descended into hell to free the spirits of those imprisoned, but "he advances the curious theory," in Spinka's words, of multiple hells as an explanation of why many of the damned continue to suffer torment (200). In discussing the Holy Spirit, Hus stayed within the bounds of orthodoxy in the Western church, affirming the procession of the Spirit from the Father *and the Son* (the *filioque* clause) rather than the original version of the Nicene Creed. Rather than speculate at length on the question of the Trinity, Hus concentrated on the issue of forgiveness of sins and the nature of the church. Christ is the one who forgives; priests are merely the mouthpieces of Christ.

Hus followed the Catholic practice of dividing the Ten Commandments (the Decalogue) into two tablets: the love of God (the first three) and the love of neighbor (the remaining seven) (202). In discussing the first tablet, he did not condemn the use of images, but he did warn against abuses. People should not be attracted to worship because of the beauty of the art (especially art depicting nude saints); nor should the church use expensive chalices, bells, and other items. The purpose of worship is to honor God and to hear his word. This emphasis was consistent with the reforms Hus instituted at Bethlehem Chapel, where scripture, congregational singing, and preaching were the focus of the service. Some of Hus's harshest words were directed against the veneration of saints' relics (204). No doubt his investigations into the "miracles" of the bleeding hosts added to his vehemence.

On the subject of using the name of God in vain, Hus steered away from the Waldensian prohibition of oaths, and the Unity eventually adopted Hus's view on this matter. Those who are baptized in the name of Christ should not blaspheme against Christ by doing evil. Neither should people use God's name vainly in prayer or in careless oaths. In the same manner, people should observe the Sabbath as a day of rest from sin, not as a day of fun and frivolity

(206).[39] Interestingly, Hus acknowledged that the biblical Sabbath was Saturday rather than Sunday, but he defended the designation of the day of rest as the day of Christ's resurrection. We see here that Hus used reason and tradition in interpreting the commandments. Likewise, in explaining the commandment to "honor your mother and father," Hus reminded his flock that devotion to Christ sometimes requires resistance to unlawful or evil commands.

The commandment against killing, for Hus, was more than just a prohibition on taking another person's life. Thoughts and words may also kill the soul. Although he was opposed to the taking of human life, Hus presented a just-war theory in the *Expositions of the Faith* that would later be rejected by Chelčický and the early Brethren (208–9). Hus used the commandment against stealing to attack simony, dishonest trade, and excessive taxation. He also promoted one of Wyclif's most radical ideas—that those who live in mortal sin, even kings, forfeit their right of dominion and use of God's property. Though it was directed against the Roman Church, this idea had the potential to undermine the legitimacy of all forms of government. This was the proposition that most angered Emperor Sigismund at the Council of Constance, and it contributed directly to Hus's execution (269–70).

In light of his own difficulties with the courts, it is not surprising that Hus gave a great deal of attention to the commandment against bearing false witness. Hus argued that it is always sinful to slander another person, especially an innocent person, but it is doubly sinful for a priest to commit slander. Those who have the responsibility to preach the Word of God blaspheme whenever they lie, including when they falsely accuse someone of heresy. Silence can also be a sin, because "not to defend truth is to be a traitor to it" (211). Finally, Hus promoted the idea of apostolic poverty as the solution to covetousness, especially for the clergy. The Unity of the Brethren adopted Hus's explication of the Decalogue for the most part, although they parted with him on the legitimacy of violence.

Hus's explanation of the Lord's Prayer was also fairly traditional, but there are some interesting aspects that illuminate the particular concerns of the Czech Reformation. His major concern was that prayer should be a matter of the heart and soul, not simply a ritual action. The one praying should understand

---

39. Spinka accuses Hus of being "puritanical" on this matter.

the meaning of the Lord's Prayer and try to live according to its petitions. Thus pedagogy must be connected to devotion. Priests need to teach the meaning of the prayer and teach people how to live properly. Hus pointed out that the Lord's Prayer offers a critique of social inequity. The first words of the prayer, "Our Father," suggests that "the common fatherhood of God places all men—popes and kings as well as their poorest subjects—on equality" (214). In discussing the prayer that God's will be done on earth, Hus asserted that God is in charge of all that happens on earth, but believers should pray that *their* wills be in conformity with God's will. Similarly, the prayer for daily bread is more than a prayer for food. It is a prayer for the bread of life, which for Hus was the Word of God (216–17). Many of these ideas were included in the catechism of the Unity, as we will see.

Hus is famous for his insistence that scripture is the true authority in the church, but he acknowledged that the church fathers played a key role in clarifying orthodox teaching. His argument that early Christianity was normative separated Hus from the reforming cardinals (conciliarists) who maintained that the church of their age, the fifteenth-century church, was superior to the early church because of the progressive nature of revelation.[40] The normative nature of the early church became a hallmark of the various Hussite parties, especially the Unity of the Brethren. The New Testament was the primary source of information on the early church, but the writings of the church fathers of the first five centuries were used as well.

Hus gave a great deal of attention to the doctrine of salvation, following the traditional Christian teaching that sin entered the world through the disobedience of Adam and Eve and left all human beings in sin and ruin.[41] This first sin of disobedience to the commandments of God was the result of human pride. Though Adam and Eve thought that eating the forbidden fruit would make them like God, the true fruits of sin are "hunger, thirst, coldness, excessive warmth, work, weariness, and death" (250–53). Humans also suffer from existential ignorance because of sin: they are ignorant of both God and themselves. John Calvin was not the first to argue that the core of doctrine is knowledge of God and of self. For Hus, the natural state of a person is fragmentation;

---

40. Quoted in Kaminsky, *Hussite Revolution*, 117.
41. Crews, *Theology of Hus*, 222 (hereafter cited parenthetically).

each man or woman is "a disjointed and terribly imperfect creature divided within himself and estranged from God and the world around him" (256). Only Christ can restore the fragmented self to wholeness.

Following the teaching of Anselm, Hus preached that sin causes infinite guilt because it is an offense against the infinite God (367). The ultimate sin is to fail to seek forgiveness from the one who has been offended. Ignorance of the fact that one is a sinner is itself a sin; therefore a refusal to avail oneself of the ministrations of the church merely compounds the guilt because it is a form of rebellion against God. Still, according to Crews, Hus "was very hesitant to say that any man was damned" (372).[42] Hus pointed to the example of the penitent thief on the cross to remind people not to stand in judgment on others. No one would know for sure who is damned until Judgment Day. "The subject of damnation was always a sorrowful one for Hus," Crews writes. "We have seen that he wept over his enemies, whom he believed to be on the way to destruction. For Hus, love was the chief Christian virtue, and this love extended even to those who rebelled against the Lord and his faithful ministers" (376).

Hus addressed the question of salvation from the perspective of God's absolute sovereignty. Salvation is the work of God, and God "is perfectly free to condemn even those who make a 'deathbed repentance,' for such men have rejected the offer of salvation when it was first given, and God is under no obligation to be bound by the last desperate wish of men" (242). We will see that the Unity of the Brethren also rejected the validity of deathbed repentance, and this was a major point of dispute between the Brethren and Luther in the 1530s.

Most important for Hus was the doctrine that salvation depends on God's free decision rather than human effort, but he did not teach a consistent theory of predestination (340–48). The basic conundrum, inherited from Augustine, is how to deal with the sovereignty and power of God without blaming God for human sin and damnation. Hus used the common distinction between those who are predestined to salvation by the grace of God and those whom God knows will be damned. The "foreknown" are not forced into sin by God; they deserve their damnation because they rebel against God. The predestined

---

42. "In damnation there is everlasting fire, darkness, excruciating suffering, and unending burning with the devils" (ibid., 375).

are equally guilty, but they are saved by the mercy of God, who chose them before the beginning of time. The elect are those predestined to receive the grace that allows them to partake of the means of salvation that God provides. "Without grace, man cannot turn to God, and so the glory for man's salvation belongs entirely to God, the giver of all grace. Grace gives man the ability to respond, but does not take away his ability to reject. In this way, the fault of damnation remains man's own" (344).

In the end, though, Hus acknowledged that he did not understand the mystery of salvation. His role was to urge all people to repent and seek the grace that God has provided, not to stand in judgment over others (348). At Constance Hus was condemned for teaching that the foreknown are not truly in the church, but he insisted that they are in the church militant, just not in the true church of the predestined.

Unlike Luther, Hus stayed within the tradition of Catholic Scholasticism, which held that grace consists in the power of God to make his creatures pleasing to himself. Humans in their natural condition are vile, but through grace they can become holy and pleasing. This grace is an undeserved gift of God given through the sacrifice of Christ. Grace gives the elect the merit they need to enter heaven. Hus also accepted the teaching that there are three types of grace: prevenient, cooperating, and confirming. The first is God's work and leads humans to salvation. Once people are awakened to their true state, they may receive further grace, which gives them the ability to cooperate with God in their salvation. Grace is conferred through the sacraments and ministrations of the church, the means of grace. Finally, grace confirms or strengthens the one being saved, preserving him from further sins (320–26).

Hus also endorsed the Augustinian tradition that there are different types of faith: believing about God, believing God, and believing in God (*credere de deo, credere deo, credere in deum*) (335). The Unity followed Hus's teaching closely in this matter, and we will revisit this concept later. The first type of faith believes that there is a God who has done what is said of him. The second type believes that what God has said in the scriptures is true. The third type of faith, saving faith, requires believing *in* God, which means placing all of one's hope in God. Furthermore, as Crews explains, "the faith necessary for salvation consists of believing that Christ is true God and true man, and in accepting the other truths of Christ's teachings" (331). The Unity of the

Brethren would refine this further in their concept of essentials, ministerials, and incidentals.

Saving faith, for Hus, is distinguished from mere belief by its being formed by love (*fides caritate formata*). There is no possibility for salvation by faith alone, if that phrase means faith without works of love.[43] In *De ecclesia*, Hus defines saving faith as the "belief of persevering love," which is possible only because of the love of God. As one is perfected through grace, one reveals more and more divine love, the "guiding force of spiritual and physical life."[44] Love is not an emotion; it is willing obedience to Christ that is manifested in works of justice and mercy. Hus frequently quoted the dictum of the Epistle of James (2:17) that "faith without works is dead."[45] He also found support for his belief that faith is inseparable from works in Augustine's instruction: "do what you believe and then it is faith." A more Christocentric way of expressing the same notion is Hus's statement "Live like Christ, and you will know Christ well."[46] This would be a major dividing point between the heirs of Hus and the Lutherans in the sixteenth century.

THE CHURCH

Hus's writings about the church and simony led to his execution. He rejected his opponents' argument that the church should be defined as a "mystico-ecclesiastical" body composed of the pope and the cardinals as the successors of Christ and the apostles. Like Wyclif, he defined the true Catholic Church as "the totality of the predestinate" (*omnium praedestinatorum universitas*). The cardinals at Constance accused Hus of teaching that the "foreknown," those destined for damnation, are not part of the church on earth, but Hus distinguished between the invisible church of the elect and the visible church militant on earth, which includes both the saved and the lost. Central to his thought is the distinction between the visible church, with the bishop of Rome at its head, and the real, true, invisible church of the elect, with Christ as the head.

43. Spinka, *Hus and the Council of Constance*, 62.
44. Crews, *Theology of Hus*, 340.
45. Spinka, *Hus' Concept of the Church*, 73.
46. Crews, *Theology of Hus*, 352.

This is the church described as "one holy catholic and apostolic" in the Nicene Creed.[47] No human authority can remove a person from the communion of this church, a conviction that sustained Hus as he faced excommunication and execution.[48]

Hus did not deny the importance of the church as the institution Christ established to serve as the conduit of grace for the elect on earth. The only foundation of the church is Christ himself, and the role of the church is to proclaim Christ and his redemption through words *and example*. In this sense the church is Mother Church, but, as Crews points out, her "womb is love, and the seed which causes life to come into being within her is the Word of God. Hus also taught that the breasts through which the church as mother gives nourishment to her spiritual children are love of God and love of neighbor." Mother Church provides the Word and sacraments for the sake of the elect.[49]

Hus recognized that the visible church, the "congregation of the faithful," is a human institution prone to error and in need of reformation. He rejected the argument of his opponents, who claimed that the Roman Church itself is "ever holy and free from all pernicious errors in morals and faith," despite the unworthiness of its officers. Hus pointed to the existence of three popes as evidence that the papacy was not infallible, and he further noted at his trial that the Council of Constance itself had deposed Pope John XXIII and convicted him of fifty-four crimes, including heresy and simony. Apparently at least one pope had erred, as had the Council of Pisa that elected his predecessor. In *De ecclesia* Hus argued that the pope had excommunicated the Greek Church in error, just as the pope erred in excommunicating the theological faculty of Prague. He even went so far as to proclaim that "to rebel against an erring pope is to obey Christ the Lord."[50] There was only one infallible head of the church, and that was Christ. All laws and actions of the church and the pope must be judged by the commandments and example of Christ.[51] This assertion played a major role in his condemnation.

Hus explicitly rejected one of the fundamental arguments for papal supremacy: that the papacy was founded by Christ when he proclaimed that Peter

47. Spinka, *Hus' Concept of the Church*, 172–74, 255–58, 387.
48. As Crews points out. *Theology of Hus*, 300.
49. Ibid., 284, 279.
50. Spinka, *Hus' Concept of the Church*, 205–6, 175, 354–57, 263, 284, 282.
51. Spinka, *Hus and the Council of Constance*, 50.

was the rock on which the church would be built (Matt. 16:16–19). Pioneering later Protestant exegesis, Hus argued that the rock was Peter's confession of faith in the Son of God, not Peter himself. The church is built on Christ the rock, not on Peter or his successor in Rome. As long as the pope demonstrates the same faith and devotion to Christ that the martyred Peter did, he is head of the church.[52] Popes who oppose the reign of Christ in the world may claim exalted titles, but in reality they are servants of the Antichrist. "Let the disciples of Antichrist blush who, living contrary to Christ, speak of themselves as the greatest and the proudest of God's holy Church. They, polluted by avarice and arrogance of the world, are called publicly the heads and body of the holy Church. According to Christ's gospel, however, they are called the least."[53]

Hus taught that the ideal and invisible Catholic Church of the saints should serve as the model for the earthly church; it is the goal toward which the institutional church should always strive. The cardinals at Constance were not wrong to recognize that Hus's zealous reform of the church, especially his demand that the shepherds protect rather than abuse the sheep, was closely connected to his definition of the church. The further the visible church strays from the teaching and example of Christ, its true head, the less authority it actually has over the lives of the faithful. The church, for Hus, is not the pope, the curia, the cardinals, or the clergy; it is the followers of Christ in every age and every nation.

One of the charges brought against Hus at Constance, which would also dog the Brethren throughout their history, was that of Donatism. In the fourth century there was a schism in the church in North Africa over the question of whether the sacraments administered by an unworthy priest are still valid. The Latin theologian Augustine of Hippo responded to the Donatists by insisting that the priest is merely a proxy for Christ.[54] The important thing is not the priest who administers the sacraments but Christ, who makes the sacraments holy. Thus worshippers need not worry that their salvation could be

52. Spinka, *Hus' Concept of the Church*, 264–68.
53. Hus quoted in ibid., 261.
54. There are numerous studies of the Donatist controversy and Augustine's anti-Donatist writings. A good starting place is Pelikan, *Christian Tradition*, vol. 1, *The Emergence of the Catholic Tradition (100–600)* (Chicago: University of Chicago Press, 1971), 307–18. See also Peter Brown, *Augustine of Hippo* (Berkeley and Los Angeles: University of California Press, 1967), 203–43.

endangered by the sinfulness of their priests. After all, as Augustine pointed out, no priest is without sin; that distinction belongs to Christ alone. Augustine's writings were originally intended to assure the faithful that their salvation did not depend on choosing the right faction in the Donatist controversy, but by the late Middle Ages this theology was often used to subvert efforts to reform the church. If the sacraments are valid despite the unworthiness of the priests, why worry about immoral or incompetent priests?

Though Hus persistently asserted his belief in Catholic teaching on the validity of sacraments administered by sinful priests, his call for reform of the priesthood and the whole hierarchy of the Roman Church bordered on Donatism. He affirmed "the validity, though not the worthiness, of the sacramental ministrations of even the most sinful priests,"[55] but his opponents had difficulty in seeing a distinction between validity and worthiness, particularly when crowds in Prague were assaulting priests they considered immoral or abusive.

Likewise, his opponents were not persuaded by his denial that he had called the pope the Antichrist. "All he had said," he claimed, "was that a pope who sold benefices, who was arrogant, greedy, and otherwise contrary to Christ in way of life, was Antichrist."[56] Since all the popes during Hus's life had done those things, presumably all of them were representatives of the Antichrist. Increasingly the official response to Hus was that he must simply submit to the authority of the church and stop his efforts to reform doctrine and practice. Páleč stressed the authority of the institutional church, especially the papacy and canon law, to the point that he defined the pope and cardinals as infallible "in all matters whatsoever."[57]

Hus responded with exasperation to the persistent attacks of his erstwhile allies: "I hope that death will sooner remove me or those two renegades from the truth either to heaven or to hell, than that I agree with their opinions. . . . Páleč calls us Wyclifites, as if we had deviated from Christianity. Stanislav calls us infidels, perfidious, insane, and scurrilous clergy. All such slanders I would have ignored, had they not strengthened the Antichrist in his wrath. I hope, however, with God's grace to oppose them until I am consumed by fire. . . . One

55. Crews, *Theology of Hus*, 279.
56. Kaminsky, *Hussite Revolution*, 40.
57. Quoted in Spinka, *John Hus*, 187.

should not sin in order to avoid the punishment of death. Truth conquers all things."[58] This last sentence became the motto of the Czech Reformation.

THE COUNCIL OF CONSTANCE

While Hus was in hiding, the great powers of Europe were in the process of convening one of the largest councils of the church in history. The Council of Pisa, which had been arranged by reforming cardinals of the rival popes Gregory XII (Rome) and Benedict XIII (Avignon), had failed to unify the church under the pope chosen at Pisa, Alexander V.[59] After 1409 there were in fact three popes competing for legitimacy, two of whom had engaged in military conflict over who could reside in Rome. The Roman Catholic Church had reached a crisis point, and increasingly people looked to the emperor to do what Constantine had done in 325. If none of the popes could invoke a council of the whole Catholic Church, then the emperor could.

The emperor and king of the Romans was Sigismund, the brother of King Wenceslas. Sigismund saw that he could greatly increase his stature among the European powers if he were to bring about the reunification of the Catholic Church and put an end to persistent dissent. After complex negotiations with Alexander V's successor, John XXIII, and with reform-minded cardinals, Sigismund called for a general council of the church to meet in a neutral city. The Council of Constance, which met from 1414 to 1417, represented the temporary triumph of the conciliarist movement, which sought to govern the church through councils rather than simply through papal authority. The Council of Constance was also the great opportunity to bring an end to the papal schism and make necessary reforms in the church without destroying the institution.[60] To John XXIII's surprise, the council he had called promptly arrested and deposed him early in the proceedings.[61]

Conciliarism had been discussed for nearly a century, but the papal schism had given urgency to the theories that canon lawyers and theologians had been

58. Ibid., 177–78.
59. Oakley, *Western Church*, 61–67.
60. Spinka gives a brief history of the council in *Hus at the Council of Constance*, 63–73, and provides a detailed eyewitness account of the council by Peter Mladoňovice (89–234).
61. Oakley, *Western Church*.

debating. Though the conciliarists in general agreed that the pope should be supreme in matters of faith, they were alarmed at the growing papal claims to infallibility.[62] The conciliarists rejected the idea that the power of jurisdiction over the church resided only in the bishop of Rome. They argued instead that the pope is chosen by the church to exercise the power of jurisdiction on its behalf, and that a pope who fails to do so should be removed from office by a general council. Only in this way, they argued, could the church be saved from the scandal of a heretical pope. Hus had tried to be part of the Catholic reformation represented by the conciliarists, but his cure proved too radical for the cardinals. Many of his statements against papal corruption echoed the sentiments of leading members of the council, including Zabarella, d'Ailly, and Gerson, but the cardinals believed that Hus had become a barrier to the reunification of the church.[63] Hus's appeal to the right of Christians to rebel against ecclesiastical abuse raised the specter of chaos and the demise of all ecclesiastical authority.

Hus was enough of a political realist to know that the journey to the council might end for him at the stake, but he appears also to have been enough of an idealist to think that by presenting his views openly to the council he could help institute broad reforms. He even wrote out a sermon he intended to preach before the council, which one biographer called an "astonishing excess of optimism." Despite Sigismund's verbal assurance of safe conduct, Hus was arrested shortly after his arrival in Constance in November 1414, and he remained in custody, sometimes in chains, until his death on July 6, 1415.[64]

Church officials questioned Hus in his cell on the forty-five articles, which had been a source of contention for a decade in Prague. Hus declared that he had never held thirty-three of them because he considered them heretical. Of the remaining twelve, he declared that they could have an acceptable meaning if read correctly. He also reaffirmed his belief in transubstantiation, to the surprise of his interrogators.[65] Páleč was asked to draw up a list of heresies based

62. Ibid., 158–74, gives a good summary of the development of conciliarist theology. For a more detailed study, see Francis Oakley, *The Political Thought of Pierre d'Ailly: The Voluntarist Tradition* (New Haven: Yale University Press, 1964). Matthew Spinka provides a good overview of the history of conciliarism and the various conciliarist theories in *Hus at the Council of Constance*, 3–86. See also Matthew Spinka, trans. and ed., *Advocates of Reform* (Philadelphia: Westminster Press, 1953).

63. Spinka, *Hus at the Council of Constance*, 21–22.

64. Spinka, *John Hus*, 226, 222–35.

65. Spinka, *Hus at the Council of Constance*, 59–60; Spinka, *John Hus*, 232–33.

on Hus's own writings, which he was eager to do. *De ecclesia* was his main source, and Hus defended the questionable articles in writing. After many weeks of debate and discussion, the leaders of the council decided on thirty-nine counts of heresy drawn from Hus's writings. Cardinal d'Ailly presented these to Hus at the trial on June 8 and Hus defended himself, often over shouts from the assembly.[66]

When the charges had been read and Hus had answered them, Cardinal d'Ailly, on behalf of the council, demanded that Hus acknowledge his error and recant.[67] Hus responded that he was willing to recant any errors that were shown to him, but that the council was asking him to recant things that he had never believed or taught. To do so would be to lie, and he was unwilling to lie to save his own life. Eventually the list of charges was reduced to thirty, but Hus was not allowed a second public hearing on the final charges of heresy.[68] Ironically, the more Hus protested his innocence, the more he confirmed the council's condemnation, in that heresy was "the pertinacious maintenance of doctrinal error by a Christian in defiance of ecclesiastical authority."[69]

There is no need to reprint the charges brought against Hus or his answers to them here. For the most part they focus on Hus's definition of the true church as the church of the elect, his rejection of absolute papal authority, and his putative Donatism. He was accused of teaching that sinners are not part of the church and that "Peter was not nor is the head of the holy catholic Church."[70] His assertion that a pope is not Peter's true successor if his life is more consistent with that of Judas was particularly troubling to the council, as was Hus's defense of the proposition that "no one is a secular lord, no one is prelate, no one is bishop while he is in mortal sin."[71] These ideas were unacceptable to the council, but they had a profound influence on the early Brethren.

Since the publication of Paul de Vooght's monumental study of Hus's theology and condemnation, *L'heresie de Jean Huss* (1960), the scholarly consensus

66. The record of the trial, including the thirty-nine articles, is found in Spinka, *Hus at the Council of Constance*, 182–223.

67. Ibid., 214; Spinka, *John Hus*, 272.

68. The final charges and Hus's response are found in Spinka, *Hus at the Council of Constance*, 260–64.

69. Oakley, *Western Church*, 175–76. The official charge against Hus states that he was "obstinate and incorrigible, and as such does not desire to return into the bosom of the holy mother Church." Spinka, *Hus at the Council of Constance*, 297.

70. Spinka, *Hus at the Council of Constance*, 261. The complete list of charges is found on pp. 260–64.

71. Ibid., 264.

has been that Hus's teachings were orthodox according to the standards of the day. This fact has been partially recognized by the modern Catholic Church. At an international symposium on Hus held at the Vatican in 1999, Pope John Paul II officially apologized for the execution of Hus, saying, "I feel the need to express deep regret for the cruel death inflicted on Jan Hus and for the consequent wound of conflict and division which was thus imposed on the minds and hearts of the Bohemian people."[72] The Vatican did not officially remove the stigma of excommunication and condemnation of Hus, however. In this regard, Hus is still officially a greater heresiarch than even Martin Luther. Though Hus's sermons and writings may have been technically orthodox at the time, they clearly opposed the authority of popes and councils to define doctrine in absolute terms. That he was condemned by a general council whose decrees were confirmed by the pope makes it difficult for the Catholic Church today to exonerate him without acknowledging that the church can err. The issues of the Hussite Reformation remain current in Western Christianity.

MARTYRDOM

On July 6, 1415, Hus was declared to be "a disciple not of Christ but rather of the heresiarch John Wyclif," who taught things that "are erroneous, others scandalous, others offensive to pious ears."[73] Hus protested loudly but was silenced by command of Zabarella. Then he was subjected to a ceremonial degradation that included being ritually stripped of his priestly robes. A paper miter with three demons drawn upon it was placed on his head. After the bishops committed his soul to Satan, Hus shouted that he committed his soul "to the most merciful Lord Jesus Christ."[74] He was handed over to the secular authorities for the final punishment, since the church could not put a man to death. His works were publicly burned in the cemetery as he was led to the stake. The wood was piled up to his chin, and eyewitnesses reported that Hus sang "Christ,

---

72. John Paul II, "Address of the Holy Father to an International Symposium on John Hus," December 17, 1999, http://www.vatican.va/holy_father/john_paul_ii/speeches/1999/december/documents/hf_jp-ii_spe_17121999_jan-hus_en.html.

73. Spinka, *Hus at the Council of Constance*, 295–96.

74. The account of his degradation and execution is found in Spinka, *John Hus*, 287–90.

FIG. 6   Hus being burned, mural in Bethlehem Chapel.

Thou Son of the living God, have mercy on me" as the flames rose. Once he was dead, the executioners ground up the remains and threw them into the Rhine River so that there would be no relics for his followers. The following year his friend and colleague Jerome of Prague suffered a similar fate, though less courageously.[75]

This effort to squelch the Czech Reformation through a public ritual of violence and intimidation had the opposite effect. During the previous three hundred years the Catholic Church had condemned many people to death on the charge of heresy, but never had it executed a prominent scholar and popular preacher whose way of life was beyond reproach. News of Hus's execution shocked and angered nobles, clergy, and commoners throughout Bohemia. More than four hundred Czech nobles sent a letter of protest to the Council of Constance with their personal seals attached, accusing the council of having executed a godly man. For many Czechs, the display of naked power and injustice at Constance completed the identification of the Roman Catholic Church with the Antichrist. Reformation quickly became revolution.

Jan Hus went to Constance as a loyal son of the Catholic Church, was declared a heresiarch, and became the symbol of a revolution. "Thus," Kaminsky writes, "only two or three months after Hus's death, the martyr replaced the actual man, the symbol of evangelical anti-Romanism suppressed the living teacher, and the man who had always tried to avoid doctrinal extremities that would have separated him from the Roman church was transmuted into the patron saint of endless sectarian innovations."[76] For the Czech Reformation, Hus the martyr was even more important than Hus the theologian or Hus the preacher. Pictures showed him ascending into heaven out of the flames of Constance, and popular songs contrasted the "Christlike" Hus with the papal Antichrist.[77] It was recently discovered that the martyr day of Jan Hus was one of the most important feast days in the Czech liturgical calendar in the fifteenth and sixteenth centuries.[78] In the midst of their internecine disputes, all Hussite parties were united in veneration of Saint Jan and his feast day, July 6.

---

75. Fudge, *Magnificent Ride*, 88–89; Spinka, *John Hus*, 292–97.

76. Kaminsky, *Hussite Revolution*, 215.

77. See the photos in Kejř, *Hussite Revolution*, 21, 41.

78. On the elevation of Hus to sainthood in the popular religion of Bohemia, see Fudge, *Magnificent Ride*, 123–35.

HUS'S LEGACY FOR THE UNITY OF THE BRETHREN

As we examine the theology of the Unity in detail, we will look at many areas in which the Brethren departed from the teaching of Hus. This was particularly the case with Hus's arguments for just war and transubstantiation. The differences between the scholastic Hus, who tried so desperately to convince the Council of Constance of his orthodoxy, and the simple brother who sought to live by the sayings of the Sermon on the Mount are so great that it is easy to overlook Hus's influence on the Unity's doctrine. Perhaps his most important contribution was his insistence that the only true head of the church is Christ. Though Hus and the Brethren differed on the role of secular authority in the church, they agreed that the primary authority for Christians is the law of Christ as revealed in scripture. Most important, Hus demystified the institutional church and showed that it is a human institution in need of constant reform and accountability, both to God and to the people it serves.

Hus was confident that simple people, farmers, midwives, artisans, and laborers, could and should understand the basic teachings of Christianity. By teaching them the Gospel and law of Christ, they would be less vulnerable to the clergy who preyed on their fears and superstitions. It was in part because Hus provided resources for the laity that someone like Gregory was confident in his ability to re-create the church of the apostles. The Brethren built their catechetical instructions around the three central elements of Hus's *Expositions of the Faith*: the Apostles' Creed, the Lord's Prayer, and the Decalogue. The Unity also accepted Hus's Augustinian understanding of the church as the invisible body of the elect, although they refined his thought in some intriguing ways.

Daniel Crews provides a good summary of the significance of Hus's theology for the Unity and the ecumenical church: "His prime contributions to theology lie in his emphasis on the love and grace of God, in characterizing works as the necessary fruits of faith, in seeing salvation as a restoration of the primary sovereignty of God over his creatures, in reminding a proud church of the authority of Scripture, and above all in stressing the ultimate responsibility of the individual before his heavenly Lord."[79] Faith must be completed in love, and love means seeking justice for one's neighbor and mercy for one's enemies.

79. Crews, *Theology of Hus*, v.

THE CHALICE

One can argue that the Protestant Reformation began on October 28, 1414, when the Czech priest Jakoubek of Stříbro first allowed the laity to drink from the chalice at communion. Giving the cup to the laity was a more dramatic break with the papacy and a more vivid symbol of the priesthood of all believers than Luther's call for scholars to debate indulgences in 1517. When Jakoubek continued the practice of the lay chalice in violation of a direct decree from the Council of Constance, he separated the Hussites from the Roman Catholic Church for good. The Latin phrase for communion in both kinds (bread and wine) is *sub specie utraque,* and the practice itself was known as *utraquism.* Those who gave the chalice to the laity, then, were known as Utraquists (or, in older sources, Calixtines, from the word for chalice).[1] The various Hussite parties disagreed on many things, but they were united in their defense of the lay chalice, and historians should not underestimate the importance of the chalice as a symbol of reform and revolution in the Reformation era. It was not accidental that all Protestant churches in the sixteenth century followed the Hussite practice of the lay chalice.

Ironically, it was the Council of Constance that brought together the two main symbols of the Czech Reformation—the chalice and Jan Hus. Not long before Hus was officially condemned, it was reported at the council that "a new

---

1. For an overview of the Hussite view of the Eucharist, see William R. Cook, "The Eucharist in Hussite Theology," *Archiv für Reformationsgeschichte/Archive for Reformation History* 66 (1975): 23–35.

scandal" had arisen in Bohemia: "the followers of this sect in many cities, villages, and places of that kingdom, laymen of both sexes, commune in both kinds of bread and wine and persistently teach that this is the way communion must be administered."[2] The council decreed that Utraquists were to repent or be excommunicated. In Bohemia, the prohibition of the lay chalice and the execution Jan Hus were clear indications that the Catholic Church had departed from the church of the apostles and fallen into heresy.

JAKOUBEK OF STŘÍBRO

Jakoubek of Stříbro (d. 1429) was Hus's successor as rector of Bethlehem Chapel, and he became the leader of the reform party in Hus's absence. Although he was less astute politically than Hus, he laid the theological and liturgical foundations for three new churches, one of which was the Unity of the Brethren. It was Jakoubek who introduced communion in both kinds, and historians have long debated the genesis of Jakoubek's practice. Kaminsky may have overstated the case when he wrote that "no one before the Hussites seems to have felt that the laity were being deprived of anything important; orthodox theology defined each of the two elements as equivalent to the full body-and-blood combination, and few even of the Hussites were prepared to deny this."[3] That all of the Protestant churches immediately adopted the Hussite practice indicates that some people felt that the laity had been deprived of something.

It seems probable that the example of the Eastern Orthodox Church, so close at hand, played a key role in Jakoubek's decision. The timing of Jerome of Prague's journey to Lithuania and White Russia in 1414, just before Jakoubek first administered the chalice, points to a possible Eastern influence.[4] The Utraquists' effort to come under the authority of the patriarch of Constantinople in the 1450s, shortly before the fall of Constantinople, was a recognition that the Orthodox, like the Utraquists, communed in both kinds. It is easy to picture the Utraquists developing into an autocephalous Bohemian

2. Quoted in Spinka, *Hus at the Council of Constance*, 128.
3. Kaminsky, *Hussite Revolution*, 97–98.
4. Ibid., 99–100; Spinka, *John Hus*, 256.

Orthodox Church. The suggestion of a Hussite-Orthodox connection is strengthened by the fact that the Hussites were the only Western church in the Reformation era to commune infants as well as adults, which is the Eastern practice.[5] Furthermore, Hus argued that the papacy had erred in excommunicating the Orthodox. However, no one has established conclusive links between the Hussites and the Orthodox.

Jakoubek himself attributed his decision to a revelation, which he defined as "a mode of knowledge coming from the scrutiny of the Law of the Lord, and from the solid expositions and authorities of the ancient saints—such as Augustine, Cyprian, Bernard, Chrysostom, and others who followed them in the same sense. By this definition I can concede that I have a revelation, for I have knowledge from the Law and from authoritative writings, and this knowledge, newly acquired in this manner, can be generally called a revelation."[6] Thus revelation, for Jakoubek, was not a direct, God-given epiphany but an intellectual breakthrough based on study and reflection. In other words, scripture, the example of the early church, and plain reason led Jakoubek to the conclusion that the church was wrong to deny the chalice to the laity.

The reason why Jakoubek gave so much thought to the nature of the Eucharist was that he endorsed Matthew of Janov's call for frequent communion. Matthew, as we saw earlier, believed that the Eucharist provided nourishment in the struggle against the Antichrist. Frequent communion was a way for individuals to nourish their souls in the struggle against evil, and it also allowed them to participate in the mystical body of Christ, which included all Christians.[7] Jakoubek, like Matthew, viewed the Eucharist more as an eschatological meal of the Kingdom of God than as a reenactment of the sacrifice of Jesus. The focus of the ritual, for Jakoubek, was the communion of the people, not the actions of the priest. He cited numerous New Testament passages about the messianic banquet and the marriage supper of the lamb as eucharistic texts.[8]

---

5. David R. Holeton has written extensively on this topic. For a summary of his research, see "Communion of Infants and Hussitism"; "The Communion of Infants: The Basel Years," *Communio Viatorum* 29 (1986): 15–40; and "The Bohemian Eucharistic Movement in Its European Context," in *The Bohemian Reformation and Religious Practice*, ed. David R. Holeton (Prague: Charles University, 1996), vol. 1. It appears that infant communion was Catholic practice until the rise of the doctrine of transubstantiation. Rubin, *Corpus Christi*, 64–65.

6. Quoted in Kaminsky, *Hussite Revolution*, 100.

7. Holeton, "Communion of Infants and Hussitism," 209.

8. Kaminsky, *Hussite Revolution*, 113; Holeton, "Communion of Infants: The Basel Years," 21.

FIG. 7   Saint Martin in the Wall Church, Prague, where the lay chalice was first used.

Jakoubek discovered that the same biblical texts that Matthew had used to support frequent communion also pointed to the necessity for the laity to receive the blood of Christ as well as the body.[9] Matthew had rejected the idea that a priest could take communion on behalf of the laity, asserting that taking communion for another person is no more possible than eating dinner for someone else. Laypersons needed to take communion personally and frequently. Jakoubek applied Matthew's statement specifically to the chalice; a priest could not drink the blood of Christ on behalf of the laity.

Nicholas of Dresden joined enthusiastically in Jakoubek's reform of the Mass. He supplied quotations from the *Decretals* of Gratian, the primary law book of the church, to show that at one time the laity were *required* by papal decree

9. Hieromonk Patapios, "*Sub utraque specie:* The Arguments of John Hus and Jacoubek of Stříbro in Defence of Giving Communion to the Laity Under Both Kinds," *Journal of Theological Studies* 53 (2002): 510.

to drink from the chalice once a year.[10] Hus's followers thus used the Catholic Church's own tradition to prove that the church had changed its doctrine and thus had committed (and even admitted) error. One of the prominent patristic sources Jakoubek used to support his teaching was Pseudo-Dionysius's *De ecclesiastica hierarchia*, which connected the worship of the earthly congregation with the worship of the saints in heaven. The saints on heaven and earth shared in the body and blood of Christ.[11]

Hus agreed with Jakoubek's conclusions but, imprisoned in Constance, urged caution. Still, in one of his writings from Constance he quoted a letter of the fifth-century pope Gelasius I instructing bishops to encourage communicants to drink the cup, "because the division of one and the same mystery cannot arise without great sacrilege."[12] He added statements from Cyprian, Augustine, and other church fathers supporting communion in both kinds, but Hus accepted the Catholic teaching that the blood is also contained in the body. Unlike Jakoubek, Hus did not insist on drinking the blood of Christ as requisite for salvation.

The *Decretals* and quotations from the church fathers were useful in the theological struggle, but Jakoubek's main arguments came from scripture, the "law of Christ." Jesus and Paul both stated that the faithful should drink of the cup. John 6:53–54 ("unless you eat the flesh of the Son of man *and* drink his blood, you have no life in you; he who eats my flesh and drinks my blood has eternal life") became Utraquism's central biblical text. When the Council of Constance forbade laity to drink of the cup, Hus openly encouraged Jakoubek and his supporters, quoting the New Testament: "as often as ye eat this bread *and* drink this cup, ye do announce the Lord's death until He come."[13] This phrase remains a part of the communion liturgy of the Moravian Church.

The Council of Constance acknowledged that Utraquism had been the practice of the church before the time of Constantine, but it rejected the notion that the early church should be the model for the modern church.[14] The anti-Utraquist theologians viewed themselves as progressive and the Czech reformers

10. Kaminsky, *Hussite Revolution*, 108.
11. Holeton, "Communion of Infants: The Basel Years," 21.
12. Patapios, "*Sub utraque specie*," 512.
13. Ibid., 520, 514–17.
14. Kaminsky, *Hussite Revolution*, 116–17; Spinka, *Hus at the Council of Constance*, 128.

as hopelessly conservative. The council's assertion that the Roman Church had the right to change the clear instructions of Christ crystallized the debate for the Hussites. Nicholas of Dresden raised the question of whether the prelates and theologians at the Council of Constance would have condemned Christ himself for serving communion in both kinds.

> Suppose as a possibility that Christ and his Primitive Church, with their apostolic life and evangelical practice, were to come into the midst of the Council of Constance, and were to say to the multitudes there, as he said and taught at Capernaum: "Except you eat the flesh of the Son of man and drink his blood, you have no life in you." And suppose that he wished to perform the sacrament as he had instituted it. Do you think that he would be listened to and would have an opportunity for this, things being as they now are? It would go hard with him. Indeed those at the Council would probably not withdraw from him scandalized, as did those at Capernaum, but would hereticate and condemn him, according to their condemnation [of the lay chalice], saying that this was not their custom.[15]

Jakoubek responded to Jean Gerson's charge that Utraquism divided the church by asserting that the true church is known by its fruits. Was the true church the one that followed the clear and simple teachings of scripture and the model of the apostles and church fathers, or was it the church that had executed Jan Hus for heresies he did not teach? Was the true church the one dedicated to rooting out corruption and greed, or the church in which sinners could condemn a blameless man? Did the true church alleviate the suffering of the poor and redeem prostitutes, or did it exact tithes, rents, and special fees from the poor?[16]

Here we see the influence of the Waldensian myth of the Constantinian fall of the church on Hussite theology. Popes and councils were the real heretics, because they violated the law of Christ and the apostles. A century later Luther took up the arguments of Jakoubek and Nicholas, proclaiming that it was the

15. Quoted in Kaminsky, *Hussite Revolution*, 115.
16. Ibid., 121–22.

Catholic Church that had fallen into heresy by forbidding the lay chalice. In his *Treatise on the Blessed Sacrament* and *The Babylonian Captivity of the Church*, Luther pointed to the Bohemians as examples of a true Christian church.[17] In his *Defense and Explanation of All the Articles*, Luther accused the Roman Church of heresy: "I say that the pope and all who knowingly abet him in this matter are heretics, apostates, under the ban, and accursed, for they teach contrary to the gospel and follow their own ideas against the common usage and practice of the whole of Christendom. Heretics and apostates are people who transgress the teaching of their fathers, separate themselves from the common usage and practice of all of Christendom and, without reason, out of sheer wantonness, invent new usages and practices contrary to the holy gospel."[18]

Jakoubek and Nicholas were not antiquarians calling for a literal application of past liturgical practice but reformers using the past to change the future. In contrast, the reforming cardinals and theologians at the council believed that the only way to ensure social justice and maintain peace was to keep the clergy on top of the social order. There must be a symbolic division between those under holy orders and everyone else. The council warned that if ordinary men and women were allowed to drink from the sacred cup, laypersons, even women, would next agitate for active participation in church leadership. The Hussites were on a slippery slope that could lead to women reading the Bible publicly and perhaps even preaching.[19] The world would be turned upside down and the social order would collapse.

Utraquism played an important role in the social experimentations of the early fifteenth century, which included vigorous discussions about the status of women in the church and society. Hus had proclaimed that women were equal to men spiritually.[20] The Hussites allowed women to drink the blood of Christ, something that had been explicitly forbidden for two centuries. Reports circulated that radical priests in Prague's New Town allowed women to preach and even to serve communion, but this was too radical for most Hussites. Interestingly, it was an assertive group of women who insisted that the town council

17. Martin Luther, *Luther's Works*, trans. and ed. Jaroslav Pelikan and Hartmut T. Lehmann, 55 vols. (St. Louis: Concordia, 1955–86), 2:178–87.
18. Ibid., 32:60.
19. Kaminsky, *Hussite Revolution*, 124.
20. Klassen, *Warring Maidens*, 159–81.

forbid the practice of women serving communion.[21] The Council of Constance's fears that Utraquism by itself would overturn the traditional social hierarchy proved to be unfounded, though it shook patriarchy momentarily.

The reformation of the Mass did not end with the restoration of the cup to the laity. Hussite theologians and priests continued to ponder the meaning of John 6:53 and the Lord's command to "drink of it, *all* of you" (Matt. 26:27). They concluded that reception of the Eucharist was a dominical injunction for all who were baptized, including children. David Holeton has called this "the greatest revolution in western medieval sacramental practice,"[22] but it was not until the twentieth century that Protestant churches adopted the Utraquist practice of communing children. It appears that it was Wenceslas Koranda, a priest in southern Bohemia, who first began giving communion to children in 1416. The next year Prague University debated a host of liturgical reforms; participants disagreed on everything from masses for the dead to exchanging the kiss of peace, but they agreed that infants should be communed.[23] The Utraquist Church held to this conviction for more than two centuries, despite persecution from Catholics and criticism from other Protestants.[24]

Jakoubek argued that many references to the New Testament (e.g., Matt. 18:3, 19:16; Luke 18:15–17; John 3:5, 6:53) support infant communion if one combines Jesus' teachings about children in the Kingdom of God with statements about the messianic banquet. He also quoted the church fathers to argue that baptism and communion are closely related sacraments. Baptism admits one into the communion of the church; therefore all the baptized must receive the nourishment of the body and blood of Christ. Holeton summarizes Jakoubek's argument thus: "Just as the newborn need physical nourishment, so too, insists Jakoubek, those who have been born again also must be nourished. If a child can receive the Holy Spirit in baptism, why cannot he also receive Jesus Christ in the Eucharist? After all Jesus said that those who wished to enter the kingdom must become like children. How can those who are held up as model citizens of the kingdom be denied access to its banquet?"[25]

21. Ibid., 199–200.

22. Holeton, "Communion of Infants and Hussitism," 217. The Moravian Church in America adopted the practice in 1983.

23. Ibid., 212; Thomas Fudge, "Hussite Infant Communion," *Lutheran Quarterly* 10 (1996): 179–94.

24. Zdeněk David makes this point repeatedly in *Finding the Middle Way*.

25. Holeton, "Communion of Infants and Hussitism," 213.

The Hussite commitment to infant communion was symbolic of the core issue of the Czech Reformation, that the Christian Church is the body of the faithful rather than merely the priests. The true church includes men and women, rich and poor, lord and peasant, adults and children. Though imperfect, the visible church was called to be an expression of the eschatological kingdom *on earth*. The Eucharist was sign, seal, and means of realization of that goal, at least partially. Jakoubek and his followers believed that the exclusion of children from communion divided the Kingdom of God and denied the power of Christ to heal all divisions of status. The abuses they sought to redress stemmed from a basic distortion of the relationship between the clergy and society.

UTRAQUISTS AND THE BOHEMIAN CHURCH

Utraquism would have been quickly suppressed by the Crown if the majority of the greater and lesser nobility in Bohemia had not provided at least some measure of support and protection for the Utraquist priests.[26] Many aristocrats, including Queen Sophie, were apparently genuinely convinced by the Utraquists' religious arguments and desire for reform, but each noble's decision to support or oppose the movement included both religious and pragmatic considerations. Kaminsky has noted perceptively that "no man's motives are pure, the complex of idealism and self-interest in any man's mind is perfectly impenetrable, and every great work of historical construction moves along by enlisting *all* the sources of energy available in the human material, which is of course tainted by sin."[27] The Czech Reformation, like that of Luther and Calvin, succeeded through a combination of theological argument, genuine pastoral concern, effective use of popular media, and shrewd application of secular power.[28]

The Hussites based their rebellion on the idea that the Bible as the law of God stands in judgment on all human institutions and systems of theology.

26. Josef Macek, "The Monarchy of the Estates," in Tiech, *Bohemia in History*, 98–116; Klassen, *Warring Maidens*, 183–210.
27. Kaminsky, *Hussite Revolution*, 155.
28. Thomas Fudge spells this out in detail in *Magnificent Ride*.

They did not advocate a naïve adherence to scripture divorced from the interpretation of the early church and plain reason, but they did encourage the laity to read the Bible on their own. Portions of the New Testament and Psalms had been translated into Czech in the fourteenth century, and the Hussites encouraged further translation from the Latin Vulgate. When Jean Gerson noted at the Council of Constance that vernacular Bible reading was the root of the Beghard and Waldensian heresies, Jakoubek pointed out that Saints Cyril and Methodius had translated the Bible into Slavonic for people in Moravia in the ninth century.[29] This reference to the missionaries from Constantinople indicates that the example of the Eastern Orthodox Church had some influence on the Hussites, at least in terms of the historical memory of an age when Bohemia and Moravia were Christian but not Catholic.

The archbishop of Prague tried to enforce the Council of Constance's decrees against Utraquism by placing the city under interdict in 1415, but this backfired. Hussite clergy simply took over the vacant pulpits and altars of Bohemia and introduced Jakoubek's revised liturgies. In the countryside, crowds of laypeople revolted against their Catholic priests and forcibly installed Utraquist clergy. King Wenceslas did not immediately intervene for fear of inciting further rioting among the people and alienating restive nobles, who had twice imprisoned him in the past.[30] By the end of 1416, much of the property of the Catholic Church in Bohemia was in the hands of Utraquists, who set about the task of reforming the church according to Hussite theology. In a few years, the Utraquist Church was the national church of Bohemia.

Jakoubek did not think that the New Testament gives a definite liturgical pattern that all churches must follow, but he asserted that no church has the authority to violate the explicit instructions of Jesus and the apostles, as the Catholic Church had done by denying the chalice to the laity. Unlike the later Calvinists and Anabaptists, Jakoubek taught that it was acceptable to follow rites and customs not mentioned in the New Testament, so long as they promoted true faith and love among worshippers. Furthermore, reformers might need to tolerate some popular practices for a while in order not to scandalize

29. Kaminsky, *Hussite Revolution*, 122–24. For more on "the apostles to the Slavs," see Dimitri Obolensky, *Byzantium and the Slavs* (Crestwood, N.Y.: St. Vladimir's Seminary Press, 1994), 204–25.

30. Kaminsky, *Hussite Revolution*, 157–61.

the weak, unless the rites were purely superstitious and stood in the way of the Gospel.[31] The debate over rites in the Czech Reformation was very similar to the conflict over the German Mass a century later in Wittenberg. Jakoubek's cautious reform of worship was based on arguments similar to those made later by Luther against Carlstadt.[32]

Expanding on the work of Hus, Jakoubek saw to it that large portions of the liturgy were translated into Czech, and he trimmed the liturgy. He argued in *De ceremoniis* that only four things were absolutely necessary for proper communion: bread and wine, an ordained priest, the words of institution from Christ, and the priest's intention in consecrating. Vestments, altars, candles, incense, choirs, and processions were unnecessary, but they were not idolatrous. Like Hus, he was concerned that the church was wasting money on luxury rather than serving the poor, but he opposed iconoclasm. Though he was suspicious of the cult of the saints and took steps to reduce the attention paid to the saints, he added a new saint's day to the church calendar, July 6 (the martyrdom of Hus). In opposition to the Waldensians, Jakoubek argued that purgatory was a biblical concept, but he was uncomfortable with masses for the dead and argued unsuccessfully for their abolition.[33]

In a series of synods and public theological disputations in 1418, the Utraquists established their basic doctrinal stance in opposition to both the Catholic Church and the radical Hussites. Kaminsky offers the following summary of Utraquist synod resolutions.

(1) Infant communion is to be given in both kinds.

(2) No one is to hold that explicit statements of holy scripture constitute all that may be believed.

(3) Purgatory is to be believed in.

(4) Masses are to be said for the dead.

(5) Prayers, alms, and other works are to be done for the dead.

(6) The saints can help the elect on earth.

(7) No one may say that oaths are never to be sworn.

31. Ibid., 191.

32. Heiko A. Oberman, *Luther: Man Between God and the Devil*, trans. Eileen Walliser-Schwarzbart (New Haven: Yale University Press, 1989), 232–45.

33. Kaminsky, *Hussite Revolution*, 193, 218.

(8) No one may say that the death penalty is never to be inflicted.

(9) A priest who sins mortally does not lose his power to perform valid sacraments.

(10) Only a priest can make the sacrament of the Eucharist.

(11) In auricular confession, various works of penance are to be imposed as necessary; mere repentance is not always enough.

(12) Extreme unction is to be given.

(13) Spiritual and temporal authorities are to be obeyed, even if evil, in legitimate matters, but lovingly resisted in illicit ones.

(14) Constitutions of the church that are not against the law of God but help it are to be obeyed.

(15) The authority of the holy doctors of the primitive church is to be respected.

(16) All ceremonies, customs, and rites of the church, helpful to the law of God and to good morals among the faithful, are to be preserved, unless something better is found.

(17) Consecration of water and benedictions of other things are legitimate.

(18) The ritual of the Mass is not to be changed without great necessity.

(19) The Gospels and Epistles are to be sung in the vernacular, the other parts of the Mass in Latin.

(20) Images can be kept in churches.

(21) Sunday, other feasts of Christ, of Mary, of the apostles, and of other saints are to be kept.

(22) Church fasts are to be kept.

(23) Evangelical priests may have necessities by divine and natural law, although not be in civil possession.[34]

We can see from this list that the Utraquists adopted the theology of Wyclif and Hus, but they retained many Catholic doctrines and practices that the Waldensians had rejected. During the disputations following the execution of Hus, the radicals were marginalized. Jakoubek never gave up hope that the Czech Reformation would become a genuine reformation of the whole Western church and that the breach with the papacy could be healed. It appears

34. Ibid., 260.

that he grew more conservative in response to the militant radicalism of Žižka and the pacifism of Chelčický, who will be discussed in later chapters.

Jakoubek was a reformer, not a revolutionary. His theological program had been informed primarily by patristic literature, respect for tradition, and pragmatism, in addition to the Bible. He was not interested in destroying the old church and creating an entirely new one based on his personal understanding of scripture. He called for the church to live according to its own traditional teachings rather than the innovations that had been introduced in the later Middle Ages. The cautious nature of his reform is seen in his conviction that the laity should not be pushed too far, too fast, even when the truth of scripture pointed toward major changes. "There are many truths," he wrote in early 1414, "that should not be pronounced in their own time, when hearts are not disposed for them; but at another time, when hearts are more ready to receive those truths, then they should be pronounced."[35] It is ironic that the later Utraquist Church would treat Jakoubek's writings as authoritative yet ignore his desire to push the Czech Reformation further. Of all of the churches created during the fifteenth and sixteenth centuries, the Utraquists were the most conservative.

One of the most radical steps the Hussites took, though, was to form a consistory, or council of priests, to govern the church independently of the Vatican. The consistory met in Prague and was led by university masters, who quickly put into practice some of the most controversial ideas of Hus and Wyclif regarding the church's secular power. They reduced the number of benefices for nonresident priests; many monasteries and parish churches were closed; and monks and friars were required to serve as regular parish priests or find secular employment. All clergy were expected to live simple and frugal lives, caring for their flocks rather than fleecing them. According to Zdeněk V. David, such reforms offered certain advantages for common people, especially in contrast to the German Reformation that unfolded in the next century: "Thus it might be said that the Czech commoners had the best of all the possible worlds: (1) enjoying their favorite liturgies of which the Protestant Reformation would have deprived them; and (2) escaping the heavy financial burden

35. Ibid., 183.

of supporting the luxuriant clerical and monastic apparatus, or facing the risk of spiritual penalties, which the Roman Church would impose."[36]

When compared to the radical Hussites or sixteenth-century Protestant churches, the Utraquist program seems quite conservative and medieval. David has compared the Utraquists to the supposed *via media* of Elizabethan Anglicanism.[37] Like most analogies, this one distorts as well as clarifies. The Elizabethan settlement was a compromise imposed on the Church of England by royal decree in the sixteenth century because that church had veered from one extreme to the other (from Lutheran, to Calvinist, to Catholic) under successive monarchs. Though conservative in comparison with the Puritans, the Church of England under Elizabeth I was more clearly Protestant theologically than the Utraquist Church. Anglican priests were expected to marry, transubstantiation was explicitly rejected, the secular monarch was the official head of the Church of England, and there was no desire for rapprochement with Rome. In contrast, the Utraquist Church was led by the priests and masters in the university, not the monarch. Jakoubek's reformation was intended to be a limited reform of Catholic practices and doctrine, particularly related to papal authority. The liturgy and theology of the Utraquist Church was more similar to the Oxford movement of the nineteenth-century Anglican Church than to the Elizabethan church. Portions of the liturgy even remained in Latin.

The Utraquist Church was the most conservative of the early modern Western churches that separated from Rome, but it is easy to overstress its conservatism. Historians should not overlook the essential fact that Jakoubek and his colleagues institutionalized the principle of rebellion against corrupt authority based on the law of Christ, or that they rejected one of the cornerstones of the medieval political structure: the political power of the church. That the church in Bohemia was rather quickly suppressed by the Counter-Reformation after 1627 should not obscure its historical significance. Though the Utraquists tried to remain within the Roman Catholic Church, historians should examine them alongside the Anglicans, Lutherans, Reformed, and Anabaptists—all paths that Christianity could have chosen to follow.[38]

---

36. Zdeněk V. David, "Utraquists, Lutherans, and the Bohemian Confession of 1575," *Church History* 68 (1999): 303.

37. Ibid., 294–336.

38. David argues that the Utraquist Church should be understood as a modern "liberal" Catholic

REVOLUTION

Until the Council of Trent, the Utraquists held out hope that the papacy would officially sanction their church, consecrate the Utraquist archbishop of Prague, and allow the laity to commune in both kinds. Such hopes were repeatedly dashed, beginning in 1419 when King Wenceslas responded to political pressure and agreed to enforce the decree of Constance forbidding the lay chalice. He was initially reluctant to do so because he feared rebellion, but he yielded to pressure from the emperor. His wife, Queen Sophie, was threatened with arrest by the Inquisition because of her support for the Hussites, and Emperor Sigismund had plans to seize the Bohemian Crown from his inept brother. In February 1419, Catholic authorities, with the aid of the king, reconsecrated Czech altars, removed Hussite priests from parishes, and made verbal renunciation of Utraquism a condition for receiving communion. The interdict was officially removed and Utraquism was forbidden everywhere but in a few parishes. By royal decree the university masters were silenced, and they observed the ban.[39] The heady period of public debate on the doctrine and purpose of the church ended abruptly in 1419.

With Jakoubek and other moderate voices silenced and Bohemian pulpits filled by enemies of the chalice, the Hussite radicals grew more determined in their opposition to Catholic authorities. A priest by the name of Jan Želivský (d. 1422) quickly emerged as the most effective and popular voice for radical reform in the New Town section of Prague.[40] Little is known about his early life, other than that he had been a monk in Želiv in southeastern Bohemia before coming to Prague. He was attracted by the Czech Reformation and became a student of Jakoubek. He actively promoted the Utraquist program until he was ousted from his pulpit at Saint Stephan's Church when the Crown enforced the decree against Utraquism. He was allowed to continue preaching at the monastery church of Our Mother of God of the Snows in the New

---

church rather than as a conservative Protestant church, but he also argues that the Utraquists should be understood in terms of the putative Anglican *via media*. It is not clear to me that both claims can be true, but had the Council of Trent been less dogmatic and more irenic, it is possible that Utraquism could have provided a model for a "liberal" Catholic church that would have been more acceptable to Protestants.

39. Kaminsky, *Hussite Revolution*, 267–68.
40. Fudge, *Magnificent Ride*, 92–95.

Town, one of the few parishes still permitted to practice Utraquism.[41] Želivský's sermons grew more incendiary after his expulsion from Saint Stephan's,
and he grew increasingly disenchanted with his former mentor, Jakoubek.

On July 6, 1419, the anniversary of Hus's execution, Wenceslas announced
that drinking from the chalice was a crime punishable by death for repeat
offenders. A large number of Hussites were imprisoned, and by November
some sixteen hundred persons had been murdered and disposed of in the mine
shafts of Kutná Hora because they had drunk from the cup.[42] When the king
removed the Hussite town councilors in the New Town and replaced them
with Catholic royalists, Želivský and other radicals saw it as a sign that the
anticipated war over the law of Christ had begun. On July 30, 1419, Želivský
and his supporters, including a one-eyed knight named Jan Žižka (d. 1424),
gathered for Sunday services at Our Mother of God of the Snows. Želivský
called upon the example of Hus and the prophets of the Old Testament as he
roused the crowd against idolatry and tyranny. He quoted Ezekiel 6:3–5: "Be-
hold, I, even I, will bring a sword upon you, and I will destroy your high places.
And your altars shall be desolate, and your images shall be broken: and I will
cast down your slain men before your idols."[43] This use of iconoclasm as a revolutionary program was a prominent feature of the Puritan revolution in England in the seventeenth century, but it was pioneered by Želivský.

The sermon ended around 8:30 A.M., and Želivský led the armed congregation in a procession through the streets of New Town while holding a monstrance with the host displayed. They went to his old parish, Saint Stephan's
Church, where they broke down the doors, threw the priest into the street,
and celebrated communion in both kinds. At about 9:30 A.M. they arrived at
the New Town hall, where some of the newly appointed magistrates were
meeting with wealthy Catholic citizens. When the crowd gathered outside,
demanding that Hussites be released from the Prague prisons, the magistrates
sent a messenger to the castle requesting troops.

It is a long way over the bridge from Lesser Town, where the royal guard
was stationed, to New Town, and by the time the troops arrived the mob had
stormed the town hall. Thirteen magistrates and burghers were hurled from

41. Kaminsky, *Hussite Revolution*, 271.
42. Ibid., 315.
43. Ibid., 292. See also Macek, *Hussite Movement in Bohemia*.

the window. Those who survived were killed by the mob below while Željiv-ský waved the monstrance in triumph. Order was quickly restored by the rebels themselves to prevent wanton rioting. The Hussites assumed command of the New Town and organized their own militia. Wenceslas had a stroke when he heard news of the rebellion; he died two weeks later.[44] The Czech Reforma-tion had turned into the Hussite Revolution.

After the death of Wenceslas, Emperor Sigismund attempted to assume the Bohemian throne, but the populace rejected the man they blamed for Hus's death. Sigismund planned to invade the country in an attempt to recapture Prague, especially the castle, and Pope Martin assisted him by declaring the invasion a crusade. Crusades had been cruelly effective in squashing the Cathar heresy in France in the thirteenth and fourteenth centuries, but this tactic failed against the Hussites.[45] The only thing, other than the chalice, that could unite the moderate and radical Hussites was the threat of crusade. In all, five campaigns were launched against the Hussites without success. The story of the Hussite Wars and Žižka's stunning victories over larger armies is beyond the scope of this book, but those crusades testified to the intensity of the Catholic Church's fear of the laity taking communion in both kinds.

THE FOUR ARTICLES OF PRAGUE

When word spread that Sigismund was going to invade Bohemia, the Utra-quist leaders in Prague called for all Czechs to defend the cause of Hus. After the defenestration in the New Town, Žižka assumed command of the militia. He organized a brilliant defense of the city, but he made it clear that in the future he would defend Prague from the crusading army only if all Hussite parties agreed on a common statement of belief. What emerged from those theological debates under threat of war were the famous Four Articles of Prague in April 1420. This simple program for church reform served as the basic instru-ment for negotiation among Hussites until the Council of Basel. Different versions of the Four Articles appeared over the years, but the basic statement remained the same:

---

44. Kaminsky, *Hussite Revolution*, 291–96.
45. Barber, *Cathars*.

FIG. 8   Chalice in battle, mural in Bethlehem Chapel.

1. We stand for the ministering of the body and blood of the Lord to the laity in both kinds, for . . . this was Christ's institution and . . . that of the first apostles and of the holy Primitive Church . . . as the Council of Constance admitted to us.

2. We stand for the proper and free preaching of the word of God and of his every truth.

3. All priests, from the pope on down, should give up their pomp, avarice, and improper lordship in superfluity over temporal goods, and they should live as models for us.

4. We stand for the purgation of, and cessation from, all public mortal sins, by each in his own person; and for the cleansing of the Bohemian realm and nation from false and evil slander; and in this connection, for the common good of our land.[46]

The Four Articles were a compromise statement that was much more radical than some of the conservative Hussites, especially the theologian Jan Přibram, were comfortable with. It was also much less iconoclastic than radicals like Želivský and Žižka wanted. For the most part, though, it was a good application of the basic theological understandings of Hus and Wyclif. It is important to note that all four of the articles were intolerable to the Catholic Church because they threatened its political and economic power. Only the first of the Four Articles was ever approved by Catholic officials (at the Council of Basel), but even it was never actually put into practice by the Catholic Church.[47] Articles 2 and 3 most clearly reflect the apostolic poverty movement that was central to the teaching of the Unity of the Brethren. The most controversial of the four articles proved to be the final one, which called upon the faithful to purge Bohemia from sin and falsehood. It was not long before Žižka took this task upon himself.

The Four Articles were an important theological statement, and they briefly brought a degree of unity to the Hussites, but tensions between the radicals and

46. Kaminsky, *Hussite Revolution*, 369.

47. Gerald Christianson, "Wyclif's Ghost: The Politics of Reunion at the Council of Basel," *Annuarium Historiae Conciliorum* 17 (1985): 193–208; Bartoš, *Hussite Revolution*, 60–98; Otakar Odložilik, *The Hussite King: Bohemia in European Affairs, 1440–1471* (New Brunswick: Rutgers University Press, 1965), 4–18; William R. Cook, "Negotiations Between the Hussites, the Holy Roman Empire, and the Roman Church, 1427–36," *East Central Europe* 5 (1978): 90–104.

conservatives grew. After the defenestration, Želivský emerged as the most effective radical leader in Prague, and his preaching went from prophetic and iconoclastic to apocalyptic. He portrayed Emperor Sigismund as the dragon of the apocalypse waging war on Christ's elect. There could be no peace or compromise with the dragon or his allies. The split between the moderates in the Old Town and the radicals in the New Town widened rapidly. Jakoubek began to fear that Želivský was the Antichrist, because he urged war, rebellion, and chaos. Fearing that the Czech Reformation was going to be crushed between the armies of the emperor and the rampaging mobs of the radicals, the Utraquist leaders decided that something had to be done about Želivský. They invited him to a public debate in the Old Town square in 1422, where they murdered him.[48] The moderates quickly brought the New Town under their control, but they could not establish their authority outside Prague. Radicalism took hold in the south and east of Bohemia, especially in the areas where the Waldensians had been influential.

Once it became clear that the emperor was never going to defeat the Hussites militarily, the Catholics came to an accord with the Utraquists at the Council of Basel in 1433, which allowed for communion in both kinds. In exchange, the Utraquists agreed to recognize Emperor Sigismund as king of Bohemia. The agreement was called the Compacta, but the radical Hussite brotherhoods of Tábor and Horeb did not agree to it because it did not affirm all of the Four Articles. After the council, Catholic and Utraquist nobles joined forces against the radicals. At the battle of Lipany in 1434 the seemingly invincible army of the Táborites was slaughtered by the combined Catholic and Utraquist forces. The Hussite Revolution was over, and the Utraquists were in control of the Bohemian Church.

ROKYCANA

Jakoubek died in 1429, and leadership of the Utraquists fell to his student and loyal supporter Jan Rokycana (1390–1473), the son of a blacksmith. Rokycana had been educated in an Augustinian monastery and enrolled in 1412 at the

---

48. Kaminsky, *Hussite Revolution*, 460.

University of Prague, where he heard Hus preach. Though he did not receive his master's degree until 1430 (because the university's charter had been revoked during the revolution), Rokycana pursued his theological studies while asserting himself as one of the leading activists at the university. In the debates and discussions of 1416–20, Rokycana agreed with Jakoubek that the radicals had abandoned true reform for dangerous fanaticism, but he still hoped to win them back to the Utraquist cause.[49] In 1424 he was a member of a Prague delegation that successfully negotiated with Žižka, who was threatening to capture the city and force it to be reformed on radical lines.

One of Rokycana's great achievements was negotiating the Judge of Cheb (*judex compactatus in Egra*), an agreement signed in preparation for the Council of Basel. On May 18, 1432, in the town of Cheb, Catholic and Hussite negotiators agreed that "the Gospel, the ways of Christ, of the Apostles and the primitive Church, together with the recognized Councils and those sentences of the Doctors clearly based on the aforementioned authorities" were the highest authorities for settling doctrinal disputes.[50] This was to be the basis for discussing the Hussite question at the Council of Basel, and it was a great victory for the reform movement. Paragraph seven stated that "the Law of God and the praxis of Christ, the Apostles and the original church, together with the Councils and teachers conforming truly thereto" would be accepted by the Council of Basel as the arbiter.[51] In other words, canon law would not be the decisive factor in determining whether the Four Articles were true; only scripture and the example of the early church possessed this authority. This was what Hus had hoped for at the Council of Constance, and it was the only time in history that the Catholic Church ever agreed to such a provision.

After the combined forces of the Utraquist and Catholic nobles decisively defeated the radical Hussite brotherhoods in battle in 1434, the majority of the Bohemian clergy elected Rokycana as the first Hussite archbishop of Prague. Despite the Compacta and years of intense negotiations with the papacy, Rokycana was never consecrated as archbishop. Even so, he served diligently

49. Frederick G. Heymann, "John Rokycana: Church Reformer Between Hus and Luther," *Church History* 28 (1959): 244–46.
50. Ibid., 246.
51. František Kavka, "Bohemia," in Scribner, Porter, and Teich, *Reformation in National Context*, 135.

as primate of Bohemia and defended Utraquism against the emperor, who reneged on the Compacta. At one point Rokycana was "kidnapped" by sympathetic nobles in order to keep him safe in the castle of Kutná Hora. When the situation was safer, he relocated to the town of Hradec Králové, where he administered the Bohemian Church for a decade.

In 1448 one of the Hussite nobles, George Poděbrady, was elected king of Bohemia.[52] The election of a "heretic" as monarch of a major kingdom sent shock waves through Europe but was a boon to the Utraquist Church. Poděbrady took charge of the government in Prague and reinstalled Rokycana to the pulpit of Týn Church on the Old Town square, which became the central church for the Utraquists. The Cathedral of Saint Vitus, across the river, remained in Catholic hands. Poděbrady did not attempt to suppress the Catholic Church. He hoped to reunite the churches on the basis of the Compacta, but when it became evident that the provisions of the Compacta would never be put into practice by the Holy Roman emperor or the pontiff, Rokycana instituted negotiations with the patriarch of Constantinople to seek union with the Eastern church. Since the Bohemian Church's doctrine and practice was close to that of Eastern Orthodoxy, the plan might have succeeded, but in 1453 Constantinople fell to the Turks, ending what hope lay in the East.[53]

Moravian Church historians have not been kind to Rokycana because of his close connections to King George Poděbrady, who launched the first persecution against the Unity of the Brethren in 1464. Because of his mediation between the Utraquists and the Catholic Church, Rokycana was seen by many as a politician rather than a religious reformer. This is unfair to the Utraquist priest and primate. In fact, he played a key role in the origin of the Unity of the Brethren and helped transmit the teachings of Hus and Jakoubek to them. His sermons inspired his nephew Gregory and a group of young men to seek a more serious approach to the Christian life. Gregory took Rokycana's preaching so seriously that he turned his fellowship into a new church in 1467, but that is a story for a later chapter. For now it is enough to note that Rokycana's passionate preaching and courageous defense of the Czech Reformation led directly to Gregory's decision to establish the Unity of the Brethren.[54]

52. For more on George Poděbrady and Rokycana, see Odložilík, *Hussite King*.
53. Ibid., 62–68.
54. Peschke, *Kirche und Welt*, 26.

Rokycana was a faithful follower of Jakoubek and Hus rather than an original thinker. Like them, he promoted the idea that the true church is the body of the elect, but as a pastor Rokycana was more troubled by the consequences of this doctrine than Hus had been. Predestination seemed to undermine one of the most basic features of Hussite theology, namely, that ethics is a central point of theology. Rokycana hoped to make sense of divine justice and mercy, and he rejected the idea that God judges people arbitrarily, like a tyrant. He also rejected the possibility that God wills some people to commit mortal sin so that he can justly damn them. Rokycana argued that it is irresponsible to shift the blame of sin onto God rather than human individuals, because then there is no motivation to choose the good.[55] Like Philip Melanchthon in the sixteenth century, Rokycana argued that God's election is ultimately a mystery beyond human understanding. God grants the means of salvation, but he does not guarantee that all people will achieve it. Election, for Rokycana, meant that some are given a chance to follow the narrow path to salvation, and those who would be saved by divine grace must pursue this path with all of their strength and will. Individuals must use the means of grace that God has granted so that they may follow the way of Christ.[56]

For Rokycana, salvation involved hard work, but not primarily works of piety. No one can truly know his or her eternal fate until the judgment; therefore everyone who wishes to be saved from damnation should be engaged in the work of salvation. He rejected the teaching that use of the sacraments alone will guarantee salvation, because this provided a false security, but he held that signs may indicate whether one is of the elect. These include "readiness to be poor, readiness to repent sins committed, great patience in suffering, generosity in helping others, and a love of God which makes the expectation of the future life in permanent union with God the most joyful, if not the only truly and permanently joyful element in human life."[57] In other words, Rokycana taught that salvation comes through faith that is formed by love.

Rokycana's published sermons, the *Postila*, influenced the theology and preaching of the Unity for decades. In these sermons he addressed in practical terms how Christians should live in the world. The Brethren took to heart

55. Heymann, "John Rokycana," 258.
56. Peschke, *Kirche und Welt*, 28.
57. Heymann, "John Rokycana," 259.

Rokycana's assertion that true Christians had always been a minority in the world. They were a righteous remnant, and this would remain true in the future. The true church would always be persecuted by the church of the Antichrist; therefore Christians should be prepared to suffer unjustly. More important, the followers of Christ, like Christ himself, should be able to do the right thing even in difficult situations, because Christ strengthens them.[58]

Rokycana repeatedly told his audience that true Christians in all times and places can be identified by their love for God and neighbor. Such love is evident in their obedience to God's law. The Ten Commandments form the basis of this law, but Rokycana also called on Christians to observe the "six smaller commandments" that Jesus gave in the Sermon on the Mount: do not respond to violence with violence, do not divorce your spouse, do not swear oaths, do not be angry without cause, do not look lustfully at someone, and love your enemies.[59] This focus on the "six smaller commandments" may have originated in Rokycana's conversations with Peter Chelčický, who is discussed in a later chapter. Gregory, the founder of the Unity, agreed with his uncle on the necessity for Christians to observe the whole law of Christ, but he accused Rokycana of not doing enough to observe the commandments, particularly the prohibition of violence.

The catechisms of the Unity repeated Rokycana's distinction between honoring the saints and worshipping them. This distinction was applied particularly to the Virgin Mary, who should be respected and held in highest esteem, but not worshipped. Rokycana rejected the Catholic Church's focus on miracles performed by the saints and their relics, arguing that miracles may dazzle unbelievers but are unnecessary for those who have faith in Christ. Worse, miracles can do the work of the devil by seducing people away from faith and true love.[60] This commonsense rationalism would remain a feature of the Unity for most of its existence.

The story of the Utraquist Church after Rokycana is somewhat peripheral to the development of the Brethren's theology, but the histories of the Unity and the Utraquists were intertwined until their mutual destruction during the Thirty Years' War. In particular, many of the leaders of the Unity, including

---

58. Peschke, *Kirche und Welt*, 29.
59. Ibid., 33.
60. Ibid., 30, 38–39.

bishops and theologians like Luke of Prague and Jan Augusta, came out of the Utraquist Church. It may be useful, therefore, to look briefly at that history.

After the death of Poděbrady, Czech nobles refused to give up the chalice and demanded that the new king respect their right to it. In 1485 the monarch signed the Peace of Kutná Hora, which granted the common people of Bohemia the right to choose whether to be Utraquist or Catholic even in defiance of their landlord's wishes. This was just the opposite of the more famous *cuius regio eius religio* decision of the Peace of Augsburg in 1555, which left the choice of a territory's religion to the ruler.[61]

Although the Peace of Kutná Hora remained a point of controversy in Bohemian politics and was never endorsed by the emperor as a permanent law, it meant that the kingdom of Bohemia was the first realm in Europe where ordinary people had a limited but legal choice of religion. The evidence indicates that most Czechs chose to be members of the Utraquist Church rather than the Catholic. The Utraquists' status as the national church was guaranteed again by royal decree in 1575. Official visitation reports from 1602 indicate that all but three royal towns were served by properly ordained Utraquist priests. Reports from foreign visitors confirmed that there were very few Catholics in the kingdom, even after the papacy restored the office of archbishop of Prague in 1561.[62]

Utraquism was in effect the established church of Bohemia from the time of Rokycana until the Thirty Years' War, even though the monarchy remained Catholic. This meant that the Utraquists could not use the power of the state to compel adherence to the Utraquist Church. Only the forced re-Catholization of the country following the defeat at White Mountain in 1620 changed this situation. In contrast, the Unity of the Brethren remained an illegal community of faith until 1609 and was subject to official persecution for most of its history. Claims for the popularity of Utraquism among the common people thus need to be modified to reflect the risk that was associated with joining the Unity.[63]

Following the rise of Protestantism after 1517, the Utraquists faced the question of whether to become Lutheran, Reformed, or pursue their own path.

---

61. David, "Utraquists, Lutherans," 303.
62. Ibid., 300, 315.
63. Ibid., 315. David's frequent assertion that the Utraquist Church was tolerant must also be balanced by the Utraquists' persistent opposition to the Unity of the Brethren and the Lutherans.

Despite pressure from Lutheran-leaning nobles and clergy, the Utraquist consistory in Prague did not fully embrace the Protestant Reformation. The Bohemian Church retained the seven sacraments, episcopal succession, vestments, saints' days, belief in purgatory, and other Catholic doctrines. Theologically, the church continued down the path set out by Rokycana rather than following Luther or Calvin. There may have been some priests, whom historians have dubbed Neo-Utraquists, who introduced Lutheran ideas, but at least one modern scholar denies this claim.[64] It appears that the majority of Utraquist priests continued to teach that good works, especially care for the poor, were an essential part of salvation and that it was good to venerate saints, especially Saint Jan Hus.

The Utraquist consistory initially opposed the effort of the Lutherans and the Unity of the Brethren to gain royal toleration for churches that signed a Protestant confession of faith (called the Confessio Bohemica) in 1575.[65] We will look at that episode in more detail in a later chapter, but for now it should be noted that the Utraquists eventually sided with the Protestants politically, though they rejected the theology of both the Lutherans and the Brethren. Again, historians should not overlook the significance of the Utraquists' continued defiance of Rome. Despite the allure of reunion with the papacy and the security it would bring, the Utraquists defended the right of the laity to drink from the chalice and the right to commune children. The Utraquist Mass continued to have portions sung in Czech according to pre-Tridentine forms of the Mass. It is noteworthy that many Utraquists, including military chaplains, joined in the Czech rebellion of 1618. After the failure of that revolt, the Utraquists were forced to reunite with Rome on the terms established by Trent, and that part of the Czech Reformation passed into oblivion.[66]

THE UTRAQUISTS AND THE BRETHREN'S DOCTRINE

Despite the Brethren's decisive break with the Utraquists and years of hostile feelings between the two churches, the theological heritage of the Utraquists

64. David, *Finding the Middle Way*, esp. 332.
65. Ibid., 187–94.
66. Ibid., 240–301. David notes that this imposition of Catholicism on Bohemia had a negative impact on the religious and intellectual life of the Czechs generally.

played an important role in the doctrine and practice of the Unity. The early Brethren defined themselves in opposition to the Utraquist Church, which clouded their own assessment of that church, but the Unity preserved the Utraquist teaching that faith must be perfected in love. In fact, in their call for Christians to be perfect, the Unity stressed good works even more than the Utraquists did. The Eucharist was vital to the life of the Unity, but the Brethren gave a different definition to the nature and purpose of the Eucharist than had Rokycana, who continued to teach the doctrine of transubstantiation.

What the Unity most objected to in Utraquism was its status as a *national* church that included the whole society, as opposed to a *voluntary* church of those who felt called to live according to the strict teachings of Jesus. The conflict between the Unity and the Utraquists can be understood using Ernst Troeltsch's religious typology of church and sect.[67] Churches attempt to build a Christian society that unites all (or most) citizens in a single sacred institution. As such, they tend to be aligned with secular authority. Churches express very hostile attitudes toward religious dissenters and may resort to persecution. Utraquist leaders' harsh criticism of the Brethren reflects their desire to enforce religious conformity.

In contrast, sects tend consciously to reject the idea that society can be made Christian. The common characteristic of sects is that their doctrine and practice mark them as countercultural. Sacramental separatism, such as believers' baptism, is connected to a sect's negative attitude toward secular society. It was precisely the inclusivity of the Utraquists that Gregory and his comrades rejected when they formed a new community in Kunwald. The Unity of the Brethren began as a typical sect, or believers' church, but it rapidly developed into a new type of Christian community: a voluntary church. Before examining that history, however, we must first look in detail at the Táborites, who were the true ancestors of the Unity.

67. Troeltsch, *Social Teachings of the Christian Churches.*

Four

TÁBOR

Jakoubek of Stříbro was more radical than Hus, and he laid the groundwork for the first permanent national church to separate from Rome, but Jakoubek and his followers grew more cautious as the Czech Reformation turned into outright revolution. The New Town was the setting for religious and political radicalism under the priest Želivský, but after his murder the Utraquists established control over most of Prague. It was in the countryside, especially in southern Bohemia, that the most extreme Hussite experiments took hold and flourished. There the Táborite Brotherhood attempted to build a millennial kingdom. In eastern Bohemia Žižka led a similar brotherhood, called the Orebites. Their combined army inspired fear throughout Europe.[1]

The Táborites and Orebites played an important role in the development of the Unity of the Brethren. Not only did the Unity establish congregations in the areas where the radicals had their centers, some of the early Brethren had been part of the brotherhoods. The memory of the gathering on Mount Tábor inspired the ecclesiology of the Brethren, and their best theologians

1. This discussion of the Táborites follows the work of Howard Kaminsky, *Hussite Revolution*, and "Hussite Radicalism and the Origins of Tabor, 1415–1418," *Medievalia et Humanistica* 10 (1956): 102–30. A brief introduction to the Táborites in the context of other millennialist movements in medieval Europe can be found in Cohn, *Pursuit of the Millennium*, 205–22, but in treating the Táborites in the context of lower-class politics of resentment, Cohn misses the intellectual and political strength of the movement. The Táborites were closer to Oliver Cromwell and the Huguenots than they were to the children's crusade. For a critique of Cohn and a more complete presentation of the Táborites, see Thomas Fudge, "Neither Mine nor Thine: Communist Experiments in Hussite Bohemia," *Canadian Journal of History* 33 (April 1998): 25–48.

FIG. 9   Jan Žižka, mural in Bethlehem Chapel.

drew heavily on the writings of the Táborites. Luke of Prague was particularly attracted to Táborite writings. In historian Erhard Peschke's words, "Táboritish is the rational tendency of his [Luke's] thought, especially his arguments against transubstantiation and the teaching on the being of Christ. Táboritish is the equality of the priestly and episcopal offices, the proclamation of the fall and corruption of the early church. Táboritish, furthermore, is his criticism of the property of the church, simony, indulgences, purgatory, and the cult of saints."[2] The opponents of the Unity were not wrong to associate the Brethren with the Táborites, even though the Brethren renounced violence. The origins of the Brethren's catechism and liturgy are found in Tábor.

MILLENNIAL DREAMS

For decades Czech reformers had been preparing people for the coming of Christ, who would punish evil people and reward the faithful. Many Czechs saw the execution of the "two witnesses," Hus and Jerome of Prague, as a harbinger of the apocalypse (Rev. 11:3–8). The laity's reception of the blood of Christ seemed evidence that the order of the Antichrist was breaking down. Anticipation of the coming Kingdom of God ran high among radical priests and their congregations, especially in the south, with its long Waldensian tradition. In 1419, when the king issued the royal decree that banned the lay chalice and removed Utraquist priests from their parishes, Utraquist priests south of Prague organized massive outdoor religious services on a hill near Bechyně Castle, not far from where Hus had gone into exile in 1412.

The hill itself was not remarkable. In fact, scholars have been unable to determine which hill in the region it actually was. But what happened there was extraordinary. Within weeks of the first meeting, it became the site of some of the largest gatherings of common people in the history of medieval Europe. Contemporary sources estimated that the size of the crowds assembled on the hill ranged from ten thousand to one hundred thousand people; modern scholars estimate that the largest gatherings may have had twenty thousand. These

2. Peschke, *Kirche und Welt*, 60–61.

were national gatherings that included throngs from Prague, the region of Plzeň in the west, Domažlice in the northwest, and Hradec Králové in the northeast. The first large gathering took place on July 22, 1419, and it appears that Nicholas of Hus, Wenceslas Koranda of Plzeň, and Jan Želivský were the leaders.[3]

The new elements in Hussite theology introduced at Tábor included a complete break with the papacy and the designation of the New Testament as the sole standard for the church. Both the Old Testament and church tradition were to be subordinate to the New Testament, which provided the model of the apostolic church for the radicals. Eschatological expectations were running high in the summer of 1419, and the Hussite priests renamed the hill Mount Tábor because, according to ancient tradition, that was the mountain where Jesus had been transfigured (Matt. 17:1–2; Mark 9:1; Luke 9:28–29) and whence he ascended (Matt. 28:16–20). Popular belief held that Mount Tábor would be the place where Jesus would return in the glory of his transfiguration in the Last Days.[4]

The gathering on the new Mount Tábor was an intense form of Utraquism. Preaching and communion in both kinds were the two focal points of the first gatherings, and we can see the influence of the Waldensians, as well as of Hus, in the themes the radicals preached to the crowds. Kaminsky summarizes the message:

(1) priests should not possess property or income by civil dominion; (2) tithes were not to be obligatory, and the clergy should be supported by freely given alms; (3) priests should abandon their legal possessions of all kinds, retaining only a limited right to live in their parish houses "with all title of civil dominion removed"; (4) the New Testament is sufficient for salvation without the figures of the Old Testament and without customs of human invention; (5) infants should be given Utraquist communion after baptism; (6) the faithful should flee from thieves and brigands— that is, the Romanist clergy—and follow Christ, the true pastor.[5]

Contrary to the claims of Norman Cohn, this represents a unified Táborite program.[6]

3. Kaminsky, *Hussite Revolution,* 290.
4. Ibid., 282.
5. Ibid., 287.
6. See Cohn, *Pursuit of the Millennium,* 210.

It was not just poor peasants who gathered on Mount Tábor; there were also persons of property and power who were drawn to the dream of re-creating the original church of the apostles as described in the fourth chapter of the book of Acts. Mount Tábor is where we find the first expression of the Radical Reformation's call for Christians to separate themselves from the corruption of the world and build a church based on the witness of the primitive church. Laurence of Březová, a contemporary chronicler who did not join the Táborites, gave the following description of the gatherings on Mount Tábor:

> Their priests indeed exercised three kinds of offices there. The people having been divided into groups, the men by themselves and the women and children by themselves, the more learned and eloquent priests, from early morning on, fearlessly preached the Word of God and especially those things that concern the pride, avarice, and arrogance of the clergy. Other priests sat continually for the hearing of auricular confession. And the third group of priests, after divine rites had been performed, gave communion to the people in both the body and blood of Christ, from daybreak to noon . . . convivial together in brotherly love, not to the extent of indulging desire or drunkenness, nor levity nor dissoluteness, but to the greater and stronger service of God. There all called each other brother and sister, and the rich divided the food that they had prepared for themselves with the poor. Not only the elders but the children, too, refrained from indulging in any dancing, dicing, ball-games, or any other game of levity. Nor, finally, could there be found any arguments, theft, or playing of pipes or lutes, as was the custom at church dedication-festivals, but all were of one heart and one will, in the manner of the apostles, dealing with nothing except what pertained to the salvation of souls and to the reduction of the clergy to its original estate, that of the Primitive Church.[7]

In this brief description we glimpse an early version of the famous Moravian settlements of the eighteenth century. Sobriety, a sense of brotherhood and sisterhood, and the sharing of communion physically and spiritually in worship

---

7. Quoted in Kaminsky, *Hussite Revolution*, 284–85.

were all related to an understanding that the eschatological vision provides the model for the earthly community. Tragically, in the case of Tábor, pacifism turned to war as expectations for the arrival of the Kingdom of God on earth were frustrated. Two decades later, the Unity of the Brethren tried to reclaim the original pacifism of 1419 in a more stable and enduring form.

In many ways, though, the gathering in July 1419 was a religious "Woodstock" in which the normal rules of competitive society were temporarily suspended and the crowds tried to create a new community in the wilderness. We can understand the gathering on Tábor using Victor Turner's idea of *communitas*, which refers to an ecstatic community that generates tremendous energy and a sense of oneness. Like many dynamic forces, though, *communitas* is unstable.[8] Like the passion of first love, it is generative and creative but is quickly spent, leaving behind the memory of what almost was and the longing for what could be. Such longing and frustrated hopes can lead to violence.

WARRIORS OF GOD

King Wenceslas died in August 1419, and his brother, Emperor Sigismund, hoped to be crowned king of Bohemia in Prague. The Hussite estates (nobility, clergy, and burghers), following ancient tradition, issued a number of demands before the coronation could take place. In general they followed a moderate or even conservative Hussite agenda, along with a pro-Czech policy, but after the Council of Constance these simple demands represented open rebellion against the Roman Catholic Church and the Holy Roman Empire. Sigismund not only rejected the Czech demands, he instituted a policy of severe repression of Utraquism. The radicals in Prague, along with the Táborite and Orebite brotherhoods, responded with violence. Monasteries and brothels were destroyed, and parish churches were taken over. The radical priest Koranda led another mass meeting on a hill near Plžen in September, and the Táborites became more clearly a political movement.[9]

On October 25, 1419, Jan Žižka led a militia against the fortress of Vyšehrad

---

8. Victor Turner, *The Ritual Process: Structure and Anti-Structure* (Ithaca: Cornell University Press, 1998), 96–140.
9. Kaminsky, *Hussite Revolution*, 298–99.

outside the New Town of Prague, and the Hussite Wars began. On November 13 the Utraquists signed a truce that allowed Sigismund to be crowned emperor in exchange for a promise to allow the lay chalice, but this proved to be an empty promise. Žižka rejected the truce, left Prague, and joined the Táborites. Later he left the city of Tábor and became the leader of the Orebites, who were more conservative theologically and socially than the Táborites. Rather than respect his promises to the Utraquists, Sigismund took advantage of the truce to step up his campaign to exterminate the Hussites. In response to his execution of hundreds of Hussites at Kutná Hora, the Táborite and Orebite brotherhoods grew more radical.[10] The original pacifism manifested on Mount Tábor quickly gave way to violent apocalyptic preaching and preparation for holy war.

Radical Hussite preachers published pamphlets that drew on the prophecy of Isaiah 19:18 urging the faithful to separate from the sinful church and flee the imminent wrath of God. The true Hussites were to fly to one of the "five cities" that would be preserved by God on the Day of Judgment. It is still not clear whether the Táborites agreed on which the five cities were, but one source listed them as Plzeň, "which they called the City of the Sun," Zatec, Louny, Slany, and Klatový.[11] It is hard to realize in our era that simply fleeing one's home was itself an act of rebellion in the Middle Ages. An imperfect analogy would be the mass emigration of people from Eastern Europe in the final days of the Soviet Union, or the flight of people from Cuba. Simply leaving a repressive regime becomes a public rejection of the legitimacy and power of the regime. This was particularly true in the Middle Ages, because flight involved forsaking one's feudal obligations. In recognition of this fact, Jakoubek publicly opposed the apocalyptically inspired call to flee to the mountains. He argued that true Christians should remain in their homes and be ready to endure even unjust suffering. Despite his efforts, thousands did answer the call to flee as word spread that the Day of Judgment would arrive in February 1420. The faithful felt they must prepare for the coming of the Lord.

Sometime in January 1420 the Táborites, led by Žižka, captured the town of Plzeň and set up a commune led by the priests. Písek and Hradeč Kravlové

10. Ibid., 307–11.
11. Ibid., 311–12.

FIG. 10   Model of Tábor, Hussite Museum, Tábor.

were also taken by radicals. Písek was soon retaken by Catholic forces, and the Táborites fled into the woods. On Ash Wednesday (February 21, 1420) they took advantage of the fact that most Catholics were recovering from the rev-els of the previous evening. They conquered the sleeping town of Ústi-nad-Lužnicí and established a communal economy. Joined by Žižka and the Plzeň radicals, who had fought a major battle en route, the radicals then took the abandoned fortress of Hradiště, repaired its defenses, and established a new community that they named Tábor, like the hill on which they had gathered in 1419. The Táborites then burned Útsi and established a new permanent community.[12]

The old fortress stood on a high hill partially surrounded by a wide river.[13] The natural defenses were supplemented with strong walls and towers that the Táborites improved. The undeveloped aspect of Tábor allowed the priests and military leaders to create a society unique in medieval Europe. Since the elect had fled from the corruption of the world in expectation of the millen-nial dawn, they could experiment with communal self-government. Kaminsky claims that "history offers no better example of the embodiment of an idea in

12. Ibid., 332–35.
13. For pictures of Tábor, see Kejř, *Hussite Revolution*, 70–89, esp. 75.

reality."[14] A vital aspect of the story of Tábor was the elevation of the common person's status.

> At Tábor, the commoner was a participant in the higher culture of his community—in its religion. In church he did not merely observe a self-contained liturgical drama, he was an actor, singing the hymns that constituted the service and listening to liturgical formulas that were kept brief and were uttered in his own language. In the religious discussions endemic in the Táborite towns, the ordinary layman could speak; having listened to countless sermons expounding the text of the Bible, he would have considerable knowledge of that book; if, as was often the case, he knew how to read, he could study not only the Bible in Czech but also the current doctrinal positions of the priests, who regularly wrote in both Czech and Latin. . . . John Přibram, who tells us that the Táborites suppressed Latin schools, also reveals that they taught boys and girls in Czech; the result was a remarkably well-educated citizenry.[15]

The Czech Reformation had made lay reading of the vernacular Bible a key component of reform, but in Prague it was primarily the aristocracy and wealthy burghers who had this privilege. The Táborites extended biblical literacy to the common people. This ideal of an educated, active laity would bear rich fruit in the Unity, especially in Comenius's advocacy of universal education.

Tábor and Prague disagreed profoundly over the meaning of church reform. The Utraquists were frightened by the social and religious reforms envisioned by the priests of Tábor and enforced by Žižka. The most to which the Utraquist leaders would agree was the Four Articles of Prague, discussed earlier, and these were interpreted very conservatively. In contrast, the Táborites wanted to impose twelve articles that were to be the basis of a righteous kingdom, similar to that dreamed of by the Puritans in England and New England two centuries later. Among the Táborite demands that the Utraquists rejected as too extreme were the following:

> That there be no toleration without punishment of evident sinners, adulterers and adulteresses, fornicators and fornicatresses, whoremasters and

14. Kaminsky, *Hussite Revolution*, 335.
15. Ibid., 486.

madams, ruffians and prostitutes whether open or hidden, idlers of either sex, thieves, and all enemies, blasphemers, and detractors of God, of whatever order or status.

That they not wear or permit to be worn prideful clothing, costly to an ungodly degree of excess, such as garments dyed purple, fringed, painted, embroidered with silver, tufted, slashed; also silver girdles, nets, and all ornaments or adornments disposed for pride.

That it be provided in the crafts and in the market that there should be no deceptions, stolen goods, usury oaths, useless or vain things, tricks or falsehood; and this under any fit punishment.

That all priests' incomes be converted to the common good, that usurious incomes on houses, commodities, or whatever else be destroyed, and that all other usurious contracts be destroyed, and that the priests be supported by the voluntary contributions of the faithful.[16]

Though rejected by the Utraquists, the austerity of this Táborite social program strongly influenced the development of the Unity of the Brethren. The Brethren would organize their discipline around these demands of higher righteousness.

APOCALYPSE

After the founding of Tábor, a new and dangerous element appeared in the preaching and propaganda of the priests. Up until then preaching had focused on the day of wrath and the return of Christ, but after 1420 preachers began to speak of a thousand-year reign of Christ on earth.[17] This belief in a millennium of true peace and harmony has a long history in Christianity, but in the late Middle Ages it was most often associated with the prophecies of a thirteenth-century Italian monk named Joachim of Fiore.[18] Joachim had written that there were three ages of the world. The age of the Father lasted until the incarnation of Christ. The age of the Son was the age of the church, and it was

16. Ibid., 482.
17. Howard Kaminsky, "Chiliasm and the Hussite Revolution," *Church History* 26 (1957): 43–71.
18. Kaminsky, *Hussite Revolution*, 351; Howard Kaminsky, "The Free Spirit in the Hussite Revolution," in *Millennial Dreams in Action*, ed. Sylvia L. Thrupp (The Hague: Mouton, 1962), 166–86.

coming to an end. The age of the Spirit would be the millennial age in which human society would be structured like an ideal monastery. There would be no need for an institutional church or a secular government because the Holy Spirit would rule in all people's hearts. There were significant differences between the Joachim vision of the millennial church and the Waldensian understanding of the persecuted church. The Waldensians believed that true Christians will always suffer, but the millennial dream envisioned a world in which suffering would be no more.[19]

In the fourteenth century the Spiritual Franciscans drew upon Joachim's prophecies in their struggle with the papacy. They tried to move the Franciscan order back to the ideal of apostolic poverty espoused by Francis in his original *Rule* and his final *Testament.* The Spiritual Franciscans were condemned for the heresy of preaching that Christ had not owned property. In the struggle over property, the Spirituals defied the authority of the pope and the general of their own order, and they popularized the idea that the institutional church of Rome would be replaced in the millennial age, which was at hand.[20] The adaptation of Joachim's ideas led to widespread interest in the millennium and the book of Revelation among religious dissenters and reformers in the early modern period.

Among them was an eloquent young Czech priest named Martin Húska who preached enthusiastically about the glories of the in-breaking millennial dawn. He was intelligent, knew much of the Bible by heart, and inspired the Táborites with a vision of the world to come. Naturally, the Táborite priests, especially those who had preached an apocalyptic message before February 1420, needed to offer some explanation for why the Kingdom of Christ had not yet been realized as predicted. The answer Húska gave the residents of Tábor was that Christ *had* come as predicted, but his coming was in secret, "like a thief in the night." Soon he would reveal himself in his glory. Before this final revelation, though, the world needed to be purified. Christ's secret return had inaugurated the period when the faithful must rid the world of evil through fire and sword, beginning in Bohemia. Until he was revealed in glory, Christ

---

19. Kaminsky, *Hussite Revolution,* 349.

20. Lambert, *Medieval Heresy,* 213–35; Leff, *Heresy in the Later Middle Ages,* 1:68–82; Bernard McGinn, *The Calabrian Abbot: Joachim of Fiore in the History of Western Thought* (New York: Macmillan, 1985).

was "not to be imitated in his gentleness and mercy, but in zeal, in rage, and in just retribution."[21] Only after evil was eradicated could Christ appear as king.

As a result of Húska's preaching on the apocalypse, the Táborites moved rather quickly from communal pacifism and voluntary suffering to defensive warfare and the establishment of a fortified city. From there they abandoned millennial dreams of complete egalitarianism and an end to oppression in favor of an apocalyptic nightmare in which even priests were encouraged to wash their hands in the blood of God's enemies. The Old Testament grew in importance in Táborite theology and preaching. The Táborite priest Jan Čápek wrote and distributed tracts that were "more full of blood than a fish pond is of water," according to one contemporary. He developed the Táborite doctrine of total warfare modeled on the holy war of the Old Testament, in which there could be no booty and no prisoners. The old world must be entirely swept away, buildings and all, to make room for the new.

"The new violence was indeed religious violence," Kaminsky writes, "orgiastic and ritualistic as well as practical in character, for its purpose was to purge the world in preparation for the 'consummation of the age,' and its sanction lay in the new situation created by Christ's secret coming, which had annihilated all traditional guides to behavior."[22] More than three and a half centuries later, the Terror of 1793 in France would echo this message. The enemies of Christ, like the enemies of the French Revolution, were easy to identify. They were all those of high rank in the state and the church. Soon the Táborites would count as "enemies of Christ" anyone who had not fled to the cities of refuge and joined one of the brotherhoods. By the end of 1420 even the warrior Žižka worried about the bloodthirstiness of the apocalyptic preachers of Tábor. He left Tábor and joined the Orebite Brotherhood, although he remained the commander of the combined peasant army of the Orebites and Táborites until his death in 1424.

This extreme religious violence lasted only a few months, but for fifteen years the Táborites maintained the most feared and successful army in medieval Europe. The story of the heroic and bloody Hussite Wars belongs in another book, but it was significant that this was the first European army made

21. Kaminsky, *Hussite Revolution*, 345.
22. Ibid., 347.

up primarily of commoners. Like Cromwell's new model army in the seventeenth century, rank was assigned according to skill rather than social status. It was also one of the most disciplined medieval armies, especially in the early days, when rape and pillage were punishable by death. Like Cromwell's forces, Žižka's warriors went into battle singing hymns, the most famous of which is the Hussite war hymn, which extols all ranks to sacrifice themselves in service to Christ rather than fight for earthly gain.

> Ye warriors of God
> And of His Law,
> Pray for God's help,
> And believe in Him,
> So that with Him you will ever be victorious!
>
> Christ will make good all your losses,
> He promises you a hundred times more;
> Whoever gives his life for Him,
> Shall gain life eternal;
> Blessed is everyone who dies for the truth.
>
> Therefore archers and lancers,
> Of knightly rank,
> Pikemen and flailsmen,
> Of the common people,
> Keep ye all in mind the generous Lord!
>
> You men of supplies and advance guards,
> Think of the souls
> That you not forfeit lives
> By greed and robbery,
> And never let yourselves be tempted by spoil!
>
> Thus ye shall shout exultant:
> "At them, hurrah, at them!"
> Feel the pride of the weapon in your hands,
> And cry: "God is our Lord!"[23]

23. Macek, *Hussite Movement in Bohemia*, 116–17; Fudge, *Magnificent Ride*, 200–202.

Though the connection between the apocalyptic warriors who sang this Hussite battle hymn and the Unity of the Brethren, with its strong commitment to nonviolence, may not be readily apparent, there was common ground. Here was a picture of the church militant organized on the principle that everyone, no matter how lowly in worldly status, is worthy of respect and has a vital role to play. Leadership was based on the ability to lead courageously rather than on birthright or status. Each soldier of Christ used what God had provided for the greater good.

THE CHURCH OF TÁBOR

After the early victories of Žižka and the decisive break with the Utraquists, it became evident to most Táborites that the Second Coming was not imminent, nor could evil be eradicated by military means. It was also clear that the enthusiastic sharing of goods that characterized the early months of Tábor could not support a stable economic system. In short, less than two years after the communal gatherings on the mountaintop, the Táborites decided to establish a firmer social and ecclesiastical structure. The Táborite and Orebite cities began to impose typical feudal obligations on the peasant population and to organize their industry on the medieval guild model. The dream of an egalitarian millennium evaporated.[24]

This did not mean that Táborite society came to an end. Unlike most millenarian movements, the Táborites made a successful transition to a stable society that provided for basic human needs while still maintaining a radically different religious and social order. As Kaminsky points out, "Tábor, and to varying degrees the other towns of her brotherhood, were new sociopolitical formations, and their religion was something that had not been seen before in European history. The new was more important than the old."[25] For our purposes, it is important to recognize that the idea that economics, community, and Christian faith were interrelated was central to the beliefs and practices of the Unity of the Brethren.

24. Cohn, *Pursuit of the Millennium*, 218.
25. Kaminsky, *Hussite Revolution*, 360, 482.

Ecclesiastically, the Táborites chose their own bishop, in defiance of the principle of apostolic succession. The man they chose was Nicholas of Pelhřimov, also known as Biskupec. Nicholas was born about 1385, was educated at the University of Prague, and was associated with Bethlehem Chapel. In 1414 he was ordained a Catholic priest, and he took a parish in southern Bohemia. He was an early participant in the ecstatic days of the Táborite movement, but he did not share the extreme apocalyptic vision of other Táborite priests. His election as a bishop indicated that the Táborites were moving away from the initial *communitas* and toward a more stable church hierarchy.[26] Nicholas was given the task of organizing and disciplining the clergy, which included setting limits on apocalyptic preaching and speculation. He was also given charge of the common funds, which gradually became a voluntary offering to support the clergy rather than a true communal system. Although the Táborites moved away from communalism, the idea of voluntary support for the clergy marked a radical departure from medieval practice. This was a tentative step toward the modern system of voluntary support of the church. It is worth noting that the Protestant churches of the sixteenth century were unwilling to depend on free gifts of the congregation for the income of the clergy. Only the Unity of the Brethren and the Anabaptists followed the Táborite practice before the disestablishment of religion in the late eighteenth century.

Nicholas wrote the main defenses of Táborite theology and political practice. Interestingly, he was one of the few medieval theorists to make extensive use of Marsilius of Padua's famous *Defensor pacis* in a practical way.[27] Drawing on Marsilius, Nicholas argued that the people had the right to establish their own government and to wage war. The "divine right of kings" was a doctrinal error. Unlike Húska and the apocalyptic preachers, Nicholas defined "just war" very narrowly, adopting the arguments of Augustine and Hus. Christians should never wage war, he maintained, for revenge, conquest, or political advantage. Unlike Augustine, though, Nicholas asserted that war was sometimes necessary to defend the truth and God's law. This included the right of Christians to defend themselves from the armies of the Antichrist, the crusaders sent to compel the Czechs to return to the Roman Catholic Church. For Nicholas,

---

26. Ibid., 387.

27. This was "one of the few moments in history when that celebrated work was made to fulfill the revolutionary promise that has so distinguished it in the eyes of modern scholars" (ibid., 485).

war was a way to liberate the oppressed, but he argued that violence should also be used to remove corrupt and abusive priests from their offices, destroy idolatry in worship, and purify the church of Christ.[28]

The Táborites felt no guilt about destroying altars or "desecrating" churches, because Catholics desecrated churches every time they performed idolatrous Masses in them. The last of the Twelve Articles urged the Hussites to "destroy and demolish heretical monasteries, unnecessary churches and altars, images kept openly or secretly, prideful chasubles, gold and silver chalices, and every antichristian institution, every idolatrous and simonical depravity, which is not of God, the heavenly Father."[29] Nicholas warned, however, that war is dangerous and should be a last resort because it tempts people into cruelty and barbarism. Christians were to wage war in a spirit of love, not hatred, if such a thing is possible.[30]

BOHEMIAN PIKARTS

Predictably, the elevation of one priest to the rank of bishop and the conscious turn away from the more extreme aspects of millennialism and apocalypticism led to a breach among the Táborites. Some of the Hussites grew more radical at the same time that Bishop Nicholas was trying to bring greater order and stability to the Táborite movement. Some of this radicalism may have come from France, original home of the Beghards, laymen who devoted themselves to poverty, chastity, religious devotions, and acts of charity. For the most part, the Beghards remained within the Catholic Church, but it appears that some of them applied Joachim's concept of the age of the Spirit to themselves as individuals. They called themselves the Free Spirits, and in their hands the millennial dream of apostolic poverty was radically transformed.[31]

Not much is known about the Free Spirits, but the fourteenth-century Inquisition in Cologne recorded the investigation of a man from Moravia who had joined them. This man, Kaminsky tells us, reported that a new member

28. Peschke, *Kirche und Welt*, 46–47.
29. Kaminsky, *Hussite Revolution*, 482.
30. Peschke, *Kirche und Welt*, 47.
31. Lambert, *Medieval Heresy*, 199–207.

of the Free Spirits would be "received into a kind of novitiate in which the emphasis was on absolute, Christlike poverty and humility: he had to sell all his goods and turn the proceeds over to the sect, and when he first appeared before the brethren he was stripped of his clothing. He was then sent out to beg with a companion to whom he owed absolute obedience; he was also required to spend time in church praying and to wash the feet of wayfarers."[32] Such conduct was similar to Franciscan and Waldensian practice and theology, but the Free Spirits saw evangelical poverty as only a step toward perfection. After fulfilling this difficult novitiate, the person was declared free of sin and the law. "The only danger was that he might submit to some restraint and hence 'fall away from the freedom of the spirit, from the perpetual to the temporal.'"[33]

Over time the Free Spirits were identified as Pikarts (also spelled Pickarts, Piccards, and Picards). The name may indicate simply that they were from Picardy in France, but it is possible that it was a corruption of Beghards (*piccardia* from *beghardia*),[34] who were often accused of heresy. Inquisitorial records indicate that Free Spirits and Beghards were present in Augsburg in 1393 and probably in Bohemia as well. We have evidence that forty Pikarts arrived in Prague in 1418 fleeing persecution in France, and there are reliable reports that they became Hussites and participated in the debates of the time. The Bohemian Pikarts' theology appears to have been consistent with that of Beghards associated with the Free Spirit movement, especially the connection between millennialism and antinomianism.[35] Rejection of the concept of transubstantiation was a distinguishing feature of these Pikarts.

The Táborite priest Martin Húska, who had introduced millennialism into the movement, endorsed elements of Pikartism in the autumn of 1420.[36] Unlike other Hussites, who venerated the host and even carried it into battle, Húska

---

32. Kaminsky, *Hussite Revolution*, 355.

33. Ibid., 355–56; Kaminsky, "Free Spirit in the Hussite Revolution." Lambert notes that accounts of the activities of the Free Spirits should be viewed with caution since there is a real possibility that inquisitors shaped the evidence to fit what they were looking for. He characterizes those accused of heresy as "a miscellaneous assemblage of suspects, suggestible women liable to say what interrogators wanted, some eccentrics, even madmen who might have remained untroubled but for investigating zeal, some religious individualists" (*Medieval Heresy*, 206).

34. Kaminsky, *Hussite Revolution*, 353–54.

35. Lambert rejects the reports of ritual nudism and orgies as typical slander against radical religious groups. He also calls the Pikarts a "red herring" (*Medieval Heresy*, 360).

36. Kaminsky, *Hussite Revolution*, 407.

and the Pikarts rejected everything associated with the new festival of Corpus Christi, especially displaying the host or using it in processions as if it were an object of worship.[37] Húska protested vehemently against what he perceived as the idolatry of transubstantiation and veneration of the host. According to Táborite sources, Húska argued that it was wrong to adore the sacrament, elevate the host in the Mass, or even to kneel before taking communion. Even more radically, Húska apparently taught that Christ may be taken sacramentally in any food at any time in any meal.[38] In essence, he turned the Eucharist into an agape meal, or "lovefeast," where the focus was on the communion among the believers rather than the enjoyment of God's grace. Opponents of the Unity often identified the Brethren as Pikarts because they refused to venerate the host. By the end of the sixteenth century, when the taint of heresy had long since faded, even the Brethren used the title for themselves, but it was always inaccurate.

Peter Kániš became the chief spokesman for the Pikarts in Tábor, and his followers went further than Húska in their attack on the Hussite Eucharist. They not only refused to kneel for communion, they even desecrated the host by taking it out of monstrances and stepping on it. This was more than just ritual desecration associated with rejection of the religious-political order; it was an attempt to disprove the miracle stories associated with the host.[39] Given the symbolic importance of the chalice to all of the Hussite parties, it was little wonder that the antisacramentalism of the Pikarts was perceived as the ultimate form of blasphemy and sacrilege. Bishop Nicholas wrote a treatise defending the doctrine of the real presence against Kániš and expelled him and Húska from the brotherhood.

Húska was arrested by a Táborite nobleman in late January 1421 and soon made his peace with Bishop Nicholas. At around the same time Nicholas ordered the expulsion of some three hundred Pikarts from Tábor. Their removal, more than anything, marked the limit of Táborite radicalism.[40] The Pikarts set up their own commune outside Tábor, where they appear to have taken the final steps toward becoming antinomian Free Spirits. Numerous reports

37. Rubin, *Corpus Christi*, 164–287.
38. Kaminsky, *Hussite Revolution*, 407–8.
39. Rubin, *Corpus Christi*, 108–28.
40. Kaminsky, *Hussite Revolution*, 427–29.

circulated that some Pikarts embraced ritual nudism so as to demonstrate that the sin of Adam and Eve had been overcome by Christ's redemption. They may have also encouraged "free love" among the perfect. Certainly they resorted to brigandage to finance their commune.

Their military captain was a blacksmith named Rohan who was no match for Žižka. The Pikarts were overwhelmed when Žižka attacked in April 1421. He burned about fifty of his captives alive. The priests of Tábor burned another twenty-five Pikarts because of their view of the Eucharist. Not long after the destruction of the Pikarts, Húska was arrested again, this time by the Orebites. When their bishop, Ambrose, failed to convert him from Pikartism, he sent Húska to Prague, where he was imprisoned by the Utraquists. But Žižka insisted on stronger measures. Húska and his companion, Prokop One-eyed, were tortured and killed in August 1421.[41] One of the bitter ironies of the Hussite Revolution was that a movement begun in protest against the burning of a man for heresy quickly adopted the same practice.

TÁBORITE DOCTRINE AND PRACTICE

After the suppression of the Pikarts, the Táborites under Nicholas created a stable doctrine and liturgy. They retained many of the rites of the medieval church but reinterpreted the sacraments and reduced the ceremonialism of all observances. Their priests remained celibate, but marriage was not viewed as less worthy than celibacy. Women were educated in scripture and doctrine, and they took part in a limited way in worship services. Priests did not hold political office or wear special vestments. Most shocking to outsiders was the fact that Táborite priests shaved neither their heads (the tonsure) nor their faces. They wore long beards, like priests in the Orthodox Church, but this may have been a reflection of the Táborites' literal reading of the Old Testament, which instructed that Israelite priests should not trim their beards. The military leader of the Táborites, a priest named Prokop, was an exception in this regard, which is why he was called Holý (shaven).[42] Even though he was

41. Ibid., 430–31.
42. Ibid., 445.

a priest, Prokop Holý became head of the Hussite army after the death of Žižka in 1424. If it was legitimate for ordinary Christians to kill, then it must be legitimate for priests as well.

The Táborites' most significant contribution to the theology of the Unity of the Brethren was Nicholas's understanding of the sacraments. Drawing upon the Antiochene school of thought that distinguished between the divine and human aspects of Jesus, Nicholas argued that it was wrong to confuse spiritual and physical things.[43] Physically Jesus was a man like all men, but God the Son is eternal and omnipresent. The resurrected body of Jesus is in heaven, but the spirit of Christ is not bound to heaven. For Nicholas, it was both nonsensical and idolatrous to adore the wine and bread of communion as if it were the *physical* body and blood of Christ. To be physical is to be bound in time and space, he argued; therefore a priest could not bring the infinite Christ down from heaven and bind him on the altar. But Nicholas also argued that the Pikarts were wrong to treat the Eucharist as no more than an ordinary meal of remembrance. The proper teaching was that Christ is *really, truly, virtually, spiritually, and sacramentally* present in the Eucharist in his divine rather than his human form.[44] The Eucharist is not a mere symbol; it is a spiritual reality that should be approached with reverence and love. As we will see, this was the definition of the presence of Christ in the Eucharist that the Unity would use throughout its existence and that it introduced to the Protestant reformers in the sixteenth century.

The description of the Táborite liturgy provided by a Catholic observer, Laurence of Březová, is illuminating.[45] In it we can see the origins of the Brethren's liturgy. The liturgy was entirely in Czech, and it included reading from the Gospels, followed by a sermon on the subject of the Gospel reading. The congregation also sang biblical psalms, recited the Ten Commandments, and sang hymns appropriate for the occasion. While praying the Lord's Prayer, both priests and laypersons knelt with their heads to the ground. For communion, the officiating priest (a bishop when possible) stood behind a simple table and consecrated everyday bread and wine using Jesus' words from the

---

43. On antiochene Christology, see Pelikan, *Christian Tradition*, 1:226–56.

44. Peschke, *Kirche und Welt*, 52.

45. Howard Kaminsky, "The Religion of Hussite Tabor," in *The Czechoslovak Contribution to World Culture*, ed. Miloslav Rechcigl Jr. (The Hague: Mouton, 1964), 210–23.

New Testament. The plate and cup were not consecrated vessels but were like those normally used for meals. After the bishop communed, the other priests came forward and he served them. Then the priests went out to the people, who took first the bread and then the wine while standing. Everyone in the town was expected to take communion.[46]

Nicholas connected his sacramental theory to the idea of liberation for the people, for, as Amedeo Molnár has written, "it was precisely through the sacraments that people were most firmly and definitively tied to the institution of the Church. . . . In the light of Christ's Law, Biskupec [Nicholas] saw the major part of the sacramental practice as a harsh means of reinforcing the clergy's superiority over the laics."[47] It is interesting that Nicholas argued that priests should not wear vestments because the robes worn by Catholic priests were based on the clothing worn by officials in the Roman Empire. Thus priestly vestments symbolized political authority and the repression of truth.[48] This was consistent with the Táborites' belief that the church had been corrupted by the conversion of Constantine.

This suspicion that the Catholic sacraments were tools of oppression was connected to the Táborite's rejection of episcopal succession. True Christianity had been preserved only by a few "witnesses to the truth," most notably the martyrs Hus and Jerome of Prague, rather than by the laying on of hands from bishop to bishop. This idea of a chain of witnesses to the truth was later incorporated into Protestant historiography in the *Magdeburg Centuries*. True priests, according to the Táborites, are not those who stand in some type of apostolic succession through ordination but those whose lives are modeled on Christ. Priests who live in poverty and bear the cross of Christ, not the Catholic bishops who assert authority over princes and kings, are the true priests, and only true priests can administer the sacraments properly. Thus the Táborites endorsed the Donatist idea that the sacraments were valid only when administered by worthy priests, an idea that Hus went to such pains to reject.[49]

The Utraquists opposed the Táborites' view of the sacraments, scripture,

---

46. Kaminsky, *Hussite Revolution*, 445.

47. Amedeo Molnár, "Peter Chelčický's Instructions on the Sacraments," *Communio Viatorum* 19 (1976): 179.

48. Peschke, *Kirche und Welt*, 51.

49. Ibid., 46, 48.

and ordination. In the early 1430s Rokycana published a tract on seven errors of the Táborites, and a second treatise defending the seven sacraments and their traditional observance.[50] He argued, contrary to Nicholas, that tradition supports and clarifies scripture. Traditional practices not specifically mentioned in scripture might be permitted so long as they did not contradict scripture. Except for requiring communion in both kinds, Rokycana followed Aquinas closely in his exposition of the sacraments.[51] The Unity of the Brethren would side with Nicholas rather than Rokycana on the question of ritual. This fundamental difference between the Utraquists and Táborites over the role of tradition in liturgy and sacramental theology would be revived among the sixteenth-century reformers as well as the English Puritans.[52]

THE TÁBORITE CONFESSION

In response to Rokycana's attack on their doctrine, Bishop Nicholas published a confession of faith, known as the *Confessio Taboritarum*, shortly before the Council of Basel. This should be considered the first Protestant confession of faith ever written. It was first printed by the Lutheran historian Matthias Illyricus Flacius in 1568 under the erroneous title *Confessio Waldensium*. Flacius used it to support his thesis that the Lutheran Reformation was not an innovation but represented the apostolic truth preserved through the centuries by witnesses to the truth. He dated the confession to the controversies "134 years earlier" (1434), but modern research has shown that the manuscript Flacius used was a redaction made after the Council of Basel. When it was republished in 1616 it was correctly identified as the *Táborite Confession*.[53] In addition to its importance for understanding the theology of the Táborites, this confession had a strong influence on the development of the Brethren's theology.

Bishop Nicholas explained that the Táborite *Confession* was intentionally written in simple rather than academic language so that "hidden matters" of

---

50. Hans Jörg Dieter, "Das Verständnis von Schrift in der Confessio Táboritarium," *Communio Viatorum* 30 (1987): 158.
51. Ibid., 160.
52. Cameron, *European Reformation*, 136–44.
53. Dieter, "Confessio Táboritarum," 157.

faith would be made clear to farmers and simple folk. The language of philosophers obscures what is simple rather than clarifying what is hidden, he maintained. Nicholas argued that the New Testament itself was written in the language of slaves in order to bring freedom.[54] This emphasis on simple language was consistent with the importance of simplicity in worship and the laity's role in the church. He was particularly critical of the elaborate Catholic Mass, which he considered a magical rite complete with robes, chants, and superstition.[55] Christian worship should include edifying preaching on the teaching and example of Christ, and the essence of the ritual was to be communion with one another and with Christ.[56] All that was needed for the Eucharist was bread and wine, the proper words of consecration, an ordained priest, the necessary intention for consecrating the elements, and remembrance of the sufferings of Christ. Jakoubek had said something similar in 1418, but the Utraquists were very critical of the simplicity of the Táborite liturgy.

The *Confession* also stresses the authority of the law of God and its sufficiency for the proper administration of the church and its sacraments. The "rule" or foundation of both doctrine and practice for Christians should be the law of Christ, which is superior to both human laws and the law of the Old Testament. The Táborite canon included the apocrypha and the Old Testament, but the Gospels had priority because the center of Táborite theology was Jesus Christ, the head to whom all members of his body must be joined in order to receive salvation and truth.[57] They were convinced that the will of Christ, which was authoritatively interpreted in the practice of the early church, was fully revealed in scripture, especially in the synoptic Gospels. Most of the rituals and symbols used in the Catholic Church, according to the *Confession*, were part of the old covenant, not the new covenant revealed in the New Testament.[58] Although Christians ought to observe what is clearly taught in scripture, they should never be compelled to participate in unbiblical practices. Those good priests, including Nicholas himself, who abolished unbiblical observances should be held in high regard rather than condemned as heretics.

54. Ibid., 164.
55. Peschke, *Kirche und Welt,* 49–50. On the elaboration of the Mass in the late Middle Ages and the superstitions associated with it, see Rubin, *Corpus Christi,* 35–48, 147–54, 310–43.
56. Dieter, "Confessio Táboritarum," 166.
57. Ibid., 167–68.
58. Peschke, *Kirche und Welt,* 43.

The *Confession* asserted that the only rites that are truly sacraments are those defined as such by Christ and the apostolic church.[59] Nicholas did not reject outright the traditional seven sacraments that Rokycana defended, but he reinterpreted them in such a way that they most lost their sacramental character. He also reduced the ceremony of the sacraments, arguing that the rituals added by the Catholic Church in the Middle Ages were the work of the Antichrist, not of Christ and the apostles. Ultimately, the most important thing was that Christians observe the sacraments according to their original sense, focusing on personal faith and moral living.

Baptism was the sign of washing the soul of sin and was based on the Gospel message of forgiveness. In addition to the washing with water, the ritual included a renunciation of evil, prayers for the person being baptized, and admonitions to live according to the baptismal covenant. The Táborites abolished anointing with oil, exorcisms, and other rites in favor of a simple "biblical baptism." Since baptism was for infants, it was necessary that adult Christians confirm their faith in a separate ritual (confirmation) that included the laying on of hands by the priest, after the model of Christ blessing the children. The confirmation ritual was stripped of the later additions, especially oils and incense. Most important, confirmation did not require the action of a bishop.[60] The Unity of the Brethren built on the Táborite idea of confirmation as a rite of passage into adulthood by strengthening the educational component of the ritual.

The Táborites did not abolish the practice of confession because they saw it as necessary in light of the human tendency to sin. They also pointed to the example of confession in Acts 2 as evidence that this was a scriptural practice. There were three types of confession, according to Nicholas. The first was genuine, inward repentance for one's sins. This was the basis for the other two types of confession. The second was spoken confession within the community of faith in worship. The third was private auricular confession before a priest. Nicholas warned that the Catholic Church often used this third form of confession to oppress people and argued that it therefore should not be required. Nicholas pointed out that if private confession was necessary for salvation, as the

59. Dieter, "Confessio Táboritarum," 168.
60. Peschke, *Kirche und Welt*, 54–55.

Catholics taught, then everyone who had died before the twelfth century (when Pope Innocent III made confession mandatory) must have been damned.[61]

Likewise, Nicholas criticized the Catholic Church for turning the sacrament of anointing into a ritual of "extreme unction" for the dying. The Bible speaks of anointing and prayer for healing in James 5. Nicholas argued that it was important for priests to return to their role of bringing comfort and hope into people's lives rather than waiting until the moment of death. Moreover, according to Nicholas, extreme unction was a ritual prone to abuse by the Catholic Church since priests used it to extort gifts from the family.[62] Speaking of death, the *Confessio* rejected the idea of purgatory, which became one of the defining differences between Utraquists and Táborites. With the rejection of purgatory came rejection of prayers for the dead, indulgences, and related practices.

The Táborites did not abolish ordination for priests because they believed that Christ himself had instituted this rite in choosing his apostles. Christ set priests aside through the rite of ordination so that they would have the authority to teach the people and administer the sacraments. But ordination by a bishop was far less important than the worthiness of the persons ordained. The ritual itself should include only prayer, fasting, testing of the candidate, and the laying on of hands. Nicholas took a commonsense approach to the sacrament of marriage as well. God had established marriage from the beginning of the human race as the way to conceive children without sin; therefore it was not distinctly Christian. It was important that the couple be instructed in the meaning of Christian marriage, had the permission of their parents to marry, and entered into the relationship freely and willingly. The Táborite marriage ritual included prayer, instruction, and fasting.[63] On the whole, the Unity of the Brethren made use of Nicholas's understanding of the seven sacraments until the time of the Protestant Reformation.

Throughout the 1420s and '30s the Táborites refined, promoted, and defended their understanding of the true church and proper worship. Though

---

61. Ibid., 56.

62. Ibid., 57; Dieter, "Confessio Táboritarum," 162. Erasmus, in his colloquy "The Funeral," recognized this potential for abuse as well. See Erasmus, *Ten Colloquies*, trans. Craig R. Thompson (Indianapolis: Bobbs-Merrill, 1957), 95–104.

63. Peschke, *Kirche und Welt*, 56–57.

FIG. 11   Statue of Táborite priest Prokop Holý, Hussite Museum, Tábor.

famous for their success on the battlefield, they did not rely on arms alone in their struggle to reform church and society. They fought with ideas, some of which would find more fertile soil during the Protestant Reformation. After the Four Articles of Prague were signed in 1424, the Táborites held out hope that Prague could be won over to a more radical reform than that promoted by the university. In the negotiations leading up to the Council of Basel in 1434, Prokop Holý insisted that scripture alone should be the rule by which to decide doctrine and church practice. The church fathers and medieval theologians, including Wyclif and Hus, were useful as long as they did not contradict the canonical scriptures and "the Law of Christ."[64] This idea was partially incorporated in the Judge of Cheb, discussed earlier, and it became a fundamental aspect of the Unity's doctrine.

In terms of worship and doctrine, the Church of Tábor may be considered the first Reformed church, but it survived as a church for only one generation.[65] When the Council of Basel granted the Utraquists permission to give the chalice to the laity, the Utraquist lords made an alliance with the Catholics against the Táborites and Orebites. On May 30, 1434, the combined Utraquist-Catholic forces overwhelmingly defeated the once invincible Táborite army at the battle of Lipany.[66] Prokop Holý died in battle, and gradually the radical Hussite brotherhoods made peace with the Utraquists and joined the national church. In September 1452 the fortified city of Tábor surrendered peacefully to the Hussite king, George Poděbrady. Thanks to the intercessions of Jan Rokycana, Bishop Nicholas was imprisoned instead of killed.[67] The great Táborite adventure had come to a bitter end, but much of the theology and ethos of the Táborites would be revived in the Unity of the Brethren.

---

64. Dieter, "Confessio Táboritarum," 157–59.
65. See Peschke, *Kirche und Welt*, 61, for a discussion of the Táborites' contribution to Protestant thought and the fundamental difference between them and Luther on the issue of justification by faith alone.
66. Bartoš, *Hussite Revolution*, 112–18.
67. Odložilík, *Hussite King*, 67.

Part Two

THE BRETHREN

Five

CHELČICKÝ

The Czech reformer who exerted the most direct influence on the theology of the early Unity of the Brethren was neither a Táborite priest nor an Utraquist professor, but he was arguably the most original thinker of the late Middle Ages.[1] Peter Chelčický (c. 1380–c. 1458) was the father of modern pacifism, and one can trace a line of descent from Chelčický to Gandhi through Leo Tolstoy, who promoted Chelčický's writings when they were republished in the nineteenth century.[2] According to the historian Matthew Spinka, Chelčický's "unyielding and unequivocal insistence on the separation of church and state, and to a somewhat less degree his pacifism, raised him to the rank of a pioneer of future types of Christianity."[3]

BIOGRAPHY

Despite his importance to the history of Christianity and political thought, Chelčický was virtually lost to history until the nineteenth century, when Czech historians began recovering the history of their nation. After more than a century of historical research, though, Chelčický's biography remains obscure. He might have also been known as Peter Záhorčí (Záhorčí was a crossroads near

---

1. Peschke, *Kirche und Welt*, 81.
2. Leo Tolstoy, *The Kingdom of God Is Within You* (Omaha: University of Nebraska Press, 1985), 26.
3. Matthew Spinka, "Peter Chelčický, the Spiritual Father of the Unitas Fratrum," *Church History* 12 (1943): 271.

Chelčice), a country squire or freeholder. If so, Peter was born in 1379 or 1380.[4] Whether or not he was Záhorčí, Peter was certainly of the upper peasantry or lower nobility. His writings show that he was closely connected to daily agricultural life, but he was prosperous enough to have the leisure to pursue education and writing.[5] It is likely that he was familiar with Waldensian literature, for he adopted many Waldensian ideas, but he made only one clear reference to the Waldensians.[6] He probably knew some Latin, but he relied heavily on the Czech Bible and Hussite literature.[7] He was a gifted if unpolished writer in Czech.

Chelčický lived almost his entire life in southern Bohemia near Hus's birthplace, Husinec. There are indications that he had heard Hus preach and talked with him about the Eucharist in 1412. Certainly he admired the writings and personal example of Hus, and he was swept up in the great excitement when thousands gathered on Mount Tábor anticipating the Kingdom of God in 1419. Chelčický was one of the thousands who came to Prague during the turbulent months following the defenestration in July 1419, and he stayed through 1420. He participated in the debates in Prague and discussed theology with some of the university masters, including Jakoubek himself. Jakoubek's assistant at Bethlehem Chapel, Martin of Volyň, introduced Chelčický to the works of Matthew of Janov, and Chelčický embraced the call for a return to the apostolic church.[8]

Chelčický was thus introduced to the main themes of the Czech Reformation by 1420, but he remained an independent and critical thinker rather than a disciple of the Prague masters or the radical priests. In his *Reply to Rokycana*, written probably in the 1440s, he acknowledged both his admiration for and distance from the mainstream of the Czech Reformation.

> And this much I say of them [Hus, Matthew, Jakoubek], not abusing
> their good works that they have done in the name of God by zealous

---

4. This was the suggestion of historian František Bartoš. See Wagner, *Petr Chelčický*, 42, for details on the research into Chelčický's biography.

5. Ibid.; Peter Brock, *The Political and Social Doctrines of the Unity of Czech Brethren in the Fifteenth and Early Sixteenth Centuries* (The Hague: Mouton, 1957), 26–27.

6. Peschke, *Kirche und Welt*, 80.

7. Molnár, "Chelčický's Instructions on the Sacraments," 190. Molnár has shown that Peter was knowledgeable about Scholastic and patristic theology as well. See also Spinka, "Peter Chelčický," 222–24.

8. Wagner, *Petr Chelčický*, 68, 67.

preaching and other good things. But I will further say, they too have drunk of the wine of the Great Whore, with which she has besotted all the nations and the people. . . . For they have written things in their works which are denied by the divine laws, especially where Master Hus has written of murder, the oath, and images. Therefore, I cannot condone what they have passed on of an offensive nature to the scandalizing of many.[9]

Unlike Jakoubek, for whom the law of Christ meant communion in both kinds, Chelčický viewed Christ's law as nonparticipation in the structures of oppression and abuse.

He pushed Hus and Wyclif's ecclesiology to a logical conclusion that they had rejected, arguing that the true church of the predestined exists outside time and space. It is eternal and not subject to change and development. The only visible manifestation of the true church was the church of the apostles; therefore only those churches that are modeled on the apostolic church share in the true church. Thus, for Chelčický, the New Testament provides a description of the true church living under the Law of Christ. He regarded the Old Testament as an inferior and incomplete revelation that must be read only in light of the New Testament. The kingship of Christ had replaced the flawed kingship of David, and Old Testament laws regarding secular authority and war were abolished by Christ's law.[10]

Chelčický valued Wyclif above all church theologians because he had "written so zealously against the poison that has flown into the church and out of which the greatest antichrist has been born with all his adversity through whom Jesus Christ and his law have been suppressed, and Wyclif has routed out the hosts of the antichrist as well as those doctors who have opposed the Law of Christ with deceptive legalities, and in this he pleases me above all others."[11] Despite his appreciation of Wyclif, he rejected one of Wyclif's fundamental principles: that the state should root out immorality in the church. Chelčický's biographer Murray Wagner summarizes his repudiation of Wyclif's political theories: "He wanted no part of the Wyclifian doctrine of magisterial

9. Ibid., 70.
10. Ibid., 86–89.
11. Chelčický, *Reply to Rokycana*, quoted in ibid., 75.

responsibility for cleansing the church of impurities. Chelčický was convinced that kings and princes enter the church as wolves invade a fold of sheep."[12]

PACIFISM

In 1420 Chelčický met privately with Jakoubek to discuss moral issues and the theology of Wyclif, Matthew, and Hus. As the imperial forces were preparing for an assault on Prague, Jakoubek spent hours with this relatively uneducated farmer discussing whether there was a Christian justification for war. Jakoubek had been a pacifist in the early days of the rebellion and was sickened by Želivský's endorsement of violence during the defenestration. But with the city under immediate threat in 1420, he felt compelled to help organize Prague's defense. According to Matthew Spinka, Jakoubek reluctantly abandoned absolute pacifism in favor of a classical theory of just war as a necessary evil that can prevent worse bloodshed: "If war is necessary and unavoidable, it still must be carried on in the spirit of love, and each soldier must feel compunction and repentance for the killing of another."[13] Jakoubek thus recognized that even if war was a necessary evil, it remained evil and should never be glorified or sanctified as a crusade.

Chelčický, however, viewed Jakoubek's position as mere scholastic hairsplitting. He accused Jakoubek and the Utraquists of violating their own teaching about the primacy of scripture and the law of Christ. In advocating war, even in self-defense, they were relying more on the tradition of the church fathers and theologians than on the clear teaching of scripture. For Chelčický, the biblical prohibition against taking human life in the Decalogue and Jesus' teaching that his followers should not resist an evildoer were absolute. Years later he reminded Rokycana "how your master Jakoubek would be angry at someone who broke the rules of the Friday fast by eating meat, but would not make the shedding of human blood a matter of conscience."[14] Chelčický saw only hypocrisy in the Utraquists' claim that they had separated from the Roman

---

12. Ibid., 73.
13. Spinka, "Peter Chelčický," 277.
14. Brock, *Doctrines of the Brethren*, 32; cf. Wagner, *Petr Chelčický*, 78.

FIG. 12   Hussite banners depicting chalice and goose (Hus), Hussite Museum, Tábor.

Church in order to live according to the law of God, since they embraced the same alliance of church and state that was the source of corruption.[15]

After the crusaders were defeated by Žižka at the battle of Vyšehrad on November 1, 1420, and the immediate military threat was removed from Prague, Chelčický was able to return to his native south. Historians think he may have lived for a while in the Táborite "city of refuge," Písek, but soon he was back at Chelčice, where he lived until his death. He remained on friendly terms with the Táborites, with whom he had much in common theologically, but he did not join them. He objected to their view of the Eucharist and their warrior cult.[16] He blamed the militancy of Tábor on the Old Testament, claiming that the devil had used that book to seduce the Táborites into abandoning their original pacifism and adopting the ideology of crusade. He was most hostile to apocalyptic preachers like Húska, who believed that the faithful

15. W. Iwanczat, "Between Pacifism and Anarchy—Peter Chelčický Teaching About Society: Hussite Views on the Organisation of Christian Society," *Journal of Medieval History* 23 (1997): 271–83.

16. Brock, *Doctrines of the Brethren*, 35; Wagner, *Petr Chelčický*, 55–64.

should purify the world of evil by violence in anticipation of Christ's return in glory.[17]

Chelčický recognized the dangers inherent in what Luther later called a "theology of glory" rather than a theology of the cross.[18] Since Christians live in a preresurrection world, they must follow the teachings of Christ on the way to Golgotha, he maintained. Christ will return in glory, he argued, but until then his followers must follow him in sacrifice, self-control, and suffering. He thought the Táborite effort to purify Bohemia in anticipation of Christ's return was doomed to failure. This theology of the cross also stood in marked contrast to the thinking of the Free Spirits, who believed that the millennial age had begun and that the faithful were already free of the law and could live in innocence. Chelčický connected the Pikarts' theology of glory with their rejection of the physical presence of Christ in the Eucharist.[19] It was not the bread and wine that were miraculously transformed into Christ's body and blood, according to the Pikarts, but the worshippers who were miraculously transformed into Christ. Húska and his followers deliberately and dramatically desecrated the host by trampling on it, which Chelčický found blasphemous. For him, the desecration of the host, the violent attempt to end evil in the world, and the reports of unconventional sexual relationships were all fruits of a theology of glory. For Chelčický, the theology of the cross included pacifism and redemptive suffering, not redemptive violence.

DESANCTIFICATION OF THE STATE

Even after Peter returned to Chelčice and assumed leadership of a small separatist community, he stayed in contact with the Táborites. He wrote several of his tracts in direct response to Táborite developments; *On the Triple Division of Society*, for example, was a brief against the Táborites' adoption of Wyclif's political theory.[20] Bishop Nicholas appealed to Wyclif's exposition of Romans

---

17. Wagner, *Petr Chelčický*, 57.

18. Alister E. McGrath, *Luther's Theology of the Cross* (Cambridge: Blackwell, 1985).

19. Wagner, *Petr Chelčický*, 60–62.

20. Peter Chelčický, "Treatises on Christianity and the Social Order," trans. and ed. Howard Kaminsky, in *Studies in Medieval and Renaissance History*, ed. William Bowsky (Lincoln: University of Nebraska Press, 1964), 1:105–79, esp. 150. Hereafter cited parenthetically.

13 in support of the political authority of the priests in Tábor and the right of the Táborite nobility to tax the peasants. For Chelčický, by contrast, Romans 13 provided no justification for a *Christian* state or even for Christians to assume political authority in the state, because Paul was not writing to the state. He was writing for Christians who were living as a persecuted minority within the *pagan* Roman Empire (147–48). The church in Paul's day suffered at the hands of the state.

Chelčický pointed out that Paul's call for Christians to obey the governing authorities was actually a call to renounce personal political power, consistent with the teachings of the Sermon on the Mount. Romans 13 thus did not sanctify the state but rejected its idolatry. Chelčický tried to remove the state's mask of piety and show its basic paganism. For him, the idea of a "Christian monarch" was a contradiction in terms.[21] The law of love and secular power could not stand more opposed. "First of all," he wrote, "the attributes of power must be understood, and we must understand that it breeds fear, for power makes it possible for cruelty to rule, threaten, abuse, do violence, imprison, beat, and kill." Since secular power can only rule through fear, secular governments must have "no qualms about grieving a man, throwing him into prison, and killing him. Power will better prosper and endure by these means than by feeding the hungry, clothing the naked, healing the sick, without ever being able to wound and grieve, as would be the case if power stood according to love. Thus there is a great difference between power and love" (138, 140).

Chelčický acknowledged that God had indeed established secular authority to restrain evildoers, but he denied that this rule of fear applied to Christians, for Christ had abolished the old law with his new covenant. "But if the Law has been commuted, and if we are liberated from the Law of death through the love of our Lord Jesus Christ, and subjected to the Law of love, then let us see on what foundation power can be placed in Christ's faith. . . . If he had wanted people to cut each other up, to hang, drown, and burn each other, and otherwise pour out human blood for his Law, then that Old Law could also have stood unchanged, with the same bloody deeds as before" (139–40). How could Christians obey the injunction of the Lord's Prayer that they forgive

---

21. Peschke, *Kirche und Welt*, 68, 70.

others as they had been forgiven, and still enforce secular justice? Would not the sword fall from the hands of one who forgave in the name of Christ?[22]

Chelčický likewise contrasted faith and power. "But since we believe that Christ won us from the Devil's power through the weakness and humbleness of his Cross, we cannot agree that he causes our perfection in the faith through secular power, as though power were more beneficial to us than faith" (147). For Chelčický, one of the marks of true Christianity was the refusal to resist evildoers with violence. The feudal order with its sanctified violence belonged to the Antichrist, but the true church belonged to Christ.[23] Since the true church must model Christian virtue, it could never participate in the violence and injustice of the secular world. Christians ought to follow the advice of Paul and obey the laws of the state and the customs of society only in so far as these do not require behavior contrary to the teachings of Jesus; they must not share in the violence of the state. Christians should pay their taxes, Chelčický wrote, but they should never shed blood or swear an oath, even at the cost of their own lives. In this, Chelčický stood on the radical side of the Waldensian tradition.[24]

THE TRIPLE DIVISION OF SOCIETY

Chelčický's rejection of the medieval and Táborite sanctification of the state went further than his reinterpretation of Romans 13. More fundamentally, he attacked the idea of the three estates (nobility, clergy, and commoners) that provided the framework for all medieval political theory and practice. Theoretically, the estates represented those who wielded the sword in defense and punishment of evil, those who wielded the power of prayer and the sacraments for salvation in this life and the next, and those who labored to provide the necessities of life for all. This "triple division" of society into those who fight, pray, and labor was assumed by all medieval theorists to be part of natural law

22. Ibid., 70.
23. Wagner, *Petr Chelčický*, 149.
24. The prohibition on oaths and killing dates back at least to the thirteenth century in Lombardy and France. See Cameron, *Waldenses*, 75–76, 84–86, 105–6. For more on Waldensian pacifism, see Biller, "Medieval Waldensian Abhorrence of Killing Pre-c. 1400," in his *Waldenses*, 81–95.

and necessary for social order. As we saw in the previous chapter, despite their initial attempt to usher in the Kingdom of God on earth, the Táborites reverted quickly to this traditional idea of the social order. The fighting class included commoners in the Táborite army, and the clergy may have dressed like commoners, but the whole social structure of Tábor depended on the power of the army to tax the peasants and to punish them if necessary.[25]

Chelčický argued perceptively that the idea of three estates was really the pagan idea of caste imported into the church, not the teaching of the apostles. In his attack on the power of the Roman Church, Chelčický was a forerunner of the late eighteenth-century Enlightenment. He accused priests of "creeping" around, spreading the idea that they were the first estate, while "those who roam about with swords are the knightly estate; those who give children to be baptized are the married estate; the peasants who plow are the laboring estate. And all together are the Holy Church. But in truth it can be said that these offices, which after all the pagans and the world also have need of, can be attributed to the Holy Church. . . . But they are necessary only to the pagans or to the world, and God does not ordain them as the parts composing his Church" (156). This was a radical rejection of Wyclif's doctrine of dominion.

Chelčický catalogued the abuses of the nobility and clergy against the common people. Drawing upon the heritage of the Czech Reformation, he argued that the shepherds were killing and eating the sheep they were supposed to protect. Those who wielded the sword were not defending the common people; they were violently abusing them and stealing the fruits of their labor. Rather than punish evildoers, they *were* the evildoers. The church was supposed to be the body of Christ, but it was a diseased body.

> How then does it happen that the crooked limbs that hold the sword oppress the other, lesser limbs, afflicting them, beating them, putting them into prison, weighing them down with forced labor, rents, and other contrivances, so they go about wan and pale, while the others, satiated and idle like well-fed horses, give them the horselaugh? And the priests, like the eyes of the body, watch sharply over both other parts, looking for a way to strip them of their property and take it for themselves. Both

25. Wagner, *Petr Chelčický*, 79; cf. Cohn, *Pursuit of the Millennium*, 217–19.

together, the lords and priests, ride the working people as they will. . . .
The working people weep, and the others plunder them, imprison them,
and extort money from them, all the while laughing at their great misery. (158)

The parts of one body should not abuse the other parts of the same body;
instead, they ought to suffer along with them. "The triply divided Christian
people, carnal and full of dissension, neither can nor ever will have that unity
and love of one another; it is the world, and it has in itself only worldly desires.
Therefore it cannot rightly be said that the Body of Christ is composed in that
triple form, for even among the pagans there is such a division of the people
into three parts" (156).

The clergy might have prayed for the common people, but in most cases
they preyed on them. Rather than lead the laity to salvation, priests used the
authority of the Bible and the church to enhance their power, wealth, and
authority. "And they twist the truth so that it lies for them when they say that
peasants and other workers have to toil to maintain the lords and priests, so
that these may be supported. Or perhaps indeed priests have no other means
of support in the Holy Church than to stuff their bellies with the fruits of the
workers' toil? But against them is the example of the Apostle [Paul] and his
assistants, who worked day and night so that they would not be a burden to
the workers, and rebuked those among them who did not work but went around
doing nothing" (172).

Chelčický was clearly drawing on the tradition of Hus and Nicholas of
Dresden by contrasting the apostles and the prelates, but he went further when
he pointed to the feudal hierarchy itself as the problem. As long as people
believed that God had ordained some to fight, others to pray, and the majority to work, there would be injustice and abuse. The way to end the abuse
would be to abolish the system itself, but Chelčický saw that as impossible.
The most that could be done was to remove its holy patina and reveal the
structures of oppression for what they really were (160–64).

Chelčický was appalled by the Pikarts' desecration of the Eucharist, but he
called for an even more radical desecration of the feudal order (151). The idea
of three estates, he wrote, was contrary to the teachings of Christ and Paul in
the New Testament. It might be the structure of secular (pagan) authority, but

it had no place in the church, because the church is the body of Christ (1 Cor. 12:21–26). "Those people [commoners] are supposed to be limbs of Christ's Body, but we cannot recognize them or consider them as such because of those inequities, and they cannot come under the rule that there should be no disparity in the Body but rather equality, without some ruling over others. For such is Christ's command (Luke 22:24–26)" (160).

SEPARATISM, POVERTY, AND PERSECUTION

Like Francis of Assisi and Valdes, Chelčický called for priests to follow the path of apostolic poverty.[26] The solution to corruption in the church was to remove temptation by stripping the clergy of their power and wealth. He went so far as to call the church's blessing of the structures of injustice "heresy," and he urged a complete separation from the state. Priests should support themselves, and the true church should separate itself from the structures of worldly power. Members of the church should voluntarily support one another, but tithes must be abolished. The Apostle Paul in 1 Corinthians (12:25–26) "requires undivided equality among the limbs of the body, so that without envy they serve each other, take care of each other, share everything with each other— if the good, they rejoice together; if the bad, they suffer together. . . . Nor will one impose on others any involuntary servitude that he would not want for himself" (173, 172). We will see that this theme of equality and mutual support in the community of faith remained a feature of the Brethren's theology and practice.

Departing from Hus, Chelčický's rejection of the papacy was part of his larger rejection of all church hierarchy and indeed of the notion of Christendom itself. The early church had no pope, king, lords, tithes or taxes, inquisition or crusade, and no pretense of being part of pagan society. It was a new community of mutual love in which all were brothers and sisters and the only lord was Christ. Chelčický was one of the most persistent defenders of the dignity and importance of common people and everyday life. He saw more Christian devotion in a farmer planting his crop than in all of the pomp and

26. Lambert, *Medieval Heresy*, 70–72.

ritual of High Mass or all the apocalyptic zeal of the Táborites. Laborers who do not try to profit from sin (whether their own or others') imitate the sacrificial love of Christ more faithfully than those who renounce the world and live in a monastery supported by the work of serfs. He perceived more genuine scholarship in ordinary people who gathered to read, discuss, and follow the law of Christ in the New Testament than in the academic squabbles of the universities. He argued that true priests must join in labor with common people. "They should set a good example to those to whom they have preached the gospel, by diligent labor day and night, so that their example may lead the others to work all the harder and thus be able to give to those who do not and cannot have anything" (165).

Many contemporaries objected to Chelčický's assertion that the Christian community must live according to the example of the primitive church, perceiving correctly that this was a rejection of the whole notion of a Christian society. The doctrine of the three estates had been a way to Christianize the social order by giving authority to spiritual leaders who could (theoretically) mitigate the violence of the nobility and improve the lives of the peasantry. Chelčický rejected this notion entirely, and he condemned those who used scripture to justify oppression. "To attempt, therefore, to use the teachings of Scripture to order the Body of Christ in this way is to order the world under the cover of Christ's faith, to disguise the course of secular affairs as the service of Christian Law. . . . But I say that to act thus is to cultivate the world under cover of the faith, to call the world the faith, and, ultimately, so to confuse the faith by mixing the world into it as thereby to make it impossible to recognize what is the world and what is the faith" (167). Chelčický recognized that this understanding of the true church was intolerable, that the forces of the Antichrist would not allow such a church to exist. The Antichrist always sought to destroy or corrupt the church; Chelčický was thus not surprised that neither the Hussites nor the Catholics supported his type of reform.

Consistent with his understanding of the theology of the cross, Chelčický argued that one of the marks of the true church was persecution.[27] Persecution could take different forms, including economic deprivation, but the true church could never persecute others. Christ was the victim of imperial injustice

27. Wagner, *Petr Chelčický*, 134.

and the mockery of the crowds, never the victimizer who promoted injustice and ignored the suffering of others. None of the Czech churches, Catholic, Utraquist, or Táborite, was the true church, for they all persecuted their enemies. The true apostolic church was not the church of the bishops; it was the church that followed the path of loving sacrifice and rejected worldly power.

Christians, especially clergy, should be prepared to follow Christ in suffering. All Christians should stand with Christ, defenseless before Pontius Pilate, ready to take up the cross.

> But if it is a true opinion that the priest is the vicar of Christ's human nature and has to follow him in toil and patient suffering, and if evil people, when he preaches, want to beat him, seize him, or hurt him, and if the vicar of divinity, its sword in readiness, does not let anything happen to him, then how will he be following Christ in patient suffering? If power will not allow anything to be done against him, and hence frustrates his following of Christ, will not the vicar of divinity be blocking Christ's human nature in its functions? And the same holds for every man in the community, for it is Christ's injunction to him that he turn his other cheek to the one who strikes him in the face (Matt. 5:39), and the Apostle's injunction that he not defend himself against wrong (Rom. 12:19, 1 Cor. 6:7). (151)

Moreover, Chelčický argued that if Christians were not suffering persecution, or at least opposition, then they had obviously become too much at home in the world. He never envisioned the possibility that the world could uphold true Christianity. He recognized that the institutional church itself might turn against him in violence because he accused it of teaching "erroneous doctrine, contrary to Holy Scriptures. . . . But if all these heresies are advantageous to the faith, then they will bear down on me, because I am spoiling something very beneficial" to the institutional church (173).

SWEARING OATHS

Chelčický's rejection of the feudal social hierarchy and his radical devotion to the suffering Savior shed light on the importance of the oath to Chelčický and the early Brethren. Feudal society depended on a complex network of relation-ships that were sealed with an oath of fealty.[28] All levels of society depended on people swearing oaths, and the power of those oaths depended in turn on the belief that oaths were sacred. Oath breakers would be punished by God in both this life and the next. One of the most effective tactics the medieval church could employ in its power struggle with secular authorities was the release of subjects from their oaths. Even today it is customary for witnesses in court to swear an oath with a hand on the Bible to underscore the sacred-ness of their obligation to tell the truth.

Chelčický affirmed the Waldensian idea of Christ's "six smaller command-ments" from the Sermon on the Mount: do not respond to violence with vio-lence, do not divorce your spouse, do not swear oaths, do not be angry without cause, do not look lustfully at someone, and love your enemies.[29] The Catholic Church had restricted these commandments to religious orders, but the Wal-densians and Chelčický insisted that Christ was speaking to all Christians. Many Waldensians tried to follow this "higher righteousness" in secret while still receiving the sacraments from Catholic priests, but Chelčický was more rigorous in his application of these commandments. For him, the oath was central. If Christians refused to swear oaths, then they would separate them-selves from the feudal order and its violence. By refusing to swear, the disciples of Christ could not participate in the military, stand in judgment of others in trials, serve as witnesses, or be justices of the peace. Economic relationships would change as well, because the charging of interest was connected with a promise of repayment sealed with an oath.[30]

SACRAMENTAL THEOLOGY

Chelčický combined this radical rejection of the traditional social order and the church with a strong sacramental theology. As part of the preparations for

---

28. Marc Bloch, *Feudal Society*, trans. L. A. Manyon, 2 vols. (Chicago: University of Chicago Press, 1963).

29. There was a great deal of variety among the Waldensians when it came to specific beliefs. In gen-eral, they were noted for their focus on the vernacular reading of scripture, refusal to swear oaths (except to avoid execution), and denial of purgatory. Beyond that, some Waldensian groups embraced much Cath-olic practice and doctrine, while others called for a complete renunciation of the Catholic Church. Lam-bert, *Medieval Heresy*, 80–85, 159–61, 170–76; Říčan, *History of the Unity*, 9.

30. Brock, *Doctrines of the Brethren*, 182–205.

the Council of Basel, he wrote a treatise on the seven sacraments that became very important in the development of the Brethren's doctrine.[31] He followed the Táborites' order of the sacraments rather than Jakoubek's, but he put confirmation last: baptism, the Eucharist, penance, ordination, marriage, anointing, and confirmation. Like the Táborites, he argued that the church should focus on those sacraments instituted by Christ and essential for salvation: baptism, the Eucharist, and penance. The other four were worthy observances that were useful to the church but not essential for all people. Extreme unction, for example, had therapeutic and emotional benefits, but people should not view it magically or as necessary for salvation. Marriage, he noted, was observed by pagans as well as Christians and thus was not required for salvation.[32] In fact, true to his asceticism and biblicism, Chelčický maintained that celibacy was a holier estate than marriage.

In dealing with the crucial sacraments of baptism and the Eucharist, Chelčický tried to protect the sacraments from those who wanted to abolish them (Pickarts), on the one hand, and from those who elevated them too highly (Utraquists), on the other. Since the apostles baptized with water, there must be great spiritual value in baptism by water, he argued. Furthermore, he asserted that the apostles themselves had baptized children; therefore contemporary Christians should not abolish the baptism of children. But he specifically rejected the idea that baptism provided entry into the body politic as well as the body of Christ. He also argued that it was wrong to baptize children and bring them under the law of Christ without caring for their souls as they matured, a view shared by the Brethren. Like the Táborites, Chelčický emphasized the importance of catechetical instruction for all who had been baptized, and insisted that priests should refuse to baptize any child who was not under the care of parents or guardians who could see to the child's Christian upbringing and instruction. Baptism, he said, could not save in and of itself, but it was a key step in the process of salvation, which also included catechetical instruction, confirmation, and discipleship.[33] The Unity of Brethren developed these ideas further.

31. The dating of this treatise is disputed, but Molnár argues persuasively that it belongs to the debates between 1431 and 1434. Molnár, "Chelčický's Instructions on the Sacraments," 177–93.
32. Ibid., 182–86.
33. Wagner, *Petr Chelčický*, 114.

Chelčický rejected the Táborites' approach to the Eucharist. Though he condemned the Catholic teaching of transubstantiation as idolatry (and was appalled by the practice of carrying the host into war like a battle flag), he was suspicious of the Táborite doctrine, defined at the synod of Klatovy in 1424, that Christ is truly, spiritually, and sacramentally present within the bread and wine. After many discussions with Táborite priests and with Bishop Nicholas himself, Chelčický decided that the Táborites really believed that Christ was only figuratively or symbolically present in the Eucharist. He concluded that despite their statements, the Táborites rejected the idea that the physical can mediate the spiritual. The difficulty for Chelčický was that this made the presence of Christ dependent on the belief of the communicant rather than on the intention of Christ. The Táborites were wrong to deny that Christ could choose to be physically present in the Eucharist.

The modern Czech theologian Amedeo Molnár has concluded that Chelčický wanted "the secret of the Holy Supper to be respected."[34] This is no doubt true, but Chelčický did argue that the presence of Christ in the Eucharist is similar to the union of body and soul, which together form a person.[35] Chelčický moved so close to the position of the Utraquists, in fact, that Rokycana enlisted his support for the Utraquist position at the Council of Basel. Chelčický's understanding that the spiritual can be united with the physical was connected to his idea that the true spiritual church must be manifested in the physical world. The Eucharist was a bridge between heaven and earth, the eternal and the temporal.

True to the concerns of the Czech Reformation, Chelčický gave a great deal of attention to the nature of the priesthood when discussing ordination. Like the Táborites, he argued that apostolic succession is not determined by the laying on of hands by a bishop; it is a matter of priests' and bishops' following the teaching and example of Christ and the apostles.[36] Part of the corruption of the medieval church stemmed from the corruption of the priesthood through

---

34. Molnár, "Chelčický's Instructions on the Sacraments," 186.

35. Wagner, *Petr Chelčický*, 101–2. Wagner claims that the Táborite position is more consistent with Peter's sectarian beliefs, but he offers little support for this view. There is no evidence of an inherent connection between rejecting the state church and a nonrealist view of the sacraments.

36. Molnár, "Chelčický's Instructions on the Sacraments," 187.

simony and immorality. For Chelčický, a priest was like the stomach in the human body. If the stomach is healthy, then the body is nourished and strengthened by the food one eats. If the stomach is unhealthy, then even nourishing food will not be helpful. Thus a bad priest could turn the good food of the Gospel into something unhealthy if he neglected or abused the people.[37] Chelčický advised that Christians should confess to a good priest, if one could be found. If there were no good priests, then confession should be made to any good Christian. Despite his rejection of bad priests, Chelčický eventually decided against the Donatist understanding that the power of the sacraments depends on the worthiness of the priest.[38] Christ, not the priest, consecrates the communion elements. Even so, the laity should avoid immoral priests; thus the people have the right to choose their confessors and priests.

Like the Waldensians, Chelčický rejected the Catholic doctrine of purgatory. He saw this as another example of how the church corrupted the teaching of the New Testament by adding its own traditions. Purgatory gave people a false sense of hope for salvation. Worse, it gave the church ample opportunity to manipulate and swindle common people into buying indulgences or paying for masses for the dead.[39] By 1430 belief in purgatory had become the litmus test for orthodoxy among the Utraquists because it was the basis for several other disputed practices, such as prayers for the dead. Because of his rejection of the doctrine of purgatory, there was no hope that Chelčický would support the Utraquists, despite Rokycana's attempt to win him to the church.

LATER CAREER

Chelčický wrote to Rokycana to protest the Utraquists' compromises at the Council of Basel, which had granted Czechs the use of the chalice and little else.[40] Chelčický repudiated this attempted reunion with the papal Antichrist, a topic he explored at length in one of his last works, *The Net of Faith*. The title comes from a parable of Jesus in Luke 5:1–11 that compares the church to a

37. Wagner, *Petr Chelčický*, 117.
38. Molnár, "Chelčický's Instructions on the Sacraments," 188.
39. Wagner, *Petr Chelčický*, 122–23.
40. Odložilík, *Hussite King*, 4–18; Bartoš, *Hussite Revolution*, 60–98.

net that has caught all kinds of fish.[41] In Chelčický's reading, the parable says that out of the chaos of the world God's law brings in God's elect. But the net also catches other fish, some of whom are predators. They seek to destroy the law of Christ and consume the good fish. The largest predator fish, who tear the net of faith, are the pope and the emperor. With this allegory Chelčický repeated his conviction that the true church will always be persecuted by both the state and the state church. The pope and emperor represent two false gods, two Baals who "together devour the land and drink the bloody sweat of the third estate, who then drenched with sweat must satisfy the gluttony of the two Baals."[42] The Utraquists were wrong to cooperate with the Baals.

It was not just the papal curia and the imperial court that oppressed the people of God, according to Chelčický; monks, priests, friars, princes, nobles, university professors, doctors, lawyers, judges, knights, merchants, and burghers were also guilty.[43] Chelčický often noted that Cain, not the faithful Abel, built the first city. It was Cain and his descendents who "invented weights and measures to disguise their devious profiteering" and established the laws of property to legitimize their thievery.[44] He called for a return to simple living, hard work, and faithful discipleship divorced from the parish system. The church of the true disciples of Christ should withdraw from pomp, hypocrisy, deception, and violence. Though they would suffer at the hands of the unrighteous, they would find peace in their own hearts and life everlasting. Five centuries later, Tolstoy would echo these sentiments.

Chelčický was highly respected by Hussite leaders on both sides, but his vision of the church was too ideal to be realized. He was the spiritual leader of a small brotherhood of like-minded people near his home, but he refused to organize them in a visible church. His importance lay in his critique of church and society rather than in leadership. In many ways he offered a pessimistic view of the world and of the institutional church, but his writings served as the major theological resource for the Unity of the Brethren for more than

41. For a German translation of the *Net of Faith*, see Peter Cheltschizki, *Das Netz des Glaubens*, trans. Carl Vogl, reprinted in *Quellen und Darstellungen zur Geschichte der böhmischen Brüder-Unität*, vol. 5 of Beyreuther, Meyer, and Molnár, *Zinzendorf: Materialien und Dokumente* (Hildesheim: Georg Olms, 1970).

42. Wagner, *Petr Chelčický*, 132, 137.

43. Peschke, *Kirche und Welt*, 77.

44. Wagner, *Petr Chelčický*, 139.

half a century. Even after the Brethren put Chelčický's treatises aside, his influence remained woven into the fabric of the Unity. The Brethren tried to combine Chelčický's honesty and integrity with a stable institutional structure. In doing so, they offered a new understanding of the church that prefigured modern developments.

In 1452 the city of Tábor submitted to King Poděbrady and surrendered the keys of their fortress city. Chelčický was not surprised that Tábor eventually fell to the forces of the state, for "those who live by the sword will die by the sword." When Chelčický himself died in 1458 or '59, the first stage of the Czech Reformation came to an end. The Utraquist Church endured for another 150 years, but much of the original reforming zeal of the Hussites was lost. It appeared certain that the Utraquists would eventually return to the Catholic Church. After years of warfare and confusion, the power of the nobility in Bohemia had increased dramatically, and the condition of the peasants had actually worsened.[45] In many respects, it seemed that Hus's reforms had finally been defeated or simply died of their own accord. Chelčický's last known work was written for a small band of young men who followed his advice to separate from the world and pursue a different path.[46] They were led by Gregory (Řehor), a nephew of Jan Rokycana, who established a covenant community on the basis on Chelčický's writings. Gregory was the founder of the Unitas Fratrum, but Chelčický was the progenitor of its theology.

45. Macek, "Monarchy of the Estates"; John M. Klassen, "The Disadvantaged and the Hussite Revolution," *International Review of Social History* 35 (1990): 249–72.
46. Wagner, *Petr Chelčický*, 151.

Six

GREGORY AND THE UNITY

The Unity of the Brethren, or Unitas Fratrum, was established in the winter of 1457–58 near the village of Kunwald by a group of serious-minded young men who represented the third generation of the Czech Reformation. In fact, these men hoped to revive the reformation that had faltered. The radical brotherhoods of Tábor and Horeb had been defeated and had capitulated to the Crown. Želivský, Žižka, Prokop Holý, and Bishop Nicholas were dead or imprisoned. The Utraquists had succeeded in creating a moderate national Bohemian church based on the theology of Hus, Jakoubek, and Rokycana, but their compromise with Rome at the Council of Basel was fruitless. For the next century and a half the Utraquists and Catholics were engaged in a type of ecclesiastical cold war that involved perpetual political intrigue and maneuvering. By the 1450s the original Hussite Reformation and Revolution had run their course, but the sermons of Rokycana inspired Gregory and his friends to challenge the status quo by establishing a new type of Christian community based on Chelčický's writings.

TÝN CHURCH

After a Hussite noble named George Poděbrady was elected king in 1448, he assumed control of Prague and Bohemia. This "heretic king" allowed the Utraquist "archbishop" Jan Rokycana to preach again from the pulpit of Týn Church in the Old Town of Prague. Rokycana assisted the king in subjugating the radical wing of the Hussites, but the Bohemian Church was still under siege by the Roman Catholic Church and barons loyal to the papacy. Rokycana was convinced that the legacy of Hus and Jakoubek was being lost through a combination of internal rot and external threat. His sermons in the mid-1450s sought to revitalize the Hussites by emphasizing the example of the martyrs, especially Hus and Jerome of Prague. He quoted liberally from the great theologians of the Czech Reformation.[1]

Like Hus half a century earlier, Rokycana attacked the ostentation of the wealthy as an un-Christian insult to the poor. He accused the nobility of oppressing the peasants in order to pay for their sinful lifestyles, and he vigorously opposed the death penalty, especially for crimes against property. His opposition to institutional violence extended to a condemnation of the common practice of hiring oneself out as a mercenary soldier. He accused Czechs of killing other people in battle merely to enrich themselves. How could the once proud soldiers of God who had fought for the right of common people to receive the blood of Christ hire themselves out as soldiers to shed the blood of Christ's people? He condemned war because it filled "the air with the cries of the poor, the earth with blood and hell with spirits," but he still promoted the idea of just war rather than strict pacifism.[2]

The rising prosperity of the merchant class also met with his stern disapproval, particularly when rising prices impoverished thousands in Bohemia. Unlike Želivský or Chelčický, though, Rokycana did not attack the medieval social hierarchy. He attacked excesses rather than the system itself. Following the early Czech reformers, Rokycana's sermons were filled with warnings about the seductions and lies of the Antichrist. Unlike Matthew of Janov, though, Rokycana did not believe that frequent communion alone could protect people from the Antichrist. Repentance and holiness of life were as important as drinking from the chalice. In fact, without repentance, the chalice could bring punishment on the worshipper. Christ's demand for righteousness meant that the elect must follow Christ's law in the apostolic writings.[3]

---

1. Brock, *Doctrines of the Brethren*, 71; Říčan, *History of the Unity*, 14–15.
2. Brock, *Doctrines of the Brethren*, 71–72.
3. Müller, *Geschichte der böhmischen Brüder*, 1:63.

FIG. 13   Týn Church, Prague, where Rokycana preached.

GREGORY THE PATRIARCH

Rokycana's rhetoric and personal charisma attracted many listeners to Týn Church, especially among the younger and poorer people. One of them was Gregory (Řehoř), who was apparently the son of one of Rokycana's sisters. She was married to a country squire of some means, so Gregory came from a background similar to Chelčický's. Like Chelčický, he had a basic education that included some Latin, but he did not become a squire even though he held the rank of knight. As a young man, Gregory moved to Prague and became the business manager for various wealthy men until he settled down as business manager of the Slavonic monastery around 1446.[4] Gregory's experience and ability

4. Říčan, *History of the Unity*, 18; Müller, *Geschichte der böhmischen Brüder*, 1:62.

in management distinguished him from the anti-institutional Chelčický, and this had a profound impact on the development of the Unity of the Brethren.

The Slavonic monastery had been founded a century earlier by Emperor Charles IV for the express purpose of celebrating the Slavonic liturgies of Saints Cyril and Methodius, the patron saints of Bohemia and Moravia. The role of the memory of Cyril and Methodius in the Czech Reformation has yet to be studied, but a number of the Hussite reformers, most notably Peter Payne, were associated with the Slavonic monastery. In fact, it is quite likely that Gregory knew Payne, for he lived at the cloister until his death in 1456. Thus we may assume a Waldensian influence on Gregory mediated through Payne and his colleagues. The experience of living in a community of celibate men may also have shaped the asceticism of Gregory and the early Brethren. Although Gregory participated actively in the life of the monastery, he did not take religious vows or become a priest. Some years later he apparently took up the craft of a tailor and was sometimes derisively called Gregory the Tailor by his opponents.

Gregory and a number of students from the university regularly attended services at Týn Church, and they transcribed the sermons of his uncle Rokycana so they could study them in detail later. For a time, this group of earnest young men, mostly students, viewed Rokycana as their "father" and were convinced by his preaching that "their very salvation was in doubt, and the Czech church was threatened with ruin." The old Hussite zeal to find good priests who lived according to the New Testament inspired the students to seek out remnants of the old Hussite "brotherhoods," including the monks of Vilémov. But even the monks fell short of the ideal. Gregory and his comrades were offended that all of the Hussite priests appeared to give the sacraments to the unrighteous and accepted tithes.[5]

They looked to Rokycana for guidance and support. The archbishop was familiar with Chelčický and his writings, and he admired him, although he did not agree with Chelčický's radical rejection of secular authority. Rokycana was impressed with Chelčický's moral rigor and rejection of violence, and the archbishop even preached on the six smaller commandments from the Sermon on the Mount, as Chelčický had suggested. It may have been Rokycana's

---

5. Říčan, *History of the Unity,* 18–20.

hope that Gregory would follow Chelčický's quietist model rather than try to resurrect the militant zealotry of Žižka or Martin Húska. In any case, the archbishop introduced Gregory and his circle to Chelčický's main works. They read them diligently, especially *The Net of Faith*, and determined that here was a Hussite who gave the true interpretation of scripture and the law of Christ.[6]

THE FOUNDING OF THE UNITY

For some time this group met for prayer, discussion, scripture reading, and mutual exhortation in the cloister while receiving the Utraquist sacraments. Initially their circle functioned much like an eighteenth-century Pietist conventicle, where laypersons gathered for prayer, mutual discipline, and the reading of scripture. But after reading Chelčický they became convinced that they must separate completely from the evil of the world. To quote Říčan, "The world had to be roused out of its indifference so that it could recognize its turning away from God and be shocked into a fear of his judgment and seek his grace. . . . The Brethren would provide a saving community where the faithful could gather as they turned away from a world falling into decay in the last age of humanity."[7] They eventually found a priest they trusted, named Michael, who served the parish of Žamberk (Senftenberg) on King Poděbrady's estate of Lititz (Litiče). With Rokycana's help they received the king's permission to establish a small community near the village of Kunwald early in 1458 (probably not 1457, as is commonly reported).[8]

After the burning of a Waldensian preacher who was close to Gregory and his band, the young men decided that they needed to separate their community entirely from the state church. At the synod of Rýchnov in 1464, the group formally organized themselves into a *jednota*, or unity. "The Brethren of the Law of Christ," as they called themselves, were led by "elders," who were the priests, and congregational lay leaders.[9] The Brethren's first priests had been

---

6. Müller, *Geschichte der böhmischen Brüder*, 1:67–70; Říčan, *History of the Unity*, 26.

7. Říčan, *History of the Unity*, 26.

8. Müller, *Geschichte der böhmischen Brüder*, 1:70; Říčan, *History of the Unity*, 27; Brock, *Doctrines of the Brethren*, 84.

9. Peschke, *Kirche und Welt*, 94.

ordained in the Utraquist or Catholic churches, and their primary duties were to teach, preach, and administer the sacraments. The lay elders assisted especially in discipline and oversight, much like the presbyterial system that John Calvin and his followers developed a century later in Switzerland. Some of the elders served as lay preachers or exhorters, but their primary task was to help "direct the community in genuine faith, love, and hope."[10] They were not to be a church, but an assembly (*sbor*) gathered for mutual discipline and instruction.[11] The Brethren associated the word "church" with the state church rather than with a voluntary Christian community.

The early Brethren adopted a Donatist stance on the issue of good priests, and they published a number of tracts on this topic. The ascetic Gregory also traveled extensively, much like an early Franciscan friar, seeking out those who were concerned about their salvation. They accepted into their new brotherhood former Táborites and other radical Hussites, including Pikarts and Adamites, as well as Waldensians. The members of the Free Spirit sect were required to do penance before being allowed to join. Many of the new Brethren in southern Bohemia came from Kroměříž in Moravia, where they had been led by a "good priest" named Stephen (Štěpán) until they were driven out by the local Catholic bishop's persecution.[12] Another important early group to join the Unity of the Brethren was made up of German Waldensians from Brandenburg who had fled persecution. Their leader had been ordained a priest by the Táborite bishop Nicholas in 1433. They urged Stephen of Basel, another Waldensian leader, to join them, but he declined.[13] In short, the early Unity attracted a wide variety of radicals in Bohemia and Moravia, including dissident priests. Fourteenth-century Inquisition records show that the areas where the Unity was most popular had a history of Waldensian and Beghard activity.[14]

At the synod in the Rýchnov Mountains in 1464, the Brethren articulated their foundational theological ideas: "Before all things we have first agreed that we will care for one another together in the faith of the Lord Jesus, be established in the righteousness which comes from God, and abiding in love, have

10. Müller, *Geschichte der böhmischen Brüder*, 1:102.
11. Říčan, *History of the Unity*, 34.
12. Müller, *Geschichte der böhmischen Brüder*, 1:73; Brock, *Doctrines of the Brethren*, 76.
13. Říčan, *History of the Unity*, 29.
14. Müller, *Geschichte der böhmischen Brüder*, 1:75, Brock, *Doctrines of the Brethren*, 76. See the map of medieval heresy in Lambert, *Medieval Heresy*, 172–73.

hope in the living God." This is one of the earliest surviving statements of the Unity's understanding that the essentials of Christianity are faith, love, and hope, discussed in detail below. A 1486 statement addressed the nature of the *jednota* and the church: "No regional assembly, however large the number of its people, is the universal communion so that it contains the whole number of the faithful. Nor does it contain all who are to be saved, so that outside of it God has none to be saved anywhere else. . . . We believe that we dwell in unity with the holy church when we observe good deeds in the unity of faith and love . . . and we share one hope of eternal life."[15] In other words, the Brethren recognized that they were a voluntary body of believers within Christ's body, the church.

Gregory's theology was Christocentric. "The essence, root, and ground of the true church is *Jesus Christ*. He is the rock on which it stands; the head of his church."[16] For Gregory this proposition meant that true Christians are those who must follow the teachings and example of Jesus rather than human authorities. The early Brethren would pay no attention to "writings that contradicted divine law, but would content ourselves with the holy Scripture and govern ourselves according to divine law. What was derived from the divine law, we would recognize and judge as good, but what was not derived from divine law, we would we judge as doubtful."[17] According to Gregory, it was not theoretical knowledge or doctrine that made a Christian but the practical transformation of one's life according to the image of Christ.[18] Gregory described the Brethren as "people who have decided once and for all to be guided only by the gospel and example of our Lord Jesus Christ and his holy apostles in gentleness, humility, patience, and love for our enemies. By this we may do good to our enemies, wish them well, and pray for them."[19] This simple approach to doctrine helped overcome the fact that so many of the Brethren came from widely different theological backgrounds.

The early Brethren agreed that the assurance of salvation included the sincere effort to follow the law of Christ; therefore they refused to grant absolution

---

15. Říčan, *History of the Unity*, 34, 55.
16. Peschke, *Kirche und Welt*, 84.
17. Quoted in Müller, *Geschichte der böhmischen Brüder*, 1:74.
18. Peschke, *Kirche und Welt*, 84–85.
19. Říčan, *History of the Unity*, 30.

and communion to those who showed no willingness to repent and amend their lives. They also agreed that it was wrong to elevate the host or to bow to it, which they equated with idolatry. Connected to this was their rejection of the idea of transubstantiation. Like the Táborites, the Brethren used normal bread and wine served in everyday vessels for Holy Communion. They also believed that the bread and wine are the body and blood of Christ only during the reception of communion; therefore the host should not be reserved in a pyx after the ceremony.[20] Along with the simplification of the Lord's Supper, the Brethren abolished the use of "sacramentals" such as holy oil, holy water, and the blessing of objects.[21] Most controversial was their promotion of the Donatist principle that sacraments given by sinful priests are not actually consecrated by Christ. In the hands of unworthy priests, bread and wine remained bread and wine, according to the early Unity. Over time, this view would change somewhat.

PACIFISM

Rokycana was unable to shield his nephew from the government indefinitely, and in 1461 the king launched the first persecution of the Brethren on the grounds that they were Pikarts who desecrated the Eucharist. Several of the Brethren were arrested, including Gregory, whose status as a knight saved him from the torture inflicted on the others. The "good priest" Michael was exiled from Lititz, and he joined some of the Brethren in southern Bohemia. Rather than destroy the young movement, the persecution sped up the process of organization and separation from Rokycana, who had reluctantly agreed to the persecution.

The Brethren repeatedly called for their enemies to recognize that religious persecution is itself sinful. Rather than protect the church or spread the Gospel of Christ, persecution actually destroys faith because "Christ is opposed to all force; whoever comes to him must do so from a free will." Following the tradition of Chelčický rather than the Táborites, the Brethren proclaimed that secular power should play no role in matters of faith. The nobility should not

20. Ibid., 30–31.
21. Müller, *Geschichte der böhmischen Brüder*, 1:77.

use the sword to defend the faith or punish heretics, and the clergy should never sanction religious violence. Christ did not come to kill, they said, but to bring new life. That the Israelites used the sword to defend the law of God merely confirmed for the Brethren that the Old Testament was imperfect and not binding on Christians.[22] Even a century later, when the Unity had abandoned absolute nonviolence as a requirement of membership, the church resolutely held on to the principle of separation between spiritual and secular authority. In opposition to medieval dissenter groups like the Waldensians, the Unity combined this rejection of secular power with a clear and coherent structure and priesthood.[23] The Unity of the Brethren, therefore, may justly be considered the first peace church.

LOVE, GRACE, AND DISCIPLINE

Gregory wrote several letters to his uncle and erstwhile mentor, Rokycana, explaining the activities of the Unity asking for his support. It became increasingly evident that the two men were on divergent theological paths, and the separation was very bitter. In his fourth letter to Rokycana, in 1468, Gregory discussed sin and grace, writing: "This not only means that the man who is devoted to Christ can keep himself from ever falling into mortal sin, but also that his inner disposition and attitudes toward his neighbors become transformed. He who by nature is impure becomes pure; angry and quarrelsome men become peaceable and patient; the proud become humble, good-hearted and merciful; mean, envious and clever spirits become generous and kind; the cruel lion and ravenous wolf turn into their gentlest counterparts, a lamb and a simple ox."[24] In other words, the Brethren were certain that redemption was possible and that people could change their actions and attitudes through God's grace. We can see parallels to the eighteenth-century preacher John Wesley, but this change of life, for Gregory, involved much more than issues of personal

---

22. Ibid., 1:86–87, 96, 99.

23. The difference in degree of organization was related to the fact that the Unity, unlike the Waldensians, faced less determined opposition from the state.

24. Quoted in Marianka Sasha Fousek, "The Perfectionism of the Early *Unitas Fratrum*," *Church History* 30 (1961): 402.

morality, such as drinking and gambling. It primarily concerned a person's treatment of other human beings: moving from violence, greed, and intimidation to generosity, humility, and peacefulness.

It is important to keep in mind that Gregory and his companions separated from the state church and its priests primarily out of a desire for a stricter discipline. In particular, they objected to the practice of giving communion to those who did not practice Christian virtue and love. As one historian has put it, "Discipline was regarded as a means of salvation from the power and deception of sin. The Brethren's connecting a justified hope of salvation with the presence of church discipline in a community shows that they thought of the discipline as being primarily an instrument of the *saving* activity of God, as a means of grace."[25] Around 1471 Jan Klenovský, one of the elders, wrote to a Bohemian nobleman, Prince Henry, to explain the Unity's teaching on sin, grace, and salvation:

> I hold this as essential to salvation, to have a will corrected by the power of God and established by his grace, by which will a man humbly wills to believe all that God wishes to have believed and faithfully wills to do all which God desires him to do. . . . In this consists the true fulfilling of the law and keeping of God's commandments, that one wills to do all which God wishes to have done; that one does what one knows and is able to do; that one submits oneself, according to God's ordinance, to receiving instruction, warning and disciplining; and that one humbly corrects or wills to correct one's trespasses which one has come to know either of oneself or by the faithful and godly counsel of those whom one can trust most securely.[26]

The Brethren held to Hus's idea that the true church is the body of the elect and that salvation occurs purely by God's election rather than by human choice. Like Hus, they also believed strongly that humans are saved by faith completed in love. Love was a matter of concrete action in the world, not a passing emotional state. Love of God was demonstrated by a rejection of worldly

25. Ibid., 397.
26. Ibid., 407.

delights and obedience to the law of Christ as revealed in the Sermon on the Mount. This law included the love of neighbor exemplified in the Golden Rule but was evidenced most dramatically in the ability to love one's enemies. Chelčický had taught that such divine love was the only visible thing that truly distinguishes Christians from the worldly. "For hypocrites can possess all the attributes of virtue, excepting divine love alone. And this can best be seen in a man in the forgiveness of injustice done by others, and in the love of enemies, and in the abandonment of beloved things or the forgiveness of offenders for the sake of God's commandment. These are the most demonstrable attributes of true divine love in man, nor can an insincere man readily have them."[27]

Such love, according to the early Brethren, is beyond human ability; it is only a product of grace working in a person. Rather than Luther's idea of "alien righteousness" imputed to sinful humans through the work of Christ, the Unity promoted Augustine's understanding that grace is the work of the Holy Spirit, which allows sinful humans to understand what God requires of them, recognize their own imperfection, and grow into the type of people God expects them to be. Justification by faith through grace, therefore, meant that through grace a person becomes righteous.[28] But the Brethren did not teach that such righteousness comes automatically. The church was expected to play a vital role in its development.

Their covenant at the synod of Rýchnov in 1464 expressed the ideal that discipline was a mark of the true church. Discipline was intended to bring about repentance rather than to punish the sinner. It was to be administered in a spirit of mutual love among the brothers and sisters. The Brethren recognized that they were joining a community of mutual admonition voluntarily:

> We have agreed to submit ourselves to a mutual obedience . . . and to receive from each other instruction, admonition and correction, in order that we might keep the covenant which God has established through the Lord Jesus Christ in the Holy Ghost . . . to help each other, according as each has received grace from the Lord . . . so that each be diligent to edify and correct the other. And to maintain Christian obedience in

27. Chelčický, *On the Holy Church*, 168.
28. Fousek, "Perfectionism of the Early *Unitas Fratrum*," 401.

that each person acknowledges his sins and lacks, humbling and lowering himself, stricken with fear and shame, and, being admonished and corrected, amend his ways.[29]

There are clear parallels here to Wesley's understanding that discipline should lead individuals to moral perfection. Brothers and sisters in the Unity who refused to confess their sins and amend their ways were denied the Lord's Supper, and they might even be removed from the brotherhood. Excommunication was based less on the severity of the offense than on a person's refusal to correct his or her actions and attitudes, because the goal of discipline was restoration of the individual to the path of righteousness.

BEGINNERS, THOSE PROGRESSING, AND THE PERFECT

In order to facilitate the work of discipline and growth in faith, love, and hope, the Unity divided its members into four categories: the perfect (or those moving toward perfection), those progressing, beginners, and the penitent. Though much criticized by both Catholics and Protestants in the sixteenth century, this system of membership, with some revisions, remained in place throughout the history of the Unity. Luke of Prague called the categories "those beginning, those moving forward, and those who have arrived." By 1600 they were officially called beginners, those proceeding, and those aspiring to perfection. This was to reduce the risk of pride among the "perfect" and to avoid offending other Protestants.[30] Some scholars have traced the practice of assigning levels of membership to the medieval Cathars, but the most likely sources for this idea were the New Testament and the practice of the early church.[31]

---

29. Ibid., 397.

30. Müller, *Geschichte der böhmischen Brüder*, 1:108–9.

31. The Cathars' asceticism was the result of a dualistic cosmology (similar to that of the Gnostics and Manicheans) that viewed the physical world and its pleasures as the work of an evil god. Salvation meant escaping the needs of the body in order to elevate the spirit. The "apostolic perfection" of the Waldenses and the Brethren was based instead on a concern for social justice. There is a vast body of scholarly literature on the Cathars (as well as a vast body of literature in the genre of "conspiracy theory"). See Lambert, *Medieval Heresy*, 52–69, 115–57, for a good introduction to the Cathars and an excellent bibliography of reliable sources.

The perfect were originally those who renounced worldly property, much like the early Franciscans. They lived communally and were supported by their own labor and the gifts of the other members. The perfect were not expected to be free from human imperfections or especially ascetic, like the perfect Cathars. They were simply experienced and proven brothers and sisters who were mature in faith, love, and hope, were eager to correct their failings, and were free from mortal, or deadly, sins such as murder and adultery.[32] As far as we can tell from surviving sources, there was no formal process for being recognized as one of the perfect. It appears to have been an informal category for those whom the community saw as exemplars of the Unity's idea of the Christian life. Though not influenced directly by the Brethren, Wesley also claimed that Christians may attain perfection, but he was less willing to identify individuals as perfect.[33]

The synod of Rýchnov decreed that "priests and teachers" should follow the example of "the first Christian leaders, about whom it is written that they held all things in common. . . . Therefore, let them be without care, putting their trust in God. . . . And whichever among them possess worldly wealth, let them do with it as the gospels ordain: give to the poor, and . . . let them earn their bread by the labour of their hands, for this is, indeed, good."[34] The perfect should be willing to suffer "hunger and cold, pain, imprisonment and death" for the sake of Christ, just like the early Christian martyrs.[35] They were also required to remain celibate. After 1467 only priests and teachers were expected to adopt such apostolic poverty and celibacy. Eventually the rules were moderated somewhat for them as well.

The second category of membership included most of the brothers and sisters. They were called the "progressing" and were expected to live according to a strict discipline that governed legitimate trades and professions, but they did not have to renounce wealth. Initially this group was made up of two distinct groups: married householders and single brothers and sisters. They had

32. Marianka Sasha Fousek, "Spiritual Direction and Discipline: A Key to the Flowering and Decay of the Sixteenth-Century Unitas Fratrum," *Archiv für Reformationsgeschichte/Archive for Reformation History* 62 (1971): 217.

33. John Wesley, *A Plain Account of Christian Perfection* (London: Epworth Press, 1952).

34. Quoted in Brock, *Doctrines of the Brethren*, 80–81; cf. Müller, *Geschichte der böhmischen Brüder,* 1:104.

35. Müller, *Geschichte der böhmischen Brüder,* 1:104.

separate sets of instructions to guide them in proper Christian living according to their estate. These instructions had their roots in medieval moral teaching. Householders were supposed to follow the household codes of the New Testament, while recognizing at all times that Christ is the true head of the house. Each home was to be a model of a true Christian community, where faith, love, and hope reigned. Martin Luther popularized this effort to make home and family the focus of religious life decades later.

Unmarried persons were expected to live under the authority of their parents, but if this was not possible they were to place themselves under the guidance of one of the elders. A female elder was to supervise the single sisters and a male elder the single brothers.[36] Like the Moravians under Zinzendorf in the eighteenth century, the Unity believed that women should exercise a degree of leadership in the congregation, particularly when it came to advising and disciplining younger women. This is an area that merits further research.

As time passed, the Unity had to decide what to do with children born into the community. Initially the Brethren did not baptize the children of members, but in 1468 they wrote to Rokycana that "children of believing Christians should be baptized in the hope of election to blessedness in the name of the Father and of the Son and of the Holy Spirit."[37] It appears, however, that the issue of infant baptism was not settled until the Brethren engaged in a formal theological debate with Prague theologians in 1478; they were persuaded then that infant baptism was indeed a practice of the apostolic church. Thus the "anabaptist" phase of the Unity's life lasted less than twenty years, but they retained many features of a "believer's church" after adopting infant baptism.[38] This is a rare example of a sectarian movement adopting the practice of infant baptism without compulsion, and it demonstrates the willingness of the Brethren to change their practice when persuaded by strong arguments.

After 1478, the Unity baptized children of members with the understanding

36. Ibid., 1:106.
37. Říčan, *History of the Unity*, 46.
38. J. Halama Jr. argues that scholars have misinterpreted the evidence regarding infant baptism in the Unity, and that the charge that they refused to baptize infants comes from their enemies. He asserts that "there existed no duty to bring a child to baptism but the practice must have existed. Otherwise the Brethren could not have promised so willingly that they would baptize children." Halama, "The Teaching on Baptism in the Unity of the Brethren" (paper given at a Unity Seminar, 1995). I have my doubts about his argument, but there is evidence of diverse opinions on this subject among the Brethren.

that their parents and baptismal sponsors would see to their religious instruction and discipline. Until adolescence they were classified as beginners. Around
age twelve they received a long period of catechetical instruction, including
instruction in the discipline of the Unity. Then they "completed" their baptism
through the rite of confirmation. This was called being "received into obedience," which sounds remarkably like the Jewish bar mitzvah. Confirmation took
place after a long and probing interview with the priest to determine the worthiness of the confirmand. After the laying on of hands and prayer by the priest,
the newly confirmed person became a progressing member and was admitted
to communion.

Adults who joined the Unity went through a similar process, modeled on
early Christian practice. First, candidates for admission made a solemn vow to
submit to the authority and pastoral care of the priest. At this point they were
"received into the obedience of the *Unitas.*" Next came "admission to the Word
of God," which meant permission to attend preaching services, which were not
public because of the threat of persecution. At this point candidates joined the
beginners and received further instruction. When the priest determined that
the candidate understood the nature of the Unity, knew what was required of
members, and showed promise of being able to live according to the discipline,
he or she was admitted to the sacraments and counted among the progressing.[39]
Until Luther's time, the Unity rebaptized adults who converted from Catholicism, a practice they defended on the grounds that the Catholic Church
forcibly rebaptized members of the Unity and their children.[40]

The fourth group was the penitents, just as in the early church. Technically
the penitents were no longer members of the Unity, but they still received pastoral care and instruction. The penitents included those whom the elders had
placed under discipline, usually for moral lapses or disobedience. Penitents
could attend most of the preaching and teaching services of the Unity but were
not allowed to partake of the Lord's Supper. For the early Brethren, this ability to exclude from communion those deemed unworthy was one of the central
features of a genuine church.[41] The Anabaptist leader Menno Simons would

39. Fousek, "Spiritual Direction and Discipline," 214.
40. Říčan, *History of the Unity*, 46.
41. Müller, *Geschichte der böhmischen Brüder*, 1:102–3, 106.

make this same claim about the "ban" in the sixteenth century, and it became a common feature of the Radical Reformation.

Readmission to communion came only after confession and absolution by the priest or an elder designated as a "judge" or "confessor." Over the years the Unity published many guides for confessors, which had their roots in medieval confessor manuals. Confessors had a great deal of leeway in determining whether a person under discipline had truly repented and was trying to reform his or her life. Confession was used primarily to determine whether a person had shown a change of heart and will rather than mere regret for having offended the community.[42] Confessors were expected to be encouraging rather than prosecutorial; the goal was change of life rather than punishment for offenses. Brothers and sisters who were recognized as morally weak were to be kept in communion as long as they were striving sincerely to make progress in faith and love.

Pastoral care was one of the main duties of the Unity's priests, and it was important that the process remain subjective rather than legalistic. Confessors were repeatedly instructed that "the same medicine cannot be given to every patient, not even in the case of the same illness." In fact, what healed one could destroy another. Confessors were to show compassion for members who were distraught over their weakness but to deal firmly with those who were merely lazy. The directives stated that penitents were to be reminded that they chose freely to join the Unity, agreed to be obedient to the elders, had come "to love the Brotherhood and have confidence in it," and were "eager to acquire righteousness, willing to receive correction and serve the faithful in love."[43] By reminding erring members why they had sought membership in the Unity, and that they had joined voluntarily, the Brethren hoped to inspire them to reform their behavior and submit to discipline voluntarily. If not, the erring member was encouraged to leave the Brethren and join the Utraquists or Catholics.

THE PRIESTHOOD

Such an intense level of pastoral care, not to mention the strict requirements of membership and the threat of persecution from outside, meant that the

---

42. Fousek, "Spiritual Direction and Discipline," 214–15.
43. Ibid., 216 and n22.

congregations of the Brethren rarely had more than two hundred members. But the Unity continued to grow, and there was always a need for qualified priests. By the time the synod at Rýchnov met in 1464, it was evident that the Unity could not continue to rely on the services of Utraquist priests who were sympathetic to their *jednota*. One of the friends of the early Unity was a Waldensian named Friedrich Reiser, who used the provocative title "Bishop of the faithful in the Roman Church who scorn the Donation of Constantine."[44] Curiously enough, Reiser had been ordained to the priesthood by the Táborite bishop Nicholas, so there was no presumption that Reiser was a bishop in apostolic succession. He and his disciple Stephen instructed Gregory and the early Brethren in both Waldensian and Táborite doctrine until the Catholic Church burned Reiser at the stake in 1458. When the Catholic bishop of Olomouc inflicted the same punishment on a member of the Unity, Jakub Chulava, the Brethren decided that they could have no further relationship with the existing churches.

Recognizing that they could no longer depend on Utraquist or Catholic priests for the sacraments, the Brethren decided to establish a new priesthood. They were concerned that their priesthood be legitimate and connected organically to the historical Christian Church, so they first considered the possibility of securing a bishop from one of the Eastern Orthodox (Greek, Armenian, or Moldavian) churches. But Gregory was not encouraged by the ceremonialism of the Orthodox Church or the behavior of the Orthodox living in Prague at the time. He also considered the Bogomils in Bulgaria, but their dualistic theology was unacceptable.[45] With the Táborites' bishop, Nicholas, in prison, that option was unavailable. There were the Waldensians, but their *barbes* (pastors) were allowed only to teach, preach, counsel, and hear confessions. They did not have bishops.[46] Gregory was also very critical of the fact that most Waldensians continued to receive the sacraments from Catholic priests.[47] So

44. Cameron, *Waldenses*, 147–50; Lambert, *Medieval Heresy*, 177.

45. Müller, *Geschichte der böhmischen Brüder*, 1:119; Peschke, *Kirche und Welt*, 93. The Bogomils were precursors to the Cathars. Müller reports that some of the Brethren even planned a trip east to find the fabled "Presbyter John" but were dissuaded by those who were convinced that he was nothing but a legend.

46. Lambert, *Medieval Heresy*, 159.

47. This was called nicodemism because of Nicodemus in John 3, who followed Jesus secretly out of fear. It was long a matter of debate in the Waldensian community. Lambert, *Medieval Heresy*, 175–76, shows that there was a wide range of opinion among the Waldenses over how far one must separate from the Catholic Church.

the Brethren decided they could not rely on the Waldensians for pastoral care and leadership.

In 1467 the Unity of the Brethren decided to break decisively from the Utraquist Church and establish their own priesthood. It is probably most accurate to date the founding of the Unity of the Brethren to 1467, because it was the establishment of a separate priesthood and episcopacy that marked the Unity's intentional decision to separate formally from all other churches: Catholic, Utraquist, Táborite, and Eastern Orthodox. Given that Gregory viewed the Roman Catholic Church and its episcopacy as the Antichrist, it is unlikely that he was much concerned with the apostolic succession of bishops through the Roman line. The origin of the Unity's priesthood and episcopacy remains a very controversial topic; many of the surviving sources were written decades after the event. It was not something the Unity publicized at the time, because it was illegal, but it is possible to piece together a fairly reliable picture of what happened, based on later reports of two participants, Gregory and Michael. That picture contradicts the later Moravian Church's claim that the first bishop and priests were consecrated by a Waldensian bishop named Stephen, who was in the apostolic succession.[48]

The Brethren did have a particularly good relationship with a Waldensian teacher named Stephen. There is no evidence that he was a bishop, but he did support and encourage the Brethren in their plan to establish a separate priesthood. The Moravian legend that the Waldensian "Bishop Stephen" consecrated the first Brethren bishop is faulty on another count as well: he was under arrest in Vienna at the time. He was burned at the stake in August 1467 in Austria on the grounds that he was a Hussite. The case for apostolic succession through the Waldensians, moreover, is based on the myth that a faithful bishop named Peter kept the true church alive after the conversion of Constantine (discussed in chapter 1). Gregory used the Waldensian idea of the Constantinian fall of the church to justify establishing a new priesthood separate from the corrupted priesthood of Rome.[49]

48. Peschke, *Kirche und Welt*, 92–95, 83–84. For the standard account of apostolic succession in the Moravian Church, see Edmund de Schweinitz, *Moravian Manual: Containing an Account of the Protestant Church of the Moravian United Brethren or Unitas Fratrum* (Philadelphia: Lindsay & Blakiston, 1859), 20–21.

49. Müller, *Geschichte der böhmischen Brüder*, 1:122–23. Pp. 144–45 gives Gregory's account of the "Constantinian fall" of the church as evidence for the need for a new priesthood consecrated directly by Christ.

For years, the Utraquist reformer Peter Payne had urged the Utraquist Church to establish its own episcopacy rather than rely on ordination through the Catholic Church. The Utraquists rejected Payne's arguments, and for two centuries they went to extraordinary lengths to have their priests ordained by Catholic bishops.[50] But Gregory decided Payne was right that New Testament bishops were not fundamentally different from priests. The ordination of a bishop was an act of the community of faith, not of the bishops themselves.[51] Thus Gregory, in Říčan's words, "came to an understanding of the universal priesthood of believers in a New Testament sense, and broke fundamentally with a sacramental conception of the office. He saw that the basis of all priesthood is in the power of Jesus Christ, who alone produces new birth in believers. In essence, all true Christians were spiritual priests. God called some believers to exercise the office of a priest, and this was made evident by his bestowing on them the personal gifts necessary for their spiritual function."[52] Gregory's view was very similar to that of Luther and Melanchthon in the next century.

The Brethren proceeded cautiously in establishing a separate priesthood. First they used the lot to determine whether God wanted them to proceed down this path. This was one of the few times that the Unity used the lot (unlike Zinzendorf), and they did so on the basis of the Apostle Matthias's selection in the book of Acts. They asked God "whether it was now the time that we finally abandon the Roman assembly and erect a new assembly according to the ordinances of the first church."[53] After a time of prayer and fasting, they reassembled and drew a lot indicating that this was the will of God. Gregory reported that they trusted in the promise of Matthew 18:19–20 that "where two or three are gathered" in the name of Christ, he will be with them.

About sixty Brethren then met in a synod at Lhotka near Rýchnov, probably on Maundy Thursday, March 26, 1467. They elected twenty elders who were to "advise, teach, and lead the people." Then they selected nine candidates for the priesthood, Gregory not among them, as he was already viewed as the "patriarch." They prepared twelve slips of paper of which nine were blank and

50. David, *Finding the Middle Way*, 143–50.
51. Říčan, *History of the Unity*, 37; Peschke, *Kirche und Welt*, 97.
52. Říčan, *History of the Unity*, 36.
53. Müller, *Geschichte der böhmischen Brüder*, 1:126.

three said "yes." It was thus possible for none to be chosen. The lot fell on three: Matthew (Matěj) of Kunwald, a farmer's son; Eliáš of Chřenovice in Moravia, a miller, and Thomas (Tůma) Přeloučský, a tailor who knew Latin. Though Matthew was only in his late twenties, he was chosen as head (or senior) priest. The lot confirmed this choice.[54]

There remained the question of who would lay hands on the new priests and ordain them. Both the Táborite bishop Nicholas and the Utraquist bishop Rokycana had been ordained priests by Catholic bishops in Roman succession. It could be argued from Scholastic theology that their consecration as bishops was permissible according to traditional teaching, even without the laying on of hands by another bishop. But what the Unity had done in ordaining its own priests was quite different, and it marked a significant theological break with all existing churches. They had chosen laypersons to be priests and let God confirm the choice directly through the lot. Many of the Brethren were satisfied with this idea; others were troubled by it.

A compromise was reached that would respect the clean break with the Roman Catholic Church while providing for the establishment of the priestly office in continuity with the historical church.[55] Michael, who had been ordained a Catholic priest before joining the Unity, consecrated Matthew as "senior." The early Brethren were reluctant to use the word "bishop" because they connected it with Catholic bishops who lived in palaces and were burning Brethren at the stake. To make things even more complete from the Brethren point of view, Matthew also received the laying on of hands from an unnamed Waldensian (not a bishop) as an additional ordination. Thus Matthew was consecrated by brothers who had both Waldensian and Roman ordination. Then, to complete the circle, Matthew reordained Michael as a priest of the Unity after he was confirmed by the lot.[56] Incidentally, the hymn sung at the first ordination is still used in Moravian ordination services. It thanks God for having raised up leaders for the community in a time of need.

After this first ordination the Unity did not use the lot to select priests but

54. Říčan, *History of the Unity*, 38–39, Müller, *Geschichte der böhmischen Brüder*, 1:126–27.

55. Peschke, *Kirche und Welt*, 99–100.

56. Müller, *Geschichte der böhmischen Brüder*, 1:129–32. Müller discusses in great detail the historical problem of determining the identity of the Waldensian elder who consecrated Michael (134–40). Suffice it to say that the evidence is clear that it was not a Waldensian bishop in apostolic succession.

employed a conferencial system. The elders verified that God had called a person into the priesthood on the basis of personal gifts and spiritual maturity. In addition to interviewing the candidate, the elders received testimony from others as to his gifts and character. The Unity always emphasized that the true high priest of the church is Jesus Christ himself and that therefore every priest must strive to follow the example and teachings of Christ.[57]

STRUCTURE OF THE UNITY

As senior, Matthew was the undisputed head of the church following the death of Gregory in 1474. He lived in Rýchnov, near Kunwald, but kept in contact with the growing number of congregations. It is estimated that by 1480 the Unity had between one and two thousand members. The lord Jan Kostka allowed the Brethren to settle on his estate in eastern Bohemia, and the towns of Litomyšl and Mladá Boleslav in that region became very important centers for the Unity. Hundreds of Waldensians fleeing persecution in Brandenburg settled on the estate of Jan of Žerotín in northeastern Moravia, where the town of Fulnek became the major center for German-speaking Brethren for more than a century. In 1481 persecution drove many Brethren into Moldavia and Hungary, where they also established congregations.[58]

One of the early histories of the Unity reports that all "were bound to obedience to Brother Matthew as bishop similar to the way the Roman church is bound to the Pope, for he was held in great respect by all in the Unity."[59] Matthew appointed an inner council of priests and laypersons to give advice and help implement decisions. One of Gregory's arguments against papal supremacy had been that even the apostles did not have a monarchal episcopacy. Peter had worked collegially with James and John. The early church had five patriarchs rather than a single pope.[60] The Unity saw the Inner Council as a continuation of this idea of conferential leadership or collegial governance. From time to time the Inner Council convened synods to make decisions that were

57. Ibid., 1:114–17.
58. Říčan, *History of the Unity*, 45–47.
59. Ibid., 52.
60. Peschke, *Kirche und Welt*, 89–91.

beyond its ken. Synods originally included priests, deacons, and congregational lay leaders.

Local congregations were served by priests under the authority of Matthew and the Inner Council. It was theoretically possible for a married man to become a priest, but the Unity preferred to ordain single men, who were required to remain celibate after ordination. Despite repeated criticism from Lutheran and Reformed leaders in the sixteenth century, the Unity maintained clerical celibacy (except for those married before ordination) until the late 1500s. Priests were assisted in their pastoral duties by deacons, who were basically priests in training—usually young men who lived in the priest's household. They assisted in household duties, and the priest in turn saw to their education and training. Priests also had several lay assistants in the congregations. Those who helped administer discipline and settle disputes between members (or between members and the priest) were called judges. Others were known as almoners; they managed the congregation's finances and saw to the needs of poorer members.[61]

THEOLOGY AND DOCTRINE

The origin of the Unity lay in a concern over the priesthood, but the leaders of the new church engaged in broader theological discussions as well. Most of their theological publications came in the form of defenses or apologies as they sought to convince the Utraquists of their legitimacy as a Christian body. Rather than write a single confession of faith that would unify the Brethren in all congregations for all time, like the Augsburg Confession, each generation of Brethren revised the church's doctrine according to the needs of the time and their understanding of scripture. This was particularly evident in the sixteenth century as the Brethren encountered new ideas from Wittenberg and Geneva. This reluctance to codify a particular confession of faith as binding for all time was itself an expression of the Brethren's theology. Doctrinal uniformity was always less important than faith, love, and hope. Miloš Štrupl counted seventeen documents that may be considered official confessions of faith for

61. Říčan, *History of the Unity*, 51.

the Unity.[62] The nineteenth-century historical theologian Phillip Schaff referred to the "astonishing number" of confessions of faith the Brethren published.[63] This did not mean that the Brethren refused to think or debate scripture, theology, and ethics. To the contrary, they wanted a higher level of theological discussion among laity and clergy than existed in the Catholic Church of their day.

The Brethren kept themselves open to new understandings and insights, and they wisely recognized that the doctrinal concerns of one era might lose their salience in another. Their attitude toward all human institutions may be seen in their understanding that this world and everything in it were temporary. As the Brethren put it, "We are pilgrims and guests here on earth placed here by the Lord Jesus in the midst of great uncertainty. Therefore separate yourself in thought from this world as pilgrims and begin your fellowship in heaven where finally you desire to enter."[64]

Though this world was temporary and all human thought transitory, it was necessary to give some form to the church's teaching. The key to understanding the Unity's doctrine is that the Brethren distinguished between things essential to salvation, things ministerial to salvation, and incidental matters. At least since Augustine, the church had distinguished between essential matters and "adiaphora," or incidental matters, but the Unity added the middle category of ministerial or ministrative things. These are the things God has provided to lead people to what is essential. Ministerial things included scripture, the sacraments, and the church. These things are obviously not incidental; they are sacred, but not in themselves: their sacred status rests in their ability to lead people into what is essential. This distinction appeared in the early confessions of the Unity, and Luke of Prague refined it as a theological concept in the early sixteenth century.[65] This may be the most important theological contribution the Brethren made to Christianity, even though it has not yet been adopted by the wider church.[66]

---

62. Miloš Štrupl, "Confessional Theology of the Unitas Fratrum," *Church History* 33 (1964): 279–93.

63. Phillip Schaff, *The Creeds of Christendom* (New York: Harper & Brothers, 1877), 1:578.

64. Říčan, *History of the Unity*, 55.

65. Štrupl, "Confessional Theology," 281.

66. After decades of intense theological discussion, the World Council of Churches was able to produce a statement on some of these issues in Lima in 1982. Despite wide acclaim, *Baptism, Eucharist, and Ministry* (Geneva: World Council of Churches, 1982) appears to have had little direct impact on most churches. For the Moravians, these three key issues all belong in the ministrative category.

The Brethren believed that confusion over what is truly essential and what is ministerial or incidental had damaged the church. The medieval Roman Catholic Church, in particular, oppressed people with unimportant things and failed to show them what truly mattered. Essential things were just that: things that are necessary for salvation. If disaster struck, or if the emperor destroyed the church, killed the priest, and burned the Bible, was salvation still assured? If persecution or war forced believers from their homes and they became aliens and refugees like Jacob of old, could they still have faith and walk with God? Even if the brothers and sisters were safe and secure in the world and attended church regularly, where did salvation lie? Was it to be found in the rituals of the church, in paying tithes or avoiding the inquisitors? Did blessedness depend on one's presence in worship or in Christ's presence with his disciples?

For the early Brethren, the only essential things were the work of the Father, Son, and Holy Spirit, along with faith, love, and hope, the theological virtues Paul promotes in 1 Corinthians 13. As one of the brothers expressed it, "First of all, we confess that salvation consists of the election of God through grace, which has come from God through his Son, Jesus Christ. . . . And that humans are able to have a part in this salvation if they come to knowledge of the Lord Christ and come to faith and to love and to direct the intention of their hearts to obedience toward God, and on that basis they will place themselves in the hope of blessedness." Like Hus, the Unity taught that individual salvation rests objectively in God's choice. "The only ones who can come to repentance and birth of the inner life are those whom God has chosen according to his foreknowledge, for Jesus said: No one comes to me unless my Father draws him."[67]

Faith is the response to being chosen by God, and in this sense one could speak of salvation through faith alone. Faith included belief in God, expressed in the Apostles' Creed, and trust in God's work, but faith has to be completed in love. Like Chelčický, the early Brethren found it impossible to separate faith from love conceptually. True faith was expressed in obedience to the law of Christ in the New Testament, including the law to love one's neighbors and one's enemies. Ethics also remained central to the Unity's view of faith.[68] "Living faith . . . creates in humans the power to do good works and live virtuous lives

---

67. Müller, *Geschichte der böhmischen Brüder*, 1:173, 218.
68. Štrupl, "Confessional Theology," 281.

so that they keep themselves far from evil ... and kill sin along with lust and build oneself up in righteousness (I John 3:7, Heb. 10:38, I Peter 1:5)." They taught that those who are saved receive the grace of righteousness. This is seen most clearly in the believer's ability to observe the commandments in the Sermon on the Mount. For the early Brethren, faith required separation from the state because the state demanded that subjects swear oaths and defend their rights in court. It always repaid evil with evil and required subjects to kill the enemy.[69]

The early Brethren wrote less about hope than about faith and love. They saw hope as the consequence of belief, obedience, and genuine love for God and one's neighbors, but this hope was directed largely to the afterlife. It was hope for heaven and the vindication of the righteous rather than hope for better times in this life. In general, the early Brethren were rather pessimistic about the world.[70] They distinguished between the true hope of those whose faith was completed in love and the false hope offered in other churches. True hope brings blessedness even in the midst of a difficult and threatening world, and consists mainly in believing that God will do what God promised.[71]

Ministerial things, in the Brethren's doctrine, mediate the work of God in salvation but do not save in themselves. The Unity recognized that humans misuse ministerial things and make them unholy by using them to oppress rather than to save. This is why they rejected the "evil priests" in the national church.[72] They knew from experience that inquisitors and executioners quoted scripture and that priests carried the chalice and host into battle. Priests absolved those who engaged in bloodshed, rape, and pillage. If the ministerials did not serve the purpose of leading people into faith, love, and hope, then they should be changed to better reflect the nature of the apostolic church. In other words, the Unity rejected outward religiosity in favor of inner disposition and ethical behavior. In Říčan's words, "Deeds flowing from the depths of a believing and repentant heart, suffering for Christ, and the life of self-denial were seen as evidence of genuine faith for which they expected as their reward salvation and eternal joy."[73]

69. Müller, *Geschichte der böhmischen Brüder*, 1:220–221.
70. Brock, *Doctrines of the Brethren*, 93.
71. Müller, *Geschichte der böhmischen Brüder*, 1:218.
72. Ibid., 1:200.
73. Říčan, *History of the Unity*, 56.

The Bible was foremost among the ministerials. It was understood less as a book of profound theological insight or eschatological mystery than as a guide to faithful living in the here and now. This attitude continued in the Unity down to the time of Comenius, but the first generation of Brethren made a clear distinction between the two testaments. The New Testament had greater force and was to be preferred in matters of faith and practice because it "neither condemns to death . . . nor coerces anyone to fulfill its commandments, but rather with loving patience calls for repentance, leaving the impenitent to the last judgement."[74] In the Old Testament, they particularly valued the Psalms, Ecclesiastes, and Proverbs. They also valued the Wisdom of Solomon from the Apocrypha.[75] It is not surprising that the last three are pieces of wisdom literature that deal with ordinary living.

After the Bible, the primary ministerial thing was the church. Salvation was not just an individual affair. The elect were joined in a heavenly community with Christ and all the faithful. True to the teaching of Hus and Wyclif, the Unity taught that the "essential church" was the invisible body of the elect throughout time and space.[76] This "catholic" church had no organization, priests, or sacraments because Christ himself was its high priest. But there is a "ministerial" or visible church that strives to be a model of the true church, in which the elect begin to live in the eschatological community.[77] This church is a gathering in time and space of humans who believe in the Lord Jesus Christ. It is a church of servants who use the ministerial things (priesthood, sacraments, worship) to lead people to the knowledge of the true God and Jesus Christ.[78] Unlike other ecclesiastical bodies, the Unity recognized that the true church could be manifested in other brotherhoods (jednota). Furthermore, the Unity taught that salvation was possible outside the visible church, but not outside the "invisible church," because by definition it is the invisible body of the saved.

The next-most important ministerials were the sacraments, especially baptism and the Eucharist. The Brethren were deeply concerned about sacramental theology and practice. They wanted to dispense with what they believed

---

74. Brock, *Doctrines of the Brethren*, 86.
75. Říčan, *History of the Unity*, 54; cf. Müller, *Geschichte der böhmischen Brüder*, 1:198.
76. Müller, *Geschichte der böhmischen Brüder*, 1:198. On Hus and Wyclif's ecclesiology, see chapter 1.
77. Štrupl, "Confessional Theology," 285.
78. Müller, *Geschichte der böhmischen Brüder*, 1:199.

were superstitious or even idolatrous sacramental practices, such as the reserved host, but they wanted to preserve the sanctity of the sacraments.[79] In discussing the seven traditional sacraments of the medieval church, the early Brethren usually put them in the following order: ordination, baptism, confirmation, Eucharist, penance, marriage, and extreme unction.[80] It is important to note that they had doubts about the status of some of the seven as full sacraments even before they encountered Luther's thought in the 1520s. It may be helpful to summarize the Unity's view of the seven sacraments here.

Ordination: The Brethren based their understanding of ordination on John 17:17–19: "Sanctify them by the truth; your word is truth. As you sent me into the world, I have sent them into the world. For them I sanctify myself, that they too may be truly sanctified" (NIV). Priests should be those who have been chosen by Christ, whose sense of being chosen is then validated by the people. No one should put himself forward as a priest; he should be called to the task of "teaching, leading, and disciplining" the community of faith. Specifically, the priest must be capable of proclaiming the word knowledgably, offering prayers for the community, administering the sacraments (except for ordination) worthily, and teaching candidates for confirmation. Ordination did not stamp an indelible character on the priest. He could be removed if he failed in his faith, duty, or example.[81]

Baptism: Although the early Brethren baptized Catholics who joined the Unity, they argued that this was not "re-baptism" because Catholic baptism was not done according to the demands of the New Testament. Gradually the Brethren were persuaded to baptize their own infants, but it was decades before they agreed to accept baptisms performed in other churches. Confirmation was needed to complete what was begun in baptism, especially for those baptized as infants. "When a child has matured and come to understanding, so that he or she can answer for him or herself, then shall [the sponsors] bring him or her before the pastor and give witness for the child that he or she has preserved him or herself in the strength of baptism and has accepted the doctrine. And the youth shall be asked whether he or she will persist in faith in

79. Říčan, *History of the Unity*, 53.
80. Müller, *Geschichte der böhmischen Brüder*, 1:202.
81. Ibid., 1:202–3.

Christ Jesus and the Christian instruction announced by the apostles."[82] Baptism alone did not save; faith had to be completed in love and displayed through one's actions.

Confirmation: The Brethren's rite of confirmation had its roots in the doctrine and practice of the Táborites. They found justification for the ritual in Acts 8:15–17, in which Peter and John lay hands on the Samaritans who have been baptized by Philip. The Brethren's ritual included public confession and absolution, and the pastor questioned the candidate about his or her knowledge of Christian doctrine and spiritual condition. Parents and sponsors publicly affirmed the worthiness of the candidate. If the priest was satisfied with the witness of the candidate and the sponsors, then he would bring the candidate before the congregation to be received through prayer and the laying on of hands. The priest then ceremonially struck the newly confirmed person on the back as a reminder that true Christians must be willing to suffer for the sake of Christ, just as Christ suffered. This was not a flogging, but, according to Müller, the priest probably used a ceremonial whip for the occasion.[83] Once the newly confirmed person was made aware of the suffering of Christ, he or she was received into the "fellowship of the body and blood of the Lord Jesus Christ." Erasmus praised the catechetical practice and discipline of the Unity, and Martin Bucer in Strasbourg introduced similar practices after meeting with representatives of the Brethren. It can be argued that the Protestant understanding of confirmation and catechism originated with the Brethren.[84]

Eucharist: The early Brethren did not alter their original understanding of the Eucharist after they established a separate church. They held to the belief that the simple words of scripture (1 Cor. 11:23–25) defined the mystery of

---

82. Ibid., 1:205–8.

83. Ibid., 1:208.

84. This thesis was first proposed by Georg Rietschel in the early twentieth century. Rietschel, *Lehrbuch der Liturgie* (1909; Göttingen: Vandenhoeck Ruprecht, 1951–52), 629–43. See also J. D. C. Fisher, *Christian Initiation: The Reformation Period* (London: Alcuin Club Collections, 1970). On the relationship of the Brethren to Erasmus and his validation of their confirmation practices, see Paul de Vooght, "Un episode peu connu de la vie d'Erasme: Sa recontre avec les hussites bohemes en 1519–1521," *Irénikon* 47 (1974): 27–47. I am grateful to David Schattschneider for sharing an unpublished paper by David Holeton, "The Moravian Origins of Confirmation," which contained this information. It is curious that Elsie McKee does not discuss the Brethren's catechism in her study of popular piety in Strasbourg, although she devotes considerable attention to the Brethren's hymnal, published by Katherina Schütz Zell. McKee, "Reforming Popular Piety in Sixteenth-Century Strasbourg," *Studies in Reformed Theology and History* 2 (1994): 1–82.

the Eucharist sufficiently without need for further theological speculation. They defended themselves from the charge that they were Pikarts who denied the presence of Christ in communion, arguing that if a faithful priest prays and says the words of institution in sincere belief and good intent, then the spiritual body of Christ is received under the form of the bread. Communicants "should believe that while they are eating the visible sacrament, they are eating the true body of Christ invisibly through faith." It was through faith that Christ was present, not physically in the host.

They asserted that the Lord's Prayer in the eucharistic liturgy was more important than the elevation of the host, "because we do not direct the faith and devotion of our hearts to visible things but to the eternal and living God." There is evidence from Inquisition records that the Brethren lacked consensus on the precise nature of Christ in the communion elements, which may explain their reluctance to define this doctrine narrowly. According to one source, "they wanted to leave up to God the question of whether the bread changed or remained bread." But they refused to reverence the host by kneeling during the consecration or reception of the bread. This alone was grounds for their arrest and torture.

The Brethren's text *Concerning Good and Evil Priests* provided an account of the communion liturgy, paraphrased here.[85] The Unity had no uniform liturgy. Some congregations used normal daily bread, while others used unleavened bread. Some priests wore simple robes, others, normal clothing. Robes and type of bread were incidental rather than ministerial things. Especially in the early days, the service often took place in the home of the priest or a member of the community. After reading from the New Testament, the priest gave a sermon explaining the text. Then the congregation remembered the life of Jesus through the recitation of the Apostles' Creed, and the people expressed their desire to receive communion. Then the priest would offer a prayer, followed by the Lord's Prayer. Next he would consecrate the elements, saying, "Our Lord Jesus Christ took bread, gave thanks, broke it, and said: take, eat, this is my body which was betrayed for you. Even so, he took the cup after the evening meal and said: drink of it, all of you. This is the cup of the New Testament in my blood that has been poured out for many for the forgiveness of sins." The

85. Müller, *Geschichte der böhmischen Brüder*, 1:209, 211.

Brethren believed that in this way they were all sharing in the community of the body and blood of Christ. "They eat the visible form of bread and wine, and they believe that they receive the invisible meal, the living bread of heaven and so have communion with body and blood of Christ." The Brethren believed that they were united in Christ through faith, just as was promised in John 6:56. The unity of the whole invisible church was contained in this unity with Christ.

Penance: Unlike the other sacraments, penance was considered something one did for oneself, but it was still necessary for the penitent to come to the priest and promise sincerely to change his or her behavior. The key thing was not the confession itself but the change of life that resulted from self-examination. In fact, the elders asserted that it would be best if no one in the community ever needed the sacrament of penance. It was expected that brothers and sisters would deny themselves and take up their crosses, as Jesus instructed. Humility and self-denial meant bringing one's will into conformity with the will of God, not using the ministrations of the church to justify one's own arrogance, greed, and self-centeredness. In the case of public offenses, especially offenses against the community, the offender might be placed in the category of penitents and denied communion until absolved by the priest.

Private sins were not revealed publicly, but the penitent had to stand before the assembly and say, "I have sinned against God the Lord and against you, as God knows, and I have revealed to these representatives, of which I present myself before God the Lord and before you as guilty, and it grieves me, and I ask you to forgive me and to pray for me to God the Lord that he will forgive me." If for some reason there was no priest to hear a confession, any of the elders could do so. At times the Brethren were advised to adopt ascetic practices of self-mortification to assist them in the change of life. These included fasting, thirsting, flagellation, all-night prayer vigils, sleeping on hard beds, and so forth.[86] Confession and penance applied only to this life, as the Brethren rejected the idea of purgatory in the next life.

Marriage: The early Brethren agreed with the Apostle Paul and the medieval church that celibacy was preferred to marriage. Marriage was for those who were too weak to preserve their virginity until death. Those who married were

---

86. Ibid., 1:213–15.

expected to be faithful to their spouse and were to have sexual intercourse *only* in order to conceive children, not for pleasure.[87] Adulterers were subject to penance, but the priests were careful not to let the offended spouse know of the offense lest the knowledge lead to divorce. Divorce was allowed only because of adultery or if one's spouse was not a believer. Over time, the Unity developed a more positive view of sexuality.

Anointing, or Extreme Unction: The Brethren recognized the benefit in visiting the dying and offering them solace; therefore they continued the Catholic practice of anointing the sick and dying as a good work (Matt. 5:26; James 5:14–15). They preferred to have elders accompany the priest and talk with the dying person about the hope of heaven.[88] Not only did this involve the laity in pastoral care, it avoided the abuses associated with last rites in the Catholic Church.

SEPARATION FROM VIOLENCE AND GREED

The Unity elders were clear that heaven was the goal of religion, but the path to heaven lay on earth; the Unity thus focused on ordinary living and daily ethics. Historians have long noted that "the bulk of early Brethren literature . . . has a decidedly utilitarian character and was written with a definite practical aim in view."[89] When pressed about their social teachings, the Brethren's leaders in the late 1460s stated simply, "If anyone would like to know how we conduct our affairs let them enquire how things stood in the early church." The early Christian model included being "humble, retiring, temperate, magnanimous, long-suffering, loving, full of pity and kindness, meek, pure, modest, peaceable, desirous only of the right, compliant, willing, and ready for every good action" (87). This view of the apostolic church stands in marked contrast to twentieth-century American religious movements that emphasized charismatic gifts as the true mark of the apostolic church.

One of the major ethical and theological concerns of the early Brethren was the relationship of Christians to the state and feudal society in general.

87. Ibid., 1:216.
88. Ibid., 1:217.
89. The following material is taken from Brock, *Doctrines of the Brethren*, hereafter cited parenthetically.

Around 1470 Gregory published a tract on worldly force, taken mostly from Chelčický's *On the Three Estates*. Gregory rejected the threefold division sanctified by the state church on the same grounds that Chelčický had done. Members of the Unity were forbidden to swear oaths or use violence and coercion; therefore they could not hold government office or become guild masters. They taught that those who follow Christ should not participate in the use of "fear, cruelty, beating, fighting, killing, reviling, violence, imprisonment, cutting-off of limbs, murder, and other physical torments," which were the main tools of secular governance (90).

In short, the early Unity adopted Chelčický's arguments for total pacifism, including the injunction against self-defense. Christ called for his followers to love their enemies, and Gregory asserted that it was simply impossible to love someone while killing or maiming them. The elders publicly repudiated the Táborites as "murderers" for having used warfare to further their cause. Gregory wrote to his uncle Rokycana, "Although it is suspected and spread abroad that we have banded together and gathered forces to overthrow this kingdom with bloodshed, yet it is not true. Such a course of action has never entered our minds; not only would we not seek such an outcome, but we would never sanction it even unto death" (96). In this early period, even the nobility were expected to follow in the path of pacifism and voluntary suffering. At least two nobles renounced their estates in order to join the Unity. Though nobles might be allowed to keep some of their property, they were expected to renounce their governing role.

When the king of Hungary launched an invasion of Moravia in 1467, most of the Brethren refused to fight in the militia. This led to a major persecution of the Unity. Though some Brethren responded to governmental threats and joined in the defense of the kingdom, the Unity officially rejected war and advocated voluntary suffering for one's faith. "True Christians must suffer every form of tribulation from the world even unto the loss of life and property, repaying good for evil" (93). The Brethren tried repeatedly to assure the authorities that they were no threat to the social order because of their commitment to the teachings of scripture. The Decree of Rýchnov (1464) stated, "In all just, proper and honest matters . . . under whatsoever authority any of us may be placed, we are taught to obey and be subject in all humility as to taxes and labour services and to be loyal in all things and to pray to God for such authorities"

(95). It was important for the Unity to convince the nobility that their pacifism included the prohibition of rebellion against secular authority, because they needed the protection of non-Brethren nobles who allowed them to live in peace on their estates. Without that protection, the history of the Unity of the Brethren would have been much abbreviated.

The conviction that the heart of the Christian message was love of neighbor went beyond nonviolence. From the early days, the elders issued decrees for Christian living that were strongly influenced by Chelčický, who was suspicious of urban life. He noted frequently that the murderer Cain had built the first city (Gen. 4:17); therefore urban economics bore the "mark of Cain" or even the "mark of the Beast." "Every kind of trade and profit-making occupation connected with the town should be avoided in order not to harm one's soul" (67).

Gregory led the first Brethren out of Prague into the countryside so that they could live more simply. There is a "puritanical" strain in the early Unity's asceticism and suspicion of refined culture. The elders warned that "lovely and delightful things, colours, fine costumes, beautiful dresses, scents, tasty dishes, out-of-the-way objects, soft raiment, fine rooms, physical beauty in man or woman" (68) threatened the souls of believers. Peter Brock notes that this attitude represented a rejection of the values of the upper classes. The early Brethren "saw, indeed, in the amenities of civilization, in art and culture, solely the privileges of the upper classes, who were only able to indulge their aesthetic tastes through the oppression of the masses" (68). In other words, the asceticism of the early Brethren was set against the aestheticism of the aristocracy, which was connected to the exploitation of the weak. By promoting simple living as a higher form of righteousness, the Brethren separated themselves from the oppressive structures of feudal society and economics.

EDUCATION

The first generation of Brethren were primarily agrarian and probably had more in common with the Amish of modern America than with Zinzendorf's *Brüdergemeine*. They formed rigorous and demanding communities that rejected the dominant culture, including university education. The Brethren knew that universities turned out lawyers, theologians, physicians, and philosophers who were merely more subtle and skillful than commoners in rationalizing injustices like the burning of Hus. Rather than use their knowledge and eloquence to reform the world, the learned sought profit and power for their own self-aggrandizement. The Brethren said of scholars, "if only they would cease to look down on the unlettered and try out instead God's gospel, proclaiming it to the people, the simple would indeed bear no grudge against them" (68). They hoped that scholars would convert and live according to the simple teachings of Christ, but this would include renouncing their social status. Members of the Unity were not allowed to teach in the university. The university and the Unity agreed on this point, but for quite different reasons.

The Brethren were not opposed to education itself, but like all things of this world education was to be integrated into a disciplined Christian way of life. Education must be judged by its moral fruits. Brock notes that the Brethren applied their egalitarian ideals to education: "While rejecting the learning of the universities as an instrument of class and religious oppression, the Brethren laid great emphasis on the spread of the rudiments of education among the simple peasants and craftsmen, who formed their rank and file" (99). Many of the early Brethren were self-educated, the Czech Bible their primary textbook, but the Unity also attracted scholars and writers. Comenius came out of this tradition, which recognized that education is a powerful force that can be used for both good and evil.

One of the reasons the Brethren encouraged literacy was so that people could read the Bible on their own. In this they followed the Táborite tradition. Aeneas Silvius, who later became Pope Pius II, was both impressed and disturbed by the erudition of peasants and artisans in the city of Tábor when he visited in the 1440s. He saw a connection between commoners reading scripture and the lay chalice. For this reason, among others, he abrogated the Council of Basel's decree allowing Utraquism in Bohemia in 1462.[90] Because the Bible includes wisdom literature, poetry, politics, and history, discussion of the Bible led to debates on philosophy, political theory, metaphysics, ethics, aesthetics, and sociology.

Brighter youths who had been selected for the priesthood received higher education. The Brethren developed their first formal school around 1482, in

---

90. Frederick G. Heymann, "Pius Aeneas Among the Táborites," *Church History* 28 (1959): 281–309.

part to educate future priests. The most important of the Brethren's schools, which soon attracted non-Brethren students as well, was founded at Mladá Boleslav in 1500. As the Brethren paid greater attention to education, they needed even more protection from noble patrons, especially, as Brock notes, "from the envy and malice which the generally high standard of education among Unity members aroused in their Utraquist and Catholic rivals," who even accused them of seeking Satanic wisdom (100). Despite the opposition of the state church, the Unity began attracting members who had university education. When the popular Prague preacher Michal Polák was tortured to death in 1480, interest in the Unity increased rather than diminished.

A friend of the Unity named Vojtěch (Adalbert) was a fellow at the University of Prague at the time. He interested two students, Jan Černý, who later became a famous physician, and Jan's brother Luke, a theology student, in Chelčický's writings. After receiving his bachelor's degree in 1481, Luke of Prague visited the Brethren's congregation at Litomyšl and soon joined. When he returned to Prague, he led other students, including Vavřinec (Laurentius) Krasonický, into the Unity.[91] This Vojtěch/Luke circle formed the core of the new generation of the Unity, but they were not the only Brethren with formal education. A wealthy layperson from Moravia named Jan Klenovský had joined the Unity during the days of Gregory and became a leading voice on the Inner Council. His allies in the doctrinal debates of the 1480s and '90s were Jan Táborský, who had been an Utraquist priest in Tábor in the 1450s, and Prokop of Jindřichů Hradec. Prokop had studied theology at the university and helped the Unity work through delicate theological debates (104–6).

THE MANDATE OF SAINT JAMES

As persecution increased, so did the size and influence of the Unity, an illustration of Tertullian's ancient dictum that "the blood of the martyrs is the seed of the church." Rather than slow the growth of the movement, a decree of expulsion from the kingdom of Moravia in 1481 helped the Unity spread to Hungary, Moldavia, and surrounding areas. In fact, so many Moravian nobles

91. Říčan, *History of the Unity*, 49–50; Müller, *Geschichte der böhmische Brüder*, 1:238–39.

FIG. 14   Modern Kutná Hora, seat of royal government in the Hussite era.

complained about losing such hardworking and law-abiding peasants that the king was forced to rescind the decree.[92] This did not mean that the Unity became a legal religion in Czech lands, though. Local magnates were merely permitted to tolerate them on their estates.

In Bohemia, the period of political instability that followed the death of King George Poděbrady in 1471 was resolved when Utraquist and Catholic nobles came to a new accord in 1485 that basically reaffirmed the Compacta of the Council of Basel granting the use of the lay chalice.[93] On the crucial question of Holy Communion, the king declared that "neither party shall insult or oppress the other, either physically or spiritually; rather, both shall preserve love toward one another. The priests of each party shall be free to preach the Word God against sin under the authority of every prince, lord, knight, and city government, but no one shall insult or call another a heretic."[94] Utraquist

92. Říčan, *History of the Unity*, 47.
93. The source of the conflict was a dynastic struggle between King Wenceslas and King Matthias of Hungary over the crown of Bohemia and Moravia. Utraquist and Catholic nobles lined up on opposite sides of the question, and there was a danger that the country would again slip into civil war. Eventually Matthias was accepted as king, but he died in 1490. The net result of the conflict was a further increase in the power of the nobility. Müller, *Geschichte der böhmische Brüder*, 1:184–89.
94. Quoted in ibid., 1:188.

lords and city governments were explicitly forbidden to interfere in Catholic services, and Catholic officials were forbidden to interfere in Utraquist practice. This fragile religious peace lasted until the Thirty Years' War, but it did not include the Unity of the Brethren.

The royal decree of toleration excluded the Unity. Only those who affirmed the physical presence of the body and blood of Christ in the Eucharist and showed reverence to the host on the altar were tolerated. Two years later the Utraquist consistory in Prague officially declared that the Brethren were "Pikarts" and heretics, despite the Unity's persistent denials. On Saint James Day (July 25) in 1508 the king of Bohemia adopted a permanent policy of persecution of the "Pikarts" (Brethren) in Bohemia. The Mandate of Saint James made permanent the earlier decision that the Brethren were Pikarts and heretics and applied this ruling to the entire realm. They were not allowed to hold meetings, preach, publish, or serve the sacraments. Their books were to be burned, and their priests were required to appear in Prague for "correction." All governing authorities, including the Utraquist consistory, were responsible for carrying out the decree.[95] Much of the Unity's theological discussion and writing after 1485 dealt with its exclusion from the decree of religious toleration. The Brethren attempted to convince their opponents of their orthodoxy and peacefulness, arguing that they were neither doctrinal Pikarts nor political Táborites.[96] Few of their opponents believed them, however, as the Brethren chose to remain outside the Utraquist Church and refused to bow before the consecrated host.

---

95. Říčan, *History of the Unity*, 95.
96. Müller, *Geschichte der böhmische Brüder*, 1:346–49.

Seven

LUKE OF PRAGUE AND THE NEW BRETHREN

By 1474 Gregory had laid the foundation for a strong and independent Protestant church, but after the death of its energetic and charismatic leader the Unity was riven by dissent. The second generation was better educated than the first, and less convinced that the agrarian ideal of the founders truly represented the teaching of Christ. They began to question whether it was proper for Christians to turn their backs completely on the world; should they not labor to bring Christian values into the world? In the 1480s and '90s the Unity underwent a remarkable transformation from a sect living apart from secular society to a voluntary church that hoped to improve the social order without compromising Christ's teachings. Two decades of discussion and debate by the younger, better-educated members of the Unity led first to schism and then to the emergence of an even more robust Unity of the Brethren under the leadership of Luke of Prague.

INSTITUTIONALIZATION

The founding of the Unity of the Brethren was an attempt at a thoroughgoing reform of the Christian Church and a return to the principles of the church of the apostles. It is thus not surprising that the Unity went through a process of development after Gregory's death similar to the process that the first Christians experienced.[1] The history of the Unity in the second generation followed a pattern familiar to students of the sociology of religion. Issues that seemed relatively unimportant during the Unity's first days became more important as children were born and raised in the community; likewise, things vital to the parents seemed less so to the children. The second and third generations did not share the formative experiences that united the first. The founder of a religious or social movement is usually a charismatic figure, like Gregory, who is able to govern because of an internal sense of authority and ability to inspire loyalty. This highly personal and somewhat unstable form of leadership is rarely matched by a successor. Subsequent leaders tend to lack the authority of the founder and need to have authority granted to them officially.[2]

The founding group is held together by loyalty to the leader who called them into community, but the second generation needs clearer structures and more formal authority. The lived experience of the first generation becomes story and tradition to the next. As Max Weber demonstrated, the children of the founders must find a way to "routinize" the first leader's charisma and ideas so that the original vision can be passed down to future generations.[3] When this vision becomes routine, a movement loses some of its initial zeal and energy, but it gains stability, effectiveness, and endurance. If an organization fails to institutionalize leadership and doctrine, it will falter and decline, or it will be continually divided without the dynamic personality of the original leader to hold it together. Thus, whether a movement institutionalizes or not, it will necessarily change over time, and the change will invariably bring conflict. This conflict often breeds division, as one faction attempts to codify the founder's vision while another seeks to reinterpret the original vision according to the changing times. Sometimes the conflict leads one faction to persecute the other.[4]

1. Good discussions of early Christian history include Peter Iver Kaufman, *Church, Creed, Bishop: Conflict and Authority in Early Latin Christianity* (Boulder, Colo.: Westview Press, 1996); Bart D. Ehrmann, *The New Testament: A Historical Introduction to the Early Christian Writings*, 2d ed. (New York: Oxford University Press, 2000); and Walter Bauer, *Orthodoxy and Heresy in Earliest Christianity*, ed. Robert A. Kraft and Gerhard Krodel (Minneapolis: Augsburg, 1971).

2. In Weber's terms, Gregory would be considered a prophet. Max Weber, *The Sociology of Religion*, trans. Ephraim Fischoff (Boston: Beacon Press, 1991), 46–59.

3. Ibid., 60–80.

4. The Franciscans offer an excellent example of this. After Bonaventure reorganized the order, a dissident group of friars who sought to follow Francis's teachings literally were eventually declared heretical. The Franciscan order itself assisted in the capture and execution of the dissident Franciscans. See

A gifted successor often becomes the "second founder" of a religious society, much as Brigham Young became the second founder of the Church of Jesus Christ of Latter-day Saints. Gregory founded of the Unity of the Brethren and was known simply as "the Patriarch." He needed no ordination, election, or other sign of office, but his successors were ordained and educated. The second founder of the Unity of the Brethren was one of the "educated Brethren," Luke of Prague (1460–1528), who served on the Inner Council for three decades and was made a senior (bishop) in 1500. Under Luke's leadership, the Brethren attempted to remain true to what they perceived as the essential aspects of Gregory's vision, while making significant changes in the discipline.

The changes in the Unity's doctrine and practice following the death of Gregory led to the only major schism in the history of the Unitas Fratrum. Those who wanted to follow the teachings of Gregory and Chelčický strictly were called the Minor Party, and those who endorsed a more flexible ecclesiology were the Major Party. In the late 1490s the two groups separated, and the Minor Party formed a separate church body with its own priesthood. The Minor Party (or Old Brethren) eventually died out as a church, but many joined the Hutterite movement that emerged in the sixteenth century.[5] Most of the surviving sources on the schism were written by historians in the Unity of the Brethren (the Major Party), and are thus biased. The debate over which party was the true heir of Chelčický and Gregory was revived in the twentieth century with the renewal of interest in Chelčický. Church historians such as Müller, Molnár, and Říčan sided with the Major Party, while social historians, especially Brock, were more sympathetic to the Minor Party's effort to maintain the ideal of a pacifist egalitarian community.

The schism itself made it difficult to recover the original teachings of the Unity, as Brock discovered: "The rapid disappearance after this date of the traditions connected with the early Brethren's social ideology, with the result that these ideas were soon quite forgotten among almost all except a handful of scholars, was linked up with the victory of the Major Party and the complete

---

Leff, *Heresy in the Later Middle Ages*, 1:139–66. A similar process occurred in early Christianity with the Montanists; see Bauer, *Orthodoxy and Heresy*, 132–46.

5. Jarold Knox Zeman, *The Anabaptists and the Czech Brethren in Moravia, 1526–1628* (The Hague: Mouton, 1969).

elimination by the middle of the century of the Minor Party."[6] Since the purpose of this book is to examine the theology of the Unity over time rather than to study the original Brethren, we will follow the history of the Major Party. Brock's keen analysis of the changes in the Unity from the first synod of Rýchnov in 1464 to the synod of Rýchnov in 1494 illuminates the significance of the transformation effected by Luke of Prague and his colleagues.[7]

DISSENT IN THE UNITY

The "educated Brethren" associated with Luke of Prague were less mystical in their devotion to imitating Christ than Gregory had been, but they had also been attracted to the Brethren by Chelčický's writings. They joined the Unity during a time of persecution, knowing the cost they might pay, and on the surface their story paralleled the story of the original Brethren, who wanted to live a more disciplined Christian life but became aware that it was difficult, if not impossible, to realize Chelčický's ideal in the real world. It was not the Major Party's intention to set aside the teachings of the Unity, but they perceived gaps in Chelčický's interpretation of the New Testament.

The Minor Party blamed the changes in the Unity entirely on the educated Brethren who joined in the 1480s, but one key figure in the transformation was Thomas (Tůma) of Přeloučský, one of the original priests ordained in 1467. Though self-taught, Thomas was so well read in Hussite and patristic literature that he ably represented the Brethren before the Inquisition in 1500. Less zealous and rigid than Gregory, Thomas wrote one of the earliest European tracts on religious toleration, arguing that the existence of several churches proves that absolute certainty in religion is impossible. Christians should be tolerant of other beliefs, Thomas maintained, until God makes his truth fully known; persecution cannot lead to truth. Thomas also provided one of the first systematic statements of Christians' right to rebel against authorities in matters of conscience. He argued that the state is not absolute, even though God can use it to enforce justice.[8]

6. Brock, *Doctrines of the Brethren*, 279. See Brock's discussion "The Old Doctrines in Unity Historiography," 277–84.
    7. For more on the teachings of the Minor Party, see Peschke, *Kirche und Welt*, 120–34.
    8. Ibid., 101, 114–15, 118.

The most pressing issue for the Brethren was their relationship to governing authorities. Since the Unity was illegal in Bohemia and Moravia, the Brethren often depended on the protection of powerful nobles. Some of the Brethren asked whether Chelčický's rejection of the nobility was too extreme. Could the elders loosen some of the original prohibitions and make it easier for pious nobles to join the Unity without renouncing their responsibilities as lords? This question weighed most heavily on the Brethren in the town of Litomyšl, where the Brethren had settled in response to an invitation from the local lord, Jan Kostka. Kostka was not a member of the Unity, but he wanted to atone for his brother's cruelty toward the Brethren during a period of persecution.[9] Like many lords in depopulated Bohemia, he also needed hardworking subjects to restore his estates. The Brethren were peaceful, law abiding, relatively well educated, and had useful skills, and so he offered them protection if they moved to Litomyšl. The connections between the Unity and Kostka grew even stronger when his son, Bohuš, joined the Unity, but in 1486 Bohuš became the lord of Litomyšl. The Inner Council faced the question of whether he could remain in the Unity without renouncing his new status as a lord.[10]

Some of the Brethren's priests and elders criticized the practice of requiring nobles to renounce their status, power, and property. They pointed out that other members of Unity did not have to make such sacrifices and that the elders would probably not be willing to sacrifice so much in the same situation. Were the elders not imposing burdens on others that they would not bear? Klenovský asked the Inner Council, echoing the words of Jesus regarding the Pharisees (Matt. 23:4). Some of the biblically literate Brethren argued further that "in the time of Christ and the apostles, equality in goods and in rank and in characters did not exist." Some of them claimed that Chelčický had exaggerated the teaching of the Sermon on the Mount, making it more extreme than it was. Luke of Prague and "others recognized that God had granted good will, in like manner as to the poor, to the noble and those in authority also, and to many, too, in certain questionable trades."[11] In other words, experience had shown that some aristocrats were also good Christians.

---

9. Müller, *Geschichte der böhmische Brüder*, 1:241; Říčan, *History of the Unity*, 45.
10. Müller, *Geschichte der böhmische Brüder*, 1:241.
11. Brock, *Doctrines of the Brethren*, 113, 125, 110.

Increasingly, it appeared that the purity and rigor the Unity valued so highly was leading to self-righteousness and pride rather than faith, love, and hope.

Other considerations arose. Perhaps it would be wise to allow ordinary Brethren to assist the governing authorities rather than anger them by refusing to swear oaths. Some of the Brethren had already renounced their faith under torture. Was it wise to invite more persecution? Perhaps a compromise on the oath could save someone from facing a trial that was too great for him or her.[12] The congregation in Litomyšl raised these questions most persistently because Bohuš Kostka had offered the Brethren freedom of religion and other incentives if they would live there, but he also pressured them to participate more fully in civic life because they were trustworthy subjects.[13] The Brethren in Litomyšl wrote to Bishop Matthew and the Inner Council in 1490 for advice on how to deal with this new situation. How could anyone abide by the decrees of the Unity and live in a city where one's livelihood depended on commerce and civil law?

The Inner Council's reply, in Brock's words, was "evasive, vague, and failed to satisfy anyone."[14] The council told them that they should have remained in the countryside, where they would not have faced such dangers. The elders criticized the Litomyšl congregation for seeking a more comfortable life in town rather than suffer like the founders of the Unity, who had abandoned their professions and retreated to Kunwald.[15] In Brock's judgment, Matthew probably wrote this reply, but "its naivety, its failure to face the issues or to pronounce definitely for one or the other course of action, its evasive style" failed to settle the matter for the Brethren in Litomyšl.[16]

They pressed the issue, asking whether they had to choose between earning a living, which required participation in a guild, and being a member of the Unity.[17] They pointed out that the early church was established in cities, not rural areas, citing Paul's letters to Corinth, Ephesus, and Rome. How, then,

---

12. Ibid., 122.

13. Říčan, *History of the Unity*, 61. Brock gives a nice description of the positive contribution of the Brethren to Litomyšl's culture and economy (*Doctrines of the Brethren*, 112).

14. Brock, *Doctrines of the Brethren*, 115.

15. Müller, *Geschichte der böhmische Brüder*, 1:242.

16. Brock, *Doctrines of the Brethren*, 115.

17. On the issue of guild membership and town government in fifteenth-century Bohemia, see ibid., 120–21.

could urban life be contrary to apostolic faith? Did the New Testament not leave room for Christians to fulfill their civic duties, such as serving on juries?[18] How far could the Unity go in accommodating the demands of the world without losing its essential character? How completely could it separate itself from the world without losing its love for neighbors outside the brotherhood? These were difficult questions.

According to Luke of Prague's account, the Inner Council "held many meetings and sessions and discussions on this matter, with prayers and fasting, according to the scriptures, seeking God's will. And through the holy scriptures they came to realize that some believers in Christ had exercised civil power and taken oaths. From this they reasoned that such things were not everywhere and in all cases forbidden by the holy scriptures. Secondly, they realized that such prohibitions arose from an unmeasured and 'high' way of thinking as well as from twisting and misusing the scriptures."[19] Luke eventually published a major work defending the swearing of oaths under certain circumstances.

THE BRANDÝS DECISION

This was not the first time Matthew and the council had addressed such questions, but it was the first time a congregation disputed the answer. The Litomyšl Brethren had a sympathetic person on the council, Klenovský, who was growing worried that the Brethren were slipping into self-righteousness. At the urging of the rest of the council, Matthew called for a synod of the priests, deacons, and congregational judges and helpers to meet at Brandýs in 1490. They prepared for the synod with prayer and fasting as they considered the following questions: How far may a brother go in exercising power, both passive and active, under a governing authority? Did the Lord forbid the saying of oaths so completely that a person might never swear under any circumstances?[20]

Klenovský opened the synod and indicated that the Inner Council did not want to decide such important matters on their own authority alone. At his

---

18. Říčan, *History of the Unity*, 61–62.
19. Brock, *Doctrines of the Brethren*, 123.
20. Müller, *Geschichte der böhmische Brüder*, 1:243.

suggestion, each participant wrote his answers to the questions on a sheet of paper. A consensus emerged that the Brethren should be allowed to use secular power, but the synod also warned that participation in some offices was dangerous because a person could be compelled to wage war or contribute to the death of an accused criminal. Clearly the issue was not participation in government itself but the taking of human life. The synod told the Brethren that it was best to avoid all situations in which they might be forced to contribute actively or passively to the death of another person. It also decreed that it could be possible for some people, with God's help, to maintain a clear conscience in fulfilling their civic duties. It might even be possible for a Christian to use secular authority to mitigate violence and injustice rather than passively allow it.[21]

Although this was a clear departure from Chelčický's original separatism, the Unity's political doctrine was still quite different from Augustine's theology of the "two cities," which had guided the Catholic Church for centuries. Augustine argued that God had ordained both secular and religious governments, and that Christians should obey authorities so long they could do so without denying Christ.[22] In fact, Augustine maintained, Christians should participate in civic life, within the bounds of Christian morality, as part of their Christian devotion. In the sixteenth century Luther reaffirmed Augustine's theory with his own concept of "two kingdoms." Good Christians should be willing even to serve as executioners.[23] The Unity's perspective differed markedly from Luther's. The Unity called for Christians within secular government to use the dictates of the Sermon on the Mount to mitigate the state's propensity to violence and cruelty. The same ethic of love applied to both civic and personal life.

Ultimately the synod concluded that the Brethren should use 1 Peter 3:1–11 as their guide in both household and civic matters: "He must turn from evil and do good; he must seek peace and pursue it." Moreover, those who chose to suffer persecution rather than swear oaths should be free to do so without

21. Ibid., 1:244.

22. Augustine, *City of God* (Garden City, N.J.: Image Books, 1958).

23. Roland H. Bainton, *Here I Stand: A Life of Martin Luther* (Nashville: Abingdon Press, 1978), 184–90; Steven E. Ozment, *Protestants: The Birth of a Revolution* (New York: Doubleday, 1992), 118–48; Luther, *Temporal Authority: To What Extent It Should Be Obeyed* (1523), trans. J. J. Schindel and Walther I. Brandt, in *Luther's Works*, 45:75–128.

criticism. In short, the synod acknowledged that the use of secular power was a complex matter, and held that members of the Unity should follow their own conscience and understanding of scripture without judging those who reached a different decision.[24] This did not mean that the Brethren divorced politics completely from the discipline of the church, only that they recognized a need for flexibility in dealing with the practical realities of living in a secular and frequently hostile society.

The Brandýs decision was unanimous, but there must have been some awareness that this decision would not sit well with all of the priests and congregations, for the decision included an explicit prohibition against open dissent:

> If, after thinking things over or for any other reasons, anyone should still find any objections he should neither speak nor act openly or in secret against this edict . . . but coming in person—or writing—to Brother Matěj [Matthew] and his Brethren [the Inner Council], he should inform them or that Brother who is charge of the province. . . . But if anyone, not out of weakness but from stubbornness and willfulness, should be unwilling to accept correction, but should cause disturbances and dissension, then . . . shall he first be excluded from the body and blood of the Lord and, should he remain obstinate, corrupting others, he shall be expelled from his congregation and, if he continue in his wickedness, from the Unity as well.[25]

THE MINOR PARTY

Two participants, Jacob and Amos, left the synod dissatisfied. They wrote in protest to Matthew and ignored the prohibition against sowing discord in the Unity by publicly and repeatedly voicing their objections to the Brandýs decision. Amos in particular found a large audience because he was a well-respected figure who had been converted by Gregory himself. Claims that he had been an Adamite before joining the Unity have not been confirmed, but he clearly represented the more radical aspects of the original Unity. Moreover, as a wax

24. Müller, *Geschichte der böhmische Brüder*, 1:245.
25. Quoted in Brock, *Doctrines of the Brethren*, 131–32.

merchant, Amos traveled extensively, advertising his views about the Brandýs synod everywhere he went. He was right that the Brandýs decision made concessions to changing social conditions that "constituted in essence a complete reversal of the Unity's official standpoint hitherto" on the question of participating in government.[26] The real question was whether this change amounted to a rejection of the faith and doctrine of the Unity itself.

The Minor Party argued that because Christ was "the way, the truth, and the life," his law was unchanging and eternal. The six commandments of the Sermon on the Mount, which include the prohibition of the oath and taking life, were absolute and binding on all Christians in all circumstances. They argued in terms of stark contrasts: light and darkness, good and evil, water and fire. Those who tolerated sin were themselves sinners, and the "educated Brethren" who favored loosening some of the Unity's rules were as bad as the pope himself. They took the old Waldensian idea of witness to the truth and applied it to the Unity of the Brethren itself. Gregory stood in the succession from "Peter Waldensky," but Senior Matthew was no better than Pope Sylvester, who corrupted the church by welcoming Constantine.[27]

In fact, Matthew himself was only lukewarm toward the Brandýs decision and was easily persuaded by Jacob and Amos's zealous arguments. The Inner Council feared that the controversy could threaten the union of the Brethren, and so Klenovský and Prokop, who had been instrumental in writing the decision, resigned from the Inner Council rather than oppose Matthew. Matthew appointed a new council of "good old brothers." The new Inner Council promptly reinstated the old prohibitions and decreed that any brother who took an oath or consented to a death sentence would be excluded from the Unity.[28] Rather than solve the problems confronting the church, Matthew's wavering leadership exacerbated the division of the Unity. The Minor Party, or Old Brethren, became more rigid in their application of the teachings of Gregory and the decrees of the early Unity.

The younger, educated Brethren led the majority who were no longer represented on the Inner Council. They sent four trusted brothers in search of

26. Ibid., 128. Brock shares Amos's view that the Unity after 1495 was no longer the church of Gregory. It was the Minor Party, or Old Brethren, that maintained the original essence of the Unity as a countercultural pacifist movement.

27. Peschke, *Kirche und Welt*, 123–31.

28. Müller, *Geschichte der böhmische Brüder*, 1:246; Říčan, *History of the Unity*, 63.

the "church of the apostles" in the hope that other churches might shed light where the New Testament seemed ambiguous. Lord Kostka arranged for their safe passage to the East and paid their costs. In 1491 they journeyed to Constantinople and then split up. Kaspar stayed in Constantinople, Mareš Kokovec went to Russia, Martin Kabátník traveled through Palestine and Egypt, and Luke of Prague explored the Balkans, where he observed Orthodox worship. The four learned much and faced many dangers before returning to Litomyšl in 1492, but they did not find the apostolic church they sought.[29] Kabátník published an account of his travels that introduced many Czechs to these exotic lands, but he found no evidence of the apostolic church in its ancient home. It was clear to all, especially Luke, that the Unity had to decide its own direction with the guidance of the Holy Spirit.

FAITH AND WORKS

In addition to the controversy over their relationship to secular authority, many Brethren raised fundamental questions about the church's understanding of faith and works. The general consensus that outward religiosity did not lead to salvation persisted. True assurance of salvation came from "deeds flowing from the depths of a believing and repentant heart, suffering for Christ, and the life of self-denial," "evidence of genuine faith for which they expected as their reward salvation and eternal joy." The Brethren had no doubt that faith must be completed in love if one was to reach heaven; but some of the more theologically literate Brethren cautioned against the belief that good works, especially mortification of the flesh, led to salvation. "Is a life of great renunciation required, which calls for constant fear of enjoying the world too much, to the extent that even to drink one's fill of water with enjoyment is considered a sin and troubling to one's conscience, yet without having peace?"[30]

This was a problem confronted in the early church as well, and the Brethren's priests and teachers searched the New Testament for guidance. In addition to the passages calling for denial of the body and renunciation of the world, which Gregory had cited, there were also passages showing that Jesus attended feasts

---

29. Müller, *Geschichte der böhmische Brüder*, 1:249; Říčan, *History of the Unity*, 63.
30. Říčan, *History of the Unity*, 56, 58.

and even made wine (John 2). It was reported that as early as the 1470s some of the Unity's priests had pointed out to the Inner Council that "many read in the scripture that Christ's yoke is easy and light, but it was actually hard and difficult." Could it be that the Unity was making the way of Christ too hard and creating unnecessary difficulties for people? The Unity had taught the laity to read and had given them the New Testament in Czech. Some of them read Paul's letter to the Galatians, which criticizes Christians who relied on the law rather than grace. Paul taught that people cannot be made righteous through the law, but only through faith. How could this be reconciled with the strict rules of the Unity?[31] Some of the priests formed what might be called a "grace party" and argued with older priests that a narrow "works righteousness" gives rise to hypocrisy, vanity, self-righteousness, pride, and contempt for others.

Matthew and others on the Inner Council feared such questioning. It seemed to them that some of the Brethren were losing their simplicity and engaging in fruitless speculation. More important, they feared that if people relied too much on the merits of Christ, they would grow lax in their discipline and even immoral in their behavior. It is important to remember the difference between the genesis of the Unity of the Brethren and Luther's break with the Catholic Church. Luther, as a devout and anxiety-ridden monk, faulted the church for emphasizing works rather than justification by grace through faith alone, as Paul had taught.[32] Gregory and the other Brethren had formed a separate community because they found the Catholic and Utraquist churches too lax, not too strict. The Brethren sought the narrow path of Christ rather than the easy forgiveness offered by the state church; so the elders were naturally concerned when some of the brothers and sisters began promoting a theology of grace in the 1480s.[33]

This issue could not be decided by administrative fiat, for it dealt with fundamental questions of biblical teaching. Those with theological training continued to press the issue. Klenovský, comprehending the ramifications, judged that both sides of the debate had merit but that both were imperfect. He published a treatise arguing that the "works party" advocated genuine righteousness, without which faith would be dead, but he pointed out that they talked

---

31. Quoted in Müller, *Geschichte der böhmische Brüder*, 1:236–37.
32. Oberman, *Luther*, 151–75; Bainton, *Here I Stand*, 39–50.
33. Müller, *Geschichte der böhmische Brüder*, 1:237.

about righteousness more than they practiced it. The "grace party," in Klenovský's view, had also erred by relying so heavily on the grace of God that they
had grown weak and were carried away with worldly things. This was a particular temptation for Brethren whose hard work and frugality had brought
them wealth.[34] Klenovský's critique of the "grace party" was particularly effective, as he came from a wealthy family but lived a simple life.[35]

Many of the Brethren blamed the new dissension in the church on the
influx of educated members, but it did not require a degree in theology to see
the trouble with justification by works. In 1489, while still a member of the
Inner Council, Prokop criticized the works party publicly. The Old Brethren
had always seen unanimity among the priests as a mark of the true church, but
Prokop argued that the Brethren had never lived up their own ideals. The
Unity and its members were not without blemish. The priests held a wide
diversity of opinions concerning the Lord's Supper, for instance, and many
faithful members found it hard to live by the church's laws. Some members of
the grace party lived moral lives, while some who promoted works righteousness sinned. "Was the Unity therefore a band of the damned, strangers to the
true church, and was it necessary to leave it?" asks Říčan. "Even the conservative Brethren admitted that their conception of the church as a society of the
perfect could not stand."[36]

The controversy over works versus grace was connected to the controversy
over swearing oaths and participating in secular government. The Old Brethren, led by Amos, aggressively pushed the older understanding, while the
younger Brethren sought modifications in the rules and greater discussion of
the church's theology. Luke gradually emerged as the intellectual leader of the
Unity after his return from his quest to find the true church. In addressing
the question of works versus grace, Luke pointed to the strengths and weaknesses in both positions and argued that this was actually a false and mislead-
ing dichotomy.[37]

34. On the tendency of sectarian churches to undermine their own opposition to the world by achieving financial success through hard work and frugality, see Bryan Wilson, *The Social Dimensions of Sectarianism* (Oxford: Clarendon Press, 1990). This is a key component of Weber's *Protestant Ethic and the
Spirit of Capitalism*, which is discussed in Richard Green, ed., *Protestantism and Capitalism: The Weber
Thesis* (Boston: D. C. Heath, 1959).

35. Říčan, *History of the Unity*, 59.

36. Ibid., 63.

37. Peschke, *Kirche und Welt*, 131, 138–39.

In 1493 Luke published a work titled *The Ship* in which he asserted that "it is not a particular manner of life marked by the negation of different regulations of the world, but rather a fundamental new beginning which makes a Christian a Christian. This involves a full dependence on Christ. Only the sacrifice of the Son of God is the foundation of the church. Without his death and the merit of his grace and sharing in his righteousness, no suffering, nor self-denial, nor merit makes for the gaining of salvation.'"[38] This early work suggests the direction that Luke would take in his later theology. Faith must be completed in love, but works of piety and asceticism on their own cannot save a person. They may, in fact, make a person less loving and Christlike. Rather than reject the teaching of the early Unity, Luke recovered some of the original meaning of the concept of faith completed in love. Love was a gift of God rather than an act of human will.

SCHISM

In part because of Luke's influence, the synod of Rýchnov in 1494 reaffirmed the Brandýs decision.[39] Membership in the Unity should be based not on complete renunciation of the world but on readiness to begin a better life. The church would maintain a strict discipline but would not turn away the weak. Instead, priests were to take special pains to help those who were weak in faith and morals.[40] It is not surprising that such changes in doctrine were controversial and remained so for centuries. Brock, who studied the history of pacifism, concluded that the new leaders of the Unity "were prepared to throw over almost all those doctrines of the early Brethren which signified their distinctive contribution to the history of political thought. They were ready to abandon the attempt to live out the ideal of the early Christian church not—as the medieval monastic orders had done—apart from the world, but within

---

38. Quoted in Říčan, *History of the Unity*, 64.

39. Crews notes a disagreement between Müller and Molnár on the translation of a key word in the original sources (*vzyzdvihnúti*). Molnár claims that the synod of Rychnov abolished rather than confirmed the judgment of the Brandýs synod. C. Daniel Crews, "Luke of Prague: Theologian of the Unity," *The Hinge: A Journal of Christian Thought for the Moravian Church* 12, no. 3 (2005): 51n33; Amedeo Molnár, "Luc de Prague devant la crise de l'Unité des annees 1490," *Communio Viatorum* 4 (1961): 223n11. Though Molnár is extremely trustworthy on early modern Czech, it seems to me that Müller's reconstruction makes more sense.

40. Říčan, *History of the Unity*, 64.

FIG. 15   Brethren's house (reconstructed), Brethren's Museum, Kunwald.

society."[41] In fairness to the Unity of the Brethren, they discovered what every radical social movement learns: that it is nearly impossible to maintain the ideals of the Sermon on the Mount in the temporal world.[42]

This is not the place to examine the details of the schism and the personalities involved, but it is helpful to remember that vigorous debate marked the Unity for at least five years following the 1494 synod of Rýchnov.[43] Initially the leadership encouraged both sides to be tolerant and loving toward their opponents, but this proved difficult. Michael, the first priest of the Unity, asked, "How many good men have suffered torture and persecution and the sacrifice of life itself for just this life? What have all our endeavors come to? We could almost have remained with the good priests." Klenovský answered, "Brother Michael, don't spoil things."[44] After the synod, some of the leading priests,

41. Brock, *Doctrines of the Brethren*, 133.

42. This is examined in detail in Troeltsch, *Social Teachings of the Christian Churches*.

43. Brock gives much more detail on the controversy leading up to the schism than do other sources in English. *Doctrines of the Brethren*, 133–81.

44. Quoted in ibid., 149.

including former members of the Inner Council, met at Přerov to discuss implementing the changes and the future organization of the Unity. Matthew was removed from his office as primate, but he retained his episcopal power of ordination. This was the earliest move in the Unitas Fratrum toward separating oversight of the church from episcopal authority. Restored to the Inner Council, Prokop took on the other episcopal functions and was made judge of the Unity. Táborský, the pastor of the Litomyšl congregation, Luke, pastor of Mladá Boleslav, and Klenovský, a layperson, formed the new Inner Council.[45]

Jacob continued to criticize the Inner Council and the Unity's priests for their laxity. He pointed out that the priests were no longer poor pilgrims following the apostles' evangelizing mission (Luke 9). "Now [they] have settled in one place and concern themselves with their parsonages . . . leading a peaceful existence." Jacob and others in the Minor Party encouraged lay brothers and sisters to refuse communion from priests who agreed with the Rýchnov synod and who taught that it was permissible to swear oaths. Eventually Jacob was threatened with expulsion, but he grudgingly repented and was eventually reconciled with the brotherhood.[46]

The members of the Inner Council did not need Jacob to tell them that they were departing significantly from the writings of Chelčický and Gregory. At a meeting in Rýchnov in 1495 they decreed that they still valued those writings. Indeed, many of the educated Brethren had joined the Unity after reading Chelčický. But they also acknowledged that the founders' works were flawed. "The views expressed there were excessive, and it was not possible to persist in them after having acquired experiences in new circumstances and also having obtained a better understanding of Scripture."[47] The Inner Council wrote to the congregations:

> Owing to God's love and effective actions we have come to realize that certain matters have been treated without moderation and intemperately. . . . We, therefore, both those who have been members from the beginning and those who joined later, have unanimously and with good intent decreed, after much heart-searching, that we should not be impeded

45. Ibid., 151; Říčan, *History of the Unity*, 65.
46. Brock, *Doctrines of the Brethren*, 154, 180.
47. Quoted in Říčan, *History of the Unity*, 67.

by these things nor keep them for future guidance. . . . But that they should be reckoned among the Apocrypha, and that those writings for long accepted by all Christians, which are set out and contained in the Bible are sufficient.[48]

In general, the council declared that the early writings were simply "insufficient" and should be used only "so long as they coincided with the holy scriptures and served the purpose of profitable edification."[49] This declaration was signed by the entire Inner Council, including Matthew, Michael, and the older Brethren.

This was an important step in the development of the Unity's theological tradition; for the first time, the leadership asserted that no human writings, not even those of its founders, set forth "unalterable laws." All doctrinal statements were subject to continual examination and alteration in light of scripture and plain reason.[50] The elders indentified the problems they had found in the earlier theological works and conceded that although the Brethren had tried to live up to Chelčický's high ideals, the result was not greater blessedness. Instead, "the Brethren came to trust more in their own good works than in the cross of Christ."[51] The practical effects of doctrinal statements were as important to the Inner Council as the logic of doctrine itself.

Similarly, the leadership reflected a sophisticated understanding of scripture. The Minor Party argued that the New Testament must be taken literally, but "Luke distinguished between the law of grace and the written word of the Bible." God imparted the law of grace directly to the believer's heart, and its content was faith, love, and hope. Luke reminded the Brethren that Christ instructed people to hear the Gospel, not read it. The Gospel preceded the writing of the New Testament; in fact, the New Testament had to be written down in the first place because early Christians began wrangling over doctrinal matters rather than holding fast to Christ's simple truths.[52]

48. Quoted in Brock, *Doctrines of the Brethren,* 161.
49. Ibid., 162.
50. Ibid., 160. Similar statements are found throughout the history of the Moravian Church, including the church's current doctrinal statement, "The Ground of the Unity." See http://www.moravian.org/; or Atwood, *Jesus Still Lead On: An Introduction to Moravian Belief* (Bethlehem, Pa.: Moravian Church Board of Publications, 2003).
51. Brock, *Doctrines of the Brethren,* 161.
52. Peschke, *Kirche und Welt,* 142–44.

This did not satisfy Jacob and Amos and their supporters, so synods were also held in 1497, 1498, 1499, and 1500. The synods consistently ruled in favor of greater freedom and toleration within the Unity. After 1500 the Inner Council approached the ongoing dispute as a matter of church discipline rather than doctrine, judging that the Minor Party was prideful and fractious.[53] Luke went so far as to publish a defense of taking oaths, based on scripture, which argued for the goodness of oath taking in certain circumstances. Such a public statement would have been unthinkable before Jacob and Amos had made the rejection of the oath the focal point of dispute.

During this period Luke traveled to Italy to visit the Waldensians and see if the Minor Party's claims about their lifestyles and church discipline were true. His negative assessment of the Waldensians no doubt reflects some of his bias against the Minor Party. He wrote that the Waldensians in the Alps were more interested in their property than in the Gospel, but he wrote a catechism for them despite his criticism. This catechism played a key role in their internal reorganization on the eve of the Protestant Reformation.[54] Luke, therefore, was almost as important for Waldensian as for Moravian history. While in Italy, Luke also witnessed the infamous burning of the reformer Savonarola in Florence, which confirmed his conviction that the church should be entirely separate from the state.

Finally, in 1500, Amos left the Unity and formed a new community, often referred to as the Old Brethren. The Old Brethren had their own priesthood, and for several decades they published polemics that only added to the Brethren's troubles with the state. In response, the Unity's writers grew increasingly hostile to the Minor Party's theology and Chelčický's writings. Gradually Chelčický faded in the memory of the Unity, and even Gregory the Patriarch was remembered as little more than an early organizer with extreme views. Traces of the Old Brethren community could be found as late as the mid-sixteenth century, but most of its adherents appear to have united with the Hutterites and other Anabaptist groups after 1528.[55]

---

53. Brock, *Doctrines of the Brethren,* 169, 176.
54. Říčan, *History of the Unity,* 70; Cameron, *Waldenses,* 227–29.
55. Zeman, *Anabaptists and Czech Brethren.*

THE SOCIAL ETHICS OF THE NEW BRETHREN

In 1500 the first bishop of the Unity, Matthew, died, marking the final passing of the generation that had known Gregory personally. Leadership of the
Unity passed to those, especially Luke, who had been educated in the university but still rejected the more secure and comfortable life the Utraquist Church
offered. Contrary to the impression Brock gives, Luke of Prague did not completely abandon the Unity's radical social ethic when he moved the Brethren
toward greater engagement with the world. In particular, he did not reject
Chelčický's insistence that the Sermon on the Mount was intended for all
Christians. He merely placed the six smaller commandments in a larger biblical context, which gave greater latitude in the matters of swearing oaths and
defending others from violence. Departing from Gregory's legalistic approach,
Luke proposed a more nuanced process of ethical discernment within the community of faith. The ideal that the Brethren held up for the community was
still characterized by the rejection of worldly values of domination, control, violence, power, and invulnerability. The blessings associated with salvation and
the gifts of the sanctifying Spirit remained those of the beatitudes: poverty of
spirit, gentleness, mourning, hungering for righteousness, mercy, purity of heart,
peacefulness, and redemptive suffering.[56]

The Unity continued to exercise a great deal of discipline over the lives of
its members.[57] In addition to the foundational biblical commandments given
in the catechism, the Inner Council issued instructions on proper secular employment and social behavior that were an integral part of the theology and
practice of the Unity throughout the sixteenth century. For instance, nobles and
scholars who were "ready to comport themselves on an equal footing with the
poor and unlettered, undergoing shame and danger with us," were welcome.[58]
The new Inner Council modified the requirements for permissible occupations in 1494 and reaffirmed the revised listing in 1501 and 1506. The criteria
for deciding what trades were permissible were based on the perceived harm
and benefit of a trade to all involved in it, whether producers or consumers.[59]

---

56. Catechism, questions 27 and 31.
57. Müller, *Geschichte der böhmische Brüder*, 1:278–84.
58. Brock, *Doctrines of the Brethren*, 221.
59. See Müller, *Geschichte der böhmische Brüder*, 1:291–92, for a discussion of occupations in the Unity.

Some businesses, such as farming, building, and most handicrafts, were obviously good. Others were obviously harmful to people in body or soul and were absolutely forbidden. Foremost among these were "dice making, acting, juggling, painting, fortune-telling, magic, usury, alchemy, houses of prostitution, worldly music, and the manufacture of gaudy and lewd apparel."[60] Tavern keeping was forbidden for a long time, and brewers and vintners were required to sell their product in barrels for home consumption rather than for drinking in taverns or the brewery. Incidentally, the Moravians put similar rules in place during the Zinzendorf era.

Unlike the old Brethren, the new Unity under Luke recognized that many occupations were not necessarily bad, but they could be dangerous. Like many medieval moral theorists, the early Unity was suspicious of any economic activity that did not involve one's own physical labor. Buying and selling for a profit seemed to be a way of cheating farmers and craftsmen of the fruits of their toil. The profit motive itself seemed closer to greed than to Christian devotion, and there was always the temptation to take advantage of the seller, whether legally or illegally. Even if there was no harm in the product sold, there was "a great temptation for falsehood, deceit, swearing, drunkenness on journeys, and easy profit, and [commerce] was allowed only to Brethren who had no other possibility of earning their living."[61]

The new Unity allowed members to engage in commerce only if they could trade honestly, without greed or conspicuous consumption.[62] In all occupations, the Unity reminded its members that business ethics was part of their Christian duty. The customer was "a neighbor, to whom was due love and readiness for service. Only a just profit was allowed and the tradesman had to love righteousness."[63] With all businesses, though, "even in the most humble trades . . . danger lurks and falsehood and deceit are found." Luke and the new Unity tried to apply Christ's teaching on the wheat and tares without abandoning their conviction that economic life is an expression of spiritual life.[64]

While this was quite a change from the original prohibition of all buying and selling for profit, it shows that the Brethren continued to make business

---

60. Říčan, *History of the Unity*, 80.
61. Ibid., 81.
62. Brock, *Doctrines of the Brethren*, 151.
63. Říčan, *History of the Unity*, 81.
64. Brock, *Doctrines of the Brethren*, 221.

ethics a part of the church's doctrine and discipline. Members whose fortune came from sinful activities were required to return the money if possible. If not possible, then they were expected to give it to the poor. This was not the Franciscan ideal of apostolic poverty for those within the religious order; it was a more flexible and yet more challenging call for all Christians to sacrifice their pursuit of profit to the greater demands of the law of Christ. The Brethren took seriously Jesus' assertion that it is hard for a rich person to enter the Kingdom of God (Matt. 19:23–24). And several wealthy Brethren did in fact divest themselves of their ill-gotten wealth by giving it to the poor.

ENGAGEMENT WITH THE SECULAR WORLD

Even more significant for future developments, the new Unity allowed nobles to join without renouncing their obligations as lords, but they were expected to practice the same discipline as the other members. The original Unity had defined lordship and power in terms of oppression. The new Unity recognized that power can be used to accomplish good, so they urged lords to rule justly and industriously rather than squander their wealth and authority through frivolous and licentious living. Instructions to nobles were based on Augustine's *City of God:*

> If the highest-born Son of God took upon himself humility and the burden of service to people, even unto death on the cross, then neither must those who rule subordinates be prideful, but they should ornament their nobility by working for the good of their neighbors and by a simple life. . . . Subjects, especially Christians, were not the property of lords, but belonged to Christ as the heir of God. The lord could not treat them arbitrarily. He was not allowed to load them down with unjust burdens. He was not allowed to extort from them taxes and forced labor beyond their capabilities.[65]

Nobles were reminded frequently that "it was always fitting to incline to mercy." The Unity also accepted the help and protection of nobles. "Brethren,

---

65. Quoted in Říčan, *History of the Unity,* 84.

then, may resort to worldly power for protection against injustices, but with the principle being preserved that the salvation of their neighbors had to be more precious to them than their own personal material concerns."[66] In order to assist Brethren in their civic duties, the elders instructed that village mayors and council members should be people of "character, self-control, wisdom and integrity, diligence in work, discretion and moderation in speech." Furthermore, the Unity under Luke recognized that ordinary Brethren could play a positive role in secular government. Members were allowed to assume public office, but they were urged to avoid sinful things, such as feasts and revels. And the Unity never wavered in its conviction that secular power should never be used to force people to profess faith.

When it came to judicial matters, Brethren were to "avoid being guilty of anyone's death." If they served on a jury, they were encouraged to take into account the motivations of the accused as well as his or her actions. For instance, if someone had stolen food to feed his starving family, then the punishment should be less severe. Brethren were also expected to ameliorate punishments wherever possible. In particular, they were instructed to resist efforts to maim or torture a convict. If called upon as witnesses or advocates in court, they were always to speak "truthfully, under the rules, quietly, without bringing in extraneous matters and without rancorous or offensive speeches towards the other side. The course of the dispute should be conducted as much as possible in such a manner that between the parties there might remain some friendship and love." Above all, they were to seek justice, not victory, reconciliation and peace rather than strife. Interestingly, Brethren were still forbidden to make their living in the law because of the temptation lawyers faced to distort truth and justice for the sake of profit.

The most significant change in the Unity's rules was the move away from strict pacifism. Military service was permitted "very unwillingly and with reservations." A brother "could take part in purely defensive wars but must never enter the service only for wages. If he was obligated to military service, he was to get a substitute to go in his place if he could. . . . If he could not avoid active military service, he was to keep to the rear." Brethren were thus forbidden to earn their living as soldiers and were expected to avoid taking life even if forced

66. This and the quotations in the following two paragraphs are from ibid., 83–88.

to defend the realm. In principle, the Unity remained committed to peace and nonresistance. It would be decades before the Unity adopted the idea that Christians should willingly take up arms against infidels and evildoers.[67]

FAMILY LIFE

The Unity gave a lot of attention to family life and provided specially trained marriage counselors for members. Since the Brethren discouraged dancing and other kinds of socializing that generally lead to courtship, marriage counselors were provided to help engaged couples get to know each other. The counselors discussed the Unity's teaching that marriage was a spiritual estate, blessed by God as an emblem of Christ and the church. The counselors were prepared privately to instruct couples in the more intimate aspects of marriage and help the couple see that all aspects of personal life were part of their service to God.[68] This type of instruction was more extensive in Zinzendorf's day, but it is interesting that the Unity of the Brethren in the sixteenth century also saw marital instruction as a Christian duty. Initially the Unity understood marriage as a sacrament, and Luke pointed out to Luther that the only time the word "sacramentum" appears in the Latin Bible it refers to marriage (Eph. 5:32), but it was not a sacrament on a par with baptism and the Eucharist, since unbelievers get married, too.[69]

Premarital counseling was merely the beginning of instruction for households. Drawing upon the household codes of the New Testament (Eph. 5:21–6:9, 1 Pet. 2:11–3:9) as well as medieval moral teachings, the Unity tried to temper the patriarchal family structure of medieval Western society with an ethic based on humility, compassion, and Christlike devotion even in the midst of suffering. Fathers were expected to serve as priests in the family, keeping order, educating the children, and providing discipline and protection without losing their priestly care and compassion. The husband was expected to honor

---

67. In response to the Turkish threat to Moravia and Bohemia after the Turks' victory at Mohács in 1526, the Unity published a manual to assist soldiers who might be captured by the Muslims. It was reprinted many times over the next century.

68. Říčan, *History of the Unity*, 78.

69. Müller, *Geschichte der böhmische Brüder*, 1:466.

and love his wife as himself, for she was "of the near, the most near" to him. Husbands were warned repeatedly not to treat wives as slaves or servants but to care for them, especially during pregnancy and in the days after giving birth.[70] Men were expected to keep the covenant of matrimony faithfully, just as wives were. If it were ever necessary to reproach a wife, the husband should do so by sensitive correction. Wives, for their part, "were to be bound by love, faithfulness, submission and respect, diligence and economy in management of the household, without contention and gossiping, without pride and pleasure seeking. They were warned against magic and superstitions, and encouraged to love and to take part in gatherings in the congregation."[71]

Householders were to include servants and hired help in the family devotions if possible. They were also encouraged to be industrious, friendly to neighbors, kind to guests, generous to the poor, fair to all, and peaceful to neighbors. Masters and fathers were to avoid both prodigality and stinginess. Most surprising for the sixteenth century, householders were forbidden to beat their servants or children. "Parents were to remember the covenant made in infant baptism," observes Říčan, "and lead their children in the awe and discipline of God, correct them sensibly, and 'have and guard' love 'in the heart.' They were to be attentive to educating children for good habits in regard to obedience and modesty." In other words, children were to be treated as the property of God, who made them in his image and who shed his blood for their redemption. The Brethren's commitment to nonviolence included the home, but this did not mean a lack of domestic discipline. Discipline was a way of living that should render punishment unnecessary.

Concrete acts of mercy, such as the collection and distribution of alms for the poor (including priests), was expected of members, although this appears to have been focused internally rather than externally. Representatives of the Unity visited the poor, orphans, widows, sick persons, and families of those in prison in order to determine the level of need. There is little evidence that the Unity felt an obligation to the poor outside their community of faith, as outsiders were the responsibility of the state church. Laypersons, known as stewards of alms, kept written records of donations and distributions. The Unity

---

70. Ibid., 1:287–89.
71. This and the quotations in the following two paragraphs are from Říčan, *History of the Unity*, 78–79.

was not naïve about the temptations of money; therefore there were always at least three almoners. One kept the money box, one the key, and one the register. The constitution and decrees of the Unity under Luke show that the Brethren still attempted to live according to the ideals of the Sermon on the Mount, but they also had a shrewd awareness of human weakness.

CONTINUED CONFLICT IN THE WORLD

The new openness to the world and the willingness to participate in most aspects of civic life did not mean that the Unity lost its sense of being a threatened minority in a hostile world. In fact, the 1503 decree "that everyone in the Unity was to be an overt and not a secret [member]" made the Unity even more visible.[72] In that same year six brothers were burned at the stake, as Catholic officials increased the pressure on the Bohemian monarch to suppress the Unity. They even sent to Prague the infamous Dominican inquisitor Henry Institoris (Henry Kramer), who had written one of the most pernicious books ever published, *Malleus maleficarum* (Hammer Against the Evildoers, or the Witch Hammer).[73] This guide for inquisitors played a decisive role in the horrifying craze of burning suspected witches in the sixteenth and seventeenth centuries.[74]

The Brethren accepted Institoris's challenge to a debate, sending two respected brothers brave enough to risk arrest. The inquisitor's attempt to impress them with miracle stories of saints was vain, of course, but he also accused the Brethren of devil worship and witchcraft, using the kind of stories he had made famous in the *Malleus maleficarum*. He said that they received the devil into their mouths as a fly, that the devil taught them infernal wisdom, and that they engaged in orgies during worship. Rather than persuading the Czech nobles and university professors that the Brethren were servants of Satan, such stories merely discredited Institoris with the audience. In fact, his attack may have improved the image of the Brethren, for they dismissed Institoris's charges with

---

72. Ibid., 89.

73. Heinrich Kramer and James Sprenger, *Malleus maleficaum*, trans. Montague Summers (Mineola, N.Y.: Dover Publications, 1971); for the online version, see http://www.malleusmaleficarum.org/.

74. There are many studies of the witch craze. A good starting point is Anne Llewellyn Barstow, *Witchcraze: A New History of the European Witch Hunts* (San Francisco: HarperSanFrancisco, 1994).

irony rather than violent rhetoric.[75] For many of the Czech nobles, it was the Catholic Church's inquisitors and cardinals who appeared to be uneducated and superstitious.

The Unity continued to defend itself by writing apologies and publishing a confession of faith that outlined the essential and ministerial things, but the royal mandates were kept in place and public worship was forbidden. The validity of the Brethren's baptisms and weddings was denied. The Mandate of St. James was entered into the permanent registry in 1508 and remained in force until 1609. In 1509, during an examination of eleven Brethren arrested on charges of heresy, an encounter took place that reveals much about contemporary views of the Unity. As Říčan records it, "And when the Brethren stood in the great hall waiting [to see] . . . where and before whom they would have to stand, Apolon, the king's fool, came by there . . . [and] he spoke thus before all: 'Are these the Pickart priests?' And when someone of those standing there answered him that they were not priests, he again said: 'But they are teachers.' And then he said to himself: 'They are not teachers, but doers.' And with this he went on his way."[76]

75. Říčan, *History of the Unity*, 91.
76. Ibid., 93–96.

Eight

ESSENTIALS, MINISTERIALS, AND INCIDENTALS

✦

Luke of Prague, the pastor of the Mladá Boleslav congregation, had become the leading figure in the Unity by 1500, but he did not become the official head of the church until the death of Bishop Thomas in 1518. Just the year before, an Augustinian monk named Martin Luther had posted ninety-five theses on the door of the castle church of Wittenberg. Luke at first welcomed the signs of reform to the north as the fruits of Hus's work, but he soon found that he needed to defend the Brethren's doctrine against the criticism of Protestants as well as Catholics. This was a critical time for the development of the Unity, and Luke responded to the challenge by penning some 170 works—polemics, biblical commentaries, pedagogical works, catechisms, confessions, and liturgical pieces.[1] He put his knowledge of the greater Christian theological tradition to good use in writing confessions of faith intended both to educate the faithful and to defend the Unity in the public arena.[2] Luke was more concerned with creating a vibrant and faithful community of Christ than with debating abstract theological issues. Part of Luke's genius was his ability to combine liturgics, ecclesiology, and doctrine with effective leadership.

---

1. Müller, *Geschichte der böhmische Brüder*, 1:535–77; Crews, "Luke of Prague."
2. Müller, *Geschichte der böhmische Brüder*, 1:457, reports that Luke knew the Latin writings of the church fathers, especially Augustine and Jerome, and the Scholastic theologians and Gratian's *Decretals*. He also studied grammar, rhetoric, and logic. He knew the Vulgate Bible very well, but he never learned Greek or Hebrew.

LUKE AND THE HUSSITE HERITAGE

In Peter Brock's view, Luke's significance lay in the fact that under his leadership the Unity "took steps toward the final eradication of the political and social doctrines of the Old Brethren," that is, the doctrines of the original Unity.[3] This assessment is too extreme, as the previous chapter demonstrates, but so is Říčan's claim that Luke led the Unity "out of the terrified ways of narrow sectarianism to a view of the universal church."[4] Although the new Unity emphasized grace and freedom more than the old Brethren, it remained separatist, persecuted, and morally rigorous. The Unity under Luke's leadership witnessed as much continuity as change, though Chelčický's name gradually disappears from the writings of the Unity after 1495. Luke rarely cited him, and Chelčický's writings were not republished until the nineteenth century.[5] In struggling with the issue of Chelčický's authority, Luke reached back into the Hussite heritage to reclaim the theology of the Táborites and early Utraquists.[6]

Despite Luke's turning away from the writings of Chelčický, we cannot say that the new Unity was disconnected from its origins as it grew less radical politically. Fousek has correctly concluded "that the revolution of the 1490s did not represent a complete break with *Unitas'* past, which was what the protesting conservative wing of the *Unitas* maintained. The official changes which came in 1494 and in the years following were not put into effect without a revolution, without pressures and scheming, and without what might be called a certain amount of intrigue. They nevertheless had an integral relationship to *Unitas'* past."[7] Under Luke the Unity brought together in a creative synthesis the three streams of Hussitism—the Utraquists, the Táborites, and Chelčický—to form a strong and stable community of faith. The new Unity departed from the rigid sectarianism of the original Unity as well as the apocalyptic worldview of the early Táborites, but it maintained its separation from the "Constantinian Church," and it continued to criticize the coercive power of the state.

3. Brock, *Doctrines of the Brethren*, 160.
4. Říčan, *History of the Unity*, 102.
5. Joseph Müller, *Die Deutschen Katechismen der böhmischen Brüder, Kritische Textausgabe mit kirchen- und dogmengeschichtlichen Untersuchungen und einer Abhandlund über das Schulwesen der böhmischen Brüder* (Berlin: Hofman, 1887), reprinted as vol. 1 of Beyreuther, Meyer, and Molnár, *Zinzendorf: Materialien und Dokumente* (Hildesheim: Georg Olms, 1982), 104.
6. Peschke, *Kirche und Welt*, 162.
7. Fousek, "Perfectionism of the Early *Unitas Fratrum*," 409.

The blending of Hussite traditions is evident in the Brethren's hymnals of 1501, 1505, and 1519. Luke composed several new hymns, but most of the texts came directly from the Utraquist and Táborite churches. Luke also translated several Latin hymns and chants from the old Latin missal.[8] This effort to bring the Unity more into the broad Christian tradition was also evident in his liturgical reform. He insisted on more uniformity in worship, and in 1501 he issued a new order of worship for the Lord's Supper that replaced the older service.[9] One of Luke's great achievements was the writing of a catechism, *Dětinské Otázky* (Children's Questions), also known as *Catechism for the Young in Faith*. Luke's catechism was based on Táborite catechisms, Hus's *Exposition of the Faith*, and Gregory's teachings. Central to the catechism was the Brethren's distinction between things essential, ministerial, and incidental, which was introduced in an earlier chapter and merits closer attention here.

ESSENTIALS

According to Luke, "all errors flow from misunderstanding of the difference between essential and ministerial things or from erroneous definition of their content or reciprocal action."[10] In clarifying the Unity's doctrine, Luke refined Gregory's original emphasis on faith, love, and hope by noting that there are *two* categories of essential things: the work of God and the human response to God. In his *Apologia sacrae scripturae* (Defense of Sacred Scripture) and his catechism, Luke stressed that the objective work of God as creator, redeemer, and sanctifier is primary. All else depends on God's work. Luke did not speculate about the inner nature of the Trinity. Rather, he followed the outline of the Apostles' Creed and presented scripture texts that were related to the threefold work of God in creation, redemption, and sanctification.[11]

Though Luke emphasized that everything God does is good, he did not write much about the doctrine of creation, because the controversies of his

8. Crews, "Luke of Prague," 46. Crews notes that fourteen of Luke's hymns appeared in the 1978 edition of the Czech Evangelical Church's hymnal.

9. Říčan, *History of the Unity*, 104.

10. Molnár, "Brethren's Theology," 406.

11. Peschke, *Kirche und Welt*, 148–50.

day focused on the nature of salvation. Unlike the Cathars and Bogomils, the Unity never questioned Scholastic teaching on God as the good creator and nature as an expression of God's laws. In the struggle with the Minor Party, Luke clearly advocated the idea that salvation is a matter of grace, not human merit. Although in his later writings he was critical of Luther's doctrine of justification by faith alone, Luke never lost his early insight that salvation, like creation, is based entirely on the work of God. He defended the Unity's understanding that faith must be completed in love, but he argued that faith is a response to the work of the redeemer, who saves. The work of the redeemer is essential, and it becomes available to the individual only through the grace of the Holy Spirit.[12] Luke, like most Unity theologians, discouraged speculation on the inner nature of the Trinity and focused primarily on the human response to the work of God in faith, love, and hope. This is most evident in his catechism.[13]

FAITH, LOVE, AND HOPE

For Luke, it is ultimately impossible to separate faith, love, and hope. All three are gifts of the Creator, revealed in the Redeemer, and made real in the believer through the Holy Spirit. The Holy Spirit, working through the preaching of the Gospel, the ministry of the community, and the visible signs of the sacraments, makes it possible for the believer to participate in the benefits of salvation in this life and have confidence when facing the next life.[14] The catechism included the Augustinian distinction between believing about God, believing God, and believing in God (*credere de deo, credere deo, credere in deum*), which

12. Štrupl, "Confessional Theology," 284.

13. For an English version of Luke's catechism, see Craig D. Atwood, "Catechism of the Bohemian Brethren, Translated and Edited from the 1523 Version," *Journal of Moravian History* 2 (spring 2007): 91–118.

14. Amedeo Molnár's discussion of these categories in his cogent chapter, "The Theology of the Unity," in Říčan's *History of the Unity*, 402, is based primarily on the writings of Luke. On p. 403 he writes, "The distinction of things essential to salvation from those things which are ministrative to salvation and those things which are merely appropriate may be called the formal principle of the Brethren's theology. According to the Brethren's belief, the failure to distinguish these things had caused a most disastrous confusion in the history of Christian thought, a corruption of proper piety in exchanging the real foundation of sure salvation for a false reliance on human arrangements."

had become part of the tradition of the Brethren. Luke taught that it is possible to have the first two levels of faith without experiencing salvation. In fact, such belief could lead to despair. Only the final stage of belief constitutes saving faith.[15]

Gregory had written that "to have faith in God is to have a living delight in the divine promises, from which humans seize God with heart-felt love and forsake earthly things while he has them as if he didn't have them, and enjoys this world as if he enjoys it not." True, saving faith is an existential faith in which one places one's life entirely in God's hands, relying on his promise for the next life and dedicating oneself to live according to Christ's teachings in this life. Humans do not save souls, even their own souls, but salvation is an active process, not a passive state. Salvation brings peace to the soul and a certain hope that one will grow in grace and obedience. "The power of faith proceeds inwardly and outwardly through visible virtues; such as humility, gentleness, unity, friendliness, doing good, seeking peace, patience, etc. and throughout the appearance of works in following the commands and not doing forbidden things."[16] True virtues flow from the faith that God makes possible.

The Unity's approach to faith, love, and hope was practical rather than theoretical: "How do you know if someone has love for God? If he has love for his neighbor." Following in the tradition of Chelčický, Luke's catechism identified the law of Christ as love of God (Deut. 6:4–5) and love of neighbor (Lev. 19:18). The Gospels recorded this as Jesus' own interpretation of the Torah (Mark 12:28–34), which "is more important than all burnt offerings and sacrifices."[17] Both the New and the Old Brethren found it inconceivable that a person could profess faith in God, love for God, and hope in God without having an active love for real people in the real world. The experience of salvation included a joyful orientation toward others expressed in sacrificial ethical living.

Personal morality and social ethics were viewed as aspects of love for God that were essential elements of human happiness and salvation. The Brethren did not understand love as emotion but as an internal orientation toward the will of God and the betterment of human life. They interpreted the statement

---

15. Müller, *Geschichte der böhmische Brüder*, 1:458–59.
16. Ibid., 1:219–20, 514.
17. Catechism, questions 18–22. Hereafter cited parenthetically.

"God is love" (1 John 4:16) to mean that the essence of God is to produce goodness through creation, redemption, and blessing. For the Unity, love is salvation and eternal life. This eternal life is experienced in this world and the next because it consists in "the knowledge of the true God and an enjoyment of him and the one he has sent." The faithful experience eternal life in this life and the next through faith. One of the major tasks of the community of faith, therefore, is to teach Christian ethics by word, example, and mutual discipline. Though Luke understood that ethics flows from the center of one's being (i.e., from having a good heart), he also recognized that those who love God and neighbor need guidance in practical matters. In his catechism he gave this guidance in three sets of biblical teachings that we have already examined in the theology of Chelčický and Gregory: the Decalogue of Moses, the beatitudes of Jesus, and the six smaller commandments of the Sermon on the Mount (questions 22–24; 32–34, 17). These portions of scripture explain the law of love that Christians should live by.

Children at confirmation and new members at baptism were questioned about sinful desires or "deadly appetites," the twin forces of self-aggrandizement and self-destruction. The Unity perceived that one of the roots of personal unhappiness and social dysfunction is loving oneself to the exclusion of loving others. Narcissism craves constant stimulation and consumption but ultimately prevents an individual from developing into a mature person. For Luke, the only cure for this condition was to "receive the truthfulness of faith and love through the gift of God and accept it through the word of God" (question 72). The Unity drew upon ancient tradition and Scholastic theology in identifying the deceptive desires as seven mortal sins: pride, greed, lust, envy, gluttony, anger, and sloth. Despite the Scholastic tone of the seven mortal sins, Luke reinterpreted these vices in terms of the Brethren's rejection of a corrupt society. Mortal sins were the source of violence, abuse, and injustice in the world. In contrast, a community of the faithful would be characterized by "humility and obedience, submission to the ordinances, with singleness of mind in the acceptance of teaching, admonition, warning, punishment, and diligent keeping of the commandments of God, and [following] the good morals of the servants of the truth [1 Cor. 15:33]" (question 75).

Though Luke had less to say about hope than about faith and love, it is also an essential. Hope is a spiritual gift that allows believers to look toward the future with confidence and expectation rather than fear. In his *Catechism for the Young in Faith,* Luke contrasted true and false religion in terms of hope (questions 63–70). True religion gives a sure hope of salvation in both this life and the next, while false religion seduces people into idolatry and immorality by giving them a fraudulent hope. According to Luke, people go astray when they do not understand who they are or where they are going. All people should place their hope in God and trust God's promises, but instead they rely on other things (questions 67–71). He cautioned against relying on the sacraments and rites of the church without experiencing an inner transformation marked by faith, love, and hope. Even "fasting, praying, and giving alms, without the true faith and right repentance," would not provide true hope. "Much hearing and reading of the Word" was likewise useless if it was merely an intellectual or legalistic enterprise. True religion is founded on the essential truth of the new covenant, which is "faith, love, and hope" in following Jesus Christ (question 65). Luke was particularly critical of many Catholic devotional practices, especially pilgrimages, saying the rosary, giving gifts to the church, hearing the Mass, or trusting that there is a purgatory. He warned against doing "works of mercy without fulfilling the commandments of God," or even fulfilling the commandments "without improvement of the heart," along with knowledge of Christ and his covenant (question 71).

This distinction between genuine and fraudulent religion was not just a matter of the afterlife; it affected people in this world. Fraudulent hope leads to religious hatred and violence, according to Luke. Those who rely on "deceptive hope and false piety" are devoted "to the words of false prophets or their works," and with "distorted love and zealous passion, follow them against godly righteousness." Such people abandon decency and reason. They "pursue their ordinances and laws out of passion and hot emotion. Or they retreat to the wilderness in order to live in a way that inures them to the body" (question 71). Luke explained the nature of the Inquisition by quoting Jesus in the Gospel of John: "they will beat you and will consider it a service to God" (John 16:2). The vehemence of Luke's attack on Catholicism and Utraquism in the catechism indicates the intensity of the Unity's desire to abolish the structures of religious violence.

FIG. 16   Linden trees in Kunwald planted by Brethren as a sign of hope before the first exile.

MINISTERIALS

Luke refined the Unity's teaching on the difference between the essentials and the things that minister to the essentials.[18] Amedeo Molnár's description is apt: "Ministrative things for them were those which the Holy Spirit uses as a tool for imparting the essential things. Because of their character as tools and objects of service, it is not permissible to call them incidental things. Ministrative things are, of course, completely dependent on the essentials. If they lose this dependence, they become at once not only void and futile but even harmful and against Christ."[19] We have seen that this idea was important in the founding of the Unity as a separate community of faith, but in Luke's hands it became a central tenet of faith.

Scripture

For Luke, "the Word of God is the first, greatest, and most necessary ministerial thing."[20] It was the basis of all other ministerial things, which get their holiness from the Word, but the Word of God was not simply the words of the Bible. The true Word of God is the Gospel of Christ and his commandments, not the words of scripture alone. Luke valued the Old Testament more than Chelčický and the first generation of the Brethren did, but he also believed that the Word of God is clearer in the New Testament than in the Old. This is the foundation of true faith (Rom. 10:14), without which no one can come to God. As Molnár puts it, "The human biblical word then is indeed only for testimony to the revelation of the Word of God, which in Christ— and only in him—became flesh."[21]

This did not diminish the status of scripture, for Luke, because scripture points to Christ. But it is Christ, not the written Bible, that is essential. The Bible is the guiding rule (*Richtschnur*) of faith, and Luke taught the Brethren's priests to distinguish "between the external writing of the law, with ink on

---

18. Crews, "Luke of Prague," 36–42.
19. Molnár, "Brethren's Theology," 408.
20. Müller, *Geschichte der böhmische Brüder*, 1:462.
21. Amedeo Molnár, *Bratr Lukáš, Bohoslovec Jednoty* (Prague: Kalich, 1948), 82, quoted in Crews, "Luke of Prague," 38.

paper or parchment, and the external reading of it, and the internal truths contained in it."[22] The biblical words become the Word only through the proclamation and reception of the Gospel; therefore priests were to follow proper hermeneutical principles. In particular, Luke instructed them to pay close attention to four things when interpreting a passage: when was it written, where was it written, to whom was it written, and why was it written.[23] Was a particular passage written in ancient Israel in the time of the Mosaic law, or was it written in the time of the early church and Christ's law of love? Luke also acknowledged that the personality of the author affected the scripture text, but, surprisingly, he criticized Luther's practice of relying heavily on philology and language study in biblical exegesis because such study was tiresome, time consuming, and prideful. The essential teachings of the Bible were illuminated through the Holy Spirit within the community of faith rather than in classrooms and libraries, according to Luke.[24] We see here the Unity's suspicion that higher education was another form of elitism in the body of Christ.

The Church as a Voluntary Community of Believers

One of the major issues facing the Brethren after the schism was that they could no longer justify their separation from the Utraquist Church on the basis of Chelčický's call for complete withdrawal from the corruption of the world.[25] The Old Brethren held to the original sectarian justification for separation from the Utraquists and Catholics. The New Brethren needed a new understanding of the relationship of the Unity to the world and the other churches. They needed a new theological perspective on how to be engaged in the world without being of the world and corrupted by it. Thus the synod of 1497 stated that the Unity was founded "in the name of the Lord Christ out of good motive, with a pure and sincere intention, and with salvation as its end, that is, for the cultivation of faith, hope, and love."[26] These three virtues, rather than

---

22. Ibid.
23. Quoted in Müller, *Geschichte der böhmische Brüder*, 1:462.
24. Peschke, *Kirche und Welt*, 170.
25. Müller, *Geschichte der böhmische Brüder*, 1:271–73. Müller lists all of Luke's writings and confessions of the Unity in 1:522–620.
26. Říčan, *History of the Unity*, 69.

the institutional authority of the episcopacy or the sanction of the state, were the marks of the true church.

The true church is also the place wherein "the gospel and the sacraments were properly ministered according to the Law of Christ and the example of the early church."[27] The law of Christ, of course, meant the law of love as revealed in the Sermon on the Mount. The Brethren argued that the Catholic Church had lost its claim to apostolicity by abandoning the poverty of Jesus and decorating holy places with gold, silver, and precious jewels that were paid for by oppression of the people.[28]

The Unity did not abandon its foundational idea of complete separation of secular and spiritual authority when it permitted members to participate cautiously in civic affairs. Secular power is granted by God but must not be seen as sacred in itself. Secular power should promote justice and well-being in the human community, but it should not be allowed to interfere in matters of conscience or the affairs of the church. By declaring that the secular power is subordinate to the authority of God rather than a representation of God's authority, the Unity preserved a principle of conscientious rebellion and non-cooperation with demands of the state when those demands were contrary to the teachings of Christ. In other words, the Unity still retained its character as a "free church" after the schism. It claimed the right to conduct its affairs according to its own understanding of the will of God.

Luke drew on Wyclif in arguing that the visible church has divinely ordained power only as long as it remains faithful. Instead of permanent authority, the institutional church has relative authority, "a gift granted for the service of faith and the establishing of salvation."[29] The foundation of the true church is Christ, who was the first head of the church, not Peter, as the Roman Catholics claimed. More important, Christ accomplishes what he proposes, and he gave spiritual power to the church for the service of the truth. As long as the church pursues the truth, the power of Christ is present, but sin, Luke warned, "adheres to the human spirit and . . . it manifests itself most dangerously on the religious plane."[30] It is dangerous to give the church political power because

27. Ibid.
28. Peschke, *Kirche und Welt*, 159.
29. Říčan, *History of the Unity*, 70.
30. Molnár, "Brethren's Theology," 410.

of the tendency of sinful humans to use religion for evil purposes. Luke, like the other Hussites, saw the Roman Catholic Church as the prime example of the tendency of churches to become so enamored of their power that they become forces of evil in the world instead of sources of salvation, but the Brethren were the most radical of the Hussites in their complete rejection of a state church.[31] Even in the catechism, Luke insisted that true Christianity must be voluntary.

Luke acknowledged that the institutional church might retain worldly power even after it abandoned the truth, but then it would be the church of the Antichrist rather than the body of Christ. For Luke, the word "Antichrist" meant the force in the world that opposes the goodness of Christ and human salvation. He used the term frequently for the Roman Church, but "Antichrist" actually meant any deceptive force that encourages sin rather than salvation. The true church of Christ speaks the truth; the other lies. "Christ gathers, but the antichrist scatters. The one gives life, the other kills. The one is humble, the other raises itself above all that God has named. . . . The one is a servant even unto death, the other is the master for whom others must die."[32] The "one, holy, catholic, and apostolic church," according to Luke, is the "assembly of those elected by God, which shall reign eternally in heaven with Christ in the choir of angels, whose names and number are known only by the one who has made them, redeemed, and made them blessed."[33]

The true church is not defined by a particular time or place, or type of structure or law, but is an invisible community called out of "all peoples and tongues from the beginning until the end." All who have a "new birth of spiritual life, renewal of the spirit and conscience, improvement of understanding, thoughts, and will in divine righteousness from faith in Jesus Christ and in practical evidence of faith in their works," are part of the true church.[34] In its earthly manifestation, this true church consists of several units (Utraquists, Roman Catholics, the Greek Orthodox, and the Brethren). While Luke thus grants legitimacy to these churches as expressions of the invisible body of Christ, "he deprived the Roman Church of its claim to catholicity, but at the same time

31. Říčan, *History of the Unity*, 71–72.
32. Peschke, *Kirche und Welt*, 155.
33. Quoted in Müller, *Geschichte der böhmische Brüder*, 1:460.
34. Quoted in ibid.

transcended the national boundaries of individual churches," in František Kavka's words.[35] In other words, the Roman Church might lead some people to salvation, but it cannot claim to be the universal or catholic church.

The true, mystical church of Christ is empirically present on earth in the "sacramental church" or "ministerial church." This church is holy because it is a visible representation of the truly holy church, but it is also a "net" that gathers up good and bad fish (Matt. 13:24–30). It reflects the holiness of Christ, who has given it his word, washed it with his blood, and made its members into kings and priests (John 17:7, Rev. 1:5–6), but it is not holy in itself. It is holy only in so far as it points to the Gospel of Christ.[36] Luke pointed to the example of Judas to show that participation in the visible church was no guarantee of personal holiness. True religion was a genuine love for God, who is the eternal Other. This love for God moves a person from self-love and self-absorption into an active love for God's creatures.[37]

Sacraments

Much of the theological writings of the Brethren concerned the sacraments, because they were forced repeatedly to defend themselves from the charge that they were Pikarts. The sacraments also figured prominently in Luke's pedagogical works because of the need to explain to new members why the Unity did not observe the sacraments in the same way that other churches did. After 1520 the Unity also participated in the sacramental debates of the Protestants, which added to the store of writings on the sacraments. In these varied works, Luke drew upon Hus, Táborite confessions, and the writings of the Utraquist archbishop Rokycana.

In his exchanges with Luther, Luke rejected the German reformer's assertion that a sacrament had to have been established by Jesus himself. Although Luke was very critical of the Catholic definitions of the sacraments, he agreed with the traditional view that the sacraments were established by Christ *and*

35. Kavka, "Bohemia," 131.
36. Müller, *Geschichte der böhmische Brüder*, 1:461.
37. I am here using the terminology of Emmanuel Levinas and Paul Ricoeur as applied by David F. Ford, who explored the idea of "the worshiping self, before the face of Christ and other people, in an 'economy of superabundance'" as a way to understand the nature of Christianity. Ford, *Self and Salvation: Being Transformed* (Cambridge: Cambridge University Press, 1999), 8.

the apostles.[38] He defended the seven sacraments as visible means to confer a spiritual blessing according to apostolic teaching.[39] Marriage, for instance, used the physical joining of two people to communicate the union of Christ and the church. But the sacraments were ministerial, for Luke, rather than essential to salvation. Christ and his apostles gave them to the church as "sign and witness" of the faith, but they were holy only in so far as they pointed believers to God. The sacraments had no power as signs and witnesses without the preaching of the Gospel.[40] Most important, they could help lead someone to faith, but they were not a substitute for faith. This is a point repeatedly pressed home in the catechism.[41] Though the teaching of the Unity on the seven sacraments was explored in a previous chapter, it may be helpful to provide a brief summary of Luke's teaching in the early sixteenth century.

Baptism: It is not surprising that Luke spent a great deal of time discussing baptism in an attempt to clarify his belief that "it is not baptism that makes a Christian but faith and truth." Those who have faith are enabled truly to repent, experience newness of life and the joy of salvation. Luke ridiculed the rituals of exorcism, taking oaths, and other aspects of the Catholic rites as witchcraft or superstition. Faith, not ritual, saves. Baptism was the outward sign of this true repentance, for Luke, and it provided two things: assurance of salvation through faith in Christ's new covenant, and acceptance into the spiritual body of Christ. God gave baptism as a way to help people manifest their God-given faith. Infant baptism made one a member of the church, much as circumcision brought one into the old covenant, but it was still necessary for an individual in the Unity to accept salvation personally. Normally, this public acceptance of salvation was part of the confirmation ceremony, when children professed their belief in Christ's redemption and accepted their responsibilities.[42] The Brethren

38. Peschke, *Kirche und Welt*, 168.

39. Müller, *Geschichte der böhmische Brüder*, 1:466. Molnár indicates that Luke was closer to the Orthodox Church in his definition of the sacraments as visible signs of grace than to the Protestants or Catholics, who both limited the number. Theoretically there could be an unlimited number of sacraments. Molnár, "Brethren's Theology," 416. There is an interesting parallel between the Brethren's deep appreciation of the ability of symbols to communicate divine truth and Paul Tillich's critique of Protestantism's rejection of sacramentalism. Tillich, "The Protestant Principle," in *The Essential Tillich*, ed. E. Forrester Church (New York: Macmillan, 1987), 80–81.

40. Müller, *Geschichte der böhmische Brüder*, 1:464.

41. Peschke, *Kirche und Welt*, 167.

42. Müller, *Geschichte der böhmische Brüder*, 1:467–69.

baptized their own children, as they could be reasonably sure that such children would be raised in the faith and discipline of the community, but in Luke's day they continued to regard believers' baptism as complete baptism.[43] The liturgy for adult baptism was clearly based on Luke's catechism. It included a declaration of desire to unite in a covenant with the Unity and with God, as well as recitation of the Lord's Prayer and the Ten Commandments, and a pledge to turn away from evil.[44]

Confirmation: Luke argued for a threefold process of entry into the church. First was Christ's embrace of a child in baptism. The next step occurred when the child, around age twelve, chose to obey Christ's teachings and was admitted to Holy Communion. Finally came the rite of confirmation, with a profession of faith and the laying on of hands in the hope of eternal salvation.[45] There was no need for confirmation when adults were baptized because they made their baptismal vows on their own. Admission to the Lord's table was restricted to those who had made a public profession of faith through confirmation or adult baptism and had given evidence of living in the covenant of grace.[46] Against Luther, Luke defended the Brethren's practice of rebaptizing those who had been baptized by Catholic priests on the grounds that Catholics did not accept the validity of the Unity's baptism.

Eucharist: The question of Christ's presence in the Eucharist was the burning issue of the day, and Luke clarified the Brethren's teaching, which rested on simple faith in the words of scripture "this is my body; this is my blood," without the need for scholarly exegesis. Luke distinguished the Brethren's understanding from that of the Catholics, Utraquists, Lutherans, and Zwinglians. He "adopted almost completely" the sacramental theology of the Táborites, who taught that Christ has four distinct modes of existence.[47] First of all, he is *substantially, naturally, physically,* and *locally* (*dimensionaliter*) present only in heaven. He will be present in this way on earth only at the Last Judgment. Second, he is currently present *powerfully* or *regally* on earth since he reigns as king (Matt. 28:18). His third mode of being is *spiritually* in the church, in the

43. Peschke, *Kirche und Welt,* 167.
44. See Müller, *Geschichte der böhmische Brüder,* 1:471–77.
45. Peschke, *Kirche und Welt,* 171–72.
46. Müller, *Geschichte der böhmische Brüder,* 1:486–88.
47. Müller, *Deutschen Katechismen,* 105; Peschke, *Kirche und Welt,* 161–65.

hearts of the faithful, and through his gifts of grace (Matt. 18:20). The fourth mode is his *sacramental* presence, which is unique to the sacrament as "a sensual sign of a spiritual truth."[48] Luke explained to Luther that the bread and wine become the body and blood of Christ spiritually or as an image (*bildlich*).[49] In light of Luke's strong opposition to Zwingli's teaching that the sacrament is a "mere sign," it is clear that he saw an image or symbol as more than a sign. Christ is not *physically* present in the sacrament, but the consecrated bread and wine communicate or confer Christ "spiritually, actually, and truthfully" to the one who eats in faith. Christ's flesh is not present, but his spirit is present (1 Cor. 11:27), and in this way the sacrament itself provides an "essential truth" to believers through the act of eating and drinking.

True to the teaching of the Unity from the beginning, Luke rejected the practice of showing obeisance to the consecrated host. In 1520 he published a tract on that topic to which Luther responded. Though Luther expressed high regard for the faith and practice of the Unity, he defended the traditional practice of kneeling before the altar as a way to honor Christ, but he agreed with the Brethren that faith in the word of the Gospel is more important than bowing. Far from being swayed by Luther's arguments, Luke's written response emphasized the Unity's belief that bowing to the host was an intolerable form of idolatry. It was worship of a thing rather than of God. This remained a point of contention between the Brethren and Lutherans for generations, and it contributed to the misunderstanding that the Brethren did not believe in the real presence of Christ in the Eucharist.

Luke's teaching on the real presence of Christ was integrated into the Unity's liturgy. The congregation first prayed for forgiveness and the gift of faith. Then they prayed that the Father would take the bread and wine and make them the body and blood of the Son in a "sacramental sense" for those who believe and partake. Though the focus of the Eucharist was on the worshipping congregation, the people were reminded that Christ's blood was "poured out for us and for many, for the forgiveness of sin" (Matt. 26:28, alt.). A key portion of Luke's liturgy was a long remembrance of the life, sufferings, and death of Jesus. Also included were special instructions about communing. The communion

48. Peschke, *Kirche und Welt*, 166–68.
49. The material and quotations in the remainder of this section are taken from Müller, *Geschichte der böhmische Brüder*, 1:443, 487–510.

service ended with a blessing that included the clear admonition to believe in the Gospel and obey Christ's commandments. For Luke, it was an error to separate one aspect of the Eucharist as the moment when Christ is made present. The remembrance of Jesus' life, sufferings, death, and resurrection, the partaking of the bread and wine, and the communicants' sincere desire to live as disciples of Christ were all necessary aspects of communing with Christ.

Marriage and Extreme Unction: Luke had little to say about the sacraments of marriage and anointing the sick, apart from repeating the Brethren's traditional understanding that the Catholic Church had misused these useful and sacred rites. He agreed with Saint Paul that the purposes of marriage were to keep those who did not choose celibacy from falling into promiscuity and to produce children. Clearly Luke did not share Luther's positive view of sexuality and marriage. In discussing the anointing of the sick and dying, he noted that in earlier days this might have been connected with miraculous healing, but in later times it acted more as a comfort and preparation for death. He rejected the ceremonialism of Catholic practice and focused instead on the moral aspects of these rituals.

Penance: Luke laid more emphasis on the sacrament of penance, which he connected directly to repentance. He distinguished three types of repentance: conversion, the sacramental confession at baptism, and the sacrament of penance. The first type of repentance was foundational: it was a turning away from both sin and self-righteousness and toward Christ. An individual could not "do penance" without being penitent. Without this fundamental reorientation toward the Redeemer, the other forms of repentance were meaningless. Luke held to the traditional Catholic teaching that sacramental penance was intended to train a person not to commit the sin again. He encouraged prayers, fasting, and giving alms as acts of penance. Prescribed prayers could help overcome the sins of the spirit, such as pride, disobedience, hate, envy, and insulting behavior. He suggested fasting for sins of the flesh such as gluttony, drunkenness, and promiscuity. Again, this was in line with Catholic teaching. Luke instructed that if the priest was convinced that a person was truly contrite in his or her verbal confession and would perform the required penance, he should pronounce the forgiveness of Christ and offer a handshake as a sign of reconciliation. He cautioned that priests should avoid any perception that they had the power to forgive sins; they were merely spokespersons for Christ.

Priesthood

Luke devoted a great deal of attention to the sacrament of ordination and the proper role of priests in the church. He provided a new liturgy for ordination in 1501 that served as a commentary on the meaning of priesthood. House-holders were to be priests in their own homes, but ordained priests were the fathers of the church as the gathered community. In 1518 the Inner Council approved Luke's *Zprávy knězké* (Instructions for the Priestly Office in the Unity of the Brethren); it was printed in 1527. This appears to have been the first work of pastoral theology ever published by a non-Catholic church in the West and thus is a very important work in the history of Western Christianity. In it, Luke set forth qualifications for priesthood that included internal calling and faith, along with proper education and intense preparation for the work of the priesthood.[50] As in all of his works, Luke reminded the church that Christ was the true priest. Human priests merely "pass on the message of hope, serving as mediators between them and Christ in the covenant and pact of the new testimony."[51] Christ's priesthood, according to Luke, is eternal, while the ministry of human priests lasts only a short while. This is another way of saying that earthly priests have relative authority rather than absolute authority; they are only truly priests when their ministry mediates the grace of Christ.

Luke further asserted that proper ordination requires five things: (1) a calling from Christ to serve as his representative on earth; (2) evidence of a calling, including a virtuous life, gifts for ministry, submission to scripture and the ordinances of the church, trustworthiness, and humility; (3) a calling from the church; (4) the laying on of hands by the church and acceptance of the ministry of Word and sacrament; and (5) confirmation of one's ministry spiritually and practically.[52]

Luke's writings on the priesthood laid stress on "the inner call to service, on the preliminary comprehensive examination . . . and on readiness for further training and development without becoming conceited with pride."[53] The

---

50. Říčan, *History of the Unity*, 103–5.
51. Ibid., 76.
52. Müller, *Geschichte der böhmische Brüder*, 1:500–501.
53. Říčan, *History of the Unity*, 75. Müller, *Geschichte der böhmische Brüder*, 1:500–506, gives greater detail on the priesthood of the Brethren.

Brethren had no doubt that an internal sense of call should be accompanied by evident gifts for ministry, such as wisdom and the ability to learn. God expected his ordained priests to prepare themselves to preach, teach, and care for souls. Their duties included counseling the fallen, hearing confessions of the penitent, showing the impenitent the way to penitence, and disciplining those who refused to repent. In addition, priests were to visit and comfort the sick, pray with them, and strengthen their hope in the face of death. Priests helped parents choose godparents for their children at baptism and guided children in the faith as they grew. Christian education was especially important at the time of confirmation. In short, priests served the community through the Word of God, sacraments, and prayer.[54]

Married men might be ordained priests in rare circumstances, but neither deacons nor priests were allowed to marry. Deacons who married lost their office, since they were then disqualified for the priesthood. Luke defended priestly celibacy against Luther's objections, arguing that married priests could not devote themselves fully to their service. Marriage would not make them "unworthy," merely ineffective.[55] In general, priests lived with other priests in the Brethren's House (manse), which served as the administrative center of the congregation. They also educated acolytes who were preparing to become priests. These young men were sometimes orphans, but most had been dedicated to the church by their parents. Deacons also lived in the Brethren's House and assisted the priest.

In keeping with the concerns of the Czech Reformation, the Unity had a small hierarchy. At the top were the "servants," or "elders of the priestly order," who were the successors of the apostles. As we have seen, they called these servants of the church "seniors" rather than bishops. Over the decades the Brethren adopted the use of the title bishop primarily to communicate better with other churches, but senior remained the official title down to the time of Comenius. Partially in reaction to the authority wielded by Senior Matthew, whom the younger generation found inadequate as a leader, the Unity divided episcopal functions among four men rather than concentrating all authority in a single senior. There were usually two seniors and two co-seniors, and the Unity

54. Müller, *Geschichte der böhmische Brüder*, 1:284.
55. Ibid., 1:502–3.

itself was divided into four administrative districts governed by the seniors. The seniors and co-seniors made up the Inner Council, which provided central administration for the Unity as a whole.[56]

Priests had great authority over the lives of individuals, perhaps more than in any other church; therefore they were carefully supervised by the seniors and the Inner Council. The Unity's attitude toward its priests was "trust, but verify." Lay judges in the congregation were expected to inform the senior if the priest was derelict in his duty or suspected of mortal sin. A priest could be demoted to the rank of layman, and only in rare instances were such priests restored to their office. When a priest under discipline was to be restored to the priesthood, he would always serve a different congregation from the one he had served at the time of his offense.[57]

The Inner Council was elected at synod, which also affirmed its decisions on fundamental matters. After the schism, the Inner Council was increasingly dominated by clergy with a theological education. The Czech historian Rudolf Říčan has argued that the reduction of lay involvement in the administration resulted from the increasing presence of nobles in the Unity. By placing control of the Inner Council in the hands of the clergy, the Brethren kept the church free from control by the nobility.[58] Though members of the Inner Council were in effect appointed for life, the council or a synod could remove a council member who was deemed in error. In fact, a synod could depose the entire Inner Council if necessary. Theoretically, therefore, all church offices were revocable, even the office of senior. So, while the Inner Council was normally the supreme authority in the Unity, its power was tempered by the synod's authority to elect and disband the council.[59]

The Brethren's priests had a demanding schedule of visitation and counseling in addition to the normal pastoral duties of administering the sacraments and preaching.[60] There was also the additional burden of earning an income, for they could not rely on tithes and endowments to support them. Thus it is little wonder that the Unity produced few scholars or creative theologians. The

56. Říčan, *History of the Unity*, 74–76.
57. Fousek, "Spiritual Direction and Discipline," 222.
58. Říčan, *History of the Unity*, 72–73.
59. Müller, *Geschichte der böhmische Brüder*, 1:281–82.
60. Fousek, "Spiritual Direction and Discipline," n47.

intellectual activities of the priests focused primarily on homiletics, pastoral counseling, catechesis, and dogmatics. In many ways the Unity's definition of priesthood was a direct forerunner of the later Pietist understanding of the role of clergy, which forms the model for most Protestant churches today. The pastor was to serve the congregation and exemplify the ideals of Christian life. In terms of income, the Unity's priests were not "professional," but in terms of expectations and standards they certainly were.

Deacons and Acolytes

Priests were assisted by deacons, but the Brethren rarely used the word *diakon* (in Czech, *jahen*) in the early sixteenth century. Usually they were just called "helpers." Deacons assisted as liturgists and might preach, but they baptized only in emergencies. During the Eucharist, deacons held the chalice, while the priest gave the bread, placing it directly on the tongue of the recipient. Deacons could lead prayers in the priest's absence, and during worship they would often read the Gospel or Epistle and lead the singing if they were able. A deacon also accompanied the priest on his frequent travels to widely scattered congregations. Priests were not allowed to travel alone lest they fall into temptation—or into the hands of the authorities.[61] After several years of faithful and industrious service, a deacon could expect to be ordained as a priest.

One of the more interesting and misunderstood offices in the Unity under Luke was that of acolyte (*Acoluth* in German), also known as subdeacon. Some Unity writings referred to these people as *Priesterschüler*, or "student priests." This was a quite different office from that created by the modern Moravian Church, which is essentially a lay pastor or lay assistant pastor.[62] The acolyte in the Unity of the Brethren was a young person preparing for the priesthood who lived in the Brethren's House with the priest and deacons. There he was educated and apprenticed into the deaconate. He prepared the sanctuary for worship and assisted the priest in the more mundane tasks of ministry. Acolytes were either given by their parents to the priests (like Samuel in the Old

61. Müller, *Geschichte der böhmische Brüder*, 1:285.
62. Moravian Church Unity Synod, *Church Order of the Unitas Fratrum (Moravian Church)*, 2002 (Bethlehem, Pa.: Moravian Church in America, 2003), sec. 691.

Testament) or they were orphans cared for by the church. Deacons and acolytes helped priests, and the priests in turn were responsible for their education, physical and emotional well-being, and discipline. In other words, these priests in training could be as much a burden as a blessing to busy priests, but it was a duty that was vital for the future of the Unity.

Lay leaders called judges or lay helpers assisted priests in their duties of administration and congregational oversight.[63] The priest and judge were to make at least one official visit to the home of each family once each quarter. The Unity appointed women as judges or elders to exercise pastoral authority over women in their congregation. They were generally called "sisters' judges."[64] This was one of the more distinctive practices of the Unity, and it merits further research. This type of female pastoral leadership was revived under the title of deaconess during the Zinzendorfian period of the Moravian Church. It remained rare in the rest of Christianity for women to be instructed and counseled by women religious authorities outside convents until the nineteenth century.[65]

Luke and his colleagues produced instruction manuals for judges and priests, which were frequently updated. In addition to advice on hearing confessions and helping people improve their behavior and attitudes, the judges were trained to settle disputes within the congregation. More important, they were expected to be wise enough to prevent disputes from developing. They were instructed to maintain strict confidentiality, except for informing the priest of necessary matters. They were expected to use "kind and gentle speech" when confronting members with their faults and to seek to understand the motives of an erring brother or sister rather than focus just on the behavior.

In other words, the process of judging within the community was supposed to reflect the ethical values of the Sermon on the Mount rather than self-righteousness, domination, condemnation, or spiritual pride. The goal was always to restore a brother or sister to the joy of salvation, not to exclude him or her. Judges, deacons, and even priests were subject to the same discipline and were supervised by the seniors. Luke frequently reminded his priests and

63. Müller, *Geschichte der böhmische Brüder*, 1:285–87.

64. Říčan, *History of the Unity*, 77.

65. Beverly Mayne Kienzle and Pamela J. Walker, ed. *Women Preachers and Prophets Through Two Millennia of Christianity* (Berkeley and Los Angeles: University of California Press, 1998).

judges to be gentle as well as firm, "for human reason is noble minded; it is more easily led than forced."[66] The brothers and sisters were always reminded that they had joined the Unity voluntarily and submitted to its discipline freely, and they were free to leave at any time. This was one of the great strengths of the voluntary principle of church membership, and it was reflected in the writings of Comenius.[67]

INCIDENTALS

In the catechism, Luke used the biblical concept of idolatry to warn members against making ceremonies and traditions, rather than God, the focus of religion. Ceremonies and traditions belonged in the realm of incidental things, and it was idolatrous to make them primary. To make this point, the catechism asked new members of the community, "In what three ways do people err commonly in the world? In three things: In idolatry, in mortal desires, and in fraudulent hope." For the Unity, idolatry was defined as giving "to a visible or invisible creature the worship and prayer that belongs to God the Lord alone, whether knowingly or ignorantly, whether physically or spiritually, inwardly or outwardly" (questions 49–50). Like the Swiss reformers later, the Brethren were suspicion of ornament and ceremony, but they did not reject them completely. Kept in proper perspective, sensory things could enhance worship. Luke, for instance, encouraged the Brethren to make more use of candles, altar cloths, and ornaments so long as they aided rather than distracted from to worship. He even restored some of the traditional Catholic feast and fast days to the Unity's calendar and encouraged use of the lectionary. In this regard, at least, Luke was closer in spirit to Luther than to Zwingli, but there was grumbling from some of the Brethren who preferred the original austerity.[68]

Naturally, the Unity's concern over idolatry was directed mainly at the Catholic and Utraquist churches, especially in relation to the consecrated host, but it was also a warning against making an idol of the traditions and practices of

---

66. Říčan, *History of the Unity*, 77.
67. It is also seen in the modern *Church Order of the Unitas Fratrum*, sec. 654.
68. Říčan, *History of the Unity*, 105.

the Unity itself. Luke asserted that the Minor Party's elevation of Gregory's and Chelčický's writings to canonical status was a form of idolatry. Under his leadership the Unity became the first Christian church to endorse what Paul Tillich has called "the Protestant principle": that the church must not make its forms and structures absolute. Continual self-criticism was necessary.[69] While the essentials of salvation did not change, the human expression of those essentials must be subject to continual examination.

This process of sifting the traditions of the church was evident in Luke's handling of the sensitive issue of the veneration of the saints, especially the Virgin Mary. The brothers and sisters of the Unity were instructed to make a distinction between believing in the saints and respecting them. This was very similar to the early church's distinction between worshipping and venerating the saints, but Luke drew the line of proper devotion further away from veneration. Christians should not worship the saints, "because they are neither God and Creator nor the Redeemer and the one who makes blessed." They were creatures of the Creator, who alone deserved praise. Believers should, however, respect and emulate the Virgin Mary and other saints because they exemplified Christian living. According to the catechism, "One properly loves them in obedience by following them in the way that they followed Christ, and by praising God through them and for their sake" (question 56).

For instance, the members of the Unity were to follow Mary's example "in her virtuous life, in which she followed Christ with living faith, and with active love, in the troubles she took for the sake of the hope of eternal life, and the law of the covenant, and in her complete pains until death, forsaking the world and its confusion and evil along with all its vanity" (question 58).[4] Far from dishonoring the Virgin Mary, as critics charged, Luke wrote many hymns in praise of Mary and encouraged the Unity to honor her.[70] The catechism taught that Mary was a virgin who "was elected by God, blessed among women, full of grace." In contrast to later Protestant thought, Luke taught that she had

69. Tillich, "Protestant Principle," 69–89. Interestingly, Tillich's critique of Protestant churches echoes the original concerns of the Unity. "A fresh interpretation of love is needed in all sections of Protestantism, an interpretation that shows that love is basically not an emotional but an ontological power, that it is the essence of life itself, namely, the dynamic reunion of that which is separated. If love is understood in this way, it is the principle on which all Protestant social ethics is based, uniting an eternal and dynamic element, uniting power with justice and creativity with form." Ibid., 82–83.

70. Crews, "Luke of Prague," 44.

been conceived without sin ("pure before birth") and remained "a blessed person on account of her humble faith well-pleasing to God, a true mother of the Lord Jesus" (question 53).

In addition to Mary, many people "were beloved saints in Christ and purified with his blood, made living from faith, and having love for God above all things, and their neighbor, and worshipping him alone, and serving him alone. Some died common deaths. Some from the throng of people departed this world, suffering anguish and martyrdom from human power for the sake of the true worship of God and for the sake of the word of God and the living hope in Jesus Christ" (question 56). By honoring the saints and their lives, Luke thought believers would gain strength and guidance for their struggles in the world. This demonstrates, again, that the Unity recognized the historical nature of the church. Each age of the church is connected in Christ and has had to struggle with the demands of the Gospel in the face of opposition. For Luke, the proper honoring of the saints helped believers face the difficult challenge of living in faith, love, and hope in a hostile and violent world. This perspective on the great tradition of the church helped moderate the Unity's harsh criticism of the Catholic Church by holding up as saints in the Catholic tradition as exemplars of faithful devotion to Christ.

LUKE'S HERITAGE

Luke of Prague died on December 11, 1528, having served the Unity for fifty years. He played the leading role in formulating the doctrine, practice, and ethos of the Unity before the Protestant Reformation. Skillfully and diligently he guided the Unity through the difficult schism of 1495 and provided a solid institutional structure for the future. He defended the Unity against the attacks of Catholics and Utraquists, and he found ways to secure the favor of powerful nobles without sacrificing the Unity's principles. He also provided the Unity with catechisms, hymns, litanies, and sacramental liturgies that were consistent in theology and perspective. It is unfortunate that his writing style was awkward and often opaque, because this limited his impact outside the Unity. As we will see in the following chapters, Luke's understanding of confirmation and catechism may have had a direct impact on Luther and Bucer, but in general his works were little known outside the Unity.

Luke, like the Unity he served, had no use for abstract theological debate or speculation on the mysteries of God and the universe. He focused on the daily life of believers and on what it meant to serve Christ in the world. He embraced the Táborites' repudiation of much medieval pomp and piety, but in some ways he was more conservative than the sixteenth-century reformers. For instance, Luke saw no need for pastors to learn Greek and Hebrew, nor did he see a reason to abandon the seven sacraments. Kavka's assessment is helpful: "Lukáš thus elaborated a truly reformational theological system, which by its teachings on justification could stand alongside Luther's doctrine, while he also anticipated Calvin's theology, both in Christology and in the notion of continual service to Christ the King. The Czech Reformation undoubtedly culminated in Lukáš."[71] Perhaps Luke's greatest achievement was making it a point of doctrine that no human doctrinal or theological scheme could be perfect and eternal. In his struggles with the Old Brethren, Luke argued successfully for the principle of theological progress. Later generations might—and should—change the doctrine of their ancestors if they found it inadequate or in error. Luke made it clear that doctrinal changes should not be arbitrary or frivolous but should come only after intense study of scripture and honest discussion. Humans should apply their reason to building up the community of faith, not to tearing one another down. Luke, like the Brethren in general, was opposed to pointless theological controversy but in favor of faithful theological discussion.

After Luke's death, the Unity entered more fully, if still cautiously, into the new Protestant world. On April 28, 1531, the Brethren's synod proclaimed "that the priests, as fellow servants of the one Lord, should feel free to use contemporary conditions as an aid in seeking out the precious truth of people's salvation and not be hindered in the quest for truth by their predecessors."[72] It is ironic that the principle of continually reforming doctrine, which Luke had made a central part of the Unity's theology, was used after his death to set aside most of his doctrinal works and liturgies in favor of more clearly Protestant expressions of faith.

71. Kavka, "Bohemia," 131.
72. Říčan, *History of the Unity*, 123.

Part Three

BRETHREN AMONG THE PROTESTANTS

Nine

THE UNITY AND THE LUTHERANS

After the execution of Hus and the beginning of the crusades against the Hussites, Bohemia and Moravia were largely isolated from the rest of Europe. Táborite delegates to the Council of Basel in the 1430s were viewed as exotic creatures: fierce and proud heretics rather than European Christians. Catholic officials throughout Europe used Hus's name to intimidate dissidents, and fathers used tales of the Táborites to frighten children into obedience. The famous University of Prague lost its charter and atrophied from lack of contact with other institutions and scholars. The power of local nobles in Czech lands increased greatly, trade decreased, and intellectual energy was spent in defending positions established in the early days of the revolt.[1] Thus the Unity was largely isolated from the main currents of Western thought and culture. Luke had glimpsed some of the glory and conflict of the Renaissance in Italy but was untouched by it. Few in the Unity were aware of the Battle of Agincourt (1415), the burning of Jeanne d'Arc (1437), the fall of Granada in Spain (1492), or even the discoveries of Columbus. They were, however, keenly aware of events closer to home, such as the fall of Constantinople (1453) and the growing threat of the Turkish military in eastern Europe. For the most part, the Unity in the era of Luke was concerned with its own affairs, unaware that the world was changing rapidly.

1. Macek, "Monarchy of the Estates," 98–116.

From the 1450s to the 1520s, the Unity's theology developed in the context of internal Czech ecclesiastical debate and politics. The Brethren's theologians drew primarily upon Hussite theological sources, especially Táborite works, and they debated primarily with Utraquist officials in government. Externally, the Unity's writings were primarily apologetic works written to those who shared a common Hussite heritage. Internally, the Unity continued to struggle with the lingering effects of the schism of 1495 and with the challenges of enduring as a separate church in Czech society. Despite internal conflicts and the threat of persecution, the Unity in Luke of Prague's era was rather stable, small, and predictable. This changed dramatically in the last decade of Luke's life, when the Unity was caught up in the maelstrom of the Protestant Reformation.

It is impossible to do justice here to an epoch as complex and momentous as the Protestant Reformation, especially given that historians still debate its nature and impact.[2] But some background is in order if we are to make sense of the history and theology of the Unity after Luke's death. In many ways, the Protestant Reformation was a continuation and intensification of the effort to reform Western Christianity that had led to the Czech Reformation of the fifteenth century. A variety of Catholic reform movements had emerged in parts of Europe in the fifteenth and sixteenth centuries, and the papacy had tried, with varying degrees of success, to keep them from undermining the unity and stability of the institutional church. Some of the reform movements remained Catholic. In Spain, for example, Queen Isabella made herself head of the Catholic Church in her realm and forced several reforms upon it. Unlike the Czech Reformation, her reforms reaffirmed traditional Catholic teaching and acknowledged the authority of the pope. In the sixteenth and seventeenth centuries, Spain provided many of the missionaries, mystics, and mercenaries who formed the backbone of the Catholic Church's effort to strengthen Catholic monarchies and reclaim areas lost to Protestantism. Spanish troops and priests also played a major role in the subjugation of Bohemia in the seventeenth century.

---

2. There are many excellent studies of the Reformation, among them Cameron, *European Reformation*; Diarmand MacCullough, *The Reformation: A History* (New York: Viking Press, 2003); Steven E. Ozment, *The Age of Reform, 1225–1550: An Intellectual and Religious History of Late Medieval and Reformation Europe* (New Haven: Yale University Press, 1980); Ozment, *The Reformation in Cities: The Appeal of Protestantism in Sixteenth-Century Germany and Switzerland* (New Haven: Yale University Press, 1975); and Roland H. Bainton, *The Reformation of the Sixteenth Century* (Boston: Beacon Press, 1952).

LUTHER

Elsewhere in Europe, especially in Germany and Switzerland, social and religious discontent led to a protest movement that shattered the Catholic Church in Europe and helped to usher in the modern age. As we know, Martin Luther (1483–1546) was the catalyst in this process, capitalizing on the demand for reform in Germany to effect a major transformation of social and political life in much of Europe. In many ways, Luther mirrored the conflicts of late medieval society.[3] He was a bright young man studying to become a lawyer when he experienced a sudden and dramatic religious conversion. Caught on the road in a violent thunderstorm in July 1505, he vowed to Saint Anne that he would enter a cloister if his life was spared. He fulfilled his vow by joining the Augustinian order, against the wishes of his father. As a monk, Luther was zealous, but he found no solace for his deeply troubled soul. Emaciated from fasting and vigils, he continually confessed his sins without feeling forgiveness. He studied theology but found no comfort in the church's teachings. Instead, by his own account, he came to hate God for the impossible demands of righteousness.[4]

After receiving his doctorate in theology, Luther was assigned to lecture on the Bible at the new University of Wittenberg. While struggling over the Psalms and the letters of Paul, he came to a new appreciation of scripture and the nature of salvation: salvation was based not on human merit but on God's grace alone. Luther's insight into the Gospel message might have become just another interesting idea for theologians to debate, but in 1517 he inadvertently ignited the tinder of discontent in Germany by posting ninety-five theses that called for a public debate on the church's practice of selling indulgences. As we have seen, the Czech Reformation became a revolution when Hus and Jerome of Prague attacked the selling of indulgences in Bohemia in 1412.[5] Luther's Ninety-five Theses posed many of the same questions that Hus had raised on the sale of indulgences, but the response to Luther's critique was much greater thanks to Gutenberg's invention of the printing press, which allowed the Ninety-five Theses to be copied and distributed throughout central Europe

---

3. The two standard biographies of Luther are Oberman, *Luther,* and Bainton, *Here I Stand.*
4. Bainton, *Here I Stand,* 44.
5. See chapter 2.

within a matter of weeks. Luther continued to ponder scripture and Christian doctrine, and by 1519 he had come to the conclusion that humans are justified, or made right with God, only through faith in Christ, not through good works. This evangelical message of salvation by faith alone was broadcast throughout Germany, and it challenged the entire sacramental structure of the medieval Catholic Church.

THE SAXON HUS

Efforts by church officials, including Cardinal Cajetan, to bring Luther quietly back into the fold failed. In 1519 the church appointed a theologian named John Eck to debate Luther on the issue of indulgences. The debate was held in Leipzig, and although the authorities promised Luther's safety, friends and foes alike reminded him of what had happened to Hus at Constance. Opponents held up placards showing a goose (Hus) burning on a stake. At a tense moment in the debate, Eck accused Luther of being a Hussite because he rejected the pope's authority to grant indulgences. During a recess, Luther went to the university library and read the account of the Council of Constance and Hus's defense. When the debate resumed, he shocked the audience by declaring, "Among the articles of John Hus, I find many which are plainly Christian and evangelical, which the universal Church cannot condemn."[6]

People began calling Luther the "Saxon Hus," some approvingly, others in condemnation. Luther's opinion of the Bohemian churches changed after the debate at Leipzig. Until then he had viewed the Unity of Brethren as heretics. Years later he recalled:

> When I was a papist, I truly and cordially hated these Pickard Brethren with great zeal toward God and religion and without any aim of gaining money or glory. When I came upon some books of John Hus unawares one time and saw that the Scriptures were treated so powerfully and purely that I began to wonder why the pope and council had burned such a great man, I immediately closed the book in terror, suspecting

6. Bainton, *Here I Stand*, 89.

that there was poison hidden under the honey by which my simplicity might be infected; such a violent fascination with the name of the pope and council ruled over me.[7]

He also reported that he had read an Utraquist tract defending communion in both kinds in 1513, when he still held the traditional view of concomitance and transubstantiation, and he had dismissed the Utraquist argument.

Luther's view of the Hussites changed completely after the Leipzig debate. In 1520 he publicly endorsed the practice of communion in both kinds, using many of the Hussite arguments he had once rejected out of hand.[8] Reformist propaganda soon circulated depicting Luther and Hus together serving the chalice to the laity and preaching from the Bible.[9] Luther also became acquainted with the writings of the Unity of the Brethren, particularly Luke's *Defense of Sacred Scripture*, which he read in 1519. He decided that the Brethren were faithful to scripture and the doctrine of the early church; it was the papacy that was heretical. In 1520 he wrote to George Spalatin, "Without being aware of it, I have until now taught and held the whole doctrine of Jan Hus. In short, we are all Hussites without knowing it. Even Paul and Augustine are really Hussites."[10]

Luther, who had once been too frightened to say the words of consecration at the Eucharist, had aligned himself with the most feared heretics in history.[11] He declared that once he read Hus for himself, "then the joy of my heart began, and, looking around at all those whom the pope had condemned and damned as heretics, I praised them as saints and martyrs, especially those whose pious writings or confessions I could find."[12] Suddenly the Bohemian churches were again at the center of controversy throughout Europe. When news of Luther's declaration of affinity with Hus reached Prague, the Utraquists welcomed him as an ally in their long struggle. They sent a delegation to Wittenberg to present Luther with a copy of Hus's *De ecclesia*. He was surprised that

7. Pelikan and Hotchkiss, *Creeds and Confessions*, 1:799.

8. Peschke, *Kirche und Welt*, 185–89.

9. R. W. Scribner, *For the Sake of Simple Folk: Popular Propaganda for the German Reformation* (Cambridge: Cambridge University Press, 1981), 221–28.

10. Pelikan and Hotchkiss, *Creeds and Confessions*, 1:796. For the letter, see *Luther's Works*, 48:151.

11. The psychoanalyst Erik Erikson examined this transformation in detail in *Young Man Luther* (New York: W. W. Norton, 1958).

12. Pelikan and Hotchkiss, *Creeds and Confessions*, 1:800.

Hus's masterpiece supported many of his own thoughts on the church, but he also recognized that this was because he and Hus had both relied on the works of Wyclif and Augustine.

In 1520 Luther published three major tracts that undermined much of the medieval church's doctrine and structure in favor of the idea of justification by faith alone.[13] He systematically and relentlessly tore down the fortress of papal authority and began rebuilding Christian doctrine on the foundation of justification by faith. He argued that it was not the sacrament of penance, or pilgrimages, or indulgences, or obedience to the papacy that saves one's soul; only faith in the redemptive work of Christ on the cross could save. Luther's assault on Catholic doctrine was more radical than Hus's, but Luther was better protected than Hus had been. Emperor Charles V needed troops from Germany to resist the Turkish invasion of Hungary; therefore he moved cautiously against the popular Luther. Pope Leo X excommunicated the "Saxon Hus," but the emperor did not have him arrested and burned. Instead, Luther was offered a chance to recant before an assembly of the German nobility at a meeting with the emperor at Worms in 1521. There, like Hus, he stood firm, refusing to recant things he believed to be true.[14]

Relations were established between Prague and Wittenberg, and Luther's key works were translated into Czech. Some of the Utraquist priests and nobles were attracted to the German reformer's ideas and formed a "Luther party" that sought to bring the Utraquist Church into closer conformity with Luther's ideas.[15] Called Neo-Utraquists by later historians, the Luther party probably had less impact on the Bohemian national church than was once believed. As Zdeněk David explains, the majority of Utraquists rejected Luther's teaching, especially "his solafideism, his principle of sola scriptura, and his rejection of sacramental priesthood in historic apostolic succession, including the papacy."[16]

13. *Address to the Christian Nobility of the German Nation Respecting the Reformation of the Christian Estate*, in *Luther's Works*, vol. 44; *On the Babylonian Captivity of the Church*, ibid., vol. 36; *Freedom of the Christian*, ibid., vol. 31.

14. Bainton, *Here I Stand*, 140–48.

15. Müller, *Geschichte der böhmischen Brüder*, 1:396–97.

16. David, *Finding the Middle Way*, 57. David disputes the claim that there was a Neo-Utraquist party. "Despite much loose talk about Neo-Utraquism, no one has yet produced a Neo-Utraquist theological text, or even made a suggestion regarding along what lines a genuine dogmatic or liturgical synthesis of Utraquism and Lutheranism should proceed" (230). I would suggest that the Utraquists' adoption of clerical marriage points in the direction of Neo-Utraquism.

Luther, in turn, was very critical of the Utraquists' commitment to apostolic succession, the veneration of saints, prayers for the dead, and other Catholic elements of their faith and practice. Although the Utraquist consistory in Prague rejected Lutheranism, several Bohemian nobles openly identified themselves as Lutheran and agitated for the right to introduce Lutheranism on their estates. In 1575 the Lutheran nobles and the Brethren signed a joint confession of faith called the Bohemian Confession, which the Utraquists eventually endorsed as well.[17] That confession will be discussed in more detail in the following chapter.

LUKE OF PRAGUE AND LUTHER

For many months after the Diet of Worms, Luther remained in hiding, working on his translation of the Bible into German. When he returned to Wittenberg, he worked with his friend Philip Melanchthon to reform the doctrine and liturgy of the local church. In doing so, they created the Evangelische Kirche, also known as the Lutheran Church. The example of the Brethren may have played a role in the early development of the Lutheran Church. For instance, when Luther rejected the Catholic doctrine of transubstantiation as absurd and unnecessary, he used the same Wyclif-Táborite arguments he had read in the works of Luke of Prague. The Brethren in turn saw similarities between Luther's theology and their doctrinal positions. As a result, they were able to establish closer relations with Luther than the Utraquists had done. Most of all, though, the Brethren were heartened by the news that a brilliant young theologian in neighboring Saxony had declared the papacy the Antichrist and was taking up the cause of Hus.

Two of the younger Brethren, Jan Roh (known in German as Horn) and Michael Weisse, were studying for the priesthood in the Unity when they came upon Luther's early works. In May 1522 they traveled to Wittenberg to study with Luther and Melanchthon. The two reformers quizzed them repeatedly about whether the Brethren really were Pikarts, as their enemies claimed. Based

17. Molnár, "The Czech Confession of 1575," *Communio Viatorum* 16 (1973): 241–47; David, "Utraquists, Lutherans"; David, *Finding the Middle Way*, 168–97.

on Roh and Weisse's account of the Brethren's teaching and his own reading of Luke's Latin writings, Luther publicly defended the Unity as a Christian church separate from Rome. He published his questions and criticisms about the orthodoxy of their eucharistic theology, however, since they denied the physical presence of Christ in the host.[18]

Roh and Weisse helped establish friendly relationships between the Inner Council and Luther, but the aged Luke of Prague, who had defended the Unity for decades from the attacks of Catholics, Utraquists, and Old Brethren, was not awed by Luther's reputation and erudition, nor was he willing to conform to Luther's teaching. He defended the seven sacraments, replying to Luther's criticisms of the Unity's doctrine that "the Brethren follow a better way, in that they actually follow thoroughly the simplicity of faith in the holy Gospel and the model of the first church; above all, they free themselves from all that runs contrary to it and give warning of such things, and they actually follow the truth of faith without anger. They do not make humans have convictions about things that God has not made us have, and they do not invite freedom where he has condemned something." In other words, Luke told Luther that the church should focus on faith, love, and hope rather than demand more precision on the nature of the Eucharist than the Bible provided. Jesus said simply, "This is my body. This is my blood." He did not, Luke noted, say of the bread and wine, "this is Christ, the true God and true Man, the Redeemer and Savior."[19]

Luther showed a degree of deference to Luke and the Unity that he denied to others with whom he disagreed. In 1522 he published Luke's *Children's Questions* in German and personally composed a preface. This meant that the Unity had the honor of publishing the first Protestant catechism. Despite its evident weaknesses in style, Luke's *Children's Questions* served as a valuable model for other Protestant catechisms.[20] In 1523 Luther also published a tract titled *Von Anbeten des Sakraments* (On the Adoration of the Sacrament) in direct response to Luke's treatment of the sacraments.[21] Luther praised the Brethren's "stance toward the papacy, human laws and traditions, purgatory, the mass and cloister, and toward prayers to the Mother of God and the saints," but he was very

---

18. Müller, *Geschichte der böhmischen Brüder*, 1:400–406.
19. Ibid., 1:407.
20. Ibid., 1:409.
21. *Luther's Works*, vol. 36.

critical of the Brethren's refusal to kneel before the consecrated bread and wine. He believed that this refusal was a denial of the real presence of Christ in communion. In Luther's judgment, their practice indicated that they were indeed Pikarts, despite their claims to the contrary.[22] There was no denying that the doctrine of the Unity, especially on the sacraments, differed on a several key points from Luther's understanding.

Luther also questioned the Brethren's approach to infant baptism based on "future faith" that needed to be completed in confirmation. He argued that original sin is washed away in baptism, which is a complete sacrament in itself, writing, "therefore it is our judgment that through the faith and prayer of the church young children are cleansed of unbelief and of the devil and are endowed with faith, and thus are baptized."[23] Luke, by contrast, argued that baptism is an act of the church that anticipates the child's future profession of faith. Baptism does not make a person Christian; repentance and profession of faith do that. Luke also emphasized that unbaptized infants are not subject to punishment but are saved by God's grace.[24] Reformation historian Elsie McKee has recently asserted that the Brethren's belief that baptism was not necessary for salvation was particularly appealing to women during the German Reformation because it removed the fear that babies were damned if they died before baptism.[25]

Formal relationships between Luke of Prague and Luther ended around 1525. It may have been that Luke was just too old to continue the debate and discussion, but Říčan has speculated that Luther's support of the princes during the Peasants' Revolt may have been decisive for Luke. "We cannot help but suspect that Lukás as leader of the Unity, constantly standing vigilant against the use of secular power for the oppression of subjects and the cruel exercise of feudal rights, had even more reason for not continuing relations with Wittenberg."[26] Říčan may be right, but evidence is lacking. Certainly the younger generation of Unity priests did not share Luke's suspicion of Luther. Soon after Luke's death, the Unity again established contact with Luther and examined the writings of other reformers.

22. Peschke, *Kirche und Welt*, 192.
23. *Luther's Works*, 36:300.
24. Müller, *Geschichte der böhmischen Brüder*, 1:468–80.
25. McKee, "Reforming Popular Piety," 56.
26. Říčan, *History of the Unity*, 116.

ZWINGLI AND THE BRETHREN

In Switzerland, a Catholic priest named Ulrich Zwingli was growing discontented with Catholic teaching and practice about the same time that Luther was preparing for the Leipzig debate. Although Zwingli later denied he had any inspiration from Luther, most historians agree that Luther's stand against the pope and emperor contributed to Zwingli's rejection of church tradition in favor of the Bible's authority alone. In 1520 Zwingli persuaded the Zurich City Council to reform the local church on its own authority, using his explication of the Old and New Testaments as a guide. It abolished compulsory seasons of fasting, turned the Mass into a simple commemorative meal, similar to the Táborite lovefeast, and abolished images in worship.[27]

Zwingli's reformation followed some of the Táborites' major themes, including iconoclasm and a call to arms in the defense of God's truth. Želivský's sermon on the need to smash the altars, which he preached before the defenestration in 1419, could have been preached by Zwingli in the 1520s, but Zwingli would not have carried the monstrance in public procession as Želivský had done. In some ways Zwingli was more extreme than the radical Hussites in his rejection of church tradition. He rejected the idea of episcopacy and clerical celibacy completely, for instance. In other ways, though, his reform of society was far more congenial to merchants and town councilmen than the Táborites' eschatological revolution, with its nascent communism.[28]

Zwingli's ideas were welcomed by a number of dissidents in Bohemia, and several priests in the Unity and the Utraquist Church read his works. A new congregation was established in Habrovany that adopted Zwinglian theology. They called themselves the Brethren, although they had no connection to the Unity. Their printing house published several polemics against the Unity, in fact, causing further problems for the Brethren in Moravia and Bohemia.[29] Some of the Brethren's priests were also influenced by Zwingli's writings. Jan Čížek and

---

27. Cameron, *European Reformation*, 108–10; 219–61; G. W. Bromiley, *Zwingli and Bullinger* (Philadelphia: Westminster Press, 1953).

28. Ozment, *Reformation in Cities*.

29. Říčan, *History of the Unity*, 119.

Michael Weisse actively promoted Zwingli's ideas within the Unity, claiming in particular that Zwingli's understanding of the Eucharist as a *Zeichen* (sign or signifier) meant the same thing as the Brethren's doctrine.[30]

After years of trying to convince the Utraquists that the Brethren were not Pikarts, Luke was not happy to find that some of his young priests were promoting the Pikart view of the Eucharist, using Zwingli's writings for support. Luke called a meeting of the Inner Council and wrote a rather harsh rejection of Zwingli and his teaching. The Inner Council called the dissidents to task for going against the doctrine of the Unity and demanded that they stop misrepresenting the Brethren's doctrine. Luke repeated the traditional formula that Christ is present sacramentally, spiritually, powerfully, and truthfully in the bread and wine.[31] The elders reaffirmed the view that "the sacrament was more than a symbol. Not only did it give honor to the grace of God, but at the same time it existed as grace and truth. God acted here, assuring a person anew for salvation; it was not at all only the person, recollecting the sacrifice of Christ for his spiritual strengthening and renewing his oath on Christ's banner, who acted."[32]

Čížek persisted in his Zwinglian teaching and was finally expelled from the Unity. In 1528 the Catholic authorities burned him at the stake as an Anabaptist. Weisse submitted to the elders, but he caused further controversy by promoting Zwingli's idea that the "keys" given to the church simply meant the word of the Gospel rather than the power to pronounce forgiveness after confession.[33] Even after the Unity ceased referring to penance as a sacrament, they retained a traditional belief in the efficacy of confession and absolution by the church. The seniors criticized Weisse throughout his career for translating the Unity's documents into German in such a way that they tilted more toward Zwingli than toward Luther. It should be noted in Weisse's defense that some of his contemporaries, especially Jan Roh, were trying to shape Unity statements in a distinctly Lutheran direction at the same time.

30. Müller, *Geschichte der böhmischen Brüder*, 1:441–43.
31. Ibid., 1:444.
32. Říčan, *History of the Unity*, 118.
33. Müller, *Geschichte der böhmischen Brüder*, 1:444.

THE RADICAL REFORMERS AND THE BRETHREN

Some sixteenth-century reformers were much more radical than Luther or Zwingli. The most famous of these was Thomas Müntzer (1490–1525), an apocalyptic prophet who was convinced that the Holy Spirit spoke directly through him.[34] More than any other first-generation Protestant reformer, Müntzer was heir to the most violent aspects of the Czech Reformation.[35] He arrived in Prague in April 1521, having spent time in Zwickau, where a group of self-proclaimed prophets had rejected all church authorities. Calling upon the Hussite heritage, Müntzer was allowed to preach in both Latin and German from many Prague pulpits. He even served Utraquist communion in the Týn Church, where Rokycana had once preached, but his effort to create a new prophetic church met with little support from the Utraquist clergy or the people. The memory of the violent Táborite priest Martin Húska was still fresh in Bohemia, and few were eager to bring a second apocalypse to the kingdom. Even the Brethren, who had the closest ties to the Táborite legacy, rejected Müntzer's message because of its violence.[36] Four years later, Müntzer helped incite the German peasants to rebel in a bloody uprising. The promised divine protection for the righteous failed to materialize. Perhaps as many as a hundred thousand peasants were slaughtered. Müntzer was captured by the nobles and brutally executed.

As in the time of Chelčický, some sixteenth-century radical reformers rejected violence. The Radical Reformation was primarily represented in Bohemia and Moravia through the pacifist teachings of Balthasar Hubmaier (c. 1485–1528) and his followers. Called Anabaptists by their enemies because they rejected infant baptism, these radical reformers called for a rigorous application of the Sermon on the Mount among the followers of Christ, much as Chelčický had taught. They understood baptism as a profession that a person had consciously committed him- or herself to the demands of Christ; therefore only adult baptisms were valid. Connected to the rejection of infant baptism was a wholesale rejection of the state church.[37]

34. George H. Williams and Angel M. Mergal, *Spiritual and Anabaptist Writers* (Philadelphia: Westminster Press, 1957); Bainton, *Here I Stand*, 201–7, 214–21.
35. Cohn, *Pursuit of the Millennium*, 234–51.
36. Müller, *Geschichte der böhmischen Brüder*, 1:399.
37. The standard history of the left wing of the Reformation is George H. Williams, *The Radical Reformation* (Philadelphia: Westminster Press, 1962).

In many ways, the Anabaptists merely took Zwingli's strict biblicism, his idea of *sola scriptura*, to its logical conclusion. Since the New Testament mentioned only adult baptism, the Anabaptists concluded that infant baptism was a later invention of the Catholic Church. It is not surprising that Anabaptist ideas first emerged in Zurich, where Zwingli had called for a reform of the church based solely on scripture, but Zwingli objected vigorously as soon as Hubmaier made his views on baptism known. The rejection of infant baptism and the promotion of pacifism threatened the government and the new Reformed Church because they undermined the connection between citizenship and church membership. At Zwingli's urging, the Zurich City Council began to persecute Hubmaier's community of believers in 1523. A number of Anabaptists made their way to Moravia, where they found a measure of protection.

Jacob Hutter emerged as the most effective leader of the Anabaptists in Moravia, and he organized a pacifist agricultural communal society, called a *Brüderhof*, with an economic discipline even stricter than that of Brother Gregory, who had allowed private ownership of property. Remnants of the Old Brethren and others who held closely to the original writings of Chelčický were still active in Moravia. A convert to the Old Brethren named Jan Kalenec had published several works against the Unity in the early 1500s, accusing them of departing from the ways of the founders.[38] His leadership helped revive the Old Brethren community for a time, but most of his followers recognized their similarity to the Anabaptists and joined up with Hutter. The Hutterites, who eventually settled in North America, were sometimes referred to as Moravian Brethren and confused with the Unity. After years of conflict with the Old Brethren and Kalenec, Luke and the other elders in the Unity were not well disposed toward the Anabaptists. The Inner Council responded with a persistent defense of the practice of infant baptism and the permissibility of swearing oaths under certain circumstances. The revival of ancient imperial laws against rebaptism may have contributed to the Unity's swift and vigorous rejection of the Anabaptists, but the Unity had moved away from believers' baptism fifty years earlier. The Anabaptist challenge merely caused the Brethren to reaffirm their doctrine on baptism for the children of believers.

38. Zeman, *Anabaptists and Czech Brethren*; Brock, *Doctrines of the Brethren*, 251–56.

A NEW GENERATION OF LEADERS

The presence of Anabaptists in Moravia meant that within a decade of the first contact with Luther, each of the main branches of the sixteenth-century Reformation (Lutheran, Reformed, Radical) was represented in Bohemia and Moravia. The Unity's social and religious context thus was much more complicated than ever before. After Luke's death in 1528, the Unity elected a new Inner Council, which included the new senior (or bishop), Jan Roh (or Horn) (c. 1485–1546). Like many Unity priests, Roh came from an artisanal family; his father was apparently a linen weaver. Senior Roh was counted among the educated pastors, although he was largely self-taught.[39] He had been ordained to the priesthood in 1518, and by the time he was elected to the Inner Council, Roh had already established contact with Luther and Melanchthon. He viewed the German Reformation with great expectation as a fulfillment of the promise of Hus's work. That he received the most votes for Inner Council at the synod indicates that his views had strong support among the clergy. A number of older Brethren expressed fears, however, that closer ties to Wittenberg and Luther's doctrine of justification by faith alone would undermine the Unity's discipline. They also feared the corrosive effect that higher education and involvement with the wider world might have on a church that had always valued simplicity, manual labor, and strict morality.

Despite such cautions, the Unity's new leadership made significant changes in doctrine and practice in response to Luther's reforms. According to Molnár, "in the face of the exclusivity and power of the Lutheran interpretation, however, it was not easy for the Brethren to maintain the emphasis which they placed, alongside the revealed Word of God, on the witness of responsibly maintaining the congregation-building community of confessors, living under the discipline of Christ's cross even at the price of the loss of their civil freedom."[40] Senior Roh established his residence in a former Franciscan cloister called Karmel in Mladá Boleslav and opened a school there. The Unity maintained a printing press there, and the Inner Council began to pay greater attention to formal education, especially higher education for the clergy. Roh was

---

39. Müller, *Geschichte der böhmischen Brüder*, 2:1–3.
40. Molnár, "Brethren's Theology," 393.

instrumental in the decision of the synod of 1531 to "set aside" the writings of Luke, which were considered dry, scholastic, and hard to understand. Many later historians agree with this assessment of Luke's writing, even while expressing admiration for Luke's leadership and theology. Under Roh, the Brethren's priests were encouraged to use contemporary theological resources, such as Melanchthon's theology texts, in their teaching and preaching, rather than simply repeat what had been said in the past. Luke's *Children's Questions* was made livelier and simpler and was reprinted as the catechism.[41]

In 1531 Michael Weisse published his German translation of the Brethren's hymnal. This *Gesangbuch* introduced many German-speaking Protestants to the theology of the Brethren and was reprinted four times in Ulm from 1538 to 1540.[42] The hymnal was divided into eighteen sections. The first eight focused on the life of Christ (incarnation, birth, circumcision, epiphany, ministry, sufferings, resurrection, and ascension), which corresponded to the major holy days of the medieval church. There were hymns on the Holy Spirit, hymns for praise, prayer, teaching, and communion, and hymns for the daily hours of devotion. The collection of hymns for use throughout the day recalls the monastic daily office, but these hymns were intended to enable the laity to sacralize their secular labors. There was a specific collection of hymns for children, reflecting the Brethren's interest in education and family life. There were even hymns for those who had fallen away from the church. In addition to hymns for funerals and the Last Judgment, Weisse included hymns designed to teach people the proper way to honor the saints, especially the Virgin Mary.[43] Weisse's hymnal conformed closely to the major themes of the Brethren's catechism. Particularly noteworthy, in view of Moravian devotion under Zinzendorf, was the heavy focus on the life, sufferings, and ministry of Jesus.

The synod of 1531 decided to simplify Luke's liturgical calendar and standardize the Unity's order of worship. The new instructions for worship were announced in 1534. Changes in communion practice, such as the required use of unleavened wafers, altar cloths, candles, and nicer chalices, suggest Lutheran influence. The elders encouraged such changes so that the Unity would "not be

---

41. Müller, *Geschichte der böhmischen Brüder,* 2:4–6.
42. McKee, "Reforming Popular Piety," 7.
43. Ibid., 18.

unnecessarily separated from other people."[44] The Brethren established a middle position between the ornamentation of the Utraquists and the austerity of the Calvinists. The Inner Council also instructed pastors to conduct a general examination, including hearing confessions of sins, for their congregations at least once a year in order to improve discipline.

One of the most significant changes concerned baptism. The new leaders published a denunciation of the practice of rebaptism, and their new instructions for baptism included having the parents and sponsors lay their hands on the baby at the time of blessing to emphasize that baptism was an act of the church and not of the priest alone. Baptism was to be done with clean water poured out three times, with the words "in the name of the Father, and the Son, and the Holy Spirit, as the Lord Christ has commanded."[45] In denouncing the former practice of rebaptism, the Inner Council affirmed the Brethren's teaching that doctrine and practice are subject to change. The new seniors were convinced that Luther was more correct than Luke of Prague, Gregory, or previous Inner Councils on the subject of rebaptism.

One of the most remarkable signs of the close ties between Luther and the Unity was that Luther published, in German translation, two versions of the Unity's confession of faith (1532 and 1535); these confessions are discussed in the following chapter. Luther wrote a preface praising the Brethren, whom he called Pickards (Pikarts), as fellow evangelicals. He had read some of the writings of those "whom they [Catholics] call Pickards, no longer as hateful to me as they had been while I was a papist. I finally found among them a unique and great miracle, almost unheard of in the pope's church, namely, that, leaving aside human doctrines, they meditated in the law of the Lord day and night and were experienced and equipped in the Scriptures."[46] The sophistication of the Brethren's theology was surprising, he noted, given their poverty and lack of education.

In 1532 Jan Augusta (1500–1572) was made a member of the Inner Council and was consecrated a bishop. He proved to be one of the most energetic, effective, and controversial leaders of the Unity. Like Roh, he was in his early

44. Müller, *Geschichte der böhmischen Brüder*, 2:12–13.
45. Ibid., 2:13. The threefold application of water and the laying on of hands by the minister, parents, and sponsors remains the practice in the Moravian Church.
46. Pelikan and Hotchkiss, *Creeds and Confessions*, 1:800.

thirties when elected, and his father was also an artisan. Unlike Roh, Augusta had been raised in the Utraquist Church. His reading of old Hussite literature, especially the works of Hus and Matthew of Janov, had inspired him to seek a more rigorous expression of the Hussite church. With the approval of his pastor, who was sympathetic to the Brethren, he joined the Unity around 1524. Throughout his career in the Unity, he maintained close ties to Utraquist leaders.

Roh and Augusta recognized more clearly than most that Luther's unexpected success in Germany meant that the Brethren were no longer pariahs. For decades theologians and kings had condemned their core teachings as heretical and dangerous, but now elements of their doctrine were being taught in universities and preached in parishes from Saxony to England. It was no wonder that for a brief, shining moment some of the Brethren believed it possible that Western Christianity could unite under an evangelical banner, with the Unity accorded honor as the pioneer of a renewed and apostolic church. Inspired by this possibility, Augusta pushed the Unity to conform more closely to Lutheran doctrine and practice, and to consider unification with the Utraquist Church if that conservative Hussite body moved toward a more Protestant stance.[47] Though he died before it was written, the Bohemian Confession of 1575 reflected his efforts at Protestant union in Bohemia.

NEW ATTITUDES IN THE UNITY

Augusta actively promoted Luther's idea of salvation by faith through grace rather than through works. Like Luke of Prague forty years earlier, Augusta had grown concerned that the Brethren were striving too hard for perfection rather than relying on the saving merits of Christ. Some of the Brethren were legalistic and judgmental in their dealings with their brothers and sisters. Luther's clear and forceful writings on the Gospel seemed like an invigorating breeze, but Augusta did not lose sight of the importance of ethics in proclaiming salvation. In keeping with Luke's *Children's Questions*, Augusta emphasized that works remain a visible sign of inner faith. In some ways the debates of the

---

47. Říčan, *History of the Unity*, 129–35.

1530s over justification by faith echoed the tension between obedience and grace that preceded the schism of 1495. Luther's expansive understanding of vocation helped move the Brethren further away from their original ascetic orientation and toward more willing engagement in the world. One of the new notes sounded in Augusta's preaching and writing, though, was the importance of joy in believing.[48] In 1532 the Inner Council modified the Brethren's traditional instructions for right living, called the *Dekrety* (Decrees), so that they endorsed the joyfulness of daily living and expressed more openness to secular society.[49] For one thing, marriage was no longer merely tolerated as a means of reproduction and a way to avoid fornication; it was now described as a blessed union of two souls who delight in one another and in the Lord.[50] Likewise, parents were told that they should view children as precious gifts of God and delight in them. They should gradually and patiently teach children the Ten Commandments, the Lord's Prayer, and the hymns of the Brethren, and should explain the meaning of the worship services. Mothers and fathers alike were instructed to repeat the story of Jesus frequently and remind their children of the grace and love of God. Augusta cautioned parents that discipline did not mean abusing children. Beating children only produced wicked adults, Augusta wrote. He also wrote that all children should be brought to worship and to school.[51] In the next century, Comenius expanded this call for universal education within the Unity to a call for the education of all children.

Augusta's first publication after being made the leading senior of the Unity was *A Conversation Between a Scholar, who Loves the Honor and Pleasure of the World More than God, and an Uneducated Man who is Merely a Farmer but who Knows God and Salvation.* Such fictitious conversations, designed to show that simple faith is wiser than the subtleties of the learned and powerful, had been a common motif in Hussite literature. In Augusta's book, a farmer uses scriptural quotations to convince a scholar that the Bible offers assurance of salvation to those who have faith. There is no need to worry about death. Catholic doctrine, the farmer asserts, was intended to keep people in anxiety about their eternal destiny so that they could be more easily led and be more

---

48. Ibid., 128.
49. Müller, *Geschichte der böhmischen Brüder*, 2:16–21.
50. Říčan, *History of the Unity*, 128.
51. Müller, *Geschichte der böhmischen Brüder*, 2:22.

willing to spend their money for masses, indulgences, and other ways of "buying" salvation.[52] Augusta's adoption of Lutheran teaching on salvation was a
continuation of the original Hussite effort to free people from the oppression
of a theology that focused on anxiety rather than faith, love, and hope. Con-
spicuously absent from Augusta's presentation of the Gospel, though, was Luke's
insistence that assurance of salvation includes a life of willing obedience to the
demands of the Sermon on the Mount.

THE LIMITS OF LUTHERAN INFLUENCE

Church historians have made much of the Unity's adoption of Lutheran teaching under Augusta's leadership, but it is easy to overstate the Lutheran influence.[53] The turn toward Lutheranism was real, but it was not nearly as dramatic
a shift as the turn away from Chelčický in 1495. Those who joined the Unity
after 1528 continued to make a public break with the world and the state
church. In Říčan's words, they "promised to follow Christ under the cross in
obedience to the priests as to servants of Christ in the bond of peace and love;
and committed themselves to an honest life and to keeping the rules of order."
Though it was not evident in some of Augusta's publications, discipline, including discipline of the priests, remained a high priority. In 1537 Augusta
wrote instructions for the inspection of congregations and the Brethren's houses
that reaffirmed the Unity's original conviction that priests and lay judges who
were derelict, abusive, or otherwise unworthy had to be removed from spiritual office. What was new was the establishment of "due process" designed to
protect priests from slander.[54]

The Inner Council continued to provide instructions for the congregational
judges and to issue lists of approved vocations. In 1538 the council handed
down a list of things forbidden "under pain of expulsion," among them suing
a brother or sister in secular court, contracting a marriage without the permission of one's parents, shameless speech, slander, visiting taverns, gaming,
dancing, and luxurious clothing. Members were forbidden to charge interest on

52. Ibid., 2:78–81.
53. Štrupl, "Confessional Theology," 280.
54. Říčan, *History of the Unity*, 153, 161.

loans, with the exception that elderly persons, especially widows, were allowed to lend money at interest, but only to the wealthy. Tavern owners were instructed not to serve alcohol to drunk or unruly people. Oaths were permitted only "if done in the name of the Lord, within given limits, and with complete sincerity in the interest of love and righteousness."[55] This list of forbidden behavior went far beyond the discipline of the Lutherans, and Luther frequently criticized the Brethren for undermining the Gospel with works righteousness. The Brethren in turn objected to Luther's reliance on secular power to promote the reformation of the church.

Clearly the Lutheranizing tendency of the Unity under Roh and Augusta was not extreme. It primarily involved modifying the Brethren's traditional teaching in ways that conformed more closely to an emerging Protestant consensus. Most significant, the Unity abandoned Luke's position on the seven sacraments and adopted the Protestant view that the only true sacraments are baptism and Eucharist. This had less impact on actual church life than one might expect, however, since the Unity retained the other five sacraments as rites of the church. As we have seen, the Unity had from the beginning rejected much of the Catholic Church's dogma on confirmation, marriage, ordination, penance, and the final anointing in favor of a proto-Protestant position. In the 1530s they stopped calling these rites "sacraments," but there was little change in either the practice or doctrine regarding them.

The Brethren's treatment of the Eucharist provides a good example of their judicious appropriation of Protestant ideas in a way that preserved the greatest possible common ground with the Lutheran position without abandoning traditional Unity teaching. The Inner Council approved of Luther's rejection of the doctrine of transubstantiation, and Roh and Augusta both used the strongest possible language to express the reality of Christ's spiritual presence in the Eucharist. But the Brethren consistently rejected Luther's idea that Christ's *physical* body and blood became present along with the bread and wine after consecration (consubtantiation rather than transubstantiation). Likewise, the Lutheran doctrine of Christ's ubiquity, whereby Christ was physically present on every altar each Sunday, made no sense to the Brethren.[56] Christ is

---

55. Ibid., 161–62.

56. Bengt Hägglund, *History of Theology*, trans. Gene J. Lund (St. Louis: Concordia, 1968), 239–44; Pelikan, *Christian Tradition*, 4:190–203; Cameron, *European Reformation*, 161–67. This was a dividing

physically present only in heaven, they taught, but he is sacramentally present in the Eucharist. The council repeatedly assured Luther that they rejected the Zwinglian and Pikart idea that the bread and wine were mere signs. Communion was more than a memorial meal. Thus, while it is correct to say that the Unity's revised communion liturgy reflected Luther's influence, this did not mean that the Unity adopted Lutheran sacramental theology.[57] Instead, it was an indication of the Unity's ecumenism and irenicism in trying to establish common ground with the German Reformation.

In their teaching on salvation, the Brethren likewise modified their preaching with the help of Luther's insight into the relationship of the law and Gospel, but they did not adopt his strict dichotomy. They maintained their traditional teaching that the covenant of grace Christ established through his death includes the law of Christ. Those who are saved by faith need to fulfill Christ's commandments; faith must be completed in love. Although they agreed with Luther that the work of Christ in redemption and the human response in faith through God's grace are essential, they continued to teach that love and hope are also essential. In general, the Brethren viewed the doctrine of the Lutheran reformers as incomplete because, as Říčan put it, "they were preaching righteousness gained from faith without any works of faith; because they were not doing justice to the full meaning of the Lord's Supper, because in the Apostles' Creed they were giving prominence to faith in Christ while passing over the other articles, because they did not base their teaching on the whole of Scripture, and particularly because . . . they taught as if salvation was obtainable through faith alone without the agency of the church and its servants."[58]

The Pietist movement, an eighteenth-century renewal movement among Protestants in Germany, made similar judgments about the sixteenth-century reformers. The Pietists hoped to "complete the Reformation" of Luther by focusing on praxis.[59] Even during the days of Augusta, who was most enthusiastic about Luther's works, the Brethren taught the importance of "the obedience of faith, which must imprint a character on the whole Christian life, in private

---

point among Protestants, most notably at the Marburg Colloquy, where Luther insisted that Christ's words, "this is my body," must be taken literally.

57. Müller, *Geschichte der böhmischen Brüder*, 2:25.

58. Říčan, *History of the Unity*, 119–20.

59. Carter Lindberg, *The Third Reformation?* (Macon: Mercer University Press, 1983), provides a good introduction to Pietism, particularly in connection with the Protestant Reformation.

FIG. 17   Cathedral of Saint Vitus, Prague.

and in association with others as well."[60] In general, the Unity remained closer in spirit to Philip Melanchthon than to Luther, and the Inner Council maintained a good relationship with the Lutherans as long as Melanchthon's voice was prominent.

It is also helpful to recall that Michael Weisse continued to offer a Zwinglian perspective within the Unity throughout the 1530s and 1540s, the period of the Brethren's strongest Lutheran orientation. Weisse was instrumental in providing German translations of the Unity's hymns and confessions of faith, but Roh sometimes reprimanded him for expressing the Unity's theology in terms that were too Zwinglian. According to Müller, the problem was not just that Weisse's translations were too Zwinglian but that Roh found the original Czech hymns insufficiently Lutheran.[61] This suggests that the Inner Council allowed a certain level of disagreement among the clergy in the sixteenth century. Doctrinal uniformity was less important to the Brethren than to other Protestant churches, but there was a consensus on the essentials.

60. Říčan, *History of the Unity*, 124.
61. Müller, *Geschichte der böhmischen Brüder*, 2:29–33.

THE UNITY, UTRAQUISTS, AND SECULAR AUTHORITY

The one area of the Unity's life that changed significantly with the Inner Council's Lutheran orientation was an increased openness to society. Now that German princes and imperial cities were endorsing church reform, formerly reluctant nobles and prominent citizens in Bohemia and Moravia were willing to risk open membership in the Unity. With Luther's prompting, the Unity adopted Hus's teaching that secular authority derives from God and is valid when used in accordance with God's law. Secular lords, they taught, would be judged by the Lord according to how they administered justice and served the needs of the people. This was quite a change from the original suspicion that nobles would be unable to live as Christians. It also went beyond the grudging acceptance of nobles as members after 1495. The Unity no longer expressed reservations about the salvation of nobles and wealthy people, but even the mighty were still held to the discipline of the church.

The number and influence of nobles in the Unity increased dramatically after the public baptism of several nobles in the Brethren's congregation of Mladá Boleslav in 1530.[62] The Unity continued to teach that people must obey their earthly lords so long as their decrees did not interfere in matters of eternal salvation, but in the sixteenth century the Inner Council emphasized the responsibility of secular lords to administer justice and rule wisely. Increasingly, educated members of the nobility served as apologists and advocates for the Unity. With their new openness to secular authorities, the Unity gained greater visibility in Czech society and government, which in turn raised anxieties about the Unity in the royal court.

Another factor in the often confusing relationship between the Unity and secular and religious authorities in Bohemia was the existence of a reform party within the Utraquist Church that sought to move the Utraquists further away from Catholicism and toward Lutheran theology. One of its leaders was the preacher at the prominent Týn Church, Václav Mitmánek, who had once been a member of the Unity. At a national Utraquist synod in 1543, Mitmánek aggressively pushed a plan for church reform that included uniting the Hussite churches into a single Czech national church that would be moderately

---

62. Říčan, *History of the Unity*, 130.

Lutheran.[63] King Ferdinand opposed Mitmánek's plan, and when the Týn preacher defended the Unity's long history of resistance to royal power, Ferdinand forbade him to preach and banished him from Bohemia. He was imprisoned for a time, escaped, and died in exile in Poland.[64]

Augusta shared Mitmánek's hope that a reformed Utraquist Church and the Unity could cooperate or even unite, but most of the Utraquist clergy and laity were opposed to the radical changes the Lutherans proposed. Around 1540 Utraquist officials renewed their opposition to the Unity. To quote Říčan once more, the Prague consistory "publicly proclaimed doubts as to the validity of the ministry of the Brethren's priests. Through this they threw into doubt the validity of marriages contracted before them. And they suspected that through the vows required by new members the Unity bound them to total obedience to the elders. They also alleged that the Unity compelled large donations from new members."[65]

These were old arguments, but the context was different in 1540 than it had been in 1508. Emboldened by the apparent success of the Reformation in Germany, the Unity ordained a dozen priests in a public ceremony in Mladá Boleslav on June 20, 1540, in open defiance of the Mandate of Saint James. Augusta published his sermon, which defended the legitimacy of the Brethren's priesthood on the basis of New Testament teaching and early church history. It is particularly interesting that Augusta's defense used neither the Waldensians nor Brother Michael's ordination as a Roman priest to justify the Brethren's priesthood. Against the Utraquist bishop Klatovský, Augusta argued that the Unity had the right to ordain priests without apostolic succession. The moderate Utraquists accused the Brethren of being combative by publicly ordaining priests. Ferdinand moved to enforce the mandates against the Brethren, but the advance of Turkish troops toward Bohemia and Moravia forced the king to turn his attention away from religious issues in 1543, sparing the Unity briefly. But Augusta's public defiance of the Mandate of Saint James made the Unity a threat to the public order.

63. It is surprising that Zdeněk David says so little about Mitmánek in his erudite presentation of the relationship between the Utraquists and the Lutherans in *Finding the Middle Way*. Though he refers to Mitmánek as a "staunch and upright Lutheran" (11), he dismisses him as the "alleged inspirer of the Evangelical trend" because he had been ordained by a Catholic bishop in Venice (136).

64. Říčan, *History of the Unity*, 157–58.

65. Ibid., 153. For the material in the following two paragraphs, see 153–61.

There was one area in which the Utraquist consistory and the Unity found important and lasting common ground. In 1541 the Inner Council published Roh's edition of the hymnal *Songs for the Praise of God*, which included 482 hymns and about three hundred melodies. The hymnal drew on more than a century of Czech hymnody stretching back to Hus. Nearly a quarter of the hymns can be traced to Luke of Prague (either as author or as translator). The Prague consistory eventually approved the hymnal for use in all Utraquist congregations, and thus it became the first Czech national hymnal. In 1544 the council also published Roh's German-language hymnal *Ein Gesangbuch der Brüder in Behemen und Merherrn*, based on Weisse's 1531 hymnal.

During this period the nobility in Moravia attempted to establish a measure of religious toleration there. The Mandate of Saint James, which was the basis for persecution of the Unity in Bohemia, had no force in Moravia, so Moravian nobles had more freedom to allow religious dissent. The region was largely Protestant by the middle of the sixteenth century. According to one twentieth-century historian, "The dwindling Roman Catholic minority was reduced to some fifty parishes (Czech and German) out of a total of over 600 in Moravia. The Unity of the Brethren experienced steady growth in Moravia and lived peacefully under the protection of the nobility."[66] In Moravia, in addition to the three traditional Czech churches, there were also Lutherans, Reformed, and Anabaptists to contend with.

When Ferdinand was crowned king in 1526, the nobles in Moravia requested that he "allow all and every one of us to persevere unhindered in the faith of the Law of God and of the Christian religion so that everyone might serve the Lord God in freedom and peace according to what one considers right following the Law and Teachings of the Lord." The king gave his verbal rather than written consent to this request. After a knight named John Dubčanský was imprisoned for his religious beliefs, the Moravian estates declared to the king, "People cannot be compelled to faith by force, for faith is but a gift from God and cannot be given to anybody by anyone else except God himself."[67] This protest marked a milestone on the path toward religious toleration in Europe, for it argued for full freedom of conscience in matters of faith rather

66. Jarold Knox Zeman, "The Rise of Religious Liberty in the Czech Reformation," *Central European History* 2 (1973): 144–46.
67. Quoted in ibid., 140–41, 146.

than trying to establish the orthodoxy of a dissenting group. It is interesting that years later Ferdinand, as the king of Moravia, managed to persuade the Council of Trent to allow the lay chalice in his lands in 1564. He drank from the chalice himself shortly before he died. This toleration extended only to the Utraquist Church, however, not to the Unity or other Protestants in Moravia.

REBELLION AND PERSECUTION

For a time it looked as though the German Reformation might proceed peacefully, but the situation changed dramatically in the 1540s. Efforts at compromise between Catholics and Protestants had failed repeatedly, and both sides grew more militant in their opposition. Having halted the Turkish advance and made peace with France in 1544, Emperor Charles V was prepared to restore order in his realm by moving against the Protestants militarily and ecclesiastically. On the ecclesiastical front, Charles finally persuaded Pope Paul III in 1545 to convene the most important general council since the Council of Constance, perhaps since that of Nicea. The council opened in the city of Trent on December 13 and met intermittently until 1563. Protestant and Catholic reformers alike had called for such a general council for decades, but hopes that Trent would resolve the religious conflict in Europe were dashed when Protestant representatives were excluded from the deliberations.[68] In its early sessions the Council of Trent formally rejected many of the central Protestant doctrines and reaffirmed traditional dogma on the seven sacraments, transubstantiation, veneration of the saints, clerical celibacy, and papal authority. Later sessions of the council addressed many of the abuses that had caused the widespread discontent that led to the Reformation.

In 1546, the year Martin Luther died, Charles invaded Germany and was opposed by the Schmalkaldic League of Protestant nobles. He was victorious, and captured the elector of Saxony, Johann Friedrich, at the battle of Muhlberg in 1547.[69] A number of Bohemian nobles either supported the rebellious Protestant lords or at least failed to send troops to assist the emperor, and they

---

68. Owen Chadwick, *The Reformation*, vol. 3 of Chadwick, *Penguin History of the Church*, 264–81.
69. Cameron, *European Reformation*, 346–47.

suffered his wrath after the war. Most of the disobedient nobles were Protestant, and several were members of the Unity of the Brethren. King Ferdinand retaliated by moving against Protestant churches and executing a handful of townspeople and nobles in Hradčaný Square in the Little Town section of Prague.[70]

Senior Augusta's aggressive attempt to increase the Unity's influence in Bohemian society had the unintended consequence of making the Brethren the primary target of Habsburg vengeance. The king blamed the Unity for the insurrection, which was not surprising since the Unity had been explicitly outlawed in Bohemia since 1508. The king also knew that an attack on the Utraquist Church, which had strong popular support, would have led to open warfare throughout the kingdom. By attacking the Brethren he could send a strong message to the Utraquists while removing a heretical group that had been a thorn in the empire's side for a century, without risking civil war. The greatest blame for the rebellion was placed on Augusta personally for stirring up dissension in the kingdom. According to later historians, the charges against Augusta "were false and were clearly either deliberately fabricated assumptions or an intentionally inaccurate interpretation of reality." It is also true, however, that under Augusta "the Unity no longer appeared only as a peaceful society cultivating religious life in the seclusion of its congregations, but rather as one ready to act as a servant of public life."[71] The intemperate senior of the Unity had made many enemies over the years, and it is not difficult to see why, given such harsh words as these:

> All the Utraquist priests are dishonorable, immoral, proud, conceited, avaricious, cruel, merciless, slanderers without goodness or holy obedience, discordant, disorderly, simonical, ignorant, unclean, fornicators, adulterous, luxurious, banqueters, worthless, impious, clownish, jokers, lazy, vagabondish, tavern seekers, gamesters, gluttons, imbibers, drunkards, flirtatious, living with concubines, mockers, rumormongers, detractors, thieves, murderers, insubordinate to the ordinances of manorial lords and of municipalities, self-willed, unmannerly, restless, stormy, vengeful,

70. Říčan, *History of the Unity,* 168.
71. Ibid., 169–70.

envious, and in brief accustomed to many sins, devoid of Christ's ecclesiastical discipline, and incorrigible, etc.[72]

In October 1547 Ferdinand renewed the Mandate of Saint James. A second mandate the following year forbade the Brethren to hold worship even in
their own homes. Churches were barricaded and preachers arrested. Utraquist
priests were required to investigate and report violators. The Crown confiscated cities in which the Unity had been active, and gave their houses of worship
to the Catholics.[73] In response, some Brethren chose to worship in Utraquist
churches, and the Inner Council permitted Brethren to be rebaptized as Utraquists in order to avoid arrest. Augusta objected to this leniency and urged the
Brethren to resist the Crown, but he was arrested, tortured, and imprisoned for
sixteen years. The Unity in Bohemia never fully recovered from the persecutions, and the center of the church shifted to Moravia, which was more tolerant.

NEW BISHOPS AND THEOLOGIANS

With the unexpected death of Senior Mach in Prussia in 1551, Augusta, still
imprisoned, became the only living bishop of the Unity. Through extraordinary means, including bribing guards, the Inner Council managed to send
secret messages to the bishop asking him to agree to an election of new seniors, but he refused. When the authorities discovered that Augusta was com-
municating with the outside world, his imprisonment was made so severe that
he became gravely ill. The Inner Council had no news for months and feared
that he had died. Finally the council decided that it could wait no longer and
proceeded to elect two new seniors in 1553. Jan Černý and Matthew Červenka
were consecrated as seniors by the oldest members of the Inner Council rather
than by a senior, as was the custom. The council justified this move in part by
using Augusta's own defense of the Brethren's right to ordain priests without

72. David, *Finding the Middle Way*, 10. Such quotations cast doubt on Dunn's claim that the Unity's
"unaggressiveness and tolerance was not only an alternative response to the aggressive, even violent context of the 15th century. It was also a means of maintaining Unity within the Unitas Fratrum." Dunn,
"Preserving the Unity," 22.

73. Říčan, *History of the Unity*, 171.

apostolic succession. Černý was appointed the Unity judge, and Červenka returned from Prussia to become the official Unity writer.[74] It is interesting that Augusta did not reconsecrate the new seniors after his release from prison. Thus the direct succession of seniors from the time of Matthew (1467) was broken.[75]

In 1559 Augusta was allowed to contact the Unity, and he expressed his opposition to what the Inner Council had done. The council explained that the consecration of the two bishops was necessary because it was normal for more than one senior to serve on the council. No senior was to rule without the agreement of the others.[76] In other words, the Inner Council reaffirmed the Unity's traditional reluctance to place authority in the hands of a single person. Instead it embraced a conferential system, over the objections of Augusta.

THE BRETHREN IN PRUSSIA

Many Brethren fled to Poland and established permanent congregations there, the most important of which was at Leszno (Lissa). That congregation, discussed in chapter 12, would become very important in the next century. A number of Brethren fled to Prussia, which bordered Poland. The borders of central Europe remained in flux for centuries, and some of the Polish cities where the Brethren were established became part of Prussia. A list of immigrants to Prussia reveals an interesting picture of the Unity in the sixteenth century. There were five millers, one baker, three cobblers, two clothiers, two coopers, at least one cutler, a locksmith, a joiner, a rope maker, a tailor, a vintner, two clerks, and a schoolmaster. They were able to establish a small, independent economy in Prussia. In general the Brethren found that they had more freedom in Poland than in Prussia, where the elders were required to submit to the rulings of the national Lutheran authorities. Under the Lutherans, the Brethren had to curtail their household gatherings, congregational discipline, and baptismal regulations. They also had to wear vestments and adopt the Lutheran way of celebrating the Eucharist. Basically, they were expected

74. Ibid., 194–96.
75. Augusta did consecrate the bishops elected after his release from prison; therefore bishops in the modern Moravian Church can still trace their succession from the first bishop in 1467.
76. Říčan, *History of the Unity*, 199.

to be Czech-speaking Lutherans.[77] It seemed to some of the Brethren that these restrictions were as bad as the conditions they had fled in Bohemia.

Conditions in Prussia worsened during the Lutheran Church's Osiander controversy. Osiander taught that Christ, rather than merely declaring a person justified, makes him or her righteous. "By his divine nature he resided in a person and thus made that person righteous."[78] This view was virtually the same as the traditional teaching of the Brethren, as we have seen, but the strict Lutherans, led by Flacius, declared it heretical. In Prussia, the Lutheran leadership required that all Protestants affirm the teaching that people are declared righteous by God rather than made righteous by Christ. In 1574 most of the Brethren left Prussia because such "theological disputes were repugnant" and because they insisted on their traditional teaching that Christians do become righteous through the grace of Christ and the agency of the Holy Spirit.[79] This was a major reason why the new elders moved the Unity away from Lutheranism, against the wishes of Augusta.

The Brethren's relationship to the German Reformation was at times controversial and even confrontational, but the discussions with Luther and Melanchthon had a lasting impact on the Unity of the Brethren, particularly in terms of sacramental theology. This was seen clearly in the most important statement produced by the Brethren after the contact with Luther. In 1535 the Inner Council approved a new confession of faith that was clearly Protestant and that served as the Unity's primary doctrinal statement long after Augusta's death.

---

77. Ibid., 187.
78. Pelikan, *Christian Tradition*, 4:150–52.
79. Říčan, *History of the Unity*, 191–92.

Ten

THE CONFESSION OF 1535

The most lasting fruit of the Brethren's theological discussions with Martin Luther was the composition of a new confession of faith in 1535, which Luther published in 1538. The Confession of 1535 was the product of eight decades of theological discussion and development from the time of Brother Gregory. Much that the Unity had taught in catechisms, sermons, and guides for pastors was presented succinctly in this confession, but its publication also marked a new chapter in the history of the Brethren's theology. The most notable difference between this confession and previous Unity writings is its clarity. The confession lacks the argumentative and Scholastic tone of previous works. Ironically, this confession, which was written for professional theologians, is in some ways more clear, concise, and understandable than Luke's *Questions for Children*. The writers of the Unity's confession clearly benefited from their contacts with the humanist scholars in Wittenberg. The Confession of 1535 remained the principal statement of faith, with minor revisions, for the Unity for the rest of its history.[1]

THE WRITING OF THE CONFESSION

The first version of the confession was written in 1532 at the urging of Margrave George von Brandenburg, a Lutheran prince with connections to Bohemia.

---

1. Müller, *Geschichte der böhmischen Brüder*, 2:111. For a summary of the changes over the next century, see Štrupl, "Confessional Theology," 278–90.

The 1532 statement was most probably written by Roh, and was translated into German by Michael Weisse. It was published in Zurich in 1533, but the Unity's elders, especially Roh and Augusta, were dissatisfied with Weisse's translation because of his use of Zwinglian terminology. A second German translation was made by an anonymous translator and sent to the margrave. Luther published this version under the title *Rechenschaft des glaubens: Der dienst und Ceremonien, der Bruder in Behemen und Mehrern, welche von etliche Waldenser genannt warden* (An Account of the Faith, Worship, and Ceremonies of the Brethren in Bohemia and Moravia, which are called Waldensians by Some). In his preface Luther highlighted his points of disagreement with the Brethren (discussed in the previous chapter).[2] Despite the erroneous identification of the Brethren with the Waldensians, the 1532 confession included a brief history of the Unity that stressed its connection to the Czech Reformation and the Four Articles of Prague. Then it dealt with the Brethren's doctrine in fourteen paragraphs.

Unlike previous statements of faith by the Brethren, this one was not structured according to the Apostles' Creed. It opened with a statement on the authority of scripture, followed by discussions of God, human sinfulness, redemption, the Holy Spirit, repentance, good works, growth in faith, and joyful hope in God. True to the Unity's heritage, emphasis was placed on the need for good works along with faith. The third section addressed order and discipline in the Unity in a long discussion of how people were received into the Unity. This was many Protestants' first introduction to the Unity's strict discipline and requirements for admission. The final section dealt with ministerial things such as the clergy, preaching, and the sacraments. For the first time in a Unity text, only baptism and Holy Communion were identified as sacraments.[3]

The 1532 confession of faith reflects the influence of Luther, but it still dealt with many of the concerns of an earlier age. It was also awkwardly written, especially in translation. At the urging of some of the Bohemian nobility, especially Lord Krajek, the Inner Council wrote a new confession, to be presented to King Ferdinand in the hope of gaining greater toleration for the Brethren.

2. Pelikan and Hotchkiss, *Creeds and Confessions,* 1:796–98; Müller, *Geschichte der böhmischen Brüder,* 2:40–42; Říčan, *History of the Unity,* 135.
3. Müller, *Geschichte der böhmischen Brüder,* 2:43–44.

The document was written in Czech and was signed by a dozen members of the high nobility and more than thirty knights in November 1535.[4] Krajek presented the confession to the king in a private audience on November 11, but Ferdinand was not impressed by a statement of faith coming from ordinary people and told Krajek, "You are neither Pope, nor Emperor, nor King. But believe what you will. We will not hinder you if you should want to drive yourself into hell."[5] Ferdinand also made it clear that the confession would not alter the law in Bohemia, where only the Catholic and Utraquist churches were tolerated. When the confession was published in Czech in 1536, it included a long apology by the elders that highlighted Augusta's efforts at uniting the Utraquists and Brethren as Czech Protestants.[6]

After the failure with Ferdinand, the Unity leadership hoped to become a part of the German Protestant alliance that Melanchthon and Martin Bucer were forming. In order to facilitate closer relations, the Confession of 1535 was translated into Latin for publication. The Latin version was more concise and precise than the original Czech had been. A delegation led by Augusta took the Latin confession to Wittenberg and met with Luther and Melanchthon, who raised objections to the articles defending clerical celibacy and rejecting deathbed absolution.[7] Modifications were made to satisfy Luther, and the confession was translated from Latin into German. Luther provided a very positive preface, and it was published in 1538 (1:799–833).

On the very sensitive question of the Eucharist, Luther wrote, "We do not want to be Christ's master, but his disciples. We do not wish to teach him but to obey him. We believe simply that the bread is the body of Christ and the wine is his blood, without troubling ourselves for the sake of physicians and mathematicians who want to know and measure everything, such as whether the divinity of Christ had been present in his hair and feet. We have nothing to do with them."[8] This was surprisingly close to the traditional position of the Brethren that Luke had presented to Luther a decade earlier. In May 1536 several prominent Protestant theologians, including Luther and Bucer, had signed

---

4. Pelikan and Hotchkiss, *Creeds and Confessions*, 1:797. Hereafter cited parenthetically by volume and page number.

5. Müller, *Geschichte der böhmischen Brüder*, 2:72; Říčan, *History of the Unity*, 142.

6. Říčan, *History of the Unity*, 144.

7. Müller, *Geschichte der böhmischen Brüder*, 2:105–6, 67, 107.

8. Quoted in ibid., 2:108.

the Wittenberg Concord, an agreement on the Eucharist that was remarkably consistent with the traditional teaching of the Unity (2:796–801). Luther indicated that after much conversation with the Brethren he had finally decided that they should serve as the apostles to the Bohemians, while he would be the "apostles to the Germans," a reference to Acts 15.

Though published in 1538, this confession is generally known as the Confession of 1535 because that is the year in which it was written. It was clearly inspired and influenced by Melanchthon's Augsburg Confession of 1530, but it is an overstatement to say that it is modeled on that confession.[9] The Confession of 1535 represents the traditional concerns of the Unity and differs from the Lutheran statement in a number of ways that are discussed below. The late Jaroslav Pelikan made the only English translation of the confession in the 1940s, and in 2003 he and Valerie Hotchkiss published that translation in their three-volume collection *Creeds and Confessions of Faith in the Christian Tradition* (1:796–833). It is regrettable that they placed the Brethren's confession at the end of the medieval section rather than in the section on the Reformation era, where it belongs. This was done no doubt because the Unity of the Brethren was founded before the sixteenth century. Certainly one could argue that the confessional statements of Gregory or Luke of Prague, with their defense of the seven sacraments, belong in the medieval era, but the Confession of 1535 is most definitely a sixteenth-century Protestant statement of faith.

The most theologically significant change from the Unity's previous statements of faith is that the Confession of 1535 does not overtly use the most distinctive aspect of the Unity's doctrine, the distinction between things essential, ministerial, and incidental. Those educated in the Unity probably recognized the continuity between this confession and the earlier writings of Luke, but this seminal idea was muted in conversations with the Lutherans, who stressed the unity of doctrine. Rather than reject the teaching on essentials and ministerials, the authors of the Confession of 1535 adapted the Unity's doctrine for a Lutheran audience. The importance of the teaching was diminished further as the Unity came increasingly under the influence of Calvinism in the late sixteenth century and adopted the terminology of Reformed theology. The tripartite distinction was not entirely lost, however; it was retained in the

9. Říčan, *History of the Unity*, 143, 148.

Brethren's hymnals and catechisms. Comenius restored this idea to its central place in the Unity's doctrine in the seventeenth century, and offered it as a means of reuniting the church.

Luke's teaching on the essentials is evident in article 3 of the confession, "Of the Faith of the Holy Trinity," which focuses on the work of God: "There are three outstanding works appropriate to him alone and to none other, namely, the work of creation, of redemption, and of preservation or sanctification" (1:803). This is a succinct way of saying that the work of the Trinity is what is essential for salvation, and is consistent with the Unity's reluctance to speculate about the divine nature. The Brethren's theology focused on what was known about God's work in the world through creation, redemption, and sanctification rather than on speculation about the inner life of the Trinity.[10] The Unity focused on the economic rather than the essential Trinity.

The authors of the confession apparently confused the Apostles' and Nicene Creeds (2:1). Article 3 gives the orthodox definition of the Trinity based on the Nicene Creed—three distinct persons with no distinction in essence—but the creed was identified as the "apostolic" statement. This confusion is understandable, as the Unity made little use of the Nicene Creed and rarely entered into theological discussions on the nature of the Godhead. There is nothing in the Confession of 1535 comparable to the first article of the Augsburg Confession, which discusses the nature of the Trinity. The Augsburg Confession also includes explicit condemnations of ancient Christian heretics such as the "Valentians, Arians, Eunomians, Mohamedans," and "Samostenes" (2:59). True to their heritage, the Brethren did not speculate on such divine mysteries; neither did they include statements condemning others. This is one of the most striking differences between the Unity's confession and the Augsburg. The latter also condemns a number of contemporary "heretics," such as the Anabaptists, but the Brethren's confession does not. It simply asserts what the Brethren believed to be true about God and the law of Christ. Their faith was based on scripture, on their experience as followers of Christ, and on the teachings of the early church. They saw no need to enter into debates about theological subtleties and metaphysics.

10. Molnár, "Brethren's Theology," 409–10.

SCRIPTURE

The Confession of 1535, like its immediate predecessor, begins with a statement on the authority of scripture rather than a creedal affirmation (1:801–2). This stands in marked contrast to fifteenth-century confessions of the Brethren that began with the Apostles' Creed, but it also differs from the Augsburg Confession, which begins with a discussion of the Nicene Creed. The Unity's confessions of 1532 and 1535 were the first Christian confessions of faith to begin with a discussion of the authority of scripture. The First Helvetic Confession (1536) of the Swiss Reformed Church also made scripture the first article of faith (2:280–91), and we should not discount the possibility that the Helvetic Confession was influenced by the Unity. The Brethren's statement on scripture was rooted in the original concerns of the Czech Reformation. The apostolic writings, it said, "should be preferred to the writings of anyone else as sacred to profane writings and divine to human ones." It is interesting that this statement defines scripture as those writings "received by the fathers and endowed with canonical authority," thus acknowledging that the canon of scripture was determined by the early church rather than given directly by the apostles. True to the heritage of Hus, the Confession of 1535 makes the translation of scripture into modern languages a point of doctrine. Scripture should not be an arcane text for the intellectual elite but should be "understood by all" and believed "implicitly and simply." Moreover, there is no need for elaborate allegorical interpretations or complex hermeneutical principles. Ordinary followers of Christ should be able to read and interpret his law in scripture. It is not surprising that the Brethren's confession, like other sixteenth-century Protestant statements, contains more than two hundred biblical quotations and allusions to support its claims.

There is no discussion of the difference between the Old Testament and the Apocrypha in the Brethren's confession, but in article 20:4, Sirach (also known as Ecclesiasticus) is quoted as an authority (1:833). It is probably wise not to place too much weight on this fact, though, since this section also includes a number of allusions to classical authors like Cicero. More important is the fact that the confession does not quite promote the idea of *sola scriptura*, or the authority of scripture alone. Scripture is uniquely authoritative, but the confession also affirms "that the writings of the Doctors of the Church, especially the ancient ones, are to be regarded as true and trustworthy." They are to be used to instruct the people, guide the church, and help in interpreting scripture unless they clearly contradict scripture (1:802). This is also consistent with the main stream of the Czech Reformation, as we have seen, but other Protestant confessions minimize the role of tradition in interpreting scripture.

Consistent with their traditional perspective, the Brethren's confession defined scripture primarily in terms of the New Testament. Scripture was inspired, not dictated, by God "through the instrumentality chiefly of Peter and Paul." The identification of Paul as the chief author of the New Testament is obvious, but it is curious that Peter is presented as equal to Paul. Most probably the elders believed that Peter was the primary source for Matthew's Gospel as well as Mark's. Surprisingly, the Apostle John, who was generally believed to have written a Gospel, three Epistles, and an apocalypse, is not mentioned. Neither are Moses, David, or the Old Testament prophets. This tells us that in 1535 the Unity continued to give priority to the synoptic Gospels and Pauline writings. Not surprisingly, there are very few quotations from the Old Testament in the confession.

CATECHESIS

Nor is it surprising that a discussion of the catechism follows the statement on scripture. The Brethren taught that children should be educated in "true religion and piety" from an early age. Unlike the Lutherans, they identified the catechism as "a spiritual law" that should be believed, confessed, and "attested to by works." Consistently the confession asserts that faith and works go together. There is no attempt to separate the theological assertions of the Apostles' Creed from the ethical demands of the Decalogue and the Lord's Prayer. This section on the catechism has two interesting features, however. The first is that it describes the catechism simply as the Decalogue, the Creed, and the Lord's Prayer, which were indeed central to the Brethren's catechism, as they would be for Luther's catechisms. But several things from the Brethren's catechism are missing in this list, especially the beatitudes and the "six smaller commandments" of the Sermon of the Mount. These had long been at the heart of the Unity's theology and practice, and they continued to play a vital role in the internal life of the Unity, but the Confession of 1535 is silent in this respect. Clearly the Brethren were trying to assimilate into the Protestant world, and over the next century their original focus on the Sermon on the Mount gradually diminished. It would be revived in the work of Comenius.

The second interesting feature is that the confession discusses the relationship between church and state in the section on educating children. Children are to be taught to obey all just laws that do not conflict with Christ's instruction, and prayers for the Holy Roman emperor are justified on the grounds that "all men, whether friend or foe, should be prayed for." What is most significant is that prayers for the emperor and obedience to secular government are both based on the requirements of love rather than on the idea that God has ordained civil authority (1:803). Clearly, though the Brethren were engaging the world more positively, they retained their suspicion of secular government. This discussion of prayers for the ruling authorities has its roots in Chelčický's exegesis of Romans 13, discussed in chapter 5, but article 16 addresses the question of secular power differently (1:826–27). Most of this section affirms Luther's exegesis of Matthew 22:21 that Christians should render to Caesar what is Caesar's, but in matters of the soul should be obedient to the Word of God (2:67). Despite the Lutheran influence, the Brethren's theology still did not allow for any notion of absolutism or the divine right of kings to rule. The state was not sacred, and neither were government officials higher than the common people.

JUSTIFICATION BY FAITH

The Brethren's Confession of 1535 follows the example of the Augsburg Confession in addressing the doctrine of original sin early on, immediately after the article on the Trinity. It depicts humans as "sinners directly by their very nature and from the womb" (1:804). The Brethren were not entirely consistent in their attitude toward inherent sin. In his study of the Unity's doctrine, Molnár pointed out that in the sixteenth century one of the Brethren's best theologians, Matthew Červenka, "held that even the original human beings were not perfect but were created for perfection so that they might come to this in their creatureliness. Yet, from its first generation the Unity taught that sin, in fact, adheres to the human spirit and that it manifests itself most dangerously on the religious plane. Sin is the free act of a person, rebellion against dependence on God, disobedience. It has corrupted humans to such an extent that they do not recognize their own corruption and do not acknowledge it. It must be revealed to them."[11] In other words, sin was associated with human finitude and imperfection rather than with God's wrath. The story of Adam and Eve illustrated the natural tendency of all humans to fall short of perfection rather than the idea of inherited guilt and punishment. Unlike the Augsburg Confession, the Brethren's confession contains no explicit condemnation of Pelagianism, although it does express the Augustinian belief that God alone can save.

The Brethren's confession maintained their traditional understanding that salvation has a subjective aspect. Individuals needed "to have a change of mind" and recognize their sinfulness if they were to have faith in the salvation achieved by Christ. God's grace works internally, leading a person to repentance and change of life. One of the longer sections of the confession deals with repentance, understood as the decision to turn away from sin and toward God. The confession acknowledges that when the Word of God makes a person aware of his or her mortality and sinfulness, the mind is "disquieted" and the heart is "anxious, broken, and trembling." Such self-knowledge could lead to despair, but true repentance required, and delivered, faith in Christ and trust in his mercy. Such repentance includes the death of the old person and his or her rebirth in Christ. This is accomplished through God's grace by faith, defined as believing "without doubting that what is promised through the keys really takes place" (1:806).

It is important to note that repentance is connected to confession and absolution. Those who do not repent "will be condemned to woeful destruction." Surprisingly, there is no mention of election in this section, but there are clear parallels to Luther's theology of law and Gospel. One distinctive aspect of the Brethren's teaching on sin is evident in the assertion that the many forms of human suffering in this life are God's punishment for sin. Since suffering is part of God's judgment on humankind, it should be borne patiently (1:805). This idea of patiently enduring suffering was connected to the Unity's understanding that one of the marks of the true church is persecution.

11. Ibid., 410.

FIG. 18   Kalich (Chalice Rocks), a legendary place of refuge for Brethren in Bohemia.

CHRIST

Unlike the Augsburg Confession, the Brethren's confession follows the discussion of repentance with a disquisition on the Son of God. The Brethren expressed their faith in the full divinity and full humanity of Christ, quoting both the Athanasian and the Apostles' Creeds. The confession also employed Luke's teaching that Christ is present to the church in different modes of being. Christ is present physically in heaven, where he rules with God the Father, but "Christ himself, true God and true man, is also with us, but in a mode and manner of existence different from the former one, namely, invisible, imperceptible, but still true and necessary for salvation" (1:807). There is no discussion of how Christ as "true man" could be present invisibly, but the point of this section is that Christ is *physically* present only in heaven, not in the Eucharist.

The Confession of 1535 interprets the work of Christ primarily in terms of the atonement for sins through his sacrifice, but this is not described in terms of mere legal satisfaction. Salvation is defined more broadly as union with

Christ, who is present in word, sacraments, and faith. Christ brings reconciliation to God through his merits, and believers experience salvation when they draw near to Christ in faith. Among the many biblical quotations used to explain the work of Christ in salvation are John 7:37 and John 6:35, which call upon those who thirst to drink of Christ by believing in him. "This sixth article is regarded among us as most important," says the confession, "since it is the sum of all Christianity and piety. Therefore our teachers explain and expound it with all diligence and earnestness and seek to impress it upon all" (1:809). Faith includes a loving relationship with the Redeemer. Hope is the result of faith in the saving work of Christ and the reality of his presence in the ministries of the church.

WORKS OF LOVE

As we would expect, the Unity's confession discusses good works as a necessary component of faith. In the Augsburg Confession (article 20), the Lutherans defended themselves against the charge that the doctrine of justification by faith denigrated good works (2:70–74). The Brethren faced the opposite problem. They had to convince the Lutherans that their emphasis on the necessity of good works was not a form of "works righteousness." In article 7, the Confession of 1535 asserts that people cannot atone for their sins through good works, nor can they be saved by them; but "good works should be performed in order to give evidence of faith" (1:809). Thus the confession explains the necessity of "faith completed in love" in terms that were consistent with Luther's teaching. Works make one's "calling and election sure," but works in themselves do not save. It is important to note that the works in question were not works of piety or asceticism, such as vigils or pilgrimages. They were instead acts of "mercy and charity toward the neighbor, the care of the sick, the instruction of others," and similar acts of sacrificial love (1:810). Although Luther personally approved this confession as an orthodox statement of faith, this idea of faith completed in love remained a point of controversy between the Brethren and the Lutherans for decades.

The Confession of 1535 asserts that human traditions should not displace the commandments of God, especially Jesus' commandments to care for the hungry, thirsty, and otherwise suffering (Matt. 25:34) (1:810). In other words, social justice and acts of mercy must never be separated from faith and worship. Faith that does not lead a person to care for the poor, despised, and suffering is a sham, according to the Brethren. The biblical quotations in this section are taken primarily from the Gospels of Luke and Matthew, which again points to the importance of the synoptic Gospels to the Unity. More clearly than in previous statements, though, the Confession of 1535 emphasizes that no one is able to follow the commandments of God perfectly. Part of the message of salvation is that humans can be freed from anxiety over their sinfulness. This meant that people of faith were free to act in love and mercy toward their neighbors rather than focus on themselves and their salvation.

ECCLESIOLOGY

Articles 8 and 9 address the nature of the church and the priesthood. In the main, the confession follows the Brethren's traditional teaching that the holy Catholic Church mentioned in the Apostles' Creed is not the institutional church headquartered in Rome. It is the body of all Christians "from all nations, peoples, tribes, and tongues, or every class, age, and station, in one faith in Christ and in the Holy Trinity" (1:811). The document states explicitly that the Unity and its congregations are not in themselves the universal church "but merely a part and member of it." The only substantive change here in the Brethren's doctrine of the church is the adoption of the Lutheran idea that the visible church should be defined in terms of word and sacrament.[12] In adopting the Lutheran formula, though, the Unity maintained its teaching that the true Word of God is Christ himself. Thus the true church is the church in which Christ is made visible in faith, love, and hope. The Brethren's confession went beyond the Augsburg Confession in asserting that the word and sacraments must be *received* faithfully, not just administered faithfully.

The Confession of 1535 includes an extended discussion of ministerial things, especially the authority, qualifications, and duties of priests (presbyters). It includes a very stern warning to those who would "cause sects or incite

---

12. Hägglund, *History of Theology*, 244–46.

sedition" in the community of faith. Those who have faith in Christ and live in his love are obligated to seek unity and peace with fellow believers rather than insist on their own way. We will see that Comenius reiterated this claim that reconciliation is an essential task of Christians. Submission and forgiveness, not self-assertion, were Christian virtues, and Brethren were urged not to focus their attention on controversial matters that would divide the followers of Christ (1:812).

Contrary to most of the churches of the day, the Unity's confession states clearly that "those who are in charge of churches should not force anyone to faith by punishment or force or threats, personally or through someone else, nor rule over the Church, nor exercise dominion over faith" (1:815). This is supported by Matthew 20:25–26, which was the basis of Chelčický's rejection of coercion in matters of faith. The confession also indicates that exclusion from the communion of the church should never be enforced by secular power. Discipline is a matter for the church elders, not secular authority. Although priests were not to rule through violence or threat, the laity should obey them as the representatives of Christ in the community of faith. The priest was to exercise authority in a congregation unless he was proved to be unworthy and removed by the elders. The confession also repeats in clear and concise terms the Unity's traditional concern about worthy priests. Moreover, it warns that no one should administer the sacraments or preach without a proper appointment authorized by the Inner Council. Despite Luther's objections, the confession also defended clerical celibacy.

The most important duty for priests was to preach the Word of God. Surprisingly, in discussing preaching, the Confession of 1535 promoted the Lutheran distinction between the law and the Gospels. This is a remarkable change from the traditional teaching on the biblical law. It is hard to conceive of "the Brethren of the Law" before 1528 referring to the law of God as "a ministry of death" (1:817). Later editions of the confession return to a more positive view of the law, a change that is often erroneously interpreted as evidence of a Calvinist influence. It is also surprising that no distinction is made here between the Old Testament law and the law of Christ, a distinction once central to the Unity's theology. Another significant change from the past is the statement that priests "should be provided and supplied with the necessities of life," which meant that the congregation should provide a living for the priest.

Although not stated in the confession, we know from other sources that this income was to be provided by voluntary contributions of the members, not by tithes collected by the secular authority. The Inner Council was obviously worried about paying clergy, however, and the confession expresses concern that priests remain active servants rather than become slothful and a burden to the congregation (1:815).

SACRAMENTS

From the beginning, the Czech Reformation focused on the issue of the proper administration of the sacraments by worthy priests. It is not surprising, therefore, to read in the Confession of 1535 that "anyone who deliberately despises them [the sacraments], or does not esteem them highly enough, or uses them in any other way than is the will and command of Christ, sins grievously against their author, Christ" (1:817). Luke's teaching on the sacraments as ministerials is also evident in the statement that those who are prevented from receiving the sacraments through captivity, religious oppression, illness, and so forth will "be saved by faith in Christ alone if he only believes the gospel." Such statements suggest greater continuity in the Unity's theology than historians have sometimes recognized, but it is surprising to read that the sacraments are "necessary for salvation." Luke's great insight that the sacraments are *ministerial* rather than essential to salvation was obscured in the Confession of 1535 because of Luther's influence. We have seen that from the beginning the Unity taught that the sacraments are the ordinary route to salvation and should be used as such, but declaring them necessary went a step beyond the traditional teaching.

Even so, the Confession of 1535 reflected the Unity's understanding that the sacraments work only through the power of the Holy Spirit and the faith of the believer. The confession reminds the reader that Judas Iscariot received Holy Communion and then betrayed Christ. It also rejects the older Unity belief that the sacraments' value is connected to the worthiness of the priest who administers them. Luther's opposition to Donatism, which was officially condemned in the Augsburg Confession, was influential in this respect. According to the Confession of 1535, the dominical sacraments, baptism and the

Eucharist, are efficacious "because of the ordinance and command of Christ," not the worthiness of the priest. The Brethren continued to recognize that the church's doctrine of the sacraments remained less important than whether the sacraments actually led people into "newness of life." This was more important than doctrinal subtleties. Again, we see the practical focus of the Unity's doctrine.

One of the longer sections of the confession deals with the issue of baptism (article 12) and acknowledges that the Unity changed its position on rebaptism to conform to the Lutheran teaching. Baptisms performed in the name of the Father, Son, and Holy Spirit are valid, even if done by Catholics or heretics. The confession reiterates the familiar claim that the Unity had rebaptized members in the past because of the corruption of the Catholic and Utraquist churches and also because other churches did not recognize baptisms performed by the Unity. The Lutherans helped the Brethren come to a different perspective, however. "This manner of rebaptizing existed in our churches until a clearer understanding of this matter was attained. But when by God's grace the light of truth shone brighter to our leaders in the course of time, and when they had examined the Scriptures more diligently, with the help of certain learned men, they came to the conclusion that the Church did not need to rebaptize, and immediately, by unanimous vote, decided to abandon the practice" (1:819–20).

The confession reaffirmed the Unity's teaching that baptism of the infant children of believers is good, but for the first time the Brethren argued that infants should be baptized because baptism is necessary for salvation (1:819). This echoes the teaching of the Augsburg Confession (2:63) but departs from the Brethren's traditional teaching. The Unity did retain its conviction that the ritual of baptism is not *sufficient* for salvation. Infants who were baptized were expected to be educated in the faith, be guided in the Christian life, and take upon themselves the demands of the Gospel as adults. Although the Unity's baptismal practice was modified under Lutheran influence, the Brethren retained their teaching that baptism is the beginning, not the completion, of Christian life. Faith, for the Brethren, remained a matter of conscious choice.

One of the most controversial matters debated in the reformations of the sixteenth century, as in the Czech Reformation, was the nature of the Eucharist. It is clear from the Confession of 1535 that the Unity continued to teach its traditional doctrine that the words of scripture are sufficient explanation in themselves and that it is dangerous to speculate further. Those who share in communion should "believe with the heart and confess with the mouth that the bread of the Lord's Supper is the true body of Christ, which was given for us, and that the cup is the true blood, which was shed for us for the remission of sins, as Christ the Lord clearly says" (1:820). The confession acknowledges that the Brethren had been accused of heresy and blasphemy for many years because they did not believe in transubstantiation, but they had also been attacked by those who viewed the sacrament as merely a sign or aid to memory. Both sides called the Brethren "any evil name they can think of, because of this faith and confession of the Lord's Supper. They do not cease to attack our teachers with this sort of curse and blasphemy. For the sake of the gospel, which commands that we pray for our enemies, our leaders bear all this patiently" (1:821).[13] Despite attacks from both sides, the Unity kept to the middle way and the plain words of scripture.

The Confession of 1535 promoted the Unity's simplified ritual of the Lord's Supper based on the model of the "primitive church." Central to this, of course, was the conviction that all communicants should receive both the body and the blood of Christ "with purity of soul, reverence, faith, and particularly with self-examination" (1:822). The communion ritual should include a sermon on Christ and his atoning death, and the minister should "urge the people to believe in the presence of Christ" in the Eucharist. The sacrament was served while the people were "calling to mind the blessings of God in hymns and spiritual songs" (1:822).

Article 22 of the Augsburg Confession repeats the Hussite argument that it is contrary both to scripture and to the teachings of the church fathers to deny the cup to the laity (2:78).[14] Article 24 also follows the basic ideas of the Hussites in simplifying the Mass and abolishing "mercenary masses and private masses, which had hitherto been held under compulsion for the sake of revenues." The Lutheran statement also rejects the idea that the Eucharist is a repetition of Christ's sacrifice for the forgiveness of sins, agreeing with the

---

13. This statement on patience does not reflect the vigor with which Gregory, Luke, and Augusta defended the Unity and its teaching, or the invective they heaped on Catholics, Utraquists, and Old Brethren who disagreed with them.

14. For the Hussite arguments, see chapter 1.

FIG. 19   Modern Protestant graffiti in Kalich.

earlier claims of the Táborites and the Brethren. The Lutherans asserted that Calvary was "once and for all," but the Brethren rejected sacrificial language because they did not believe that Jesus was physically present on the altar. There cannot be a sacrifice without a victim. The Reformed tradition followed the Unity's doctrine in this respect.

The Brethren's pronouncement on confession and absolution (article 14) is consistent with earlier practice as well. It distinguishes between "traditions, rites, and customs which in no way interfere with piety" and those that "obscure grace or the glory of Christ, draw and attract the people away from truth and faith" (1:824). This article thus addresses the category of "incidentals" or "things appropriate," though without using those terms. These things were not to be matters for controversy unless they in some way interfered with faith, love, and hope. In the preface, Luther agreed that uniformity in worship is neither possible nor even desirable.

Article 18 treats fasting as an incidental matter, asserting that moderation in food is always better than fasting but that fasting may be useful at times.

The Unity called for members to fast during times of persecution and crisis. The most important thing was that food should not become a cause of offense to others (1:830). In contrast to the Reformed churches in Switzerland and the later Puritans, the Unity reaffirmed the observation of "many old church rites," including matins and vespers, saints' days, days to honor the Virgin Mary, and especially days associated with the life of Christ, such as Christmas and Easter. This was certainly the case in Luke's day, so this statement should not be interpreted as a sign of Lutheran influence. Although such human traditions were not "inviolable and eternal" and could not be disregarded, the confession condemns in strong language those who "take offense at, despise, hate or persecute another because of the differences in ceremonies, customs, and rites which do not interfere with nor militate against piety" (1:825). Rites and rituals were not to be used as excuses for sedition or disunity in the church.

Likewise, the saints were to be honored because of their faith in God, but believers would honor the saints most clearly by emulating their good deeds and having faith in God. The Confession of 1535 gives a prominent place to the Virgin Mary, affirming devotion to Mary. But the confession states emphatically that Mary was the "Mother of the Savior," rather than the mother of God, and that she was a sinner saved by grace (1:828). This is reminiscent of Nestorius's decision, in the fifth century, to call Mary the mother of Christ (*Christokos*) rather than the mother of God (*Theotokos*). Though the Brethren did not call Mary the mother of God, they celebrated her festival days and sang hymns to her honor, unlike most Protestants.

The Unity's confession also taught that living people may be called saints and should be honored as such. "For all who believe in Christ, regardless of the nation in which they live, are saints" (1:829). This idea of the sainthood of all believers (rather than the priesthood of all believers) informed the Unity's ecumenism, but the love ethic was an even stronger impetus to toleration of other churches. Those who follow the law of Christ "ought especially to embrace all Christians in love, also the evil ones, and offer a helping hand to them, both at times of need and at other times." Even Christians whose life and doctrine were inconsistent with the teachings of scripture and the example of Christ "should be humanely corrected and charitably tolerated" (1:829). Prayer, not violence, was the proper means of bringing the erring to the way of salvation.

POINTS OF CONTROVERSY

The distinctiveness of the Brethren's doctrine in the sixteenth century can be seen most clearly in comparison with the second part of the Augsburg Confession, which addresses several specific points of controversy with the Catholic Church, especially with respect to priestly celibacy and monastic vows. The Unity also had to address those issues in its confession, but it was no longer defining itself only against the Catholics, Utraquists, and Old Brethren, who all had celibate priests. Now the Unity had to defend its doctrines and practices against the arguments of Protestants, too. Both the Augsburg Confession (article 23) and the Confession of 1535 (article 19) address the question of priestly celibacy, arguing from scripture and the example of the early church that priests can marry, but the Lutherans and the Brethren arrived at different conclusions about actual practice. Rather than blame priestly incontinence on the immorality of priests, as the Hussites had, the Augsburg Confession argued that "immorality and abominable vice" was a natural consequence of denying priests a normal Christian marriage (2:82). Celibacy should not be required of clergy because it is unnatural and destructive. Over Luther's strong objections, the Confession of 1535 defended the practice of clerical celibacy (1:830–32). The Brethren argued that the servants of Christ must devote themselves fully to their ministry and "be willing to renounce everything, even life itself" (1:831). Clerical celibacy, for the Brethren, was less a matter of asceticism than a daily preparation for exile and martyrdom.

The Augsburg Confession devotes a great deal of attention to the question of private confession, arguing that confession should be used for the benefit of the laity rather than as a way to oppress them. The Lutherans rehashed arguments that had been used a century before in the Czech Reformation and were so widely accepted in Bohemia and Moravia that the Unity's confession did not address them in detail. Though the Protestants moved away from private confession, the Unity continued to give detailed instructions on the proper nature of private confession in its instructional manuals for priests and congregational judges.

The Augsburg Confession devotes several pages to the question of the spiritual and secular authority of bishops (article 28), which for the most part repeat the concerns of Hus and the Czech Reformation: church officials should not wield secular authority. The Lutherans largely did away with the office of bishop (the Church of Sweden was an exception), arguing that the New Testament made no distinction between presbyters and bishops. The Brethren, as we have seen, retained the threefold ministry of the Catholic Church, although they called their bishops "seniors." As we would expect, the Confession of 1535 contains no defense of the apostolic succession of bishops.

One of the most revealing differences between the Augsburg Confession and the writings of the Unity was the former's sharp focus on monastic vows (article 27). Many of the Protestant reformers, including Luther himself, had taken monastic and priestly vows. In many ways the sixteenth-century Reformation itself was a struggle over monasticism, but the history of the Unity was quite different. Few Brethren came out of monasteries or had experienced the type of angst that tormented Luther before his breakthrough. Rather than abolish the demands of the monastery, the Unity taught that the true church should be guided by the strictures of the Sermon on the Mount, much as the original monasteries were. For the Unity, the rejection of the sword in matters of faith meant that all vows had to be voluntary.

The final article of the Confession of 1535 addresses another point of controversy between the Brethren and the Lutherans, and Luther insisted on revisions before he would publish it. As we have seen, the Brethren were very suspicious of deathbed conversions and were most reluctant to confer absolution on people whose lives had not demonstrated faith, love, and hope. They doubted that a lifetime of evil could be absolved in a moment of contrition on one's deathbed. The original draft of the confession asserted that deathbed repentance was fruitless, but the final version reluctantly conceded the possibility of salvation at the eleventh hour. Still, the language was grim: "It is indeed to be feared that he who has so slothfully and incorrigibly abused the time which God granted him for repentance will receive a reward worthy of his deeds" (1:833). Those who died without repentance and faith would be "subject to eternal judgment." With Luther's encouragement, Augusta added the words "the time of grace lasts as long as life itself." Even so, the confession ends with the elders' exhortation that all repent and find their true rest and peace with Christ, "before the sun is darkened" (1:833). People should turn away from sin and toward Christ early in life so that they could enjoy the blessings of salvation long before facing the terrors of death. "Being made firm in his grace and walking and going forward in good works, he should surely believe that when his soul is freed from the bonds of the body, it does not pass over into any punishment, but, like the soul of Lazarus, will be carried by angels into eternal blessing, where it will remain forever with Christ the Lord" (1:832).

REVISIONS TO THE BRETHREN'S CONFESSION AFTER 1535

The Confession of 1535 demonstrates clearly that eight decades after the founding of the Unity, the Brethren continued to focus on practical matters of Christian living rather than on theological and metaphysical speculation. Ethics and church order were not peripheral to Unity doctrine; they were central. Although the confession expresses general Protestant concerns about personal salvation and personal faith, this was understood within the context of the community of faith. Over time, the Brethren moved increasingly into the Reformed tradition of Protestantism, and this is reflected in later editions of their confession of faith. In general, the Brethren used the Old Testament, especially the law of Moses, in later versions of the confession. In keeping with this turn toward the Old Testament was a more favorable view of secular government. Most dramatically, the last edition of the confession before the Thirty Years' War relinquished the view that celibacy was preferable to marriage, even in the case of clergy. The Brethren had defended clerical celibacy for decades, but in the end they gave in. Later editions of the confession portrayed Adam and Eve as living in matrimony even before the Fall.

Predestination also assumed a more prominent position in later versions of the confession; this change reflected Calvinist influence, but the Brethren interpreted the doctrine of predestination in interesting ways. For example, all infants who died before being baptized were held to be saved by God's election, even though they had never had the chance to profess their faith.[15] This position reaffirmed the Brethren's traditional teaching on the salvation of infants through the grace of Christ, but now in the language of election. This approach to infant salvation stood in marked contrast to much Reformed theology of the time.

---

15. Štrupl, "Confessional Theology," 289.

With the Confession of 1535 the Unity of the Brethren brought its doctrine on the sacraments more in line with the Lutherans, but it did not reject the fundamental convictions that had defined the church from its beginnings. The Unity remained a voluntary community of faith that rejected the use of secular power in matters of faith. Despite their appreciation for Luther and Melanchthon, the Brethren continued to insist that faith must be completed in love. Orthopraxy rather than orthodoxy remained the defining characteristic of the Brethren's theology throughout the sixteenth century. The final edition of the Brethren's confession of faith was written by Comenius in the mid-seventeenth century, when it appeared that the Unity was destined for destruction and oblivion. Comenius once again elevated the distinction between essentials, ministerials, and incidentals that had been increasingly neglected over the course of the sixteenth century.[16]

16. Ibid., 288–90.

Eleven

CALVINISTS, HUMANISTS, AND BRETHREN

Historians have sometimes characterized the Unity's theology in the sixteenth century as a pendulum swinging between the two poles of Protestant thought, first toward Luther and then toward the Swiss Reformation.[1] Too much can be made of this observation, especially if one overlooks the evidence for continuity in the Unity's doctrine. The gradual reorientation of the Unity away from Wittenberg and toward Geneva was less a matter of change within the Unity than continuity with its theological heritage. As we saw in the previous chapter, the Brethren learned a great deal from Luther and reformulated some of their doctrine and practice to be consistent with his ideas, but they also retained key aspects of their traditional doctrine in their confession of faith. Throughout the sixteenth century the Brethren tried to express their teaching and practice in terms congenial to their fellow Protestants, both Lutheran and Reformed, but they always represented a "third way" within Protestantism. As "Brethren of the Law of Christ," they shared many of the ethical views of the Anabaptists, yet they practiced infant baptism and sought out fellowship with other churches. Like the Anabaptists, they persistently rejected the idea of a state church, but they came to accept a legitimate role for Christians in government. By focusing on orthopraxy rather than orthodoxy, the Unity of the Brethren could be ecumenical in a very confessional age.

Since the Brethren argued that the true church is a voluntary rather than a

---

1. Štrupl, "Confessional Theology," 279–93; Říčan, *History of the Unity*, 261–75.

territorial church, they had little difficulty acknowledging the legitimacy of other churches as communities of faith. The Unity understood that it could affirm another community of faith as Christian without sacrificing its own independent status, an idea that churches that endorsed the parish structure found baffling. The Unity also rejected the growing tendency of Protestant theologians and pastors, after Luther's death, to focus on divisive issues like predestination and the Eucharist, rather than on those things that united people and inspired them to greater devotion and service. As we have seen, the rise of doctrinaire Lutheranism in Prussia contributed to the Unity's tendency to look toward Geneva, but the Brethren were not alone in their conviction that theologians should focus on uniting rather than dividing. This was a common theme of the sixteenth-century humanists with whom the Brethren had close ties.

HUMANISM AND THE BRETHREN

It may seem odd that the Unity, which distrusted universities and had few scholars, would be attracted to the humanist thinkers of the sixteenth century. Two factors help explain this. One was that the humanists, like the Unity, viewed the universities of their day with suspicion. Many of the great minds of the time, like Erasmus and Petrarch, believed that the academic world was moribund and trapped in pointless academic debates. Writers and scientists alike saw that the excessive rationalism of the universities was disconnected from lived experience. Too often, formal education was a matter of books talking to books and authors quoting authorities rather than engaging creatively with the world. Though few of the Brethren had the education or inclination to participate in the "community of letters," they shared many of the religious and moral concerns of the humanists. The Brethren, with their focus on practical Christianity, shared the humanist conviction that scholarship should not be divorced from life.

Second, the Brethren had no objection to the exercise of reason, a faculty that did not depend on higher education. The Unity's leaders were craftsmen, farmers, and artisans, not bureaucrats or theologians. These people valued practical reason and knowledge of the natural world more highly than they did metaphysical speculation. The Unity was founded on the conviction that ordinary people could and should think for themselves, even about the Bible. They did not object to the doctrinal tradition of Christianity; they simply rejected the notion that Christian truth was only for the educated elite. They saw ordinary people as rational beings who could understand and interpret that doctrine. Christ did not establish a university; he established a community of disciples who lived the truth.

Humanism was one of the most important intellectual and cultural movements of the early modern period, but, like all important social movements, it cannot be easily defined.[2] During the Renaissance an informal society of scholars emerged who called themselves *humanistae*, that is, those who taught humane studies (the humanities): grammar, rhetoric, history, ethics, and poetry.[3] Twentieth-century definitions that set humanism against Christianity distort our understanding of the vitality of sixteenth-century humanism and its importance for the Reformation. In general, we can describe Renaissance humanists as Christian scholars who had rediscovered the classics of the ancient world.[4] The humanists focused primarily on the Greek and Latin classics, including the church fathers, but their chief interest was human society and virtue. Some of the most important figures in early Protestantism were humanists, most notably Melanchthon, Zwingli, Calvin, and Bucer. In fact, it is hard to imagine the Protestant Reformation without the humanist reformers.[5]

The humanists' motto *ad fontes*, "to the sources," was a call to return to the classics themselves rather than to rely on authoritative commentaries. This return to the sources had profound implications for Christian theology. Humanist theologians became experts in scripture, hermeneutics, and rhetoric. The historian William Bouwsma has characterized the humanists thus: "They looked for inspiration not to the philosophers of antiquity but to its orators, poets, and historians. Their preference for persuasion over rational conviction was associated with a view of human being as passionate, active, and social rather

2. For a good analysis, see Myron P. Gilmore, *The World of Humanism, 1453–1517* (New York: Harper & Row, 1962).

3. Kristellar, *Renaissance Thought*, 9–10, 121. Donald R. Kelley, *Renaissance Humanism* (Boston: Twayne, 1991), extends Kristellar's work on Italian humanism to the early Enlightenment. Particularly useful is his presentation on Lorenzo Valla, who debunked the donation of Constantine.

4. Kristellar, "Paganism and Christianity," in *Renaissance Thought*, 70–91, esp. 86.

5. James D. Tracy, "Humanism and the Reformation," in Ozment, *Reformation Europe*, 33–58.

than intellectual. Accordingly they saw language less as a medium for conveying truth about the world than as an essential ingredient of life in society through its ability to move the feelings and stimulate the will to act."[6] This literary approach seems far removed from the concerns of the Unity of the Brethren, but there was common ground in their mutual emphasis on reading the Bible directly and focusing on morals rather than metaphysics. The humanists' appreciation for scriptural narrative rather than abstract theology corresponded with the Unity's focus on the synoptic Gospels. The humanists and Brethren shared the view that the Bible is a guide for proper living in this world while preparing for the next.

ERASMUS AND THE BRETHREN

The most famous of the sixteenth-century humanists was Desiderius Erasmus (1466–1536), who published the first edition of the New Testament in Greek. Generations of historians since the Enlightenment erred in seeing Erasmus primarily as a skeptic rather than as a devout follower of Christ, but that misperception has largely been corrected since World War II.[7] Part of the difficulty in understanding the profoundly Christian aspect of Erasmus's humanism lies in its intimate connection to his criticism of Scholastic theology and contemporary church practices. According to John Dolan, Erasmus believed that Scholasticism had "first of all subverted theology to a ludicrous and profitless concatenation of quarrels. Theology is far from *pure docere Christum* [pure teaching of Christ] when it has become a prestigious intellectual gymnastic. Further, dialectic leads men to an obstinate pertinacity in their own opinions, dangerous to the peace and unity of the church."[8] Luke of Prague would have agreed.

6. William J. Bouwsma, *John Calvin: A Sixteenth-Century Portrait* (Oxford: Oxford University Press, 1988), 114. Even Calvin, contrary to his stereotype as a rigid dogmatist, argued in interpreting scripture that "each may use his own judgment, provided no one tries to force all others to obey his own rules" (120).

7. Among the many biographies of Erasmus, the best include Johan Huizinga, *Erasmus and the Age of Reformation* (New York: Harper & Brothers, 1957), M. M. Phillips, *Erasmus and the Northern Renaissance* (New York: Macmillan, 1949), and Roland H. Bainton, *Erasmus of Christendom* (New York: Scribner, 1969). A handy brief biography is provided by John P. Dolan, ed. and trans., *The Essential Erasmus* (New York: Meridian, 1964), 17–23.

8. Dolan, "Introduction," *Essential Erasmus*, 13.

Erasmus described his theology as "the philosophy of Christ" because it was based on the example of Christ and his teachings, especially the Sermon on the Mount, which was "more real and precious than any material relics of him that could be found."[9] Like the Brethren, he believed that morality rather than ritual was the central aspect of Christianity, and he criticized those who "believe the greatest piety is repeating as many psalms as possible every day, though they scarcely understand them."[10] He dismissed much popular Catholic devotion as superstition, arguing that faith is expressed more clearly in a well-ordered home and in public acts of mercy than in pilgrimages, fasts, and extraordinary acts of devotion. People should understand scripture and live according to its teaching rather than kiss relics. A character in one of Erasmus's *Colloquies* explains his understanding of Christianity to a neighbor: "I watch what my servants, male and female, are doing. Then to the kitchen, to see if any instruction is needed. From here to one place and another, observing what my children and my wife are doing, careful that everything be in order. These are my Roman stations."[11]

This rejection of the traditional Stations of the Cross in favor of a well-ordered home parallels the Unity's instructions for righteousness in the home, which promoted benevolent patriarchy. It is therefore not all that surprising that Erasmus, in 1519, was the first western European writer to defend the Brethren publicly. The Brethren came to his attention because some humanists in Prague in the early 1500s were not impressed with the rustic and unrefined Brethren.[12] One of them, Jan Šlechta, wrote a long letter to Erasmus describing the three Czech churches: Catholic, Utraquist, and Pikarts (the Unity). He depicted the Brethren as ignorant heretics, but to everyone's surprise the urbane Erasmus replied to the letter with a defense of the Unity.[13]

Erasmus expressed approval for the Unity's conscientious efforts to remove unworthy priests from office and impose stricter discipline in the church. He even offered the heretical Unity as a model that the Catholic Church should emulate. Erasmus drew on his knowledge of early Christianity to defend the

9. Quoted in Phillips, *Erasmus and the Northern Renaissance*, 81.
10. Erasmus, "Handbook of the Militant Christian," in *Essential Erasmus*, 38.
11. Erasmus, "A Pilgrimage for Religion's Sake," in *Ten Colloquies*, 91.
12. One of the humanists, Jakob Ziegler, wrote a polemic against the Brethren in which he depicted them as ignorant heretics. Over time, he moderated his views somewhat. Peschke, *Kirche und Welt*, 173–78.
13. Müller, *Geschichte der böhmische Brüder*, 1:392–94.

fact that the Brethren chose their own priests, noting that this had been the practice of the early church. In the fourth century, for instance, the people of Milan elected Ambrose bishop even before he was ordained a priest. Erasmus even affirmed the Brethren's practice of calling each other "brother" and "sister," but only so long as their actions matched their language.[14]

The one area of the Brethren's doctrine that Erasmus did not endorse was their teaching on the Eucharist, because it seemed to him impious not to kneel before the consecrated host. He approved of their simplified liturgical calendar and worship, however, noting that the many festivals in the Catholic calendar might be fine for wealthy parishes but were a burden on poor people. He argued that it was better for a poor person to work with his hands for the sake of his wife and children than to spend his time and money on religious festivals. On the whole, Erasmus's defense of the Brethren was consistent with his call to reform the Catholic Church on the basis of the New Testament. His popular *Enchiridon* (Handbook of the Militant Christian) was in many ways a sophisticated and stylish expression of the main themes of the Unity's theology.

The Brethren were so encouraged by this unexpected defense from one of the most respected scholars of the age that they sent a delegation to present Luke of Prague's *Apology of Sacred Scripture* to Erasmus, in the hope that he would publish it with his seal of approval. Erasmus expressed his general support for their simple approach to the Christian life, but, to the Unity's great disappointment, he prudently noted that it would be extremely dangerous for him to publish the *Apology* when he was already suspected of heresy. Moreover, he informed the Brethren, his endorsement would actually do little to help the Unity's cause.[15] Erasmus was aware of the limits of his influence in the halls of power.

Here we see the crucial difference between Renaissance humanism and the Hussites. The heirs of Hus identified martyrdom as one of the ultimate marks of faithfulness. Truth conquers only if one is willing to lay down one's life for the sake of the truth. Correct doctrine and elegant writing were less important to the Brethren than witnessing to one's faith even in the midst of violent opposition. Although younger humanist reformers like Calvin and Melanchthon

14. Ibid., 1:394.
15. Ibid., 1:394–95.

were willing, unlike Erasmus, to break with the Catholic Church and risk the wrath of the state, even they did not identity persecution as a mark of the true church.

Still, it is illuminating that the Unity recognized a kindred spirit in Erasmus, who seems so different from them on the surface.[16] Though Erasmus lived in a sophisticated world far removed from the village life of the Brethren, he was also concerned with the obligations and possibilities of ordinary life. Rather than engage in academic debates or seek dogmatic precision, Erasmus used the Bible as a guide for practical Christianity in a complicated world. He believed in the God-given rationality of ordinary people, who could, with the grace of Christ, make moral choices. Education had the potential, if properly directed, to help people make better use of their intelligence in daily living. This is why Erasmus rejected Luther's idea that the will is in bondage, either to Christ or to the devil.[17]

Like Erasmus, the Brethren did not share the pessimistic view of the human will that one sees in Luther and Calvin. The Brethren certainly understood that sin is pervasive and deceptive, but their writings did not dwell on human weakness and depravity. They argued that human beings cannot save themselves without the help of Christ, but this did not mean that human creatures lacked any goodness at all. Salvation may have been predetermined by the grace of God, but humans had the freedom to make moral choices.

The first question in the Brethren's catechism defined a human being as "a rational creature of God." This confidence in the rationality of the ordinary people was a pillar of the Unity's faith and practice, as it was for Erasmus. The humanists and the Brethren shared a mutual interest in pedagogy, and both worked on the assumption that faith and ethics can be taught and learned. Their contexts were quite different, however. The humanists educated the children of the aristocracy and the bourgeoisie in the classical disciplines of grammar and rhetoric. The priests of the Unity were teachers, but they were also pastors. More important, they were educating the children of farmers, craftsmen, and other common people.

16. Molnár, "Erasmus und das Hussitentum," *Communio Viatorum* 30 (1987): 185–97.
17. For the debate between Erasmus and Luther, see E. Gordon Rupp and Philip S. Watson, with A. N. Marlow and B. Drewery, eds. and trans., *Luther and Erasmus: Free Will and Salvation* (Philadelphia: Westminster Press, 1969).

MARTIN BUCER AND THE UNITY

One of the sixteenth-century reformers with whom the Brethren had the warmest relations was the humanist Martin Bucer of Strasbourg. Bucer played a key role in the Reformation in central Europe and England, but he is little studied today. As one biographer put it, "few figures of the Reformation era are so thoroughly forgotten."[18] This is unfortunate, because Bucer did more than anyone else to promote unity between the German, Swiss, and English Reformations. In addition, as Elsie McKee explains, "the city of Strasbourg was among the most important loci of liturgical development and renewal, for its leaders were especially interested in the doctrine of the church and the shaping of its practice." It is not surprising that the Brethren, who had pioneered new forms of ecclesiology, worship, education, and church discipline, would come to the attention of the reformers in Strasbourg. It is interesting that it was Bucer who did the most to promote catechesis as a central aspect of the rite of confirmation in Protestantism, and it seems reasonable to conclude that he was influenced by the Brethren.[19]

Bucer was a Catholic priest who had become increasingly frustrated by the corruption and inertia of the Roman Catholic Church in the early sixteenth century. He responded immediately to Luther's call for reformation and was instrumental in convincing the town council of Strasbourg to abolish the Mass and adopt Protestantism. Like other Protestant reformers, the former priest married and settled down to domestic life as pastor of his flock. Though not as brilliant as Luther or Calvin, he participated actively in many of the councils of his day, and he was invited to England during the reign of Edward VI to help the Church of England make the transition from Catholicism to Protestantism.[20] Like Erasmus and the Unity, Bucer's primary concern was that believers learn how to live according to the teachings of Christ and the apostles

---

18. Martin Greschat, *Martin Bucer: Ein Reformator und seine Zeit, 1491–1551* (Munich: Beck, 1990), 9, quoted in Thomas A. Brady Jr., "'The Earth Is the Lord's and Our Homeland as Well': Martin Bucer and the Politics of Strasbourg," in *Martin Bucer and Sixteenth-Century Europe: Actes du colloque de Strasbourg (28–31 août 1991)*, ed. Christian Krieger and Marc Leinhard (Leiden: E. J. Brill, 1993), 129.

19. McKee, "Reforming Popular Piety," 3, 14.

20. Bucer's energetic activities are explored in Krieger and Leinhard, *Bucer and Sixteenth-Century Europe*, and David F. Wright, ed., *Martin Bucer: Reforming Church and Community* (Cambridge: Cambridge University Press, 1994).

in their daily lives. One modern biographer has concluded that "Bucer came to the Reformation as an Erasmian and he remained one. He acquired a certain theological orientation to evangelical ideas but his fundamental concern was for the conduct of the Christian life, and he remained true to it, no matter what the cost."[21]

Bucer knew the Brethren by reputation and expressed interest in their church order and discipline before the Brethren had even heard of him.[22] More research is needed to establish to what extent the Brethren's doctrine and practice influenced the development of Bucer's ecclesiology and plans for Strasbourg, but there are clear parallels between Bucer's plans and the Unity's constitution. In 1540 the Unity's Inner Council received one of Bucer's most important works, *On the True Care of Souls and the Proper Service of the Shepherd,* which pleased them because it was so similar to Luke of Prague's instructions to the priests.[23] In response they sent a letter to Bucer, delivered by Matthew Červenka and two companions, along with the Confession of 1535. The Brethren were warmly received in Strasbourg and became acquainted with Bucer's colleagues Wolfgang Capito and John Calvin.[24] Calvin was a refugee in Strasbourg at the time, and he wrote to Augusta, "Therefore I will consider our congregations to be properly cultivated only if they are bound together by this union of order and discipline."[25] Shortly thereafter Calvin returned to Geneva, where he instituted a strict church discipline not unlike the Unity's. The major difference in Calvin's approach was that the consistory in Geneva was part of the civil government and had the power to punish those convicted of immorality or heresy.

When Bucer read the Brethren's account of their church life and discipline, he told them, "You have a great gift of God, namely, the bond of love, the unity of the Body of Christ, the church, an order and community of all your members. Where that is lacking the Lord Christ can neither be preached nor

---

21. James Kittelson, "Martin Bucer and the Ministry of the Church," in Wright, *Martin Bucer,* 94.
22. Müller, *Geschichte der böhmische Brüder,* 2:116.
23. Martin Greschat, "The Relation Between Church and Civil Community in Bucer's Reforming Work," in Wright, *Martin Bucer,* 17–31, points to the correspondence between Bucer and the Brethren as evidence of "how flexible and versatile Bucer could be in developing his understanding of the proper relation between the spiritual and political exercise of authority and power in the community."
24. Müller, *Geschichte der böhmische Brüder,* 2:117.
25. Quoted in Říčan, *History of the Unity,* 151.

learned."[26] He singled out for praise their attention to the proper education of children, premarriage counselling, the work of judges in the community, and wise exercise of discipline according to Matthew 18:15–17. For his part, Capito declared that the Brethren and the Strasbourgers were united in doctrine and practice, and he urged them to make a common case at the Reichstag, but the Brethren were reluctant to get involved in imperial politics outside Bohemia. The Brethren were also critical of Bucer's willingness to use civil authority to impose church discipline.[27]

Bucer was not the only reformer in Strasbourg to be impressed by the Brethren. Katherina Schütz Zell was one of the few women to publish material in support of the Protestant Reformation, and she was active in the theological debates of the sixteenth century.[28] When she married Matthew Zell, a priest turned Protestant reformer, in 1523, the couple took communion in both kinds. As part of her effort to reform the religious life of the laity, Zell edited and published Michael Weisse's 1531 German version of the Brethren's hymnal. For the most part she left the hymn lyrics alone, but she did change the musical settings in many cases. She also wrote a preface defending the practice of congregational singing. It is interested that she assured the laity that Weisse's hymnal contained hymns for the major festival days of the church, some of which were being removed from the Reformed liturgical calendar.[29]

Zell noted specifically that the Brethren's hymns were good for use in family devotions, while at work in the home, and as lullabies for children. McKee emphasizes that Zell focused on women as singers of the hymns, which suggests the laicization and domestication of devotional life in the sixteenth century. But McKee overlooks the possibility that Zell might have been drawing on the Brethren's tradition of using women in pastoral roles (the sister judges), including the religious education of women in the home.[30] In other words, Zell's suggestions may not have been innovative. The important point, though, is

26. Quoted in Müller, *Geschichte der böhmische Brüder*, 2:118.
27. Martin Greschat, *Martin Bucer: A Reformer and His Times*, trans. Stephen E. Buckwalter (Louisville: Westminster John Knox Press, 2004), 204–5.
28. For more on Zell, see Elsie McKee, *Katherina Schütz Zell* (Leiden: E. J. Brill, 1998).
29. McKee, "Reforming Popular Piety," 17, 34. Zell did not name the person who introduced her to the Brethren's hymnal. McKee speculates about that person's identity, but she does not mention Matthew Cerevenka, a likely candidate, who had come to Strasbourg specifically to acquaint the Protestants there with the Brethren and their devotional literature.
30. Ibid., 40.

that Zell and other Strasbourg reformers recognized that the Brethren's doctrine, as communicated in their hymns, was useful for Protestant worship and
instruction. Reformers recognized the traditional doctrine of the Brethren as
orthodox before the Brethren were attracted to the Reformed Church.

Few scholars have studied the Unity's contributions to the early development
of Reformed theology, but Bucer's mature ideas on infant baptism and confirmation were so close to the Brethren's teaching on these sacraments that one
must suspect a direct influence. Bucer regarded baptism as more than just a sign;
it signaled entry into the *koinonia*, or true community of the church, that placed
a mutual obligation on the one baptized and the church. He argued that when
the apostles baptized people, "they admitted them only into a school of piety
and an apprenticeship in Christianity."[31] Like the Brethren, Bucer saw baptism
as a "sacrament of education"; thus catechism and confirmation were necessary
components of a Christian community.[32] Bucer's understanding of confirmation as "the public profession of faith and obedience, accompanied by congregational prayer and the imposition of hands," reflected the Brethren's doctrine.[33]

It is also probable that Bucer made use of Luke's idea of the "sacramental"
presence of Christ in the Eucharist when attempting to mediate the dispute
between Zwingli and Luther.[34] Bucer moved away from his earlier Zwinglian
idea of the Eucharist as a mere mnemonic device of remembrance of Christ's
sacrifice to an understanding of the Eucharist as part of the self-giving of Christ
to the believer.[35] Like the Brethren and the Utraquists, Bucer used John 6 as
a Eucharistic text, while rejecting any notion that Jesus spoke of eating his body
and drinking his blood *physically*. For Bucer as for the Brethren, the believer
in faith, through the power of the Holy Spirit, receives the real, spiritual body
and blood of Christ that unites every Christian in the invisible body of Christ.

---

31. Quoted in Bucer's commentary on John in David F. Wright, "Infant Baptism and the Christian
Community in Bucer," in Wright, *Martin Bucer*, 104. Bucer emphasized the role of the Holy Spirit more
than the Brethren did, however. W. P. Stephens, *The Holy Spirit in the Theology of Martin Bucer* (Cambridge: Cambridge University Press, 1970), 221–37.

32. Wright, "Infant Baptism," 104; Amy Nelson Burnett, *The Yoke of Christ: Martin Bucer and Christian Discipline* (Kirksville, Mo.: Sixteenth-Century Journal and Northeast Missouri State University,
1994), 74, 147–48.

33. Burnett, *Yoke of Christ*, 140.

34. Müller, *Geschichte der böhmische Brüder*, 2:115–16.

35. Ian Hazlett, "Eucharistic Communion: Impulses and Directions in Martin Bucer's Thought," in
Wright, *Martin Bucer*, 72–82; Stephens, *Holy Spirit in the Theology of Bucer*, 238–59.

Maligned by more doctrinaire contemporaries, such as Heinrich Bullinger, who accused him of being a "vacillator" and opportunist, Bucer shared the Unity's conviction that Christians should cooperate rather than oppose one another.[36] It is illuminating that the Reformed theologians Bucer and Wolfgang Capito, whom the Unity valued most highly, were the driving forces behind the Wittenberg Concord, signed in 1536.[37] The final version of the Concord was drafted by Philip Melanchthon, another friend of the Brethren. The statement on the Eucharist echoes the language of the Unity, going back to Gregory: "with the bread and wine the body and blood of Christ are truly and substantially present" only during the act of communion.[38] The Concord avoids the notion that Christ is physically present, while affirming that he is truly spiritually present. As Capito wrote in 1530, "In this sacrament he gives of the true body and of the true blood truly to eat and drink for the nourishment of your souls and eternal life, that you may remain in him and he in you."[39] This had been the teaching of the Brethren since the fifteenth century, and it might have become general Protestant teaching, but confessionalism militated against ecumenism in the years following Luther's death.

THE ECUMENICAL CHURCH

One reason why the Unity resonated so well with Bucer and Melanchthon is that the Brethren shared the humanists' irenic understanding of the church. They agreed that reconciliation was central to the message of Christianity and that cooperation was more fruitful than competition. The Unity certainly agreed with the declaration in Bucer's Tetrapolitan Confession (1530): "For as love is greater than faith and hope, so we believe that those things which come nearest—that is, such as bring assured profit unto men—are to be preferred above

---

36. Pelikan and Hotchkiss, *Creeds and Confessions*, 2:796; James Kittelson, *Wolfgang Capito: From Humanist to Reformer* (Leiden: E. J. Brill, 1975), 158–59, 165–66. It is no accident that the 1532 statement of the synod of Bern, which was written by Capito, is one of Reformed statements of faith acknowledged in the modern Moravian Church's "Ground of the Unity."

37. For more on Capito's role in the sacramental controversy and the Concord, see Kittelson, *Wolfgang Capito*, 143–65.

38. Pelikan and Hotchkiss, *Creeds and Confessions*, 2:799.

39. Quoted in a draft of the Tetrapolitan Confession, in Kittelson, *Wolfgang Capito*, 156.

all other holy functions."[40] The Unity was attracted to the Reformed Church's emphasis on discipline and order, which resonated with the Unity's primary reason for separating from the Utraquists.[41] The Brethren, in Molnár's estimation, correctly perceived "that the Calvinist teaching in great part set forth . . . their own understanding of the gospel of Christ, the gracious demanding sovereign will of God, trust in the election of God, and a congregational community bound by discipline."[42] It is intriguing that Bucer proposed the creation of voluntary, disciplined Christian communities (*Christlichen Gemeinschaften*) within a commonwealth *after* his encounters with the Brethren.[43] Bucer's idea of little churches within the church would be revived by the Pietists in Germany in the eighteenth century.

There were two aspects of the Reformed Church that the Unity did not embrace until late in the sixteenth century. One was the desire of Reformed ministers to establish "godly" magistrates who would govern according to the biblical law, especially the Old Testament.[44] The Unity consistently rejected the idea that the secular authorities should use their coercive power to assist the church. The Brethren objected to Bucer's plans to unite sacred and secular authority on theological grounds, but the magistrates of Strasbourg rejected Bucer's plan on practical grounds. As Thomas Brady observes, they "opposed every form of compulsory religious discipline, for, having rid Strasbourg of one pope, they were not about to establish others."[45] From the Unity's perspective, the Reformers' use of secular authority in church discipline seemed closer to the Táborites than to the New Testament. In this matter, the Unity was more modern than the other Reformation era churches.

The Unity also rejected the tendency of later Reformed scholars to engage in speculative theology and enter into destructive theological controversies. According to Molnár, "the tangle and contention of theological disputes in the

---

40. Pelikan and Hotchkiss, *Creeds and Confessions*, 2:226.

41. Bucer's church discipline is examined in detail in Burnett, *Yoke of Christ.*

42. Molnár, "Brethren's Theology," 396.

43. Gottfried Hammann looks at Bucer's idea of small Christian groups, but he does not mention the contacts with the Brethren who pioneered the type of community Bucer envisioned. Hammann, "Ecclesiological Motifs Behind the Creation of the 'Christlichen Gemeinschaften,'" in Wright, *Martin Bucer*, 129–43.

44. Bouwsma, *John Calvin*, 191–234; Theodore Dwight Bozeman, *To Live Ancient Lives: The Primitivist Dimension in Puritanism* (Chapel Hill: University of North Carolina Press, 1988).

45. Brady, "Earth Is the Lord's," 135.

bosom of the western Reformation about the limits of orthodoxy, into which the Unity did not wish to be drawn, acted as a brake on the development of the individuality of the Brethren's approach to theology."[46] It also kept them from simply uniting with the Reformed churches. It is significant that within the Reformed world, the Unity maintained closer ties to the Rhineland churches and schools, such as Heidelberg, rather than enter into the controversies that led to the synod of Dort and the Westminster Confession.[47] Here again, the Brethren were close in spirit to the humanist theology of Martin Bucer, and, like him, they taught the idea of predestination without denying human freedom and moral responsibility.[48]

RECLAIMING THE BRETHREN'S THEOLOGY

By the time Luther died in 1546, the Unity's leaders were losing some of their initial enthusiasm for his theology. In that year the Inner Council decided it had been wrong to abandon the works of Luke of Prague. The council members had at first wanted "to see if there might be something better to be found outside the Unity," but after fifteen years they decided that they had been seduced by Luther's eloquence.[49] Even Roh and Augusta, who had been the most excited by Luther's works, agreed that those pastors who preached justification by faith alone had the least order and discipline in their congregations. Though they had gained a great deal from the writings of "the Saxon Hus," the Brethren felt they were losing important aspects of Hus's reformation, such as the teachings that faith must be realized in works of love and that the local church should be a disciplined school of Christ.

The Inner Council turned to Luke of Prague's instructions for priests for help in restoring the discipline and order of the Unity. In the words of one council member, "therefore we have turned with our heart and mind to that which God out of grace was pleased to give to the Unity at the first, and we

46. Molnár, "Brethren's Theology," 396.

47. For more on these schools and their relationship to Calvinism, see Howard Hotson, *Johann Heinrich Alsted, 1588–1638: Between Renaissance, Reformation, and Universal Reform* (Oxford: Clarendon Press, 2000), 15–65.

48. Stephens, *Holy Spirit in the Theology of Bucer*, 23–36.

49. Quoted in Říčan, *History of the Unity*, 163.

took the aforementioned book with diligence before us and read it all thoroughly and judged it and found the wholeness of faith and its sense in all truths necessary for salvation, and that it is not necessary for us to look for something better, but to use with gratitude what is given at home by God's grace for the Unity to know."[50] By reclaiming Luke's instructions for the priests, the Brethren reaffirmed their conviction that congregational discipline, social justice, pastoral care, and practical Christianity were more important than doctrinal pronouncements.

BLAHOSLAV

The turn away from Luther was accelerated by changes on the Inner Council. Jan Roh died in 1547 and Augusta was imprisoned the next year. Younger leaders like Jan Černy and Matthew Červenka became the voices of a rising generation that wanted to be true to the theological heritage of the Brethren while making stronger connections with humanism. They had already established good relationships with Bucer, Capito, Zell, and Calvin in the 1540s. The most important of the new generation of Unity leaders was a young Czech humanist named Jan Blahoslav (1523–1571). In his short life, he would do the most to reclaim Luke's works and interpret them in light of the Protestant Reformation.[51]

Unlike most of the Unity leaders before him, who had been Utraquists, Blahoslav was raised and educated in the Unity. According to the biographical entry on Blahoslav in the *Necrology of the Unitas Fratrum,* he was educated by the priest of his congregation, and as a child was delighted by the history of the Unity. At age seventeen he moved into the home of Senior Martin Michalec for further education, as was the custom with boys destined for priesthood, and he remained with Michalec until the bishop died in 1547. As a result, he had a strong sense of tradition and appreciation for the witness of the Brethren. Blahoslav also attended the Latin school in Goldberg in Silesia led by

---

50. Ibid.

51. The most complete account of Blahoslav's life in English is that of Miloš Štrupl, "Jan Blahoslav: Father and Charioteer of the Lord's People in the Unitas Fratrum," *Czechoslovakia Past and Present* 2 (1968): 1232–46. See also Říčan, *History of the Unity,* 165–66.

Valentin Trotzendorf, one of the great classicists of the period. Later he was sent to Wittenberg along with other Unity theology students and attended the lectures of Luther and Melanchthon. Not surprisingly, he was especially attracted to Melanchthon, from whom he adopted the definition of Christian scholarship as "the perpetual task of a Christian who has consciously received his intellect and his talents from God with the obligation of using these gifts for the understanding of God's things and in God's service."[52] It was not long before Blahoslav became one of the great Czech humanists. Like Comenius after him, he exemplified the union of humanism and simple Christianity.[53]

After completing his theological education, Blahoslav was sent to the prominent Unity congregation of Mladá Boleslav as assistant pastor in 1547. That year he wrote his first book in the midst of the conflict caused by Augusta's efforts to reconcile the Unity and the Utraquists. It was a defense of the Unity's separatism titled *On the Origin of the Unitas Fratrum*. His intention was to strengthen the Brethren's conviction that God had willed their existence, and this remained a major theme of his later works. Recognizing his talents and interests, the Inner Council encouraged Blahoslav to pursue higher education. First he enrolled in the new university in Königsberg, but he did not stay long, thanks to a doctrinal dispute among the Lutherans over Melanchthon's theology. He supported Melanchthon but did not wish to get involved in fruitless theological debate. He then tried to study at Basel, but illness forced him to return to Moravia.[54]

Blahoslav taught briefly at the Brethren's school in Prostějov, but he soon returned to Mladá Boleslav, which had become the major headquarters of the Unity in the 1520s. There he assisted Senior Černy in establishing an archive to preserve Unity documents. The *Acta Unitatis Fratrum* grew to fourteen folio volumes covering the period up to 1589.[55] In the nineteenth century the *Acta* were rediscovered in Lissa, Poland, and purchased by the Moravian Church. The Lissa Folios, as they are commonly known, were housed in the archives in Herrnhut until the mid-twentieth century. Having barely survived destruction during the last days of World War II, the folios were taken to Prague,

---

52. Štrupl, "Jan Blahoslav," 1233.
53. Říčan, *History of the Unity*, 208.
54. Štrupl, "Jan Blahoslav," 1234–35.
55. In Czech, *Akty Jednoty bratrské*. Ibid., 1237.

where they were microfilmed. The original documents remain one of the treasures of the Czech people and are housed in a secure underground vault in the National Museum in Prague, but they remain the property of the Moravian Church. Joseph Müller, the Moravian archivist in Herrnhut, translated the Czech portions of the *Acta* into German, and his monumental three-volume history of the Unity follows the *Acta* closely. An English translation of the *Acta*, made from the microfilm, is housed in the Moravian Archives in Bethlehem, Pennsylvania.[56] The *Acta Unitatis Fratrum* remains one of the most important collections of primary source material for the history of central Europe during the fifteenth and sixteenth centuries.

In 1553 Blahoslav was made a priest and was chosen to be the official Unity spokesperson to the outside world. Miloš Štrupl summarized his importance to the Unity during the tense years of the sixteenth century: "his excellent knowledge of the history of the Unitas, as well as of the issues confronting it, his splendid command of humanistic Latin, and his almost aristocratic polish made him an ideal representative of the church. As an apologist and diplomat, he rendered his Unitas most valuable service."[57] This diplomatic activity included a failed attempt to meet with Emperor Maximilian in Vienna. Blahoslav did meet with the Lutheran theologian and historian Matthias Illyricus Flacius, whose history of the church (known popularly as the *Magdeburg Centuries*) exerted great influence on Protestant historiography. Flacius appreciated Hus, whom he saw as a "witness to the truth" before Luther, and he published the catechism of the Brethren, whom he confused with the Waldensians. In 1556 Blahoslav personally gave Flacius the Latin version of his history of the early Brethren, in which he distinguished the Brethren from the Waldensians and the Pikarts. Unfortunately, by this time the Lutherans were becoming divided between the Gnesio-Lutherans (strict Lutherans), led by Flacius, and the followers of Osiander. As we saw in chapter 9, the Brethren rejected the doctrinaire approach of the strict Gnesio-Lutherans. Despite Blahoslav's efforts, Flacius cooled toward the Brethren.[58]

The Unity acknowledged Blahoslav's talent by electing him senior in 1557,

---

56. I am grateful to Rüdiger Kröger, the current archivist in Herrnhut, and Daniel Crews, archivist of the Moravian Archives in Winston-Salem, for this information.

57. Štrupl, "Jan Blahoslav," 1237.

58. Ibid., 1239; Říčan, *History of the Unity*, 211.

along with George (Jíří) Izrael (c. 1510–1588), who was made supervisor in Poland. They joined seniors Jan Černy and Matthew Červenka on the Inner Council. Blahoslav and Červenka were made the official scholars and writers of the Unity and were expected to read everything published on the Unity, including negative literature, and to write defenses when necessary.[59] In this capacity Blahoslav wrote his most important works, among them two versions of the Czech hymnal, published in 1558 and 1569; the first complete translation of the New Testament from Greek into Czech; a Greek grammar for Czech students; and a rhetorical manual for preachers titled *Preachers' Defects*, which served as the main textbook for educating Unity priests for decades.

After his release from prison in 1564, Senior Augusta opposed Blahoslav's emphasis on education, but the young humanist fought back in a work titled *Enemies of Refined Education*. He pointed to Luke of Prague as a man who used his education and knowledge for the good of the Unity and "had opposed anyone who equated intellectual indolence and cultural backwardness with having true faith."[60] The two bishops remained at odds until Blahoslav's death in 1571. It was hard for someone like Augusta to understand that humanist scholars like Blahoslav could reject the apostolic authorship of the Apostles' Creed and still regard the creed as authoritative.[61]

Blahoslav's hymnals clearly reflect his concern for clarity of doctrine, beauty of expression, and usefulness for daily living. Blahoslav followed the traditional Unity practice in organizing his hymnals according to the triad of essentials, ministerials, and incidentals, which was one of the key Unity doctrines that he hoped to preserve. He improved the meter and music of the hymns and added several new works to the collection. The hymnal contained 735 hymns, seventy of them by Blahoslav himself, and 450 melodies. Augusta contributed twice that many, earning Blahoslav's admiration despite his genuine disagreement with Augusta on many issues.[62] In 1566 Blahoslav also produced a new hymnal in German that included many hymns from the Weisse original, along with 108 Lutheran hymns, most of them by Luther. This hymnal was reprinted

59. Říčan, *History of the Unity*, 165–67.
60. Ibid., 210.
61. Molnár, "Brethren's Theology," 403.
62. This statement and the following two paragraphs rely on Říčan, *History of the Unity*, 204–20.

in the seventeenth century and became one of the Brethren's primary hymnals in later generations.

While Augusta was in prison and the Unity was facing a direct threat from the emperor, the Inner Council rejected Augusta's efforts to unite with the Utraquists and Lutherans. Červenka and Blahoslav were the Unity's primary public defenders, and they rejected union for several reasons. The most important was their conviction that the Unity reflected the teaching of scripture, including the law of Christ, better than any other church. They felt that other churches focused too closely on doctrine and ritual and too little on discipline and sacrifice. They pointed out that the Brethren had established congregations that were intimate and caring expressions of Christian love and service, which they had not seen in other churches. Finally, they were convinced that God had called the Unity into being and had blessed it through many years. It would be wrong to abandon their church in the hope of a more secure life in the world. Persecution was a sign that they were still obedient to the law of Christ and had been chosen to suffer with Christ in order to share in his glory.

The Unity was also under pressure to unite with the Reformed churches in Switzerland and the Rhineland. Although it recognized a close affinity with the Reformed churches, the Inner Council was reluctant to adopt a new confession or enter into political alliances with the Reformed magistrates. While they generally avoided theological disputes, the Brethren's leaders repeatedly criticized Lutherans, Utraquists, and Reformed churches for becoming entangled in secular politics and looking to the state for assistance in matters of faith. As we will see, whenever the Brethren signed joint confessions of faith with Lutherans and the Reformed, they did so on the condition that they could retain their own confession. Unlike other churches, the Unity saw no problem in a "diversity of confessions and church orders," for Christ might deal differently with different people.

Blahoslav responded to the specific criticisms of Reformed theologians by defending the Unity's traditional practices, especially calling its clergy "priests" and requiring them to remain celibate. "Priest" was simply the shortened form of the Greek word for "presbyter" or "elder"; the church fathers had used it as well. By calling their pastors priests the Unity was asserting its continuity with the early church. As for clerical celibacy, the elders agreed that it would be difficult for a priest of the Brethren to support a family, given that his salary depended on voluntary contributions and was not guaranteed. Blahoslav also defended the practice of preaching from the traditional lectionary of the Catholic Church, because this forced pastors to address scriptural texts that they might otherwise ignore.

Internally, Blahoslav warned young priests not to be tempted by the Calvinist practice of pondering the mystery of predestination too deeply or preaching too often on that obscure topic. The Brethren, including Blahoslav, affirmed predestination of the saints but were deliberately silent on "double predestination," the idea that God had predestined some souls to heaven and others to eternal damnation, regardless of their works.[63] This approach to the question of predestination goes back to the beginning of the Unity and should not be seen as evidence of Calvinist influence. In fact, the Brethren rejected aspects of Calvin's teaching. According to Senior Červenka, the doctrine of predestination illuminated "the boundless grace and love of God to the church and to those who are saved," but scripture, unlike the Calvinists, said nothing about double predestination.[64] In other words, predestination assured the salvation of the elect, not the damnation of others. Rather than wander into labyrinths of theological speculation and confusion, Blahoslav told priests to direct their flocks' attention to Christ's simple invitation: "If any wish to become my followers, let them deny themselves and take up their cross and follow me" (Matt. 16:24). Faith, for Blahoslav, meant trust in Christ, who would never disappoint, but this faith always included obedience and self-sacrifice.[65]

The bishops of the Unity repeatedly cautioned clergy and laity alike about the perils of metaphysical speculation. Reason, they believed, worked best when it stayed within the bounds of what can be known rather than seeking answers to questions invented by speculative philosophers. Only in the late eighteenth century did Immanuel Kant give philosophical precision to this idea of the limits of reason, but the Brethren had an intuitive grasp of Kant's concept two centuries earlier. The Brethren's preference for practical, or "simple," reason was not a rejection of reason or education, far from it. By exercising caution in the use of speculative reason, the Brethren maintained their confidence in the innate reasoning ability of ordinary people. Excessive speculation into divine

---

63. Hägglund, *History of Theology*, 260–62.
64. Molnár, "Brethren's Theology," 412.
65. This and the following four paragraphs rely on Říčan, *History of the Unity*, 215–16, 265–67.

mysteries could lead one into doubt rather than faith, despair rather than hope, apathy rather than active love. Along with the humanists, the Unity questioned the usefulness of the doctrine of election if the elect failed to live as God had instructed. True faith, they averred, does not rob people of hope, nor does it replace active love with doctrinal purity.

GENEVA AND THE BRETHREN

Blahoslav's death in 1571 at the age of forty-eight was a serious blow to the Unity. No one in the Unity other than Comenius ever matched Blahoslav as a scholar, leader, councilor, and diplomat. He had guided the Unity safely through the most difficult days of the Reformation and helped the Brethren maintain their distinctive voice among Protestant churches without retreating from the world. He ensured that the Brethren would continue to value an educated clergy and that the church could intelligently and faithfully engage the issues of the age.

After Blahoslav's death the Brethren relied heavily on schools associated with the Reformed Church for the training of priests and scholars. The academy Calvin founded in Geneva became the premier Protestant educational institution of the sixteenth century, and it attracted many Brethren as students. The Inner Council maintained good relations with Calvin's successor, Theodore Beza, in Geneva, although they were concerned about his emphasis on double predestination and his endorsement of the persecution of "heretics" like Michael Servetus. Some of the Brethren at the academy were preparing for the priesthood, but many children of wealthy families attended the academy in pursuit of secular careers. After Blahoslav's death, these Geneva-educated nobles increasingly moved the Unity into the Reformed political camp.

As a result, the Unity grew more Reformed in doctrine and practice after 1547, but, as with Luther's influence, this development should not be overstated. The Unity continued to define the church as the community of the elect without being unduly concerned about who were not of the elect. The Brethren also rejected the notion that the church should be identified with a particular geographical area or political unit. They made no attempt to create a "holy commonwealth" like Geneva, the Palatinate, Scotland, or New England. They insisted instead that "the body of the elect" must by its nature be a minority community within any society. The Brethren maintained a discipline that was at least as strict as that of Geneva (in fact, it seemed almost monastic to other Protestants), but they emphasized that discipline was always to be tempered by love. The Unity remembered the excessive violence and cruelty of their Táborite ancestors and saw the potential for such abuses in both the Calvinists and the Anabaptists. To put it bluntly, the Unity was one of the few European churches that never killed or maimed a person because of his or her beliefs.

Calvin's famous "third use of the law" was very appealing to Brethren who had always been suspicious of Luther's rigid division between law and the Gospels. Calvin believed that the biblical law was more than a means of restraining evildoers or convincing people of their need for grace. It was also aspirational in that it showed how believers could and should live.[66] This appealed to a community that referred to itself as "brothers of the Law of Christ," but the Brethren remained suspicious of the Calvinists' mingling of the Mosaic law of the Old Testament and Christ's law as expressed in the new covenant. For the most part, they retained their Christocentric hermeneutic in their reading of scripture and in their social ethic. The teachings and example of Jesus remained the norm for interpreting both the Old and New Testaments.

Perhaps the most significant Calvinist influence on the Brethren concerned clerical celibacy. We have seen that the Unity's elders repeatedly defended clerical celibacy in response to criticism by Lutheran theologians; but one of the Brethren's priests in Moravia, George Strejc (1536–1599), became convinced by Calvinist arguments on the benefits of clerical marriage. Rather than try to persuade the Inner Council of the wisdom of allowing priests to marry, he simply married without permission. The elders disciplined him, but he was elected to the Inner Council in 1577.[67] After that, clerical marriage became the norm in the Unity rather than the exception.

Another sign of the growing connection with the Reformed churches came in 1581, when the Latin version of the Brethren's confession was printed in Geneva in a collection of Reformed confessions of faith without the permission

---

66. John Calvin, *Institutes of the Christian Religion*, ed. John T. McNeill, trans. Ford Lewis Battles, 2 vols. (Philadelphia: Westminster Press, 1960), 1:348–66; Pelikan, *Christian Tradition*, 4:212–17.

67. Říčan, *History of the Unity*, 269. Quotations and material in the following seven paragraphs are from ibid., 227, 231, 233, 238, 242, 244–46, 250–51, 269.

of the Inner Council. Future collections of Reformed confessions also included the Brethren's confession of faith, and increasingly the Brethren's congregations in Poland, Moravia, and Bohemia were listed along with Reformed churches. The rising generation of Unity priests in the late sixteenth century pushed for even closer connections to the Reformed. For instance, Brother Strejc translated portions of Calvin's *Institutes of the Christian Religion* into Czech for the use of the Brethren's priests. By 1600 the Unity was on the verge of becoming simply the Reformed Church of Bohemia and Moravia.

ECUMENICAL AGREEMENTS

As a result of persecution following the Schmalkaldic War in 1547, the center of the Unity shifted from Bohemia to Moravia and Poland, where the Brethren found greater toleration and protection. Mladá Boleslav in Moravia became the Unity headquarters in Czech lands, while Leszno (Lissa) in Poland became the Polish headquarters. The Brethren established a strong presence in Leszno, which became even more important after 1620, but the church was never fully integrated into Polish society; it remained a Czech community in Poland. In the Czech lands, the Unity had been built up by farmers and craftsmen, but in Poland the church depended on the patronage of powerful nobles who exerted great power over "a people spiritually destitute and materially enslaved." These nobles pressured their subjects to attend worship in the Brethren's churches. Despite the power of noble patrons and protectors in Poland, however, Senior Izrael did not allow the secular authority to take over the governance of the Unity completely. The Unity's traditional separation from the state impeded its growth in Poland because many nobles preferred the more compliant attitude of the Lutherans and the Reformed.

The Unity of the Brethren in Poland played a key role in one of the milestones of ecumenical theology. In 1555 representatives of the Brethren and the Reformed in Lesser Poland met in Kozminek to discuss greater cooperation and even the possibility of merging. The Reformed pastors agreed to accept the Unity's confession of faith and to use the Unity's order of worship, though the Reformed remained a separate church. When the Polish reformer Jan Laski (1499–1560) returned from England, he affirmed the close ties of the Brethren and the Reformed, and he promoted union with the Lutherans as well. Laski even wrote a history of the Brethren and their church order in Latin, a portion of which was republished by Comenius in the next century.

Despite real disagreements over doctrine and discipline, the Protestants in Poland recognized that they had much in common and could work together. The three Protestant churches issued a joint pronouncement (*reces*) that presented the basic doctrine of all three churches, leaving room for personal interpretation. After much negotiation, the Protestant leaders in the new Polish-Lithuanian empire signed the Consensus Sandomiriensis (Sandomierz Agreement) in 1570. Each church was allowed to keep its distinctive confession but agreed to recognize the validity of the other confessions. The Lutherans and Brethren agreed that they could share or exchange pastors and that neither would try to convert members of the other church. On the divisive issue of the Eucharist they declared, "We are agreed, that we believe and confess that the essential presence of Christ is not only implied, but to those who partake of it in the Supper it truly presents itself, distributes and gives the body and blood of Christ, at which to the matter itself are joined by no means mere signs: according to the name of sacraments." Luke of Prague would probably have been quite pleased with this.

The Unity was reluctant to move too far toward a full merger, though. This reluctance was due in part to the fact that the Polish branch of the Unity was officially under the authority of the Inner Council in Moravia, which opposed merger. The Brethren were reluctant to sacrifice their separate identity as a community of faith or to undermine the Unity's cohesion. The insistence of the Protestants in Poland on giving secular officials a deciding voice in the administration of the church was the biggest barrier to merger. In a major departure from the past, however, the Brethren in Poland allowed the nobility to collect tithes from the peasants to support the clergy.

True to their commitment to social justice as a part of Christian ethics, the leaders of the Unity in Poland urged the nobility to ameliorate the sufferings of the peasants living under feudalism. They called for nobles to decrease the labor requirements of the peasants so that they would have time to raise food for their own families. And they demanded that lords use transparent bookkeeping methods so that the ignorant would not be cheated out of their due. The Brethren demonstrated their independence and integrity when the leaders excommunicated Count Lukáš of Górky for adultery and Lord Peter Maczyn-ski of Poznaň for insubordination toward the congregational judge. As a result, a number of nobles left the Unity to join the Lutherans, who did not pry so deeply into the affairs of the nobility or publicly challenge their treatment of the poor and defenseless.

In Bohemia the Brethren took part in another major ecumenical undertak-ing. Maximilian II, who ruled as emperor from 1564 to 1576, was not crowned king of Bohemia until 1575. He had been interested in Lutheranism in his youth but turned solidly to Catholicism when he assumed office. Like many rulers of the time, he had grown weary of the Protestants' continual doctrinal disputes. As befitted a king of Bohemia, though, he received a special dispen-sation from the pope to receive the chalice. Drinking from the chalice did not make him more welcoming of the Brethren in his realm, and he encouraged Catholic polemicists to work freely. In response, Protestant nobles and schol-ars agitated for complete religious freedom.

Eventually Maximilian called a meeting of the estates, in September 1575, to discuss the religious situation before he was crowned king. Lutheran nobles and some of the Utraquist leaders called for a new confession of faith to be written for the meeting. It was to be a joint confession of all the Protestants in Bohemia, including the Unity. The Brethren had agreed on the condition that they could retain their own confession, which had been republished in 1573.[68]

In 1575, after a period of intense negotiation, the Lutherans, Utraquists, and Brethren in Bohemia presented King Maximilian with a joint Confessio Bohem-ica (Bohemian Confession). Among the signatories were seventeen lords and nearly 150 lesser nobles who were members of the Unity.[69] The Utraquists and the Unity both provided a preface to the confession. The Utraquist preface is much longer and more politic than the Unity's, which is simple and straight-forward. It is significant that the Unity did not replace its confession with the Confessio Bohemica, as some historians have assumed, nor was the con-fession written by the Brethren. As noted above, the Unity agreed to sign the

68. There has been a lot of confusion among historians regarding the Bohemian Confession of 1575 and the Brethren's Confession of 1573 because an English translation of the latter was erroneously pub-lished in the 1590s under the title the "Bohemian Confession."

69. Otakar Odložilík, "A Church in a Hostile State: The Unity of the Czech Brethren," *Central Euro-pean History* 6 (1973): 119; Molnár, "Czech Confession of 1575"; David, "Utraquists, Lutherans"; cf. David, *Finding the Middle Way*, 168–204.

confession only if they could retain their own statement of faith for use in their congregations.

The Bohemian Confession was based on the Augsburg Confession and is basically a Lutheran statement of faith. Though approved by the Utraquist consistory in Prague, the confession was actually binding as a rule of faith only on Lutherans, who were a small minority in Bohemia. Many people suspected that this was simply a ruse designed to make the nation Lutheran. Maximilian refused to sign the Confessio Bohemica into law, but he assented verbally to toleration for all those who had signed it. Unfortunately for the Brethren, Maximilian also renewed the old Mandate of Saint James shortly after his coronation, which meant that the Unity remained illegal in Bohemia despite having signed the new confession.[70] Although the Bohemian Confession ultimately failed, it represents a significant ecumenical achievement during the confessional age. It is illuminating that the Unity was instrumental in bringing about reconciliation among Protestant churches in both Bohemia and Poland in the sixteenth century.

THE BRETHREN'S BIBLE

The greatest achievement of the Reformed humanists in the Unity was the production of the Brethren's Bible, which became known as the Kralice Bible in the nineteenth century. The first edition of this Bible appeared in several volumes over a period of many years. Blahoslav translated the New Testament from Greek into Czech, and after his death some of his students took on the task of doing the same for the Old Testament. They worked from the Antwerp Polyglot, an edition of the Bible that included both the Hebrew and Greek scriptures, which had been published by Catholic scholars in 1569–72. The Brethren's Bible was printed on the Brethren's press at Kralice on the estate of Count Žerotín, one of the great protectors of the Brethren in Moravia. The Pentateuch appeared in 1579. Finally in 1588 the Unity published the Apocrypha, completing the project. In 1594 Blahoslav's original translation of the New Testament was revised and published.[71]

70. Říčan, *History of the Unity*, 252–55.

71. Ibid., 270–71. Quotations and material in the following two sections are from ibid., 270–72, 301–20.

The Brethren's Bible included extensive interpretive notes taken primarily from the works of Reformed biblical scholars and theologians in Geneva, Heidelberg, and at Herborn Academy. Thus the publication of the Bible in Czech moved the Brethren even closer to the international Reformed community of scholarship. In 1596, in another great ecumenical achievement, the Unity published a one-volume version of this Czech Bible without notes or commentary, which was adopted by Lutherans, Reformed, and Utraquists as the official Bible in Czech-speaking lands. The last printing of the whole Czech Bible was completed in 1613, shortly before the Thirty Years' War. In Czech lands during the seventeenth-century Counter-Reformation, the Kralice printing press was destroyed and copies of the Czech Bible were burned. A few copies survived, however, and in the nineteenth century Czech linguists adopted the Brethren's Bible as the guide for Czech grammar and style. Thus the Brethren played a significant role in the recovery of the Czech language during the rise of Czech nationalism in the nineteenth century.

DISCIPLINE AND PASTORAL CARE IN THE
SIXTEENTH-CENTURY UNITY

The Unity changed a great deal after the death of Luke of Prague, but it remained a distinctive expression of Christianity until end of the sixteenth century. Members were still organized according to the tripartite scheme of beginners, those progressing, and those moving toward perfection. Beginners were admitted to sermons and instructed in the ways of the Unity, but they were not admitted to the Eucharist until they were received among those progressing (also known as the proficient). As late as 1600, the third category of membership, the perfect (or those moving toward perfection), was defined as "members who were mature in knowledge of the things of God and so rooted in faith, love, and hope that they could guide others." The perfect included priests, judges, and other congregational leaders. This division of membership was more pedagogical than judgmental, as it provided a system of instruction for those entering into serious Christian living. It was also intended to assist pastors in their duties, because more was expected of the perfect than of beginners.

Even after the turn toward Calvinism, the Unity continued to issue instructions for appropriate occupations, but the list of accepted vocations mushroomed. The instructions prepared in 1611 included advice for physicians, watchmakers, goldsmiths, printers, engravers, and other skilled trades that had once been forbidden. But members were still instructed in how to conduct their secular affairs according to the law of Christ. For instance, in the second half of the sixteenth century Brethren were allowed to become lawyers only if they used their education for the sake of the poor and defenseless rather than a means to wealth and prestige. As the Unity entered more fully into society and attracted more members of the nobility, members had to be reminded that power and wealth made salvation more difficult, not easier: "The poor who are not nobly born are exalted above the highborn, for whom humility is especially fitting, so that they might acquit themselves well." The Brethren still preached on Christ's parable of the camel and the eye of the needle to warn the well off that prosperity was not a sign of blessedness, and nobles were as likely to be excluded from communion as less powerful brothers and sisters were.

Priests, increasingly known as pastors or ministers, were the backbone of the Unity, and they spent most of their time in pastoral care. They had great authority, but they were not absolute rulers. They were always accountable to the Inner Council, which had authority to remove unworthy priests. Priests worked with congregational judges and other lay leaders in disciplining and guiding their congregations. For the most part, priestly education remained an apprentice system rather than a process of formal education. Acolytes lived in the Brethren's House and became deacons when they were older. This allowed them to assist more directly in pastoral work. Deacons preached on occasion, but their sermons were written in advance and approved by the priest. Deacons also taught in the schools and led the catechism for the young; this was how Comenius began his work as an educator. Ordination to the priesthood came only after a long period of preparation, trial, and questioning. At ordination the new priest formally received a personal copy of the Unity's worship books.

The chief duties of the priests were preaching, administration of the sacraments, and overseeing church discipline. They typically led worship three to five times on Sundays and held services on Wednesdays and Fridays. Communion was given four times a year, and private confession of sins was required of all communicants. Priests were trained in the difficult art of counseling. "It is noteworthy," Říčan writes, "that the Brethren in these instructions for improvement did not restrict themselves to admonitions for moral action, but started ever anew from the bases of Christian life, from the need of 'internal rehabilitation to God,' that is, the awakening of faith, love, and hope, so that from this welled forth all further remedy (or reform). Let reform touch every power of the spirit, mind, and members. Let it include also the renewal of a proper relationship to the Unity, especially that close connection to its services and servants, but also to one's fellows (in the Unity), to one's poor neighbors, and to people in general." As with the Brethren of old, it was the practical concerns of Christian living that occupied the attention of the Unity's priests and seniors.

The office of judge or helper remained important after the turn toward Protestantism, even though this office was frequently criticized by Lutherans who feared works righteousness and judgmentalism. The Inner Council provided instruction books for judges that taught them how "to be the eyes and ears" of the pastor. They were, Říčan notes, "to keep an index of members in their assigned area. They also watched over the diligent consecration of Sunday and were to call attention in a timely manner to defects in family life." They even quizzed the youth on the contents of sermons. One could draw parallels to seventeenth-century Puritan practices here.

One interesting aspect of the Brethren's polity illustrates the humane values of the church. As with the Rule of Saint Benedict for monasteries, in meetings of elders and helpers, "the youngest one of them had the first word, the older and more experienced ones gave their opinions, and then the administrator closed the discussion. This is the way things were done in all the Brethren's meetings so that the younger members would not be embarrassed to express their own opinion." It was important for the health of the community that all felt free to air their opinions and raise questions.

As they had done since the beginning, the Brethren continued to choose judges who were skilled in reconciling individuals in conflict with others or the church. They also visited those troubled in body, mind, or spirit. Female judges and elders were chosen by the women of the congregation to care for their spiritual needs. They offered maternal advice, mentored younger women in the church, and helped resolve disputes. They were inducted into office by a bishop, just as priests were. This was as close to the ordination of women as any church in Europe came before the eighteenth century. Girls as well as boys received a basic education and were expected to read and understand scripture and doctrine. True to the Hussite heritage, the elders noted that "women also excelled at times in courage for confessing their faith."

Over time, the title of senior gave way to that of bishop, but the duties of the office remained essentially the same as it had been in the days of Luke of Prague. Bishops served as supervisors or overseers of the three provinces of the Unity (Bohemia, Moravia, and Poland). In particular they were responsible for providing congregational leaders. They saw to the recruitment and training of priests, appointed them in their charges, disciplined the clergy, and oversaw the support of clergy and their families (after 1570). Bishops also kept a list of the laity in their dioceses and maintained contact with the heads of households. They conducted regular inspections of the local congregations and "looked after the doctrinal and moral purity of the priest, and took care if an external danger threatened." Bishops were also entrusted with the Unity's archives and produced literature for use in the church. Co-bishops served on the Inner Council, which unified the three provinces.

PRESERVING THE BRETHREN'S HERITAGE

Under the leadership of Bishop Strejc, the Unity in Moravia and Bohemia moved ever closer toward full union with the Reformed churches at the end of the sixteenth century. By 1600 the Unity's most gifted priests and scholars were educated primarily at Herborn Academy, Geneva Academy, and the University of Heidelberg. But some of the leaders retained Blahoslav's perspective that the Unity should learn from its own heritage and speak with a distinctive voice within Protestantism. The most important of these theologians and church leaders was Simeon Turnovský (1544–1608), the bishop in Poland. He had been educated by George Izrael, and in his ecumenical work in Poland he was careful to distinguish the Brethren's theology from that of the Calvinists and Lutherans, without offending the other churches. Like Blahoslav a generation earlier, he criticized those who were "duped into casting aside the Brethren's writings without reading them, not having seen the Unity's own light and not even being aware of it."[72] It was Turnovský who rescued the Brethren's key insight about essential, ministerial, and incidental things from near oblivion at the beginning of the seventeenth century.

Turnovský was not an antiquarian trying to revive the "good old days" of the old Unity but the bishop of a vibrant community of faith who skillfully guided his flock through the turbulent waters of late sixteenth-century Poland.[73] He recognized that the Unity was threatened by extinction on two fronts. One was the real likelihood of Catholic persecution; the other, the demand of Protestant churches that the Unity simply merge with them. Like Blahoslav and Červenka, Turnovský believed that God had indeed called the Unity into existence to bear witness within the wider Christian church. The unique history of the Unity gave its members a perspective missing in other churches. Although their doctrine and worship were compatible with the Lutheran and Reformed churches, the Brethren shared many of the qualities and convictions of the Radical Reformation. Their concern for social justice, the separation of church and state, and witness for peace was communicated to the two main Protestant churches through continual ecumenical dialogue.

Turnovský opposed the growing influence of the Zwinglian perspective on the Eucharist among the Calvinists and in the Unity. He emphasized the traditional teaching of the Brethren that Christ is truly, spiritually present in the bread and wine.[74] Turnovský likewise rejected the Calvinists' insistence that Christ's descent into hell in the Apostles' Creed was symbolic rather than literal. The Calvinists saw this as a poetic description of Christ's suffering on the cross, but Turnovský insisted on the Brethren's traditional understanding that Christ truly preached to the souls in prison, where he offered redemption to the dead. Turnovský proclaimed that Christ was indeed a victor who had defeated death and bound Satan.[75] This idea of Christus Victor was not fully developed in the theology of the Unity, but it was an intriguing alternative to the dominant Protestant theories of the atonement based on Anselm.

Turnovský argued that the Brethren should maintain their mediating position between the Calvinists and Lutherans. By focusing on their own theological

72. Molnár, "Brethren's Theology," 398.
73. See Říčan, *History of the Unity*, 224–49 and 276–96, for the details on the Unity's precarious existence in Poland.
74. Ibid., 273–74; Molnár, "Brethren's Theology," 398.
75. Říčan, *History of the Unity*, 273; Molnár, "Brethren's Theology," 411.

heritage, the Brethren could help reconcile and reunite the two main branches of Protestantism. They could endorse the Augsburg Confession and the Bohemian Confession as ecumenical statements of Christian faith, but not as binding authorities. They could also affirm Reformed confessions. Not surprisingly, neither Lutheran nor Reformed theologians in the age of orthodoxy and confessionalism were thrilled by Turnovský's proposals. Surprisingly, however, the Inner Council rejected Turnovský's proposals and would not allow his works to be printed. Even his historical writings were suppressed, because they provided evidence that the Inner Council was deviating from the Unity's distinctive theological heritage.[76]

That the Inner Council suppressed Bishop Turnovský's texts shows that the other elders did not want the past to influence their plans for the future. Educated at Reformed schools and convinced that only Reformed doctrine and exegesis were orthodox, the new generation of elders, led by Strejc, saw no need to address the theological heritage of their ancestors. Turnovský considered it foolish to ignore the wisdom of previous generations of Brethren in order to adopt the theological agenda of Calvinist and Lutheran officials, but he submitted to the decision of his fellow bishops, and his works remained in manuscript form. He obeyed even though he "rejected the overblown claims to the authority of the Brethren's elders by referring to the communal nature of theological activity in the preceding generations of the Unity."[77] A few decades later, his works would be read by Comenius, who used them to pass on the heritage of the Unity to the modern church.

76. Říčan, *History of the Unity*, 273–75.
77. Molnár, "Brethren's Theology," 398.

Twelve

THE LABYRINTH OF THE WORLD

At the beginning of the seventeenth century the Brethren were no longer an isolated community worshipping in the hills of Bohemia. They had become deeply involved in European affairs, and their most important bishop and scholar, John Amos Comenius (Jan Amos Komensky) (1592–1670), would become an international celebrity. But the promise of a new age for the Unity was to end in tragedy. It is ironic that the greatest flowering of the Brethren's intellectual heritage came at the same time that the Unity itself was virtually destroyed. This chapter focuses on the history of the Brethren in the seventeenth century and the life of Comenius.[1] The next chapter looks more closely at Comenius's work. In many ways, Comenius's life was a microcosm of the history of the Unity in the seventeenth century. Just when it appeared that he and they had achieved success and security, it was all consumed by fire, sword, and plague. One of the great scholars of the seventeenth century was an exile and a pilgrim with no fixed abode, but he became the "teacher of the nations."

---

1. The most recent biographies of Comenius available in English translation are Daniel Murphy, *Comenius: A Critical Reassessment of His Life and Work* (Dublin: Irish Academic Press, 1995), and Jaroslav Pánek, *Comenius: Teacher of Nations* (Prague: Orbis, 1992). Still very useful is Matthew Spinka, *John Amos Comenius: That Incomparable Moravian* (New York: Russell and Russell, 1943). Říčan, *History of the Unity*, 335–80, gives a good account of Comenius's life and work. The most comprehensive biography is Milada Blekastad, *Comenius: Versuch eines Umrisses von Leben, Werk, und Schicksal des Jan Amos Komensky* (Oslo: Universitetsforlaget, 1969). Other useful biographies are Jan Jakubec, *Johannes Amos Comenius* (1928; reprint, New York: Arno Press, 1971); František Kozik, *Comenius*, trans. Stephan Kolar (Prague: Orbis, 1980); and Jan Milíč Lochman, *Comenius* (Hamburg: Friedrich Wittig, 1982).

HISTORICAL SETTING

In order to place the story of Comenius and the destruction of the Unity in context, we need to look briefly at the historical situation in the first half of the seventeenth century. The history of the Unity was part of a wider history of religious and political conflict that affected much of western Europe in the wake of the Reformation. After much bitter strife, the Netherlands eventually succeeded in gaining independence from the Spanish Crown. The Dutch rulers settled religious conflict in their realm by granting a remarkable level of religious toleration, including toleration of Anabaptists and Jews. The Dutch jurist Hugo Grotius laid the foundations for international law based on reason and human rights during this period. Comenius would eventually settle in Holland, and he drew heavily upon Grotius's ideas in his own political theories.

In England, the reign of Elizabeth I ended in 1603, and her settlement of the religious conflict in the Church of England unravelled under her successor, James I. In an effort to avert rebellion, he allowed some of the most vocal Puritan dissenters to emigrate to New England in 1620 and 1630, and there they founded the "godly commonwealths" of Plymouth and Massachusetts. James also sponsored a new translation of the Bible, which bears his name, but that did not quell dissent. In 1649 the British Parliament rejected the divine right of kings and executed Charles I after convicting him of treason against the nation. The head of the army, Oliver Cromwell, established a commonwealth in England in 1653.[2] The Brethren were caught up in this struggle, and for a time it appeared that they might relocate to either Ireland or New England with the assistance of Parliament.

War between Protestant and Catholic rulers ravaged central Europe for nearly thirty years (1620–48), decimating the population and disrupting the social order of many territories. The movement toward religious toleration discussed in the previous chapter ended with the reassertion of Habsburg control over Czech lands in 1620 and the forced re-Catholicization of the population. The Unity of the Brethren suffered greatly during this period, and the church barely managed to survive in Poland, but it was doomed to extinction

---

2. For a good account of this period, see Christopher Hill, *Intellectual Origins of the English Revolution* (Oxford: Oxford University Press, 1965).

when its headquarters there was destroyed during the Swedish-Polish war of the 1650s.

Against this backdrop of war and turmoil, some of the great thinkers of European history worked to uncover the secrets of nature, society, and the human mind. René Descartes and Baruch Spinoza used mathematics as a guide for the pursuit of truth in philosophy. By doubting everything, Descartes asserted, one could eventually arrive at certainty through logic alone. In medicine, William Harvey discovered the circulation of blood in the body and how the heart functions. Paracelsus began the process of transmuting alchemy into a medically useful form of chemistry. The recently invented telescope and microscope revealed that the universe was much larger and more complex than ever imagined before.[3] Magellan circumnavigated the globe, and Jesuit missionaries translated the Gospels for the emperor of China.

Galileo rejected Aristotle's authority in physics, much as Luther had rejected his authority in theology. Galileo's efforts to explain motion by means of observation and mathematical calculation led to a new understanding of the natural universe, but his writings were condemned by the Roman Inquisition and he was imprisoned. Scientific advances could be dangerous. The Inquisition burned Giordano Bruno at the stake because of his scientific theories, but by the end of the century Isaac Newton was using Galileo's theories in his formulation of the law of gravity, creating a new scientific understanding of the universe. Also in England, Francis Bacon proposed that empirical research should form the basis for knowledge of the natural world.

The seventeenth century was a time of unprecedented intellectual, technological, and social change, and it is thus no wonder that many philosophers and theologians dreamed of creating a new and perfect society.[4] Thomas More had written his *Utopia* in the sixteenth century, but the seventeenth century was the age of utopian literature. Johann Valentin Andreae's *Christianopolis*, Samuel Hartlib's *Macaria*, and Thomas Campanella's *The City of the Sun* envisioned new worlds in which faith, reason, and virtue would work together for

3. Charles Webster, *From Paracelsus to Newton: Magic and the Making of Modern Science* (Cambridge: Cambridge University Press, 1982).

4. See Charles Webster, *The Great Instauration: Science, Medicine, and Reform, 1626–1660* (New York: Holmes & Meier, 1975).

the betterment of humankind.[5] The printing press sped the sharing of discoveries and new ideas, allowing a simple cobbler in Görlitz named Jacob Böhme to propose a new Christian cosmology and path of redemption that inspired Germany philosophers for two centuries.[6] Comenius drew upon this utopian literature in writing his classic *The Labyrinth of the World and the Paradise of the Heart*, discussed below.[7] Comenius's *Labyrinth* was quite different from the visions of his friends Andreae and Hartlib, because the utopian dream was tempered both by the Brethren's theology and by Comenius's own experience of war and grief. His work was one of the first negative utopias (or dystopias) ever printed, but it does bear some resemblance to Sebastian Brandt's *Ship of Fools* and Erasmus's *The Praise of Folly*, which depict human folly in all walks of life as part of social critique.[8]

Comenius and the Brethren were swept up in the intellectual and social ferment of the age. In 1583 the emperor Rudolf II, one of the most interesting Habsburg rulers, moved the imperial capital to Prague for the first time since the days of Charles IV.[9] Bohemia again became the center of European affairs, and Prague was the focus of intellectual life. Rudolf was a patron of the arts and sciences, and his support for the work of the astronomers Tycho Brahe and Johannes Kepler had a lasting impact on science. It was Kepler who developed the laws of planetary motion that helped prove Copernicus's heliocentric theory, but Rudolf's interest in the heavens had as much to do with astrology as with science. He was also a patron of alchemists, magicians, and other practitioners of occult arts, like Robert Fludd.[10] Although Comenius was not part

5. See Frances A. Yates, *The Rosicrucian Enlightenment* (Boston: Routledge & Kegan Paul, 1972), 208–16; Dmitry Čiževsky, "Comenius' *Labyrinth of the World*: Its Themes and Their Sources," *Harvard Slavic Studies* 1 (1953): 86; C. Daniel Crews, "Through the Labyrinth: A Prelude to the Comenius Anniversary of 1992," *Transactions of the Moravian Historical Society* 27 (1992): 33–34; Karel Kučera, "An Analysis of the Vocabulary of *The Labyrinth of the World and the Paradise of the Heart*, by J. A. Comenius," *Acta Comeniana* 4 (1979): 339–53. For Campanella, see John M. Headley, *Tommaso Campanella and the Transformation of the World* (Princeton: Princeton University Press, 1997), and Charles Andrews, ed. and trans., *The New Atlantis and the City of the Sun: Two Classic Utopias* (Minneapolis: Dover Publications, 2003).

6. Andrew Weeks, *Boehme: An Intellectual Biography of the Seventeenth-Century Philosopher and Mystic* (Albany: State University of New York Press, 1991).

7. John Amos Comenius, *The Labyrinth of the World and the Paradise of the Heart*, trans. Andrea Sterk and Howard Louthan (New York: Paulist Press, 1998).

8. Erasmus, "The Praise of Folly," in *Essential Erasmus*, 94–173.

9. Josef Válka, "Rudolfine Cuture," in Teich, *Bohemia in History*, 117–42; E. R. W. Evans, *Rudolph II and His World* (Oxford: Oxford University Press, 1973).

10. See Yates, *Rosicrucian Enlightenment*.

of Rudolf's court or closely associated with Prague, his writings display the eclectic blend of religion, science, and philosophy that marked the intellectual life of the early seventeenth century.

WORLDLY SUCCESS FOR THE BRETHREN

We have seen that the Unity had become more like other Protestant churches over the course of the sixteenth century, but it remained a voluntary church with strict demands for membership. It was still an illegal organization, except for a brief period from 1609 to 1620. As such, it remained a small community of faith compared to the Lutherans, the Reformed, and the Utraquists. Říčan has estimated that there were at most two hundred congregations of the Unity in Bohemia, Moravia, and Poland, with a total of about fifty thousand members.[11] Though it is possible that the church was twice that large, it remained a fairly intimate community that focused on practical Christianity rather than on speculative theology. Although theologian Matouš Konečný (1569–1622) was charged with the task of writing a systematic theology for the Unity similar to other Protestant dogmatic works, he never finished his *Loci communes theologici*. Konečný instead published a book on Christian duties and a manual for household devotions. He also wrote a work on natural science as a way of understanding the work of God in the world, which represented a new approach for the Brethren.[12]

One result of the influence of Reformed theology on the Unity can be seen in the Inner Council's allowing secular leaders greater say in the church's governance in the early seventeenth century than had been the case in the time of Blahoslav and Augusta. Authority gradually shifted from the Inner Council and synods to assemblies of nobleman in the Unity. As one historian has noted, "It is not at all surprising that the seniors, although respected for their knowledge and moral integrity, retreated from the forefront, and that in moments of crisis eminent laymen acted as the Unity's spokesmen. The Unity preserved its

---

11. Říčan, *History of the Unity*, 299. It is not possible to determine the precise membership of the Bohemian, Moravian, and Polish branches of the Unity, but it is unlikely that it ever exceeded one hundred thousand.

12. Ibid., 335.

doctrine and regulations for everyday life in the congregations, but entertained amicable relations with the Reformed churches."[13] With the increase in authority for the nobility and greater involvement with the Reformed churches of Europe, the Brethren entered more deeply into the labyrinths of contemporary politics.

Emperor Rudolf had been educated at the court of Phillip II in Spain, the leading opponent of Protestantism among the European rulers. It was Phillip who had attempted to invade England in order the remove the "heretical" queen Elizabeth in 1588. During Rudolf's reign many Catholic Czech aristocrats established ties with the Habsburgs in Spain and joined in the Habsburg effort to abolish Protestantism throughout Europe.[14] Because Prague was now the capital of the Holy Roman Empire, the papal nuncio to the imperial court exerted pressure on Rudolf to re-Catholicize the country. Like many aristocrats of the time, Rudolf was personally tolerant of unorthodox ideas in his court, such as astrology and alchemy, but he was less tolerant of heterodoxy among the people.

Under Rudolf, the Jesuits gained greater authority in Bohemia, and they targeted the Unity for special attention, as it was the smallest and weakest politically of the Protestant parties. Prominent supporters of the Unity were pushed out of public office, most notably Charles of Žerotín, who had fought for the Huguenot Henry of Navarre in the French religious wars.[15] With nobles sympathetic to the Unity out of office, the Jesuits encouraged Rudolf to reissue the Saint James Mandate outlawing the Unity, but the plan backfired when the Utraquist and Lutheran nobility in Bohemia and Moravia rose in protest. Czech historian Otakar Odložilík summarizes the effect of Rudolf's pro-papal policies: "No extensive propaganda was needed to present Rudolf as a captive of the intolerant court party and a passive instrument in its hands. Dissatisfaction with his rule after 1602 reached such an intensity that a showdown became inevitable. In 1608 the estates of Austria and Hungary rose against Rudolf, and Moravia went over to them."[16]

13. Odložilík, "Church in a Hostile State," 121.

14. Válka, "Rudolfine Culture," 120–21.

15. František M. Bartoš, "Wenceslas Budovec's Defense of the Brethren and of Freedom of Conscience in 1604," *Church History* 28 (1959): 220.

16. Odložilík, "Church in a Hostile State," 123.

The major defender of the Unity in the imperial diet was Vaclav Budovec (1551–1621), a nobleman raised and educated in the Unity. He had traveled and studied in the Protestant centers of western Europe and counted Theodore Beza, of Geneva, among his friends. Budovec wrote an elegant defense of the Brethren titled *Description of how, in the Kingdom of Bohemia, the Royal Mandates and Many Other Senseless Things and Torments Directed against the Brethren of the Unity, Were and Still Are Being Issued.*[17] He not only catalogued the abuses the Brethren had suffered throughout their history, he also defended the Unity using Sebastian Castellio's *Concerning Heretics.*[18] Religious persecution, he argued, hurts the body politic more than unorthodox beliefs and practices do. Budovec also pointed to the popularity of the Brethren's hymnal and Bible as evidence of the Unity's positive contribution to the social and political life of Bohemia.[19]

As the years passed, the emperor's habitual melancholia increased and he became reclusive and volatile.[20] His attempt to impose Catholicism on Protestant Hungary led to a revolt in 1604, weakening the empire's defenses against the Turks. His brother Matthias, with the support of the nobility, forced Rudolf to cede the governorship of Hungary, Austria, and Moravia to him in 1608. On July 9, 1609, Bohemian nobles forced Rudolf to sign a decree of religious toleration, called the "Letter of Majesty," in order to prevent another revolt in his realm. This decree granted freedom of worship in Bohemia to the Utraquists, Lutherans, and Brethren on the basis of the Bohemian Confession of 1575. Budovec was the author of the royal decree.[21]

For the first time in its history, the Unity had the right to public worship in Bohemia. Bethlehem Chapel was given over to the Brethren in recognition of their role in preserving the Hussite heritage. The Brethren were also active participants in the proposed merger of the Czech Protestants into a single national church, but they insisted on maintaining their own church order, discipline, and priesthood until the Bohemian (Utraquist) Church demonstrated

17. Bartoš, "Wenceslas Budovec's Defense," 222.
18. Valentin Urfus, "Jurisprudence in Comenius's Times," in Pešková, Cach, and Svatoš, *Homage to Comenius*, 97–105.
19. Bartoš, "Wenceslas Budovec's Defense," 223.
20. Some scholars have gone so far as to suggest that Rudolf was a paranoid schizophrenic. See Válka, "Rudolfine Culture," 124.
21. Bartoš, "Wenceslas Budovec's Defense," 224.

that it would "stand in good order according to the example of the apostolic church." The Unity's elders provided the Bohemian parliament with a comprehensive statement on their church order and discipline that was eventually published in Leszno, Poland, in 1632.[22] The process of social assimilation begun in 1495 was now almost complete. The Unity had become a church like the others—but its rise in status and apparent security led to its rapid demise.

There was growing concern over Rudolf's fitness to rule, and in 1611 his brother Matthias deposed him as king of Bohemia and Holy Roman emperor. Matthias and his chief ecclesiastical official, Bishop Klesl of Vienna, followed a policy of reconciliation with the Protestant nobility in an attempt to bring greater stability to the empire. When he deposed Rudolf, Matthias reaffirmed the provisions of the Letter of Majesty, much to the anger of some of the more stridently Catholic members of his family. It was an unstable arrangement, especially since the new emperor was an old man who was facing death without an heir. Unfortunately for the Unity, he was unable to prevent Ferdinand II, the grandson of Ferdinand I, from being chosen as his successor in 1618.

Even before he was given the crown, Ferdinand and his allies encouraged anti-Protestant violence in Bohemia and Moravia. Some of the Brethren's schools and houses of worship were destroyed or confiscated by Catholic lords.[23] When the Bohemian crown passed to him in 1618, he made it clear that he had no intention of honoring the Letter of Majesty or respecting the rights of "heretics" in his realm. In a bitter meeting of Bohemian nobles at the Hradčany castle in Prague in May 1618, some of the Protestants expressed their anger at Ferdinand by hurling the most aggressive Catholic lords, Slavata and Bořita, out the chancellery window.[24] This second defenestration in Prague was the first act of the Thirty Years' War (1618–48), the bloodiest conflict in Europe until the twentieth century. We will return to the war and its impact on the Unity of the Brethren, but first let us look at the life of Comenius before 1620.

22. Říčan, *History of the Unity*, 332.
23. Ibid., 340.
24. De Schweinitz, *History of the Church Known as the Unitas Fratrum*, 481–82, gives the colorful details of the episode.

FIG. 20   Defenestration window in Prague Castle.

COMENIUS THE STUDENT

Comenius is remembered today primarily for his brilliant work on pedagogical reform, but he was also a theologian, bishop, cartographer, hymnist, novelist, lexicographer, and social reformer.[25] Just one indication of Comenius's continuing relevance is that one of the European Union's twenty-first-century educational reform programs is named for him.[26] Though he achieved international renown, he came from a humble background. He was born in 1592, probably in Nivnice, a small village in Moravia near Uherský Brod. Because his family had originally come from the village of Komna, he adopted the Latinized surname Comenius in school. He was orphaned at the age of twelve and was sent to Strážnice, where he attended school until he was sixteen. He referred frequently to the cruelty of education in his day, in part on the basis of his experience in Strážnice.

At the age of sixteen Comenius was able to study at the Brethren's premier school in Moravia, Přerov, where he would later teach. His talents were evident in school, and his teacher, Bishop Lánecký (Lanecius), gave him the name Amos, a pun on the Latin *amor*, because of his love of learning. Later Comenius associated himself with Amos the biblical prophet, a zealous advocate of social justice. Because of Comenius's promise as a scholar, Count Žerotín provided the funds for him to study at the Hohe Schule (Reformed Academy) of Herborn in Nassau from 1611 to 1613.

Herborn was one of the most distinguished schools in western Europe, although it did not have the credentials of a university because the empire did

25. The literature on Comenius is vast. The following works cover important aspects of his life and work: Pešková, Cach, and Svatoš, *Homage to Comenius*; P. van Vliet and A. J. Vanderjagt, eds., *Johannes Amos Comenius (1592–1670): Exponent of European Culture?* (Amsterdam: North-Holland Press, 1994); Josef Brambora, Josef V. Polišensky, et al., "Research on the Life and Work of J. A. Comenius (1957–1970)," *Acta Comeniana* 3 (1973): 443–94; Joseph Needham, ed., *The Teacher of Nations: Addresses and Essays in Commemoration of the Visit to England of the Great Czech Educationalist Jan Amos Komensky (Comenius), 1641–1941* (Cambridge: Cambridge University Press, 1942); and Klaus Schaller, ed. *Comenius: Erkennen, Glauben, Handeln* (Sankt Augustin: Richarz, 1985). Facsimiles of Comenius's major works can be found in *Johann Amos Comenius: Ausgewahlte Werke*, ed. Dmitrij Tschizewskij and Klaus Schaller, 4 vols. (Hildesheim: George Olm, 1973–83). His complete works were published as *Johannes Amos Comenii: Opera Omnia*, ed. Otalar Chlup, 18 vols. (Prague: Academia Scientiarum Bohemoslovakia, 1969).

26. The overall program is called SOCRATES. COMENIUS is for the lower schools and ERASMUS is for higher education. It is very appropriate that these three names remain linked. http://europa.eu.int/comm/education/programmes/socrates/comenius/moreabou_en.html.

not recognize the Reformed Church as a legal institution at that time. The political theorist and Reformed leader Johannes Althusius had served as rector of the academy from 1597 to 1604, and Comenius drew upon his political theory of federalism in his own plans for social improvement.[27] Herborn was a new form of educational institution that sought to escape the dominant influence of Aristotle in science and philosophy. The faculty adopted the methods of the logician Pierre Ramus, who rejected Aristotelian dialectics, with its syllogisms, in favor of a type of logic that worked through the classification and ordering of ideas. Practical reason was more important to Ramus than abstract ideas. He and other Protestant intellectuals were convinced that devotion to Aristotle prevented human advancement because scholars were too bound by prejudice to learn new and better methods. Herborn's publicity materials declared that "praxis not theory is the goal of education."[28]

The teacher who became Comenius's mentor at Herborn was Johann Heinrich Alsted, who attempted to include all areas of human knowledge in his *Encyclopaedia*.[29] In the judgment of his biographer, Howard Hotson, "Rarely has one man attempted to expound so systematically and comprehensively the whole of reality: the breadth of human knowledge in his philosophical encyclopedia, the height of divine wisdom in his theological *summa,* and the depth of universal history in his chronological and millenarian writings."[30] Comenius shared Alsted's conviction that humans could truly understand the world if knowledge were organized logically according to the Ramist system. It was also from Alsted that Comenius picked up the concept of a millennial age of peace and harmony, which helped shape his vision for social reform.[31]

After studying at Herborn, Comenius spent time at the University of Heidelberg in the Palatinate. Though more sophisticated and humanistic than Herborn, the university and the academy were bound together by religious faith and a commitment to "further reform," meaning that both institutions hoped

27. Johannes Althusius, *Politics,* trans. Frederick S. Carney (Boston: Beacon Press, 1964).

28. Hotson, *Johann Heinrich Alsted,* 22.

29. Gerhard Michel, "Komensky's Studien in Herborn und ihre Nachwirkungen in seinem Gesamtwerk," in Schaller, *Comenius: Erkennen, Glauben, Handeln,* 11–21; and Franz Hofmann, "Der enzyklopädische Impuls J. H. Alsteds und sein Gestaltwandel im Werke des J. A. Komensky," ibid., 22–29.

30. Hotson, *Johann Heinrich Alsted,* 9.

31. Howard Hotson, *Paradise Postponed: Johann Heinrich and the Birth of Calvinist Millenarianism* (Dordrecht: Kluwer Academic, 2000).

to reform Christian life, not just doctrine.[32] Frederick V, the prince of the Palatinate, was the chief among the seven electors of the Holy Roman emperor, and was therefore second only to the emperor in status. He was married to Elizabeth, the daughter of King James I of England, and during his reign Heidelberg was the center of a network that included Protestant intellectuals, politicians, and religious reformers in Bohemia, the Netherlands, and England. Heidelberg Castle was one of the most celebrated castles in Europe, and its gardens were famous for their beauty, diversity, and ingenuity. Intellectual stimulation, aesthetic pleasure, and social reform were united in Heidelberg, as they were in Comenius's writings. Comenius suggested that every school should have its own gardens, smaller versions of those in Heidelberg, for the enjoyment and use of the students. The idea that Christ would restore the primal garden of paradise played a role in his theological works.[33]

While in Heidelberg, Comenius attended the lectures of the famed professor David Pareus.[34] Though Pareus disagreed strongly with Alsted's theology, especially the idea of a millennial age on earth, he shared Alsted's dream of peace among Christians. During the years that Comenius was his student, Pareus was writing his *Irenicum,* published in 1614. *Irenicum* offers an ambitious plan for overcoming the differences between the Lutherans and Reformed both theologically and politically. The Unity's influence (perhaps mediated through Comenius) is evident in the *Irenicum*; Pareus used both the Consensus of Sandomierz and the Confessio Bohemica to show how Protestants could work together.[35]

During his time at Heidelberg, Comenius established a lifelong friendship with the Württemberg pastor and writer Johann Valentin Andreae, the author of *The Chemical Wedding of Christian Rosenkreutz* and *Christianopolis.*[36] We see the same eclectic blend of science, alchemy, religion, magic, and social reform in the *The Chemical Wedding* that was displayed in the court of Rudolf II. Andreae may also have been the author of the famous manifestos of the Rosicrucians,

---

32. Hotson, *Johann Heinrich Alsted,* 26–28.
33. Yates, *Rosicrucian Enlightenment,* 13–23, describes the gardens of Heidelberg and their influence.
34. Wilhelmus Rood, *Comenius and the Low Countries: Some Aspects of Life and Work of a Czech Exile in the Seventeenth Century* (New York: Abner Schram, 1970), 22–24.
35. Howard Hotson, "Irenicism and Dogmatics in the Confessional Age: Pareus and Comenius in Heidelberg, 1614," *Journal of Ecclesiastical History* 46 (1995): 432–53.
36. Yates, *Rosicrucian Enlightenment,* 42–44, 201–2, 218.

a brotherhood of intellectuals who had dedicated themselves to the healing of individuals and society. Historian Frances Yates has concluded that there was no actual Rosicrucian society in the early seventeenth century, when the manifestos appeared, but she argues that there was a network of reformers connected to Andreae and the Rosicrucian manifestos. She has provided ample evidence that Comenius was part of this informal network of Protestant intellectuals and reformers.[37] It should be noted that the seventeenth-century Rosicrucians, if they existed, had no connection to later movements that adopted that name.

An indication of Comenius's broad interests as a student can be seen in his purchase of a first edition of Copernicus's *De revolutionibus orbium coelestium*, the book that transformed our understanding of the heavens.[38] Comenius, however, was not impressed with Copernicus's theory, and he maintained a belief in a geocentric universe throughout his life. (It should be noted that it was not until the eighteenth century that Copernicus's theory was generally accepted.) Comenius's rejection of Copernicus, though, is a reminder that he was neither a scientist nor a mathematician. He was very enthusiastic about the technological advances of his age, even if he did not always appreciate the scientific methods and theories behind them. Comenius ignored the work of Kepler in Prague, but he was profoundly influenced by Francis Bacon's *New Organon*, which called for observation and experimentation in science. Bacon asserted that "idols" of the mind prevent humans from perceiving the natural world correctly: idols of the tribe, idols of the cave, idols of the marketplace, and idols of the theater or dogma.[39] Each of these is a type of presumption or habit of mind that clouds and distorts perception. Comenius used this idea in his classic *Labyrinth of the World*, as well as in his pedagogical works, arguing that prejudice, greed, and dogma warp our perception of things. People need to overcome their assumptions and dogmas before they can truly see, learn, and build a better world.

37. Ibid., xi–xv, 278–93. Clare Goodrick-Clarke asserts that Comenius was an important Rosicrucian, but a number of mistakes in her article raise questions about the depth and breadth of her knowledge of Comenius. Goodrick-Clarke, "The Rosicrucian Afterglow: The Life and Influence of Comenius," in *The Rosicrucian Enlightenment Revisited*, ed. Ralph White (Hudson, N.Y.: Lindisfarne Books, 1999), 193–217.

38. Spinka, *John Amos Comenius*, 31.

39. Francis Bacon, *The New Organon*, ed. Fulton H. Anderson (Indianapolis: Bobbs-Merrill, 1960), 48–49.

EARLY CAREER

When Comenius left Heidelberg in 1614, he walked home to Moravia. This lengthy walking tour was not just a way to save money; it allowed Comenius ample time to learn the geography and culture of Europe outside his native Moravia. Upon his return home he was ordained a deacon in the Unity and assigned to teach at the school in Přerov. There he published his first Latin textbook and began two lifelong projects: a Czech dictionary and a Czech encyclopedia, *Theatrum universitatis rerum* (Theater of All Things), modeled on Alsted's encyclopedia. These manuscripts were destroyed when his home was burned in 1656.

In 1616 Comenius was ordained to the priesthood of the Unity, and in 1618 he was named pastor of the Fulnek congregation, the Brethren's most important German-speaking congregation. Before taking up his position, Comenius married Magdalena Vizovská, the daughter of a wealthy burgher in Přerov.[40] At the age of twenty-six, Comenius was settling down to a rather comfortable life as a husband, pastor, and scholar, but he did not neglect the Brethren's traditional emphasis on social justice as a central component of true Christianity. One of his earliest publications was the 1619 *Letters to Heaven*, in which he protested against many social injustices, echoing the themes of the original Czech Reformation.[41] Comenius, like the original Brethren, argued that Christ condemns those who enrich themselves from the sweat and blood of the poor, but he also judges the poor who forsake the law of love.

REBELLION AND WAR

In 1618 the Czech nobles tried to assert their ancient right to elect a king of Bohemia in defiance of the Habsburg emperor, Ferdinand, who had a claim to the throne. The nobles chose as king the only Calvinist elector in the Holy Roman Empire, Frederick V of the Palatinate. Many Protestants in Europe looked on Frederick as an almost messianic figure because he and his spouse

40. Spinka, *John Amos Comenius*, 36.
41. Ibid., 33; F. M. Dobias, "Aspects of Social Ethics in the Works of J. A. Comenius," *Communio Viatorum* 4 (1961): 72–82, 181–91.

were devout, intelligent, handsome, and energetic. There was widespread hope that the coronation of Frederick and Elizabeth as the king and queen of Bohemia would lead to a new age of scientific advancement and religious reform.[42] Czech nobles prepared for the arrival of the newly elected king by banishing the Jesuits from the kingdom and giving their beautiful church, the Klementina, to the Brethren. The sect that had begun with a small group of serious-minded young people who rejected the pleasures of the world now had representatives in the royal court and could worship in one of the most beautiful churches in the capital. For the first time in its history, the Unity was a worldly success. Ignoring strong evidence that their rebellion could not succeed, the Czech nobles crowned Frederick on October 31, 1619 (Reformation Day). Bishop Cyril of the Unity participated in the coronation, abandoning the Unity's traditional separation of church and state.[43]

Unfortunately for the Czech Protestants, the Calvinist Frederick proved to be as intolerant in his way as Ferdinand was in his. He chose the beautiful Saint Vitus Cathedral as the castle church, but he stripped it of much of its artwork, angering Utraquists and Lutherans as well as Catholics. He also imposed the Reformed liturgy on an unwilling population. Even the Brethren, who were close to the Reformed theologically, objected to the austerity of this liturgy. The nobles in Moravia, including those in the Unity, kept their distance from the new king and did not support the Bohemian rebellion. Frederick and the rebellious nobles lacked support among the common people, and the new king failed to secure alliances with other Protestant monarchs. James I of England refused to help his niece even though his British and Scottish subjects strongly supported Frederick and Elizabeth.[44] The Bohemians wrongly assumed that the ruler of neighboring Saxony would support a Protestant king, but the Lutheran Johann Georg II, elector of Saxony, proved unwilling to help a Calvinist. Johann Georg was a shrewd politician. In exchange for supporting the emperor, Saxony received Upper and Lower Lusatia, historically part of Bohemia. The Zinzendorf estates, where a group of Moravian refugees would seek refuge a hundred years later, were located in Upper Lusatia.[45]

42. Yates, *Rosicrucian Enlightenment*, 25–34.
43. Říčan, *History of the Unity*, 341–42.
44. Yates, *Rosicrucian Enlightenment*, 32–33.
45. Říčan, *History of the Unity*, 342.

Not surprisingly, Emperor Ferdinand responded to the coronation of Frederick with extreme force. Unfortunately for the Czech Protestants, there was no Jan Žižka to lead the Protestant army this time, nor were there legions of peasants determined to fight against oppression, as there had been two centuries earlier. The battle of White Mountain, fought just outside the walls of Prague on November 8, 1620, was an overwhelming victory for the Catholic lord Wallenstein, the emperor's most brilliant military strategist. Frederick fled the country in disgrace. He not only lost the crown of Bohemian, but the Palatinate was soon taken from him as well. The magnificent gardens, fountains, and art of the palace in Heidelberg were destroyed, and his extensive library was plundered and scattered. The Palatinate fell under Catholic control, and the Protestant population was oppressed for years.[46] So many Palatines eventually fled to the New World that the word "Palatine" became a synonym for "German" in colonial America.[47]

In Bohemia and Moravia, Emperor Ferdinand ordered mass arrests of leaders of the rebellion, and on June 21, 1621, twenty-seven people were beheaded in front of the Old Town Hall. Seven of those killed, most notably Budovec, were members of the Unity; one was Catholic. Twelve of the heads were placed in iron cages and displayed on the towers of the Charles Bridge.[48] In 1621 Spanish troops destroyed the Brethren's house in Fulnek, where Comenius lived, and his library was destroyed by Capuchin friars. Comenius had been warned of the attack and fled before the troops arrived. His wife had already returned to her family in Přerov, for she was expecting their second child, but the next year she and both children died of a plague that followed in the wake of the imperial army. Comenius found refuge at Brandýs on the Bohemian estate of Count Žerotín along with two dozen other Unity priests. It was there, in 1623, that Comenius composed one of the masterpieces of European literature and spirituality, *The Labyrinth of the World and the Paradise of the Heart*.[49]

46. Josef Petráň and Lydia Petráňová, "The White Mountain as a Symbol in Modern Czech History," in Tiech, *Bohemia in History*, 143–63.

47. A. G. Roeber, *Palatines, Liberty, and Property: German Lutherans in America* (Baltimore: Johns Hopkins University Press, 1993), 2.

48. Říčan, *History of the Unity*, 345.

49. See Crews, "Through the Labyrinth"; Jan Milíč Lochman, "Chiliasmus versus: Eschatologie und Weltgestaltung in der Perspecktive des Comenius," *Theologische Zeitschrift* 35 (1979): 275–82; H. Schroer, "Reich Gottes bei Comenius," in Schaller, *Comenius: Erkennen, Glauben, Handeln*, 87–93. Dagmar Čapková argues that *Labyrinth* contradicts Comenius's other works; see Čapková, "Some Questions of the

FIG. 21   Memorial marking place of execution on the Day of Blood, 1621.

During this time, Comenius also remarried, in the hope of better days to come. His new wife was Dorothea, the daughter of Bishop John Cyril.

The State Counter-Reformation Commission, established by Ferdinand, was very efficient. In 1624 all Protestant clergy were expelled from Bohemia and Moravia.[50] Places of worship were seized, Protestant books and Bibles were burned, and the chalice was taken away from the laity. Adults were forced at bayonet point to attend Catholic services. Some Protestant children were forcibly taken from their families and raised in Catholic schools. In the new

---

Integrity of Education and the Development of Man in Consultatio Catholica," in *Consultationes de consultatione*, trans. and ed. Dagmar Čapková, J. Dohnalek, and E. Turkova (Prague: J. A. Comenius Institute of Education, Czechoslovak Academy of Sciences, 1970), 85–118. It is interesting that William Bouwsma titles the second section of his provocative biography of John Calvin "The Labyrinth." Bouwsma, *John Calvin*, 67–127. Like Comenius, "Calvin did not doubt that the world needed setting to rights" (69). Bouwsma's portrayal of Calvin helps explain why the Brethren were initially attracted to Geneva but turned away when Calvin's successors became more dogmatic than their teacher.

50. Adolf Vacovský, "History of the Hidden Seed," in *Unitas Fratrum*, ed. Mari P. von Buijtenen, Cornelius Dekker, and Huib Leeuwenberg (Utrecht: Rijksarchief, 1975), 35–54.

constitutions written for Bohemia (1627) and Moravia (1628), the nobility lost the right to protect non-Catholics, and it was soon decreed that nobles who did not convert to Catholicism would be banished from the kingdom.[51] In 1625 Comenius was a key member of the delegation that met with Count Leszczynski of Poland to secure permission for a large immigration of the Brethren to Leszno, where there had been a congregation since the 1540s. In 1627 Comenius was forced into permanent exile from Czech lands along with many of the Brethren, including Count Žerotín, his patron.

After two centuries, the Czech Reformation was brought to a brutal end by the Spanish troops of the Habsburg emperor. By the time the war ended in 1648, the population of Bohemia and Moravia had been reduced by half. Ferdinand had come close to fulfilling his vow that he would rather rule a desert than a nation of heretics. Those loyal to the legacy of Hus remained, "although they had no preachers, churches, or meeting halls," Vacovský tells us.[52] In a few Bohemian and Moravian villages where the Unity had once been well established, a faithful remnant tried to maintain the church, using some of the Brethren's hymnals and catechetical materials. Remnants of the Brethren survived in isolated pockets in Prussia, Poland, and Hungary for some time. The Unity of the Brethren was virtually destroyed during the seventeenth century, but the writings of Comenius gave it an enduring legacy.

THE LABYRINTH OF THE WORLD

As a pastor, theologian, and man of faith, Comenius was called upon to make sense of the disaster that had struck the Brethren. He was able to draw upon the Unity's long tradition of facing life and death with honesty and integrity in *The Labyrinth of the World and the Paradise of the Heart*, an extended allegory about the complexities and tragedies of life.[53] His own personal grief is

---

51. Říčan, *History of the Unity*, 345.
52. Vacovský, "History of the Hidden Seed," 36, 38.
53. Dmitry Čiževský points out that Comenius's use of allegory differs from most allegorical writings. Rather than obscure the meaning of the symbol or create wooden associations, Comenius's allegory "does not diminish the liveliness, the full vitality, and the richness of the pictures drawn. Instead, it allows the author to spread the colors more thickly, to give his lines exaggerated sharpness, to intensify his contours to the point of caricature." Čiževský, "Comenius' Labyrinth of the World," 90.

evident in his statement, "The arrows of Death struck my three companions [his wife and two children]. Being left alone in anguish and stunned with terror, I did not know what to do."[54] Nearly four centuries later, the reader can feel the heartbreak of a bright young man who has seen his future destroyed by war, plague, and the folly of the world: "Time and again you have shown me and promised me riches and knowledge, comfort and security. But what do I possess? Nothing. What have I learned? Nothing. Where am I? I myself don't know. I only know this, that after so much confusion, so many labors, and after having been exposed to so much danger and having thoroughly wearied and exhausted my mind, I have finally found nothing but pain in myself and hatred toward me in others" (164).

There is a long tradition of Christian devotional works that use the motif of pilgrimage to describe the process of spiritual growth, but the pilgrim in *Labyrinth* does not go on a journey through the world.[55] Instead, he explores a single city whose streets are like the labyrinth in the Greek myth of the Minotaur on Crete. The pilgrim finds no monster to slay at the center of the labyrinth, but an abyss, from which he turns in despair (chapter 36).[56]

The *Labyrinth* is based on the book of Ecclesiastes, one of the few Old Testament books the Brethren valued.[57] In Ecclesiastes, the teacher, traditionally identified as King Solomon, "saw all the deeds that are done under the sun; and see, all is vanity and a chasing after wind."[58] Most of the people Comenius's pilgrim encounters on his journey through the labyrinth of the world do just this: they chase after the wind, and in the end they reap precisely what they sowed—nothing. In despair, the pilgrim hears God's voice calling him to "return whence you came, to the home of your heart, and shut the door behind

54. Comenius, *Labyrinth of the World*, 83. Hereafter cited parenthetically.
55. Čiževsky, "Comenius' *Labyrinth of the World*," discusses in detail the possible sources behind Comenius's use of the metaphors of pilgrimage, the theater of the world, and the mirror of the world, demonstrating that Comenius employed these traditional metaphors in quite distinctive ways.
56. In the Middle Ages, labyrinths were sometimes constructed so as to help people who could not go on a pilgrimage experience some of its spiritual benefits. Prayer books or living guides were available to help a pilgrim walk through the twists and turns of the labyrinth while meditating on the twists and turns of life. Walking along the path allowed people to detach themselves from the distractions of the world, gradually letting go of the cares that cloud the mind, until they reached the quiet center. There are many books on the labyrinth in modern and medieval spirituality. A good starting place is Lauren Artress, *Walking a Sacred Path: Rediscovering the Labyrinth as a Spiritual Tool* (New York: Riverhead Books, 1996).
57. See chapter 7.
58. Eccles. 1:12–14.

you" (187). In turning inward, he discovers Christ, and he is then able to re-enter the world with greater security and more wisdom.

A detailed examination of *The Labyrinth of the World and the Paradise of the Heart* goes beyond the scope of this work, but we can delineate some of the themes most clearly connected to the Unity's theology. When the pilgrim first comes upon the city, it looks beautiful and well ordered. Its main streets represent different social classes and callings: domestic, productive, academic, religious, political, and military. "The first class," Comenius tells the reader, "produces all; the second sustains all; the third teaches all; the fourth prays for all; the fifth judges and preserves all from disorder; the sixth fights for all. Thus all serve one another, and everything is harmonious" (68). This is a more elaborate version of the three feudal estates that Chelčický had criticized.[59]

From a distance, the city appears to be a perfect system of interlocking and interdependent parts, but on closer examination it is revealed as a scene of chaos. "When I listened, everything was filled with beating, banging, rustling, whispering, and shouting" (69). The pilgrim is given two guides who will lead him through the labyrinth, Ubiquitous and Delusion (63). When Ubiquitous says, "I walk through the whole world, explore all corners, and inquire into the words and deeds of every person," we are reminded of the young Comenius who walked from Heidelberg to Moravia. But when the pilgrim tells his guide, "I trust that God and my eyes will not lead me astray," Ubiquitous rebuffs him, warning him against thinking too much about what he sees, "or you will come to evil and I along with you" (64). Ubiquitous's warning is repeated by the second guide, Delusion, sent by the queen, "for it is not Her Majesty's will that whoever enters her kingdom should interpret what he sees and hears as he pleases."

Delusion's role is to lead people "to joy and contentment" (65). He intends to keep the pilgrim from learning the truth of what he sees, and he insists that the pilgrim wear special spectacles, their lenses made from "presumption" and their frames, from "habit" (66–67). The glasses make "what was ugly beautiful, and beautiful, ugly." Throughout the book the two guides try to prevent the pilgrim from using his senses and his reason to observe and understand the city through which he is journeying. But, like Hus and Chelčický, the pilgrim

---

59. See chapter 5.

is unwilling to follow Delusion's counsel that "all will be well. . . . Only believe, and let us go onward" (69).

Here Comenius addresses one of the great themes of modern literature and philosophy: does human happiness depend on self-deception? Do ideals and virtues merely mask the grinding force of opposing power structures, or is there a deeper reality and hope to which those ideals may lead?[60] The pilgrim manages to see things clearly because he has inadvertently put the eyeglasses on askew. He also refuses to let his mind be twisted by his guides, declaring, "I trust God that you will not bind my mind and reason" (67). True faith and true reason go hand in hand in the Brethren's theology. One of the tasks of the theologian and pastor was to *disillusion* people so that they could freely and willingly embrace the truth about themselves, the world, and God. Chelčický had boldly desacralized the feudal social hierarchy and revealed it as a structure of oppression; Comenius did the same for the early seventeenth-century social order.

Entering the city, the pilgrim is immediately struck by the ceaseless activity and noise. Ironically, Delusion unintentionally speaks the truth about humans: "They bear the image and likeness of immortal God, which can be recognized by the variety of their praiseworthy deeds. Here you can see as in a mirror the dignity of your race." But the pilgrim sees only hypocrisy (71). Society turns out to be a masquerade, and behind their masks people are deformed and monstrous. Rather than bear God's likeness, the city's inhabitants have pig lips, ox horns, dog teeth, fox tails, and other animal features symbolic of their greed, rapacity, cunning, and other vices. Delusion explains that the masks covering such monstrosity are necessary for public life, but "alone one can be as one is."

The labyrinth's denizens rush from one activity to another and are never satisfied. Some raise themselves on stilts so that they can appear better than their peers, only to have the envious trip them and leave them in the mud. (This may be an allusion to the coronation of Frederick.) People are deformed by their labors rather than ennobled by them. Each task requires almost all of

---

60. The literature on this question is too vast to cite, but one thinks immediately of Karl Marx, Sigmund Freud, Jean-Paul Sartre, Michel Foucault, and Franz Kafka. As Sterk and Louthan point out in their introduction to the *Labyrinth*, Václav Havel was an heir to Comenius when he wrote that proclaiming the simple truth is an act of treason in a regime based on lies (7–8).

a person's energy and attention, but honest workers still cannot feed themselves and their families. Apart from providing for one's family, the goals of most of the commercial and manufacturing activity the pilgrim sees are pointless (86). Here we see the influence of the Brethren's teaching on economic life: one's work is an expression of one's relationship with God, and it ought to be beneficial to others.[61]

Nor are marriage and family spared the pilgrim's disillusioning investigation. Stripped of the delusions of romance and desire, marriage loses its luster. First the pilgrim notices how poorly couples are paired when money and status, rather than compatibility and companionship, determine the match. A couple might marry for economic reasons, but once they are bound, they are joined by heavy chains that cannot be broken except by death. Many of the married people the pilgrim observes are horribly mismatched and even abusive to each other (82). Even in a happy and successful marriage like his own, the pilgrim finds that "sweetness is mixed with bitterness," especially the bitterness of grief.

The most disturbing image the pilgrim sees is Death strolling through the marketplace. "No one avoided Death. They only took care not to look at her" (76). On closer inspection, the pilgrim notices that people actually give Death the weapons she uses against them: disease, drunkenness, war, gluttony, and so forth. The pilgrim is horrified, and since he is evidently too sensitive for manual labor, his guides suggest that he take up the occupation of scholar. To his surprise, however, the pilgrim learns that even scholars are deformed: some cannot hear, others are unable to see or speak. One of the more memorable sections of the *Labyrinth* involves the pilgrim's visit to the library. Books, like medicine, are meant to improve the health and happiness of human beings, but only a few scholars choose their books carefully and eat the contents slowly in order to digest what is consumed. Most "behaved very greedily, stuffing themselves with whatever came into their hands. . . . I also saw that what they crammed into themselves came out of them again undigested. . . . Some of them fainted from dizziness or went mad. Others grew pale, pined, and died" (96). Still others merely carry their books in their pockets without ever reading them.

---

61. This was also part of the creed of the eighteenth-century Moravian Church. See Craig D. Atwood, *Community of the Cross: Moravian Piety in Colonial Bethlehem* (University Park: Pennsylvania State University Press, 2004).

Then there are those who prepare "beautiful cases" for their books. "They looked at the books, putting them on and taking them off the shelves again. They packed and unpacked them, and approaching and withdrawing, they showed each other and strangers how beautiful they looked. . . . Occasionally some also looked at the titles so that they would know what they were called" (97). Others merely copied what others had written, rather than think for themselves. The city's few wise scholars, by contrast, have "an inner store of knowledge," and their wisdom would survive the loss of their libraries—an allusion, no doubt, to Comenius's own situation.

The pilgrim observes that academic disputes are marked by hatred, envy, and malice. When Delusion describes this wrangling as part of the educational process, the pilgrim replies, "But I see wounds, blood, anger, and murderous hatred of one toward another. Even among the working class, I have seen nothing like this" (100). These passages clearly reflect the Unity's dislike of theological disputation. Hatred is hatred, no matter how refined the weapons.

The pilgrim's two guides conclude that he is too sensitive and scrupulous for academic life and that the religious profession might suit him better. They lead him on a tour of the world's religions: paganism, Islam, Judaism, and Christianity. Unfortunately, Comenius's assessment of non-Christian religions falls short of disinterested inquiry. His pilgrim dismisses Jewish worship as irrational and incomprehensible, "not unlike the howling of wolves" (123). He is only slightly less critical of Muslims, "those white-clad and well-washed people with rolled-up sleeves and sparkling eyes, biting their lips and roaring frightfully, running about, putting to the sword whomever they encountered, and wading in human blood" (124–25). His description of Judaism and Islam appear to rely heavily on Boehme.[62]

Had Comenius applied the same condemnation of violence to his own religion, he would have had to reject Christianity as well, but instead he sought the reformation of the Christian Church. The pilgrim's account of the violence, drunkenness, and lustfulness of Christians reads like Gregory's original complaints about the Catholic and Utraquist churches. Comenius, like generations of Brethren before him, argued repeatedly that knowledge of doctrine and scripture was meaningless without corresponding behavior. The clergy

---

62. Weeks, *Boehme*, 203.

came in for special condemnation, "the mind trained in Scripture, the heart exercised in cunning; the tongue full of piety, the eyes full of wantonness" (128).

Moving on to the city government, the pilgrim is persuaded to join a rebellion against one of the princes and install a new ruler, but the affair ends in violence. This episode, too, reflects Comenius's own despair, in this case over the political situation after the brief reign of Frederick, the Winter King, as he was known. "I gladly left this place and resolved never to return," says the pilgrim (141). He then examines the military profession. Delusion assures him that the military contributes to the well-being of society by "clearing away obstacles," but the pilgrim soon learns that the obstacles in question are other human beings. When he expresses horror during a battle he witnesses, his guide attacks him for being "squeamish" and "a sissy." Like Chelčický, Comenius demystified the art of war by stripping away the illusions of glory associated with it. War is nothing more than the brutal death and dismemberment of human beings undertaken to settle disputes among rulers. Throughout his life, Comenius repeated the pilgrim's cry: "Oh what barbarity and beastliness! . . . Are there not other paths to peace?" (144).

Turning away from warfare, the pilgrim sees that the wealthy voluntarily bind themselves in chains and are proud of their enslavement. Some of the wealthy "tied so many of their possessions onto themselves that they could neither walk nor stand but could only lie panting and groaning. Seeing this, I said, 'But in the name of all the saints, are these people supposed to be happy?' In all the work and human striving I observed below, I have never seen anything more miserable than such happiness" (153). With his unshaded eyes, the pilgrim sees the results of such gluttony and hedonism: disease, misery, and meaninglessness (153–59). Teetering on the brink of the abyss at the center of the world's labyrinth, he faces the final emptiness of life without faith, love, and hope. "Is this the goal of your learning and great wisdom with which you are so puffed up? . . . Oh God, God, God! God, if you are God, have mercy on me, a wretched man!" (186).

The pilgrim hears a voice calling him back to his true self: "Return whence you came, to the home of your heart, and shut the door behind you!" (187). He answers by closing his "eyes, ears, nostrils, and all external passages" and turning his consciousness inward. Once he is able to observe the condition of his own heart without distractions, he finds that it is dark and grimy. The virtues within (prudence, humility, justice, purity, and temperance) are faded and distorted, but in the quiet of his heart, the pilgrim waits.

Through the grimy upper window, a light bursts forth and God appears in human form. "Although his face shone greatly, yet it could be looked upon with human eyes; nor did it inspire terror, but radiated a loveliness such as I have never seen anywhere in the world. Then he, the epitome of kindness and good will, addressed me . . . embraced me cheerfully, and kissed me" (188). This passage strikes a note of exuberance and joy rarely found in the writings of the Brethren.[63] Christ persuades the pilgrim that all the earthly desires he has witnessed in corrupt and chaotic form can be transformed by making Christ the goal of his existence.

Christ tells the pilgrim to renounce the allure and cares of the world and to contemplate God, but this does not mean entering a monastery or living the life of an itinerant preacher.[64] He can "work faithfully, uprightly, and quietly" in his earthly profession (191). Christ instructs the pilgrim to follow the Sermon on the Mount: "for the sake of the peace of all, give up even yourself," and do not return violence with violence. In religious matters, he should not "stir up disputes" but "serve me in quietness." Rather than attempt to rule others, the pilgrim should devote himself to governing his own body and soul. The true meaning of heroism is the courage not to wage war but to master one's own desires (194).

Instructed by Christ in a few basic aspects of Christian life, the pilgrim is sent back into the labyrinth to seek the "invisible church" of true Christians (196). True to the theology of the Unity, Comenius emphasizes that Christianity is by its nature communal rather than individualistic. By finding Christ in the center of his own being, in solitude and quiet, the pilgrim is redeemed from his isolation and alienation. He learns that the true church is called *praxis christianismi*, which literally means "the practice of Christianity" but which Comenius translates as "the truth of Christianity" (197). Like generations of Brethren before him, Comenius defines Christian doctrine in terms of Christian practice. There can be no orthodoxy (right belief) without orthopraxy (right practice).

---

63. Říčan, *History of the Unity*, 375, 383.

64. Max Weber identifies the idea of "worldly asceticism," or renouncing the world while still pursuing a secular vocation, as a key factor in the rise of modern capitalist society. Weber, *The Protestant Ethic and the Spirit of Capitalism*, trans. Talcott Parsons (Los Angeles: Roxbury Publishing, 1996).

FIG. 22   Memorial of the Brethren's exile, Rixdorf, Germany.

The pilgrim learns that those who wish to enter the true church must endure an examination that includes a painful process of "new birth." It is difficult to give up the habits of the old self, but the reborn Christian becomes healthier, wiser, and more whole than before. Comenius and the Brethren were not concerned only with the question of whether a person would be admitted into heaven because of Christ's atonement but also with the experience of new birth and salvation in this life. Once the pilgrim is transformed, he sees a world that is the inverse of the one he has fled in terror. He finds the beautiful harmony for which he had longed from the beginning. It is the same world he has left behind, but rightly ordered according to light, truth, order, peace, joy, abundance, freedom, and safety (198).

The pilgrim's despair is not a descent into hopeless cynicism and apathy, as one finds in Voltaire's *Candide* or in existentialist writers like Sartre. It is the necessary disillusionment that allows the pilgrim to glimpse a better, more beautiful, and truer society. The *imago Dei*, or image of God, has not been completely destroyed. Though distorted and perverted by human greed and arrogance, the image of God is still visible. Through faith and love, there is hope even in the midst of tragedy. The Brethren viewed Comenius's allegory as a truthful statement about life and faith. They carried copies of the *Labyrinth* with them into exile. Some even claimed that they left their homeland with nothing but their Bibles and Comenius's *Labyrinth*.

Czech hopes for a Protestant victory over the Habsburgs were dashed when King Gustavus Adolphus of Sweden, leader of the Protestant cause, died in 1631. Soon Frederick of the Palatinate also died, and with him the hope of a Protestant regaining the Czech throne in Prague. Recognizing that their exile would continue for years, the Brethren made Leszno in Poland their permanent headquarters, reestablished the printing press there, and appointed Comenius rector of the school. Dissatisfied with existing textbooks and methods, Comenius turned to the work of contemporary pedagogical reformers like Eilhard Lubinus, Wolfgang Ratke, and the Jesuit William Bateus for advice and inspiration. Building on their ideas and on his own experience as a student and teacher, Comenius composed *Janua linguarum reserata* (Gate of Tongues Unlocked), one of the first books the Unity published in Leszno. For decades it was one of the most widely used textbooks in Europe, and it brought him international fame.[65]

In addition to his work in the Brethren's school, Comenius was elected cosenior of the Brethren in 1632, and was assigned the duties of secretary for the church, which included defending the Unity in print. During this time he translated the Puritan classic *The Practice of Piety*, by Lewis Bayly, into Czech for the Brethren's use.[66] He recognized the similarities between the piety of Bayly and that of the Brethren. Bayly's book later became a standard text for German Pietists.[67]

During this period as secretary of the Brethren in exile, Comenius wrote his first works on ecumenical theology and ecclesiastical reconciliation, *Haggaeus*

---

65. See Johannes Amos Comenius, *Orbis sensualium pictus*, facsimile of the third London edition of 1672, ed. James Bowen (Sydney: Sydney University Press, 1967), 11; Gerhard Michel, *Schulbuch und Curriculum: Comenius im 18 Jahrhundert*, Schriften zur Comeniusforschung 2 (Ratingen: Henn, 1973).

66. Spinka, *John Amos Comenius*, 53–55. Bayly's book was one of the most popular devotional works for the Pietists, according to Ward, *Protestant Evangelical Awakening*, 48.

67. Willem J. Op t'Hof, "Protestant Pietism and Medieval Monasticism," in *Confessionalism and Pietism: Religious Reform in Early Modern Europe*, ed. Fred van Lieburg (Mainz: Verlag Philipp von Zabern, 2006), 40–45.

redivivus (Haggai Reborn) (1632) and *Via pacis* (The Way of Peace) (1637).[68] It was in Leszno that Comenius began work on his idea of a grand synthesis of knowledge, faith, and social improvement, discussed in the next chapter. He called this "pansophy," which means universal wisdom, a term he probably learned from Boehme.[69] This "synthesis of beliefs and ideas" was part of the common currency of the early seventeenth century, especially among the followers of Paracelsus and Renaissance Platonism.[70]

Sometime earlier, Comenius had become acquainted with Samuel Hartlib (1595–1662), a scholar and reformer born in Elbing, which was in Prussia at the time. Since 1628 Hartlib had lived in London, where he had close connections to the English court through his wife. He became one of the leaders of an international group of like-minded reformers that included John Dury in Prussia and John Milton in England. The English Puritans' esteem for Hartlib can be seen in Milton's dedication of his treatise *Of Education* to him.[71] Comenius sent his friend Hartlib a sketch of his pansophy, asking for his criticism, but in 1637 Hartlib took the liberty of publishing it in England, without Comenius's consent, under the title *Pansophiae prodromus*.[72]

This early pansophic work was praised by the French luminary Marinus Mersenne, who was in close contact with Descartes, Pascal, Galileo, and other leading scholars and scientists of the age. It was probably through Mersenne's influence that Cardinal Richelieu offered Comenius an opportunity to establish

68. Spinka, *John Amos Comenius*, 57.

69. Klaus Schaller, *Pan: Untersuchungen zur Comenius-Terminologie* (The Hague: Mouton, 1958); Jaromír Červenka, "Die Grundlagen der pansophischen Idee des Johann Amos Comenius," *Acta Comeniana* 1 (1969): 77–84; and Červenka, "One Hundred Years of the Views on Comenius' Pansophia," in Čapková, Dohnalek, and Turkova, *Consultationes de consultatione*, 21–84.

70. Weeks, *Boehme*, 48ff.

71. John Milton, *Areopagita and Of Education*, ed. George Holland Sabine (Wheeling, Ill.: Harlan Davidson, 1987). For more on Hartlib's work on educational reform, see Charles Webster's collection of Hartlib's writings, *Samuel Hartlib and the Advancement of Learning* (Cambridge: Cambridge University Press, 1970).

72. Spinka, *John Amos Comenius*, 63. G. H. Turnbull wrote the first works on Hartlib's circle. See his *Samuel Hartlib: A Sketch of His Life and His Relations to J. A. Comenius* (New York: Oxford University Press, 1920), and his *Hartlib, Dury, and Comenius: Gleanings from Hartlib's Papers* (London: Hodder & Stoughton, 1947). Charles Webster built on Turnbull's work in *The Great Instauration*, arguing that this Hartlib circle was central to the development of English science and medicine. H. R. Trevor-Roper offers a much more negative reading of the Hartlib circle and especially of Comenius. Trevor-Roper, "Three Foreigners: The Philosophers of the Puritan Revolution," in his *Religion, the Reformation, and Social Change, and Other Essays*, 2d ed. (London: Macmillan, 1972), 237–93. See also Čapková, "The Comenian Group in England and Comenius' Idea of Universal Reform," *Acta Comeniana* 1 (1969): 25–34.

a pansophic college in France, an offer he declined.[73] At Mersenne's urging, Descartes read the *Prodromus*, but he objected to its blending of philosophy and theology, preferring his own strictly rationalist method. In 1642 Comenius and Descartes had a four-hour conversation at Endegeest, near Leiden, in the Netherlands. Rather than coming closer together, each thinker raised substantive objections to the other's work, but they parted on good terms.[74] They would also both be called into service for the Swedish Crown.

One of the most serious objections to pansophy came from within the Unity. Jerome Broniewski, a Polish nobleman, protested that pansophy mixed "matters divine and human, theology with philosophy, Christianity with paganism, and thus darkness with light."[75] Unlike Descartes, who rejected Comenius's use of revelation, Broniewski felt that Comenius was too rationalistic rather than too religious. He tried to have Comenius removed from his position as rector of the Brethren's school, even though he was co-senior. Comenius was forced to defend his ideas and methods at a synod of the Unity, where he argued that the Brethren had always seen the benefits of combining faith and reason. His works were warmly approved by the synod as expressions of the Brethren's theology.

Comenius's pansophy generated the most immediate interest in England, thanks in large part to the activism of Hartlib, who published *Prodromus* in English under the title *A Reformation of the Schooles* in 1642.[76] At Hartlib's suggestion, several members of Parliament invited Comenius to come to England in 1641 and discuss the possibility of establishing a pansophic college in Chelsea. (Interestingly, a hundred years later Zinzendorf would make Chelsea his headquarters in England.) Comenius accepted the invitation, in large part because he hoped that Parliament would support the Czech Protestants in

---

73. Spinka, *John Amos Comenius*, 57, 91.

74. Rood, *Comenius and the Low Countries*, 118–62; Pavel Floss, "Komensky's Auseinandersetzung mit dem Cartesianismus in seinen naturwissenschaftlichen Schriften," in Schaller, *Comenius: Erkennen, Glauben, Handeln*, 189–96; U. Kunna, "Komensky's Stellung zum Cartesianismus in seinen Spatschriften," in Schaller, *Comenius: Erkennen, Glauben, Handeln*, 197–204; Nicolette Mout, "Comenius, Descartes, and Dutch Cartesianism," *Acta Comeniana* 3 (1973): 243–45; Mout, "The Contacts of Comenius with the Netherlands Before 1656," *Acta Comeniana* 1 (1969): 221–31.

75. Spinka, *John Amos Comenius*, 68.

76. Comenius, *A Reformation of the Schooles*, trans. Samuel Hartlib (facsimile of the 1642 London edition), ed. R. C. Alston (Menston, England: Scolar Press, 1969); see also Lawrence Stone, "The Education Revolution in England, 1540–1640," *Past and Present* 28 (1964): 41–80.

their cause against the Habsburgs. He wrote *Via lucis* (The Way of Light) in preparation for this meeting with Parliament, but it was not published until years later. In it Comenius called for the establishment of a "college of light" that would examine nature and human society without prejudice.[77]

Those involved in the pansophic project had connections to Gresham College, which advocated educational reform. Some historians trace the origins of the Royal Society of London to the work of the Gresham circle, Comenius, and Hartlib.[78] Comenius never got to meet with the British Parliament, only with a few members who were part of Hartlib's circle. The outbreak of the English Civil War prevented plans for a pansophic college from proceeding, but Comenius was able to establish close ties in England and the bishops of the Church of England recognized him as a peer, a fact that Zinzendorf exploited in the next century.[79] It is possible that during or shortly after his sojourn in England, Puritan leaders in New England recruited Comenius to serve as president of Harvard College and establish a pansophic school system for the colony of Massachusetts. In his history of New England, Cotton Mather reported, "That brave old man, Johannes Amos Comenius, the Fame of whose Worth hath been Trumpetted as far as more than Three Languages (whereof every one is Endebted unto his Janua) could carry it, was agreed withal by our Mr. Winthrop, in his Travels through the Low Countries, to come over into New England and Illuminate this Colledge and Country in the Quality of President: But the Solicitations of the Swedish ambassador, diverting him another way, that Incomparable Moravian became not an American."[80] There is no additional evidence to corroborate Mather's claim, but it is hard to believe that he simply made it up. Even if Mather did manufacture a connection between Harvard and Comenius, it is a sign of the high regard in which the American Puritans held him.[81] His textbooks were used in New England as late as the early nineteenth century.[82]

77. Spinka, *John Amos Comenius*, 73–77.

78. Webster, *From Paracelsus to Newton*; Yates, *Rosicrucian Enlightenment*, 220–46.

79. For more on Comenius's visit to England, see Robert F. Young, *Comenius in England* (London: Oxford University Press, 1932).

80. Cotton Mather, *Magnalia christi americana, or, the Ecclesiastical History of New England* (London, 1702), book 4, p. 128, quoted in Spinka, *John Amos Comenius*, 84–86.

81. G. W. Schulte-Nordholt, "Comenius and America: Some Remarks on Some Relations," *Acta Comeniana* 2 (1970): 195–200.

82. David A. Schattschneider, "Three Examples of Comenius' Legacy in America," (paper given at

Comenius accepted the generous offer of Louis de Geer, a Walloon businessman with close connections to the Swedish Crown, to pursue his educational reforms in Sweden. De Geer had an exclusive lease on iron and copper mines in Swedish territories and was the largest arms manufacturer for the Protestant armies in the Thirty Years' War.[83] In *Labyrinth of the World*, Comenius raised serious questions about manufacturing weapons. His pilgrim asked how those "whose work consisted in fashioning instruments of cruelty . . . all for the destruction of humanity . . . can have clear conscience and such cheerful thoughts" (87). This was a strong expression of the Brethren's pacifism, but one wonders whether Comenius ever asked his patron this question. We do not know and must be content with the observation that Comenius could not avoid the contradictions and confusions of the labyrinth of the world.

In Sweden Comenius met with Queen Christina, who had learned Latin from his *Janua*. Chancellor Axel Oxenstierna offered him the job of establishing a national school system for the kingdom, noting that a "Hussite bishop" would be more acceptable than a Calvinist pastor to the Lutheran bishops in Sweden. Comenius declined the position, but he agreed to relocate to Elbing, in Prussia, where he would write textbooks for use in Sweden.[84] Comenius worked diligently for the Swedish Crown, but he ran afoul of church politics when he participated in an ecumenical gathering in Thorn, Poland, in 1645. The colloquy was an attempt to bring together Lutherans, Reformed, Catholics, and the Brethren in Poland, but it served only to highlight their differences and mutual animosity.[85] To complicate matters, the Brethren's representatives were officially listed among the Calvinists, prompting officials in the Church of Sweden to call for Comenius's removal from his post on the grounds that he was a Calvinist.[86] In reading Comenius's proposals for church reform and his criticism of church officials, it is important to remember that he was speaking from personal experience.

---

the conference "Comenius' Heritage and the Education of Man for the Twenty-first Century," Prague, March 1992), 3

83. Spinka, *John Amos Comenius*, 90. For more on the de Geer family and Comenius's relationship to them, see Rood, *Comenius and the Low Countries*, 67–117.

84. Spinka, *John Amos Comenius*, 93–97.

85. Ruth Rouse and Stephen Charles Neill, eds., *A History of the Ecumenical Movement, 1517–1948* (Philadelphia: Westminster Press, 1954), 88–91.

86. Spinka, *John Amos Comenius*, 103–7.

FURTHER EXILE

After ending his service to Sweden, Comenius rejected offers of patronage from several sources and returned to Leszno, where he was elected senior of the Bohemian and Moravian branch of the Unity in 1648. Shortly thereafter, his wife of twenty-four years died. They had four children, the youngest of whom, Daniel, was only two years old. Comenius married Jana Gajusová, the daughter of a fellow pastor, in 1649. A short time later, Comenius's daughter Alžběta married his scribe Peter Figulus, whom Comenius would later consecrate a bishop.[87]

The Thirty Years' War was finally brought to an end by the Peace of Westphalia in 1648. The treaty acknowledged that there was no real victor in that titanic struggle. There was, however, one clear loser. The parties to the peace treaty chose the religious geography of 1624, not 1618, as the norm for the treaty. The Czech lands had been overwhelmingly Protestant in 1618, but by 1624 the Habsburgs had established firm control of Bohemia and Moravia. Thus the treaty granted them freedom to continue persecuting non-Catholics in those regions. Moreover, the Unity of the Brethren was not included among the churches that could receive legal status anywhere in the Holy Roman Empire. The Reformed churches could be tolerated, but the church of Gregory, Luke of Prague, and Michael Weisse could not.

The mid-seventeenth century had one bright spot for Protestants in eastern Europe. By 1645 the Magyar nobles in northern Hungary and Transylvania had embraced Calvinism and gained a measure of sovereignty from the Habsburgs, including freedom of religion. The reigning prince, George Rákóczy I, capped his military victories with a vigorous program of religious and cultural advancement for his realm. Comenius's old professor, the famed encyclopedist Alsted, taught in Transylvania until his death in 1638.[88] Prince George's younger brother, Sigismund Rákóczy, invited Comenius to follow in Alsted's footsteps and teach in Sárospaták, the summer residence of the ruling family.

Comenius arrived in Sárospaták in November 1650 with a royal mandate

---

87. Pánek, *Comenius: Teacher of Nations*, 44.

88. Josif Antochi, "Alsted und Comenius in Transylvania," in Schaller, *Comenius: Erkennen, Glauben, Handeln*, 38–48; Petr Rákos, "Genti cuique splendorem addit: Comenius Among the Hungarians," in Pešková, Cach, and Svatoš, *Homage to J. A. Comenius*, 270–80.

to establish a school that would be a laboratory for his educational vision.[89] It was to be a *schola ludus*, or school of play, where students would be inspired by the joy of learning rather than the fear of punishment. Unfortunately, the conditions in Sárospaták were not as good as Comenius had expected, and he faced continual opposition to his *schola ludus* idea from the rector of the school, János Tolmai. Comenius wrote in complaint, "My whole method aims at changing the school drudgery into play and enjoyment. That nobody here wishes to understand." The two men clashed angrily over Comenius's desire to adopt the Jesuit practice of using drama as a teaching method. Comenius wrote several plays for students, including some on biblical themes that Tolmai considered impious because they mixed God's word with theater. Finally, in 1654, Comenius's students were allowed to perform a simple drama on the theme of learning Latin. It was such a success that it had to be repeated many times, but by that time Comenius had decided to leave Hungary.[90]

Comenius expressed his sense of failure in Sárospaták in his *Gentis felicitas* (The Happiness of the Nation).[91] Many contemporaries and later scholars agreed that Comenius had failed in Sárospaták, but modern scholarship has challenged that negative assessment.[92] Comenius's biographer Milada Blekastad notes that Comenius was sent off from Sárospaták by a crowd of admirers, some of whom had originally opposed his plans. She concludes, "Comenius has achieved the peak of his endeavours in Hungary."[93] It was during his time at Sárospaták that he prepared one of the most influential textbooks ever written, *Orbis sensualium pictus*. This text was designed to teach Latin to children by incorporating pictures with the study of language. As James Bowen points out in his introduction to an English translation of the work, "For the first time in the history of Western education a text book attempted to make the symbolic abstractions of language meaningful to the schoolchild in terms of

---

89. Eva Foldes and Istvan Meszaros, eds., *Comenius and Hungary* (Budapest: Akademiai Kiado, 1973).

90. Spinka, *John Amos Comenius*, 129–30. Comenius had hoped that Prince Sigismund would be the next great Protestant warrior against the Habsburgs. He officiated at the wedding of the prince to Henrietta Maria, daughter of King Frederick, raising expectations that Sigismund could take the Bohemian crown. But the prince and princess both died in 1654, and once again Drabík's prophecy of Habsburg defeat went unfulfilled.

91. Rákos, "Genti cuique splendorem addit," 275.

92. See Istvan Meszaros, "On the History of the Sárospatak School in the Fifteenth–Sixteenth Centuries, and on Comenius' *schola trivialis* There," in Foldes and Meszaros, *Comenius and Hungary*, 111–32.

93. Blekastad, *Comenius*, 517; Rákos, "Genti cuique splendorem addit," 274.

personal experience."[94] When published in 1658, it was an immediate success, and it went through hundreds of editions in more than a dozen languages, including Turkish, Arabic, and Mongolian.[95] That "incomparable Moravian," in Mather's words, had become an internationally renowned scholar and pedagogue, but he took little comfort in his personal success.

LATER WORKS

Following the disappointing Treaty of Westphalia, Comenius published a short book titled *The Bequest of a Dying Mother, the Unity of the Brethren*, in 1650. In this work, Comenius wrote in the voice of a woman (the Unity) admonishing her family members, namely, the various branches of Christianity. The "dying mother" called for repentance and renewed faith. She recalled the importance of the Brethren's ecumenical efforts, as well as their commitment to the law of love. The remaining Brethren should join other congregations rather than turn to unbelief and worldliness. She chastised them, though, because their "distrust, suspicions, quarrels, controversies, and self-seeking" had contributed to their exile and dispersion. She noted in particular that the Brethren were learning bad habits from other Christians: "their brains are befuddled with speculations and with everything else but the simplicity of Christ and of our worthy ancestors." She urged them to return again to the essential things, "genuine faith in Christ, fervent piety, and hope of the sweet age to come."[96]

Comenius returned to Leszno and assumed his duties as a senior of the Brethren, but he was sixty-four years old and wanted to complete his pansophic works. Once again, war interfered with his plans. Charles X of Sweden invaded Poland, and the Brethren supported him. Comenius even published a panegyric to King Charles when it appeared that Swedish victory was certain, but the Poles rallied. Polish nationalism and Catholic devotion were united when Queen Louisa Mary of Gonzague declared that the "black Madonna" of

---

94. See Bowen's introduction to *Orbis sensualium pictus*, 27.

95. Kurt Pilz, *Die Ausgaben des Orbis sensualium pictus: Eine Bibliographie* (Nurnberg: Selbstverlag der Stadtbibliothek Nurnberg, 1967).

96. Comenius, *The Bequest of a Dying Mother, the Unity of the Brethren*, trans. Matthew Spinka (Chicago: National Union of Czechoslovak Protestants, 1940), 10, 18, 19, 22.

the monastery of Czestochowa had ensured a Polish victory over Sweden in 1655.[97] As the victorious Polish forces drove the Swedes out of the country in April 1656, they took revenge on the Protestant center of Leszno. Three days of looting and burning left the city in ashes. Comenius lost his home, life savings, library, and numerous manuscripts prepared for publication. Among them was the Czech-Latin dictionary on which he had worked for more than forty years.[98]

A refugee once more, the elderly Comenius accepted the offer of Lawrence de Geer, son of his former patron, to move to Amsterdam with his family. De Geer supplied him with a home and a good salary, and the town council of Amsterdam offered to pay the costs of publishing his collected pedagogical works, *Opera didactica omnia*. For a time he enjoyed celebrity in Amsterdam, but when the prince of Transylvania invaded Poland to assist Charles X, Comenius abandoned his pacifism and supported the war effort by publishing the anti-Habsburg prophecies of three Czech prophets: Christopher Kotter, Christina Poniatowska, and Nicholas Drabík. Comenius had been collecting their bizarre prophecies since the 1620s and had even presented a collection of them to Frederick in his exile. The prophecies appeared in two editions: *Lux in tenebris* (Light in Darkness) in 1657 and *Lux e tenebris* (Light from Darkness) in 1665.[99]

When the prophecies of the end of Habsburg domination of central Europe failed to come true, Comenius was ridiculed throughout Europe. It was evident to many readers at the time (and even more so today) that the prophecies were merely the wishful thinking of displaced persons who longed for the destruction of the Habsburg Empire.[100] Comenius's reputation as a scholar was permanently harmed.[101] The Enlightenment critic Pierre Bayle used Comenius as

97. Atwood, *Always Reforming*, 163.

98. Spinka, *John Amos Comenius*, 135–36; Jiří Hrubes, "On the Panegyric of Comenius," *Acta Comeniana* 3 (1973): 247–53.

99. Spinka, *John Amos Comenius*, 137–40. An English translation of *Lux in tenebris*, titled *Prophecies of Christopher Kotterus, Christiana Poniatovia, Nicholas Drabicius*, was published in England in 1664 and is available on microfiche. The original is in the Bodleian Library, Oxford.

100. Trevor-Roper, "Three Foreigners," 237–93, points to Comenius's fervid belief in prophecy as proof that he was not part of the scientific revolution and that his pedagogical reforms were based on religious yearnings rather than sound practices.

101. See Turnbull, *Hartlib, Dury, and Comenius*, 377ff.; Yates, *Rosicrucian Enlightenment*, 203–9; Trevor-Roper, "Three Foreigners," 237–93; Klaus Schaller, "E revelationum labyrinthis tanden repertus in planum exitus," *Communio Viatorum* 25 (1982): 123–26; and Rood, *Comenius and the Low Countries*, 163–225.

an example of religious folly in his *Dictionaire historique et critique* in the early eighteenth century. Since this was one of the most influential books of the Enlightenment, Bayle's ridicule had a lasting impact on Comenius's reputation.[102] As a coda to the story, the Austrians executed Drabík as an enemy of the realm in 1671. They, at least, took Drabík's words seriously.

In one of his last works, *Unum necessarium*, an older and chastened Comenius addressed some of the mistakes in his own life and writings, including his publication of the prophecies. "This brought with it not only much labor and trouble, but also much fear, hatred, and danger, and, along with these, ridicule on account of my credulity, and threats on account of distrust and delay."[103] It is tempting to dismiss *Lux e tenebris* as evidence of senility, but passages in *The Labyrinth of the World* show that Comenius's belief in angelic messengers and divine prophecy was firmly established early in his career (212). Such beliefs were not unusual among seventeenth-century scholars, however. Many of the men associated with the scientific revolution, including Isaac Newton, John Dee, and Francis Bacon, were involved in what might be termed occult or mystical science, and believed in angelic messengers.[104] Modern scholars, moreover, have recognized that Comenius's view of divine prophecy was also an expression of his conviction that God remains active in the world.[105]

While belief in prophecy was not unusual in the seventeenth century, even among the educated, Comenius's zealous convictions about it raise a disturbing question about his theology. One of the major themes of *The Labyrinth of the World* is that people need to overcome worldly delusions in order to find true happiness. But were these delusions any worse than the delusions of Drabík? George Rákóczy risked his kingdom in a futile military venture against Poland in part because he believed in Comenius's anti-Catholic prophecies. For more than a century the Brethren had held to the simple teachings of Jesus and rejected speculation about the end times as a needless distraction.

102. Peter Gay, *The Rise of Modern Paganism*, vol. 2 of Gay, *The Enlightenment* (New York: W. W. Norton, 1966), 293.
103. "John Amos Comenius, *Unum necessarium*," trans. Vernon Nelson (BD thesis, Moravian Theological Seminary, Bethlehem, Pa., 1958), 114.
104. Webster, *From Paracelsus to Newton* and *Great Instauration*.
105. Joseph Smolik, "Das Eschatologische Denken des Johan Amos Comenius," *Evangelische Theologie* 43 (1983): 191–202; Amedeo Molnár, "Notes de lecture sur Comenius le theologian," *Acta Comeniana* 2 (1971): 305–11.

But in the midst of the turmoil of the seventeenth century, it was easy to lose perspective and to seek dramatic confirmations of one's hope rather than rely on faith alone. Comenius turned toward prophecy, and at the end of his life he suffered bitter disappointment and disillusionment. The world's labyrinth is extremely complicated, even for the faithful.

THE END OF THE UNITY OF THE BRETHREN

In the 1950s Rudolf Říčan calculated that five to six thousand Bohemian Brethren went into permanent exile during the Thirty Years' War. Leszno, in Poland, served as the center of the Unity after 1627, but the church there never recovered from the destruction in 1656. The Brethren were scattered over central Europe, but in general they sought out areas where the Reformed Church was strong. After the Treaty of Westphalia extinguished hopes for the restoration of the Protestant churches in Bohemia, Comenius urged his scattered flock to join Reformed churches, and most did so. A few Brethren congregations in Poland and Prussia endured until the nineteenth century, but they were basically Polish Reformed churches that used the Czech language in worship.[106] One of the last Unity congregations was in Thorn, Poland, where Bishop Sitkovius served as pastor in the early eighteenth century. As late as 1724 the Brethren in Thorn were persecuted when the Catholic authorities closed the Protestant school and executed twelve Protestant leaders.[107] Sitkovius supported the consecration of David Nitschmann in Herrnhut as a bishop of the Unitas Fratrum in 1735. The Polish branch of the Brethren maintained its separate episcopal succession, despite numerous difficulties, until the last bishop died in 1841.

In 1971 Marianka Fousek posed the question, "What caused the disappearance of the *Unitas Fratrum*, the noblest flower of the Czech Reformation? Was it simply the Thirty Years War and the persecution of Protestants in Bohemia and Moravia after the defeat of the Bohemian uprising against the Hapsburgs in 1620?" Fousek argued that the Unity was already on the road to

106. Müller, *Geschichte der böhmischen Brüder*, 3:317–89.
107. Ward, *Protestant Evangelical Awakening*, 21–23.

extinction before the battle of White Mountain, and that the ease with which the Brethren joined Reformed churches was evidence that their church had lost its distinctiveness. "The Brethren had been under foreign theological influences for several generations. They had no theological faculty of their own. While most of their candidates for the ministry prepared themselves for their vocation under the guidance of their pastors, in whose households they apprenticed and lived, the Brethren's best students were being sent to the Protestant universities abroad."[108] As a result, by 1620 the Brethren had assimilated into the Protestant world and were abandoning distinctive practices like private confession. Fousek's argument has merit, and it reminds us that the Unity of 1620 was not the same disciplined community of faith that it had been in the time of Blahoslav, but Fousek overstates her case. The Unity of the Brethren was not the only church destroyed or severely damaged during the Counter-Reformation in eastern and central Europe. All forms of Protestantism (Utraquist, Lutheran, Reformed, and Anabaptist) were nearly extinguished in Habsburg and Polish lands in the seventeenth and eighteenth centuries. The situation did not improve until Joseph II's edict of toleration in 1781. After that, the Unitas Fratrum was reborn in Czech lands.

Comenius spent his final years producing resources that would preserve the heritage of the Unity of the Brethren, and in that effort he was largely successful. "The congregations of the Unity pass away," he wrote, but the teachings of the Brethren might still bring about reformation and unity in other churches.[109] The institution was dying, but Comenius hoped that its message would live and bear fruit in the wider church. He prepared a new hymnal, a history of the church, a description of the Unity's discipline, a catechism, and a reprinting of the Confession of Faith of 1535. One of his most important publications was his account of the history and church order of the Brethren called

108. Fousek, "Spiritual Direction and Discipline," 209.
109. My reading of the *Bequest* is quite different from that of Truman Dunn, "Facing the Death of the Moravian Church with Courage and Vision," *The Hinge: A Journal of Christian Thought for the Moravian Church* 8, no. 4 (2001): 2–9. Dunn argues that the "idea that the Moravian Church as we know it must die before a new church can be formed . . . comes from our own history, from none other than Bishop John Amos Comenius" (8). But Comenius was not looking forward to the death of the Unity in the hope of resurrection; he was facing the tragic end of a vital community of faith, hoping that its heritage would be carried on in a general reformation of the churches. The *Bequest* was about preserving a heritage, not destroying it in order to create a new church.

Ratio disciplinae. This work provided an important link between Comenius and the German Pietists, including the residents of Herrnhut.

Comenius consecrated his scribe and son-in-law Peter Figulus a bishop of the Unity in "hope against hope," but Comenius outlived Figulus. Thus Comenius was the last senior, or bishop, of the Moravian and Bohemian branch of the Brethren when he died in 1670. The Polish branch of the Unity later consecrated Comenius's grandson, Daniel Ernst Jablonsky, bishop, even though he was a Reformed minister serving as chaplain to the king of Prussia. Jablonsky would pass the episcopacy of the Brethren to the Herrnhut community sixty-five years later, but that is a story for another book. Comenius was buried in the Walloon Church in Naarden, where the governments of the Netherlands and Czechoslovakia erected an impressive mausoleum in the twentieth century to honor his legacy, in the hope that the world would learn from the great educator.[110] Comenius brought the theological heritage of the Unity to fullest flower, and he offered that heritage to the world in ways that still challenge and inspire.

110. Müller, *Geschichte der böhmische Brüder,* 3:354, 359.

Thirteen

COMENIUS'S THEOLOGY AND PANSOPHY

John Amos Comenius, the brightest light of the Unity of the Brethren, had ambitious plans for the reformation of church and society based on his idea of "pansophy," or universal wisdom.[1] Pansophy united Comenius's pedagogical, theological, pastoral, philosophical, and political efforts in a more or less coherent system. It was Comenius's direct challenge to the fragmentation and specialization of the emerging modern world, especially the tendency to separate the material and the spiritual worlds.[2] The three most important elements of this pansophic reform were education, religion, and politics. Comenius summarized his project in this way:

> (1) We must make *education* easily available and introduce the *universal* culture of men's minds, so that the inter-change of books and wisdom is just as common-place as the use of the senses and the tongue among all

---

1. See Amedeo Molnár, "Zum Theologieverstandis des Comenius," *Communio Viatorum* 27 (1984): 227–41; Jan Marinus van der Linde, "Der andere Comenius," *Unitas Fratrum* 8 (1980): 35–48; Renate Riemeck, *Der andere Comenius: Bohmisher Brüderbishof, Humanist, und Pädagoge* (Frankfurt am Main: Stimme-Verlag, 1970); Z. Kučera, "John Amos Comenius: A Theologian of Universality," in Pešková, Cach, and Svatoš, *Homage to Comenius*, 190–98; Dagmar Čapková, "On the New Image of Comenius," *Acta Comeniana* 2 (1970): 470–81.

2. "Man has lost what Comenius and many with him called 'nexus hypostaticus,' fundamental link, man's bond with God as a being among the other creatures, as a partner among fellow-beings in the created world, the important among them as 'imago Dei,' entrusted with the role of a careful manager co-responsible for the destiny of the world." R. Palouš, "The World of Comenius," in Pešková, Cach, and Svatoš, *Homage to Comenius*, 12.

humankind. (2) Likewise the Reform of the *Ministry of the Church* is necessary to ensure that the sons of men therein are most truly born again to become the sons of God. (3) The *political system* requires to be reconstituted so that the whole body of human society is maintained in true peace and very pleasant order. In a word, the enlightenment of men must not depend on the wearisome infliction of a great host of text-books, and the increase of the sons of God must proceed without undue pressure from the ministry, rather like dew on the grass, brought to birth by the sunrise, and men must adopt a policy of tolerance instead of relying so much on the fear of the sword and other instruments of violence.[3]

Philosophers should attend to things, politicians to human affairs, and theologians to God, but Comenius posited that all three professions must work in concert for the benefit of the world. He connected these three professional orders to the essentials of the Brethren's doctrine: philosophy dealt with faith, politics with love, and religion with hope (1993:140).

Pansophy was based on the conviction that the revelation of God is threefold. "The story of Nature, the text of Scripture, and the register of Universal Ideas are man's alphabet, displaying the mystic meanings and the inter-play of God's wisdom to the sons of a more mature Wisdom" (1995:178). This universalism was inspired by the encyclopedic enterprise of Comenius's teacher Alsted, but pansophy differed from encyclopedism in two major respects. It focused on the practical reform of society, and it attempted to penetrate to the essential unity of things. Pansophy worked from the simple to the complex and back to the simple. It was not an attempt at an exhaustive knowledge of the world but a search for a true understanding of reality, which Comenius thought would lead to harmony among peoples and nations.[4]

For years, scholars dismissed pansophy as a misguided medieval exercise that distracted Comenius from his practical educational reforms, but in the latter half of the twentieth century students of Comenius recognized that pansophy

---

3. John Amos Comenius, *Panorthosia, or Universal Reform, Chapters 1–18 and 27*, trans. A. M. O. Dobbie (Sheffield: Sheffield Academic Press, 1995) (hereafter cited parenthetically as 1995 plus page number), and *Panorthosia, or Universal Reform, Chapters 19–26*, trans. A. M. O. Dobbie (Sheffield: Sheffield Academic Press, 1993) (hereafter cited parenthetically as 1993 plus page number), 1995:172.

4. See Hofmann, "Enzyklopadische Impuls J. H. Alsteds"; Robert Alt, "Die Consultatio und ihre Beziehungen zur enzyklopadischen und utopischen Literatur," *Acta Comeniana* 1 (1970): 87–92.

FIG. 23   Apostolic clock in Old Town Square, Prague, a symbol of harmony for Comenius.

was central to all of his work.[5] Comenian scholar Dagmar Čapková expressed this growing appreciation of Comenius's pansophy: "The important contribution to European culture by Comenius is his methodological emphasis on an integrated whole of spiritual, mental, practical, individual, and social activity of mankind which will lead to a new system of culture, based on the defence of and respect for life, on universal life-long all round education for everyone based on truth, love and tolerance, and on the participation of all men in discussing *emendatio rerum humanarum* [reform of all human affairs]."[6] What

5. Jaromír Červenká, "Die Grundlagen der pansophischen Idee des Johann Amos Comenius," *Acta Comeniana* 1 (1970): 77–84; Červenká, "One Hundred Years of the Views," 21–84. Vladimir Jelenik takes a negative view of the relationship between pansophy and pedagogy: "Whatever the benefits of these efforts, it must be admitted that preoccupation with them had an unfortunate effect upon his didactic works. The genial, imaginative, and inventive qualities of his earlier works made not only for instruction but also for charm, whereas the later didactic works and the revisions of his earlier works are ensnared in the net of system and represent a less vigorous and penetrating thinker." Jelenik, *The Analytical Dialectic of Comenius* (Chicago: University of Chicago Press, 1953), 5.

6. Dagmar Čapková, "The Cultural Inheritance of Comenius," in Vliet and Vanderjagt, *Johannes Amos Comenius*, 17.

follows is a sketch of Comenius's pansophy and its relationship to the theology of the Brethren.

CONSULTATION ON THE REFORM OF HUMAN AFFAIRS

As we saw in the previous chapter, Comenius first sketched his pansophic reform in *Pansophiae prodromus*, which led to his invitation to England to establish a pansophic school.[7] Although that plan failed, he continued to refine and elaborate on his reform ideas throughout his life. Unfortunately, he died before completing his *De rerum humanarum emendatione consultatio catholica* (General Consultation on the Reform of Human Affairs). The *Consultatio* was to be composed of seven books, covering different aspects of the pansophic reform: (1) *panegersia*, or universal awakening, (2) *panaugia*, or universal light, (3) *pansophia*, or universal wisdom, (4) *pampaedia*, or universal education, (5) *panglottia*, or universal language, (6) *panorthosia*, or universal reform, and (7) *pannuthesia*, or universal warning. The manuscript of the *Consultatio* was lost until the 1930s, when it was discovered by Professor Dimitri Čyzevsky (Dmitrij Tschizewskij) in an orphanage in Halle, Germany. The Latin original was published for the first time in 1966 in Czechoslovakia, and it has been the object of great interest among Comenians ever since.[8] Portions of it were translated into English in the 1990s.

The only part of the *Consultatio* to be printed in Comenius's lifetime was *Panegersia, or Universal Awakening*, which appeared in 1668 in Amsterdam.[9] It provides a nice entrée into the overall program, and it was an important bridge between the Brethren and the Pietists in Germany. In 1702 August Hermann Francke, a leading figure in German Pietism, reprinted this work along with some of Comenius's other writings. Nicholas von Zinzendorf, leader of the

7. Comenius, *Reformation of the Schooles*; Comenius, *The Way of Light*, trans. E. T. Campagnac (London: Hodder & Stoughton, 1938).

8. Comenius, *De rerum humanarum emendatione consultatio catholica* (Prague: Czechoslovak Academy of Science, 1966); Johannes Schurr, *Comenius: Eine Einfuhrung in die Consultatio Catholica* (Passau: Passavia Universität Verlag, 1981); Robert Kalivoda, "Comenius' Consultatio und Comenius' Philosophie," *Acta Comeniana* 1 (1969): 113–16. For more information on the discovery itself, see Dagmar Čapková's introduction to *Consultationes de consultatione*, 7–21.

9. The original text was in Latin but was translated into Czech and Russian in the nineteenth century. The first English version appeared in 1990.

Herrnhut community, had been a student of Francke's at Halle and was familiar with some of Comenius's works.[10] The question of Comenius's direct influence on Herrnhut belongs in another book, but we can identify one reason
why the Herrnhuters and other Pietists were attracted to Comenius. Like the
eighteenth-century Pietists, Comenius based his proposed reforms on simplicity, spontaneity, and unity. Reform must begin with an understanding of the
basics: "Let our *philosophy* be simpler provided that it satisfies moderate minds
and circumstances! Let our *religion* be simpler provided that it satisfies God,
the fount of simplicity, and men of upright conscience! Let our *political system*
be simpler, provided that it satisfies its purpose, namely, that mankind shall be
preserved in peace!" Comenius saw his program as a part of salvation history,
but he defined salvation in broader terms than simply forgiveness of sins: "*Firstly*,
let us recognize THE SALVATION OF MANKIND as our goal! Let us take steps
to rescue our schools, churches and political systems (1) from partisanship
which infinitely divides us, (2) from multiplicity which infinitely embarrasses
and perplexes us, and (3) from compulsion and violence which endlessly afflict
and torment us! Let the world revive its passion for universal and total salvation and for the simplest truth and perfect peacefulness everywhere."[11]

Comenius lived in an age that had become aware of the vastness of the
earth and the diversity of peoples within it, and he broadened his gaze beyond
that of Gregory the Patriarch or Luke of Prague to include the universal welfare of all the earth's people. He believed that European Christians had much
to offer the world, particularly the teachings of Jesus, but they could also learn
from the other children of the Creator. "We know that God is everywhere and
spreads his gifts variously among peoples and nations and languages and ages,
so that the whole earth is filled with his glory, so all men's hearts could be filled
with his light. But in the past, Alas! We have stubbornly refused to combine
our little sparks and torchlights." One of his boldest proposals was the establishment of a world assembly or ecumenical council that would represent all
the inhabited continents. Comenius lamented the fact that humans divide the
world into nations, declaring some enemies and others friends: "mother earth
bears them and nurses them all for a time; air and winds breathe upon them

10. Rýdl, "Comenius in the Development of European Thinking," 171–79.

11. John Amos Comenius, *Panegersia, or Universal Awakening*, trans. A. M. O. Dobbie (Warwickshire: Peter I. Drinkwater, 1990), 60, 70.

all and make them grow. The same sky protects them all; the same sun and stars traverse all regions in turn so that all men may enjoy a common life and thrive with a common spirit. Therefore since we are all fellow-citizens of one world, what is to prevent us from combining into one political state with one set of laws?"[12] In order for the assembly to reform the world, its members would have to commit themselves to three principles:

> 1. *The need to avoid prejudice.* No one should be deceived into claim-
> ing universality for himself or his religion. We should never expect to
> reach true unity, universality, and true reform until we are firmly con-
> vinced that ours is at best only partial perfection. Prejudices of this kind
> must be destroyed and banished from our minds, and generally speak-
> ing men should be entirely free of prejudice before taking part in this
> saintly assembly;
> 2. *The need for impartiality,* so that no one considers anything as exclu-
> sively his own affair but everything is of common concern. We should
> adopt as our motto *"the safety of the people must be the supreme law."* . . .
> The third duty will be *to establish a new philosophy, a new theology or
> religion, and a new political system.* (1993:135, 140)

Comenius's proposal represents one of the earliest calls for structured and sus-tained interfaith dialogue in the history of Western culture. This was a remark-able statement on ecumenism and the pursuit of truth and justice in the world, but Comenius's awareness of the relative nature of truth was consistent with the Unity's teaching. Comenius's global perspective went far beyond the vision of Gregory or Luke of Prague.

ESCHATOLOGICAL HOPE

In part six of the *Consultatio,* titled *Panorthosia* (universal reform), Comenius offered his thoughts on the reformation of the world based on the expecta-tion of the millennial Kingdom of God promised in the Bible (Rev. 21:9–10,

12. Ibid., 25, 70.

19:7–8).[13] Unlike modern fundamentalists, Comenius's eschatological expectation was based on the conviction that God intended that humans participate in bringing about the restoration of the world. The world suffers from the curse of Babel, but Christians can anticipate and work for the creation of Zion, the city of God, by establishing a just social order. It was time to call people together for a general discussion on reform that would lead to "the quick and complete overthrow of the great Babylon of our confusions and the establishment of God's Zion in its sublime light for the nations of the world" (1995:41). Chaos and confusion could be overcome through education, communication, and the ethic of love.

Comenius used the Old and New Testaments to buttress his belief in the dawning of a new age, when the world would return to the original blessings of Eden.[14] The "Philadelphia church" of Revelation 3:7–9 was emerging, and the defeat of Satan was at hand. This last age of the world would be an age of enlightenment, true religion, and peace. But the millennial kingdom would not arrive unless humans played an active role in bringing it about. This millennial dream was quite different from that of the Táborites, who sought to establish the Kingdom of God through war and bloodshed. "Men need a true relationship," Comenius wrote, "with Nature through Philosophy, with each other through true Politics, and with God through true religion, and this would produce a true reform of human affairs in contrast to previous attempts which have been fraught with strife and violence" (1995:47).[15]

Comenius had seen enough of war to know that there was no such thing as a holy war. He reclaimed the pacifist heritage of the Unity of the Brethren

13. See Schroer, "Reich Gottes bei Comenius."
14. The scripture passages quoted in *Panorthosia*, 2:60–65, are Dan. 12:4; Rev. 20; Hos. 3:5; Jer. 31:34; Joel 2:28; 2 Esd. 6:20–21, 15:20, 26; Zech. 8:20–22, 9:10, 14:15; Mal. 4:5–6; Isa. 2:2, 2:4, 11:6–9, 30:26, 62:16, 66:12, 66:18; and Luke 17:26–27.
15. Comenius accepted the new historical understanding of Johannes Coccejus, who proposed that there were seven ages of the world, corresponding to the seven days of creation. The last age is the great Sabbath age, the millennial kingdom. For more on this idea, see Douglas H. Shantz, "Discovering the Key to Reformed Pietist Chiliasm: The Influence of Johannes Coccejus upon Horch, Reitz, and Bröske," *Covenant Quarterly* 61 (2004): 17–37. Comenius emphasized the active role of humans in the modern world as part of this scheme of salvation. "On the *sixth* day, the rational creature, Man, was formed after the image of God, and this corresponds to the rational age of the world which has brought a revival of the arts, a love for sacred literature and a reasonable investigation of countless subjects." *Panorthosia*, 1995:64. He most probably learned Coccejus's schema from Alsted, whose 1627 *Diatribe de mille annis apocalypticis* was instrumental in developing and popularizing millennialist thought in Calvinist circles. Hotson, *Paradise Postponed*, 176.

and eloquently proclaimed irenicism in many of his works.[16] "Mankind has had enough of folly and war," he wrote in the *Consultatio*, "and it is to be hoped that the time will come when all men are exhausted with wars and return to peace, and the state of this world nearing its end becomes one of peace and tranquility" (1995:57). The goal of human history was the return to the original blessing of creation, where God, nature, and humankind worked in harmony. We saw a similar perspective in Luke of Prague's catechism, but Luke had envisioned the restoration as coming within the community of faith rather than in the world as a whole. Comenius expanded the Brethren's eschatological perspective.

Following the theological tradition of the Unity of the Brethren, Comenius consistently taught that faith in God as Creator, Redeemer, and Sanctifier leads to positive engagement with the world that God has created, redeemed, and sanctified. In other words, faith was an active concept, and humans were active agents of God's work in the world. "Christ does all his work apart from that of Redemption through others" (1995:73).[17] God made humans rational because he intended that they use their minds to work for the restoration of creation; therefore the church should not interfere with the pursuit of truth. "It would surely be absurd if God equipped Man with an intelligent and inquiring mind and commanded him to be especially mindful of his salvation only to find that Man in his turn insulted him by refusing."[18] In this Comenius was consistent with the Brethren's confidence, from the beginning, in the ability of ordinary people to think for themselves and create a disciplined and orderly community. The rational nature of mortal humans was the first answer in Luke's catechism.

Comenius united two cardinal theological concepts, creation and redemption, in his understanding of the restoration of all things. The idea that God

16. His classic statement on the peace witness is *The Angel of Peace*, ed. Milos Safranek, trans. W. A. Morison (New York: Pantheon Books, 1945), which he wrote in 1667 in the hope of stopping war between England and the Netherlands. Josef V. Polišensky analyzes Comenius's efforts on behalf of peace in the context of seventeenth-century politics and notes that his efforts were not well received. See Polišensky, "Comenius, the Angel of Peace, and the Netherlands in 1667," *Acta Comeniana* 1 (1970): 59–66, and "The Social and Political Premises of the Work of J. A. Comenius," *Acta Comeniana* 4 (1979): 5–26.

17. Amedeo Molnár, "Comenius' theologica naturalis," *Communio Viatorum* 8 (1965): 53–64.

18. *Panegersia*, 46. "It is well-known that from the beginning of creation God took no immediate action by himself in dealing with his creatures, but always used them as his agents. It is most important that every creature should be able to rule by itself. That is why God endowed everyone with an element of self-love, a desire for self-preservation, and the ability to seek ways of survival" (46).

created all things good and had made humankind in his own divine image meant that nature, including human nature, reflected the goodness of God, in spite of the existence of sin and corruption in the world. Redemption through Jesus Christ, "the new Adam," addressed the issue of sin and correction. For Comenius, Christ was "capable of restoring everything" (1995:72). Christ was the source and model of redemption, "the first supreme model and pattern of all God's works, the very creation (and subsequent incarnation) of God's Wisdom" (1993:23). Redemption, for Comenius, was not simply the justification of the individual before the judgment seat of God; it was the restoration of the original blessing of creation. If humans recognized their true nature as created in God's image, and if they committed themselves to cooperating in the redemption of the world, "then the light and peace would return to the world, which would work like an elaborate clock with all its components well connected, well balanced and functioning together for a common purpose. Every man in creation would return to the image of God within him (I Colossians 1:26–29) and similarly every family group, every state and church, and finally the entire world" (1995:50).

A true reform of human affairs would begin when Christians recognized that *all* humans bore God's image. This was the primary guide for ethical decisions: "Whenever you encounter one of your neighbours, regard him as yourself in another form (which he is), or indeed as God in another form, for he is the image of God, and God will be watching to see how reverently you treat him" (1993:22).[19] Comenius's millennial dawn began with the awareness that all humans shared in the divine image and reflected, however imperfectly, divine nature. The quest for social reform would succeed only if people respected the axiom that each person was "a Creature with his own free will, made in the likeness of his Creator. . . . Hence God brings no compulsion to bear upon mankind, even when it has recovered from its fall and is restored to its true self; but deals with it only by persuasion, using promises to attract it to the good and threats to deter it from evil, and teaching it how to see the ways of

---

19. The basis of ethics for Comenius is the awareness of the image of God in all people. "1. Men should behave in the same way towards the image of God (which means himself and his fellow men) as he should behave towards God. 2. Since mankind is God's image, we should show the same behaviour towards it as God does, for God is setting us an example" (1995:190).

salvation before it but to guard against surrounding pitfalls leading to destruction, and so to take thought for its own best interests" (1995:94).

No one could be led through the labyrinth of the world to salvation by violence, force, or deception. "Force, coercion, fraud, and treachery are illegitimate ways to obtain the obedience of a rational creature." Comenius urged political leaders to do "everything freely, without the application of force, and reasonably, without trickery or fraud. For human nature wishes to be ruled in humane ways, more by leading than dragging, more by persuasion than forcing; this is because it has been made rational according to the image of God, and free, and, in fact, its own authority."[20] Here again Comenius expressed clearly the Brethren's perspective that coercion has no place in matters of faith, but he extended this insight to the social and political realms as well. Peace, for Comenius, was more than the cessation of armed conflict or a state of divine bliss; it was the ability to view the world from God's perspective and act as God acts toward his own creation. Compulsion violated creation and demeaned the image of God. Comenius's motto was *omnia sponte fluant; absit violentia rebus* (let everything flow of its own accord, let violence be absent from the process), or "let everything flow freely in the absence of violence."[21]

For two centuries the Brethren had struggled for religious toleration and freedom of worship. Comenius pursued that struggle on an even larger scale. Love, not dogmatic certainty, was one of the three essentials of salvation, and Comenius, like Chelčický, rejected the notion that anyone could show love for others while attacking them, let alone while burning them at the stake for heresy. But Comenius went well beyond the Unity's perspective in arguing that Christian love and respect should include all people, of whatever faith.

> Firstly we should have no hatred toward *Christians*, because they are servants of Christ, or at least profess to be so. We should not adopt a hostile attitude towards *Mohammedans* [Muslims], because they acknowledge our Christ as a great prophet, and do not allow any blasphemy towards him. . . . We should be tolerant towards the Jews because theirs is "the

---

20. *Unum necessarium*, 78.

21. In his introduction to a selection of Comenius's writings on religion, Amedeo Molnár points to the influence of the Brethren's theology on Comenius's motto. See J. L. Hromadka and Amedeo Molnár, eds. and trans., *J. A. Comenius—A Perfect Reformation* (Prague: Comenius Faculty of Theology, 1957).

adoption, and the glory, and the covenants, and the giving of the law, and the service of God, and the promises, and of them as concerning the flesh Christ came" (Romans IX 4, 5); and we have only been taken up into salvation through their unbelief which befell them in times past (Romans XI, 11). . . . Lastly, we should be tolerant towards all *Gentiles*, because they are blind, and deserve compassion rather than hatred. (1995:119)

This respect for all people would not rule out evangelism, but it rejected all forms of persecution and coercion. Evangelism was to be based on love and respect, according to Comenius. If the evangelism did not reflect the character and witness of Jesus, then it was not Christian, regardless of the content of the doctrine. True evangelism, for Comenius, was based on "kind and humane treatment" and respected the rationality and integrity of others (1995:246).

POLITICS

Comenius argued that God established three estates for the good of the world. These were not the three estates of medieval social hierarchy but the realms of education, religion, and justice. It is interesting that Comenius did not include the household in this schema, as Luther had. This was probably because each estate, in Comenius's scheme, entrusted its own professionals—teachers, pastors, and magistrates, respectively—with the task of supervising these areas of life. Moreover, Comenius argued that the household encompassed each estate in miniature because each household was its own school, church, and government, with the father being responsible for the well-being of everyone, including servants and boarders. It is worth noting that Comenius's detailed "instructions for the household" were based on the Unity's household instructions, discussed in chapter 7 (1993:31–37).

Beyond the household, each of the three estates had its proper task, but Comenius believed that each was in need of reformation. In particular, each estate needed to learn to work in concert with the others rather than impede their work. "The task of theology," for example, "will be to seek the face of God and to foster the desire to walk unfailingly in his sight, but it will avail itself of the services of philosophy and politics to supply the light of things and the laws of happiness respectively. Politics for its own sake and in its own right will deal with ways toward peace, but it will look to philosophy for enlightenment on things, and in theology for the hope of a better life and its own establishment in Heaven" (1995:159–60). If the professionals in each estate did their work as instructed by God, then greater knowledge of the natural world, peace on earth, and peace of conscience would result (1995:167). In keeping with the Unity's established convictions, Comenius maintained that clergy sinned when they laid "claim to secular power which does not belong to them." Politicians likewise sinned when they assumed authority over the church and wished "to keep it under their control" (1995:161). The sword had no place in matters of salvation, but neither should theologians dictate the laws of the state.

This perspective on human society stands in marked contrast to Thomas Hobbes's *Leviathan*, which appeared during Comenius's lifetime.[22] Hobbes presented a nightmarish picture of human beings in the state of nature. Without government, they would have no industry and would starve. Moreover, they would engage in perpetual warfare unless a greater power restrained them through threat of force. Human life was by nature "poor, nasty, brutish, and short," but an absolutist state with complete mastery over its citizens could enforce a civil order for the good of all. For Hobbes, peace could be achieved only through the coercive violence of the state. Peace was merely the repression of violence by the threat of violence.

Hobbes provided intellectual support for the emerging absolutist states, but Comenius rejected absolutism on several grounds. First, humans were made in the image of God, and the attempt to coerce them led to rebellion and dissent rather than peace and harmony. Repression ultimately failed to bring peace. Second, there was no divine right of monarchy or any other governmental system. In A. M. O. Dobbie's words, "Neither kings nor politicians hold power by divine right, and autocratic rule is a piece of gigantic effrontery" (1995:31). Instead of an absolute monarchy, Comenius advocated Althusius's concept of federal government, which consisted of interrelated units. Such a government, like the ecclesiastical government of the Unity of the Brethren, which had bishops, an Inner Council, and congregational councils, would combine the

---

22. Comenius identified several utopian writers as influences in his *Consultatio*, among them Francis Bacon, Augustine of Hippo, Thomas Campanella, Johann Valentin Andrea, and Plato, but he approached each critically. *Panorthosia*, 1995:21, 34.

best aspects of monarchy, aristocracy, and democracy. The concentric circles of authority would include a world assembly, to meet every fifteen or twenty years, much like the modern United Nations, to adjudicate claims and maintain peace among nations (1995:222).

This is not the place for a detailed discussion of the laws that Comenius proposed for the state, such as a tax on inheritance to provide relief for the poor, but throughout his writing we see an attempt to build on Chelčický's original awareness that the wealthy and greedy fed off the labor and misery of the poor (1993:98).[23] Following the Unity's original doctrine, Comenius taught that part of the solution to the world's misery lay in individuals' looking toward heavenly riches rather than seeking earthly pleasures and power. "Wealth is sure to bring anxiety, political power vanishes like smoke, and pleasure is a sweet drug leading to all kinds of vice, assuming that we pursue these ambitions in the usual way to the exclusion of better things."[24] Unlike the original Brethren, though, Comenius called for active engagement in the reform of society rather than withdrawal from a corrupt world. Comenius's willingness to propose changes in civil law indicates how far he had moved from the original sectarianism of the Brethren, but Comenius agreed with the Brethren that the world of politics, commerce, and law was corrupt. Good politics should not be naïve, but it must begin with the knowledge of the vanity of the world. People could not find their way out of the labyrinth unless they acknowledged that they were stuck there in the first place.

In *Unum necessarium* (One Thing Necessary), one of his last works, Comenius returned to this theme of the vanity of the world.[25] He claimed that all people were afflicted by three woes, which could be summed up in the classical myths of the labyrinth of Minos, the Sisyphean mountain, and the delights

23. See also Rudolf Říčan, "Motifs et modeles de l'Unite des Freres dans la consultation," *Acta Comeniana* 1 (1970): 47–57; Amedeo Molnár, "Comenius et l'Unité des Freres tchèques," *Communio Viatorum* 1 (1957): 110–15; Eva Foldes, "Comenius' Connections with the Anti-Feudal Movements," in Foldes and Meszaros, *Comenius and Hungary*, 51–68; J. Hřbek, "Comenius and His Endeavours to Reform Human Society," *Acta Comeniana* 3 (1974): 17–20.

24. *Panegersia*, 16–17.

25. *Unum necessarium*. Unfortunately, Vernon Nelson's translation—which constituted his bachelor of divinity thesis at the Moravian Theological Seminary (1958)—has never been published, but a German translation of the *Unum necessarium* is readily available. The original Latin text was published twice, with minor variations, first in 1668 in Amsterdam, and again in Amsterdam in 1724, during the heyday of the Pietist movement.

of Tantalus.[26] These represented confusion, futility, and grief, respectively. In discussing these myths, Comenius distinguished between the essential goodness of God's creation and its current corrupt state. Neither age, nor class, nor status, nor gender, nor profession would exempt anyone from confusion, futility, and grief, but human nature remained basically good. Most important, God wanted his creatures to be happy in the world he had made. "Why did it please God to sow such deep-rooted desires in the human heart, if he never wished them to be full grown?" The problem flesh-and-blood humans faced was the gap between the goodness of creation and the current corruption. Humans could achieve true happiness only when their eyes were opened to what is worth desiring, and when they had the freedom to pursue truth and happiness.[27] In a pluralistic society it was necessary for the state to be tolerant even of error so that people might be free to pursue truth and lasting happiness. Comenius considered toleration one of the Christian virtues and a sign of the believer's strength (1995:119–25).[28]

PEACE AND JUSTICE

Though Comenius's program appears complicated on first reading, it is rather simple. In fact, Comenius taught that one should always begin by examining first principles. In the case of social and ecclesiastical reform, one should first inquire about the real purpose of the church, state, or school. Then one could judge how well such institutions functioned and where reform was needed. Governments were not to be judged by their ideology or national pride but by how effectively they achieved their purpose. Comenius's definition of the purpose of the state is still relevant today. "Since the aim of human society is general peace and security," he wrote, "and the safety of the people ought to be the

26. The labyrinth in myth was a cunning path of confusion and deception. The mythical Sisyphus was doomed to spend eternity rolling a stone up a hill, only to have it roll back again each time. And Tantalus, in Hades, offered the thirsty water they could not drink and food they could not eat. It is interesting that the myth of Sisyphus was revived by existentialist philosophers, like Albert Camus, in the twentieth century. For Camus, though, Sisyphus represented the triumph of consciousness in the midst of absurdity.

27. *Unum necessarium*, 8–9, 17, 7.

28. Some people cannot "bear discord whatsoever. But it is only a weakling who cannot bear anything. A man of character tolerates everything, and if possible, he improves things." *Panegersia*, 72.

supreme law of every state and kingdom, our immediate task is to put a stop to everything that can distress, trouble, or upset human society in any way or break the bonds of peace and security whether of the state or the individual" (1993:102). For Comenius, this meant that war always represented a failure of the state, for war endangers rather than protects citizens. Though Comenius allowed for national self-defense, he believed that good government, diplomacy, and decency would reduce the threat of aggression. "The end or aim of this Political System will be to gather the nations of the world together again into the harmony of peace among mankind by abolishing wars and cutting away the causes of war" (1995:187).

Comenius did not consider the state absolute. The worst of all forms of government was tyranny, where the state was at war with its own citizens, endangering their lives and souls through oppression. Civilized nations respected international law, natural law, and human rights.[29] Comenius did not expect that laws and institutions alone could restore the proper function of politics; forgiveness was necessary as well. As long as humans were divided into rival camps, there would be no peace. As long as each camp harbored grudges and sought revenge for wrongs, real or imagined, peace would elude human grasp. Three hundred years after Comenius, Desmond Tutu and Nelson Mandela pursued a similar line of thought by establishing a truth and reconciliation commission in South Africa. Without truth, there can be no reconciliation, and without forgiveness there is no hope for peace. Comenius noted that disagreements lead to hatred and heated emotion, which in turn lead to "injustice and persecution which erupt from our hatred to our mutual destruction." Social reform must therefore include ways to resolve disputes reasonably.

Because ignorance, prejudice, and stubbornness combined to prevent the changes necessary for improvement, reform must overcome these things. The path to peace required forgiveness and mutual love ("they should believe it unworthy of humanity to pursue one another in hatred, no matter what the cause may be"); mutual tolerance ("no one should force his opinion on philosophy, religion, or politics upon others, but should allow everyone to use his senses to the full, and to enjoy his possessions in peace"); and reconciliation

---

29. Valentin Urfus discusses the influence of Hugo Grotius and Samuel Pufendorf on Comenius's political theories. Comenius knew Grotius personally and quoted his work. Urfus, "Jurisprudence in Comenius's Times," 97–104.

("we should all carefully combine to inquire into what is best and to seek to reconcile our feelings, our wills and our policies with those of our fellowmen") (1995:109–10).[30] The church's proper role in society was to promote the spiritual virtues that allowed for a peaceful social order. Church should be a place where people learn to resolve their differences in love.

UNIVERSAL EDUCATION

The centerpiece of Comenius's pansophic reform was universal education, or *Pampaedia*,[31] and his pedagogical magnum opus was *Didactica magna* (The Great Didactic), a compilation of his writings on education.[32] Comenius developed his educational theories and methods as a teacher and administrator in the Brethren's schools in Moravia and Poland. He also acknowledged his debt

30. One can make the case that Comenius promoted an early Enlightenment understanding of freedom in civil society. See Jan Blahoslav Čapék, "Comenius as Predecessor of the Enlightenment and of Classicism, with Particular Regard to Panaugia," *Acta Comeniana* 1 (1969): 35–45.

31. The literature on Comenius's importance for modern education is vast and, unfortunately, of unequal quality. The more useful studies and anthologies include John Edward Sadler, *J. A. Comenius and the Concept of Universal Education* (London: Allen and Unwin, 1966), and the related anthology edited by Sadler, *Comenius* (London: MacMillan, 1969); Klaus Schaller, *Die Pädagogik des Johann Amos Comenius und die Anfange des pädagogische Realismus im 17. Jahrhundert* (Heidelberg: Quelle, 1967); C. H. Dobinson, ed. *Comenius and Contemporary Education: An International Symposium* (Hamburg: UNESCO, 1970); M. S. S. Buchenall, "A Comparative Historical and Philosophical Study of the Educational Theories of John Amos Comenius (1592–1670), Friedrich Froebel (1782–1852), and Maria Montessori (1870–1952)" (Ph.D. diss., University of Denver, 1970); Sook Jong Lee, "The Relationship of John Amos Comenius' Theology to His Educational Ideas" (Ph.D. diss., Rutgers University, 1987); Manouchehr Pedram, "A Critical Comparison of the Educational Theories and Practices of John Amos Comenius with John Dewey's Concept of Experience" (Ph.D. diss., University of Kansas, 1963); James D. Pope, "The Educational Writings of John Amos Comenius and Their Relevance in a Changing Culture" (EdD thesis, University of Florida, 1962); C. Paul Roberts, "Comenian Philosophy and Moravian Education from 1850 to the Present Day" (EdD thesis, Rutgers University, 1979); Jerome K. Clauser, "Comenian Pedagogy and the Moravian School Curriculum" (EdD thesis, Pennsylvania State University, 1961); S. S. Laurie, *John Amos Comenius: His Life and Educational Work* (London: Cambridge University Press, 1904); Will S. Monroe, *Comenius and the Beginning of Educational Reform* (New York: Scribner and Sons, 1900). Brambora, Polišensky, et al. provide a helpful bibliography in "Research on the Life and Work of J. A. Comenius." The Comenius Gesellschaft in Germany maintains an extensive website at http://www.deutsche-comenius-gesellschaft.de/.

32. *The Great Didactic of John Amos Comenius translated into English and edited with biographical, historical and critical introductions*, trans. and ed. M. W. Keatinge, 2 vols., 2d ed. (London: Adams and Charles Black, 1923). Though dated, volume 1 includes a useful biography of Comenius, and Keatinge skillfully places Comenius's work in its historical context. Volume 2 is *The Great Didactic* proper. The citations of *The Great Didactic* below refer to vol. 2. The book is available online at http://core.roehampton.ac.uk/digital/froarc/comgre/.

to other educators, primarily those in the humanist tradition, especially Erasmus. Despite his lifelong enmity toward the Jesuits, he recognized what was useful in their educational theories and methods and adopted it.[33] Not that all of Comenius's pedagogical ideas were original, but his importance lies in his ability to draw upon many sources to create a powerful and coherent vision of education.[34] As Jean Piaget noted, "Not only was Comenius the first to conceive a full-scale science of education but, let it be repeated, he made it the very core of a 'pansophy' which, in his thinking, was to constitute a general philosophic system."[35]

As with politics, Comenius argued, educational reform ought to begin with an examination of whether schools were achieving their primary purpose, the development of wisdom. Comenius was very critical of the educational methods of his day, and he lamented the way in which his own youth had been wasted by an educational system that was ineffective at best and cruel at worst. "Most schools adopt a method of compulsion and violence which is contrary to nature and more of a deterrent than an incentive, turning schools into drudgery instead of play, or labyrinths instead of gardens" (1993:45). Such schools deformed the minds of the young: "For five, ten, or more years they detained the mind over matters that could be mastered in one. What could have been gently instilled into the intellect, was violently impressed upon it, nay rather stuffed and flogged into it." In contrast, he argued, "the proper education of the young does not consist in stuffing their heads with a mass of words, sentences, and ideas dragged together out of various authors, but in opening their understanding to the outer world, so that a living stream may flow from their own minds."[36]

He reminded magistrates that Martin Luther had called for the establishment of schools in every town and village, but this had not been done.[37]

33. Amedeo Molnár, "Comenius und die Gegenreformation," *Communio Viatorum* 19 (1976): 97–108; Ivana Čornejová, "The Jesuit School and John Amos Comenius," in Pešková, Cach, and Svatoš, *Homage to Comenius*, 82–95.

34. One recent book to highlight this aspect of Comenian pedagogy is Murphy, *Comenius: A Critical Reassessment.*

35. Jean Piaget, "Introduction," in *John Amos Comenius, 1592–1670: Selections in Commemoration of the Third Centenary of the Publication of Opera didactica omnia, 1657–1957* (Lausanne: UNESCO, 1957), 12.

36. *Great Didactic,* 78, 147.

37. Ibid., 76. Modern scholars agree with Comenius's assessment of Protestantism's failure to improve basic education significantly. See Strauss, *Luther's House of Learning.*

Comenius set forth his pansophic purpose on the title page of *The Great Didactic:* "The whole art of teaching all things to all men or a certain inducement to found such schools in all the parishes, towns, and villages of every Christian kingdom, that the entire youth of both sexes, none being excepted, shall *Quickly, Pleasantly, & Thoroughly* become learned in the Sciences, pure in Morals, trained to Piety, and in this manner instructed in all things necessary for the present and for the future life."[38] By "teaching all things" Comenius did not mean that he would teach every fact about the world to every student, but that everything that should be learned could be learned if one employed the proper method and attitude.

Comenius was one of the few persons of his time to assert the need for the education of every child in a society to allow for the "development into full humanity not of one particular person or a few or even many, but of every single individual, young and old, rich and poor, noble and ignoble, men and women—in a word, of every human being born on earth."[39] The goal of education for the poor was consistent with the practice of the Brethren since the fifteenth century, as was the call for the education of girls and women, an area in which Comenius's ideas were radical for his day, though still of course bound by his historical time and place. While he asserted the equal worth of women as children of God, and even recognized that some women were smarter than men, he saw the primary purpose of educating women as preparation for their role as wives and mothers.[40]

Comenius combined indoctrination, socialization, and education in his proposals, and he stressed throughout his work that education must address the entire person, not just the intellect. Schools must teach morals and piety as well as reading. Education must "illumine the intellect, direct the will, and stimulate the conscience. . . . It is impossible to separate those three ornaments of the soul, erudition, virtue, and piety." Comenius had no conception of what John Dewey would later call value-free education. The primary purpose of education, as he saw it, was to form character. "The seeds of knowledge, of virtue, and of piety are, as we have seen, naturally implanted in us; but the actual knowledge, virtue, and piety are not so given. . . . Let none believe therefore,

38. *Great Didactic*, 3.
39. Comenius, *Pampaedia*, trans. A. M. O. Dobbie (Dover: Buckland Publications, 1986), 19.
40. *Great Didactic*, 68.

that any can really be a man, unless he have learned to act like one, that is, have been trained in those elements which constitute a man."[41]

TEACHING AND LEARNING ACCORDING TO NATURE

Comenius's work was based on the conviction that all truth comes from God, regardless of the immediate source. Every person should make full use of the gifts God has given, including intelligence. Comenius believed that there was unity in all knowledge and that humans were part of the greater unity of creation. "The world is a simple organism," he wrote, "not dead matter; it is a tree with roots and branches, and God is the root of that tree. . . . God's principles are visible in the world-system; therefore, the world cannot be anything else but perfect and dominated by an order that is continuous."[42] Students had to be given a unified approach to education so that they would know "the principles, the causes, and the uses of all the most important things in existence."[43] At every level of education, students would learn the same basic things, but in increasing detail. Proper education should be a spiral leading to greater complexity and better understanding of the essential unity of creation and the human's role in God's world.

Comenius believed that life was a gift from God and should not be wasted or shortened; therefore schools should prolong life as well as educate the intellect. Recreation, amusement, and refreshment were also important. Comenius favored a four-hour school day, two hours in the morning and two in the evening. The time between should be spent in preparation, organized recreation, and the exploration of nature. Play was important in teaching because play imitated life; therefore teachers should use "recreation, amusements, games, merriment, music, and such-like diversions, and thus to refresh the inner and outer senses."[44] "For since God in His compassion for our youth has at last revealed the art of turning all our schools into games," Comenius wrote, "it is

---

41. Ibid., 72, 58, 52.
42. Quoted in P. van Vliet, "The Utopian Ideas of Comenius and the Dutch Republic: An Uneasy Relation," in Vliet and Vanderjagt, *Johannes Amos Comenius*, 86.
43. *Great Didactic*, 70.
44. Ibid., 108.

insufferable that any school should survive in the style of a treadmill or a torture-chamber for the mind. Therefore Colleges of Light will take the utmost care to see that all schools develop into gardens of delight, ensuring that they are administered as far as possible without ruthless discipline, though not altogether without it when occasion demands" (1995:225). It is hard to imagine the original Unity endorsing such a view of play and amusement.

One of the most important advancements in education was Comenius's recognition that different methods were required for people at different stages of cognitive development, moving from the concrete to the abstract.[45] He proposed that there should be four types of schools: the school of motherhood (birth to age six), the vernacular school (age six to age twelve), the Latin school (age twelve to age eighteen), and the university. Each school should deal with tasks appropriate for those ages. Within the schools students should be divided into age-specific classes, with textbooks specially prepared for each age division. At each stage, the more experienced would guide the learners along natural lines of development.[46] Freedom to explore and experience the world was to be combined with discipline and respect for others.

Because learning began in the home, the family was to be responsible for helping children develop necessary sensory skills, the ability to identify objects, learn manners, and cultivate a sense of justice.[47] Throughout his instructions to parents, Comenius emphasized the goals of harmony, virtue, peacefulness, piety, and obedience. Each member of the family should be active in either

45. "Comenius may undoubtedly be considered as one of the precursors of the genetic idea in developmental psychology, and as the founder of a system of progressive instruction adjusted to the stage of development the pupil has reached." Piaget, "Introduction," 16. Piaget also warned against anachronistic evaluations of Comenius: "Nothing is easier, or more dangerous, than to treat an author of three hundred years ago as modern and claim to find in him the origins of contemporary or recent trends of thought. . . . Comenius could likewise be represented either as a precursor of evolutionary theory, genetic psychology, teaching methods based on child psychology, functional education and international education; or as a metaphysician who had no idea of the requirements of experimental psychological or even educational research, and who substituted the discussion of ideas for the analysis of facts. Yet all these extreme judgements would be incorrect" (ibid., 11–12). Daniel Murphy argues that Comenius's theory of education and development are closer to those of the early twentieth-century Russian theorist Lev Vygotsky than to Piaget, given Comenius's recognition of the importance of social context and the positive role of the teacher. Murphy, *Comenius*, 182–94, esp. 188.

46. For more analysis of this system, see Jean Auba, "Comenius and the Organization of Education," in Dobinson, *Comenius and Contemporary Education*; and Janusz Tomiak, "Comenius and the Notion of a Differentiated Analysis of Education," *Acta Comeniana* 3 (1973): 177–83.

47. Comenius, *The School of Infancy*, trans. and ed. Ernest M. Eller (Chapel Hill: University of North Carolina Press, 1956).

work, learning, or play. Luxury was discouraged, but the home should not be deprived of necessities. Most important, each home ought to earn the right to have this inscription over its door: "THIS IS THE DWELLING PLACE OF VIRTUE, ORDER, AGREEMENT, AND GOD AMONG MEN! Therefore let nothing that is evil ever enter it!" (1993:37). Luke of Prague would have assented wholeheartedly.

The primary or vernacular school was to be for all children, boys and girls, rich and poor, with instruction in the local language. Use of the vernacular would ground education in the student's social and cultural context. Instruction should reflect the culture, traditions, values, and aspirations of the local community and the nation. It would build on what was familiar to the student in order to teach what was unfamiliar, including foreign cultures and languages. In the vernacular school, students would work on such skills as reading, writing, painting, singing, counting, and gardening. Despite his generally platonic philosophical orientation, Comenius adopted much of the Baconian method of direct observation of nature. People "become wise by studying the heavens, the earth, oaks and beeches, not by studying books; that is to say, they must learn to know and investigate the things themselves." Comenius drew his examples not from Aristotle but from trees, birds, and craftsmen. A key component of his approach was the need to learn by doing. A carpenter does not tell an apprentice how to build a house but shows him. Likewise, people do not learn their first language from grammar rules but by imitating their parents. "Rules," Comenius wrote, "are like thorns to the understanding."[48]

In his proposals for primary education, Comenius praised such inventions as the printing press and the mechanical clock as examples of what the mind could create when freed from habit and prejudice.[49] He rejected a system of education that focused on ancient authorities rather than contemporary experience. The teacher's task was to ignite the inner light of reason, not to carry about "torches of strange opinion."[50] Students should learn various mechanical arts at school so that they might discover their occupational calling, rather

---

48. *Great Didactic*, 150, 196.

49. Josef Polišensky has examined Comenius's ambivalence toward the new science in "Comenius and the Seventeenth-Century Social and Scientific Revolution," *Acta Comeniana* 2 (1970): 139–46, and "Comenius, Huygens, and Newton, or: The Social and Scientific Revolutions of the Seventeenth Century," in *Jan Amos Comenius: Geschichte und Aktualitat, 1670–1970*, ed. Heinz Joachim Heydorn, 2 vols. (Glashutten: Detlev Auvermann, 1971), 2:187–200.

50. *Great Didactic*, 44.

FIG. 24   Comenius statue, Rixdorf, Germany.

than be subject to the hand of faith, as in *The Labyrinth of the World*. One of Comenius's most interesting suggestions was that schools should have gardens so that students could study plants and learn the rudiments of medicine, a field in which Comenius encouraged humane Christian values. When the plague struck Leszno, Comenius and the Brethren insisted that victims be treated humanely rather than left to die in isolation.[51]

Children who were destined for farming or a craft might stop their education after the vernacular school, but Comenius hoped that most would continue on to the Latin school. There students could acquire the tools necessary for further education and participation in the wider world. They were to learn Latin, some Greek and Hebrew, dialectic, grammar, rhetoric, arts, and sciences. Only the best intellects (regardless of social standing or wealth) would be selected to continue on to the university, where they would study theology, law, medicine, or philosophy. Like Bacon, Comenius insisted that all education should be practical. "With every subject of instruction the question of its practical use must be raised, that nothing useless may be learned." The student who asked why she needed to know geometry deserved an answer, otherwise she would not learn it well. Comenius considered language study to be particularly important because humans by their nature must communicate. Latin was the universal language for scholars, but it was not necessary for all pupils.[52] Ultimately, Comenius hoped to replace Latin with a new universal language that all Europeans could speak. He attempted to create such a *panglottia*, which he thought would overturn the curse of Babel and reduce misunderstanding and conflict. Though his work has been praised by modern linguists, he did not complete this project.[53]

51. J. Neuwirth, "Comenius and the Plague in Leszno," in Pešková, Cach, and Svatoš, *Homage to Comenius*, 106–13.

52. *Great Didactic*, 155, 204. For more on Comenius's method of teaching language, see *The Analytical Didactic of Comenius*, trans. Vladimir Jelinek (Chicago: University of Chicago Press, 1953). This is a translation of the tenth chapter of the *Novissima linguarum methodus*, which was first separated out and so named by the Czech scholar F. J. Zoubek in 1874. See also Jean-Antoine Caravolas, "Comenius (Komenský) and the Theory of Language Teaching," *Acta Comeniana* 10 (1993): 141–62.

53. Hana Sychrova, "Language as One of the Means of 'the Reform of Human Affairs' and Its Function in the World of the Scientific and Technological Revolution," *Acta Comeniana* 3 (1973): 365–75; V. T. Miskovska-Kozakova, "Comenius's Linguistic Theory and Experiment," *Acta Comeniana* 4 (1979): 291–317; and Miskovska-Kozakova, "Elements of Syntaxis in the Constructed Language of Comenius," in Čapková, Dohnalek, and Turkova, *Consultationes de consultatione*, 119–40.

Comenius repeatedly insisted that he was a theologian and that the purpose of education was not just temporal happiness or fame but preparation for eternity. He viewed the world itself as the school of the soul, created in God's wisdom to prepare persons for eternity, and teachers should take this task seriously. The study of nature, history, and morals, as well as theology, should have as their ultimate goal the love of God.[54] Drawing on the Brethren's humanistic tradition, Comenius asserted that "it is clear from Scripture that piety itself is teachable, i.e., not immediately or miraculously infused by God, but transmitted in the ordinary course of instruction."[55] He rejected the Calvinist belief in the utter depravity of humankind articulated by the synod of Dort.[56] As the Creator, God is the lord of nature who implanted a good nature in all people. Adam's disobedience weakened the human ability to live as God intended, but Christ's redemption overcame this weakness. "It is base, wicked, and an evident sign of ingratitude, that we continually complain of our corrupt state, but make no effort to reform it; that we bring forward what the old Adam can work in us, but never experience what the new Adam, Christ, can do."[57] Christ reversed the curse of Adam so that the innate knowledge of God might function again. Education merely assisted in the work of Christ in the world, and "Christian philosophy teaches the knowledge of nature and salvation."[58] Therefore it was vital that teachers work with God's creation, including human nature, not against it. The human potential to know all things would unfold like a plant, because everything in nature, including humans, seeks its end willingly.[59]

Because Comenius believed strongly in the goodness of God and the redemption of Christ, he could look at all children as images of God called to imitate Christ. Teachers must cooperate with God and teach as Christ himself taught. "Teaching means leading from the known to the unknown, a kindly

54. *Great Didactic*, chapter 2.
55. *Pampaedia*, 46. For more on this, see Murphy, *Comenius*, 136–73, esp. 164–68.
56. Alsted taught that the image of God had been destroyed in the Fall but could be restored (instaurated) through the redemptive work of Christ, but there was an unreconciled tension in Alsted's thought. Comenius departed from his teacher, drawing instead upon Erasmus and Melanchthon. Hotson, *Johann Heinrich Alsted*, 66–82, 229.
57. *Great Didactic*, 50.
58. Van Vliet, "Utopian Ideas of Comenius," 88.
59. *Great Didactic*, 42.

and non-violent activity born of love and not hatred. When I wish to lead any-one, I do not push nor bully him nor knock him down. Instead of forcing him, I take him by the hand and walk gently beside him, or I go ahead of him on the open road and beckon to him to follow me."[60] Time and again, Comenius asserted that one cannot educate through beatings and threats. The teacher's duty was to inspire students to learn, not to frighten them. The way to build peace in the world was through modeling peacefulness in the home and the school.

Teachers and parents were responsible for protecting children from all that might harm them, especially violence. Comenius restricted corporal punish-ment to grave moral offenses that threatened to harm others. Moreover, he asserted that punishment should never be used in anger, because then it became abuse rather than discipline. Parents and teachers should remember that "the object of discipline should be to stir us up to revere God, to assist our neigh-bors, and to perform the labours and duties of life with alacrity."[61] Punishment should be swift and effective, but never cruel. Discipline helps form an indi-vidual's character and allows him to live freely and joyfully in the world as God intended. This conviction, as we have seen, reflected the Unity's understand-ing of discipline in the church and home.

In short, Comenius believed that God had provided a world filled with wholesome delights that were to be enjoyed as a way to grow in the knowledge and love of God. "We must therefore begin by implanting faith, charity, and hope in the hearts of men," he wrote, "and we must work one and all to reform ourselves according to the image of Him who has restored all things, making it our earnest desire that our faith, charity, and hope should be full, orderly, and clearly true" (1993:65–66). Comenius, like previous generations of Breth-ren, believed that the essentials of the Christian religion showed the path to personal fulfillment, social harmony, and human happiness. Comenius shared the conviction of Luke of Prague and Blahoslav that God speaks through both faith and reason, and that therefore it was possible to understand what was essential for salvation and happiness in this life and the next. Coercion could only impede faith. Leaders must remember that since all people are made in

60. *Panegersia*, xv.
61. *Great Didactic*, 250.

God's image, they will tend toward God so long as they are not forced. "Anyone choosing to use compulsion only embitters, poisons, and alienates men,
and either makes them hypocrites or prepares the way for a fresh and perhaps
greater breakaway. Fear is a poor guarantee of friendship" (1995:120).

CHURCH REFORM AND THE UNITY

Comenius's proposals for church reform were consistent with his pansophic
vision, and they reflect the direct influence of the Brethren's doctrine and practice. First of all, Comenius insisted that churches should focus on deeds rather
than theories. "*Knowledge* which does not produce deeds must perish. The same
applies to *Faith* which does not operate through acts of charity, and to a *Political System* which fails to maintain human affairs in peace" (1995:182). Those
entrusted with the task of guiding people in religious matters must concentrate on what is most important rather than become ensnared in trivialities.
"There is every reason to expect that we shall be as brothers," he wrote in the
Panorthosia, "if in accordance with God's word we concentrate on seeking Faith
in God, combined with Charity and crowned with Hope" (1995:125). Once
again, we see the centrality of the Brethren's idea that the essentials of Christianity and human happiness are faith, love, and hope.

In the *Consultatio* Comenius held up the doctrine of the Unity as the basis
for restoring the church to its proper role in society. The purpose of religion
was to restore all souls to God and to begin the heavenly life here on earth, but
"the Means are either Essential or Ministerial or Accessory. I. The Essentials
are faith, charity, and hope in God the Father, the Son, and the Holy Spirit. . . .
II. The Ministerials are all things essential to the instilling of God's word, the
keeping of the keys in order, and the sealing of sacraments. . . . III. The Acces-
sories are the statutes of the Church, universal or particular, and the customs
built around them" (1995:196–97). With this perspective it should be possible
to remove "anything which for any reason destroys or diminishes faith, hope,
and charity, or confuses or obscures or debases or undermines them," he insisted. This included superstition, atheism, pharisaism, hypocrisy, and despair
(1993:61). Comenius identified several things that needed to be removed from
churches, among them "polemic assemblies and the itch of disputation," "buying

and selling in religion," "the use of violence in matters of conscience," and "inquisition instead of discipline" (1993:62–63). The Calvinist influence on the Brethren can be seen in Comenius's call for the abolition of clerical celibacy.

Just as the best-governed states had a few laws understood by all rather
than a labyrinth of rules and regulations that enriched lawyers and sowed discord, the best-organized churches would have a few doctrines that could be
easily understood, a simple ritual in harmony with the requirements of daily
living, and a form of discipline that maintained order and harmony without
being oppressive or arbitrary (1995:197–98). This is a good description of the
Unity throughout its history. According to Comenius, other reform movements,
including those of "Wyclif, Huss, Luther, Zwingli, Calvin, Menno, Socinus,
and even the Pope himself," achieved only partial reform of the church. Further reform was needed to abolish "the *Religion of Cain*, which . . . is jealous of
the grace of God to man, and establishes sects, and starts persecutions because
of disagreement in religion, and causes bloodshed, and seeks earth instead of
heaven. We should install the *religion of Abel*, humble faith, active charity, and
hope directed towards heaven and eternity" (1995:201). Comenius may have
been drawing here on Boehme's writings, which also contrasted the religions
of Abel and Cain, but his presentation lacks the mystical dimension of Boehme's
use of the patriarchs.[62]

Comenius focused on practical faith, and he urged Christians to recognize
that moderation is itself a part of Christian faith. Satan works by inflaming
unholy passions and pushing people to extremes of rationalism empty of faith,
or to fanatical devotion devoid of reason. "We must therefore oppose Satan by
keeping to a middle course 1. between neglect and abuse of the Scriptures,
2. between a life of profanity and one of superstition, 3. between neglect of
discipline and harmful rigidity. Instead of discipline, violence is done to truth
and conscience is tortured by excommunication, the Spanish Inquisition, or
auricular confession" (1995:204). Moreover, if the path ahead is uncertain, he
advised, it is safer to keep to the middle so that you can move to the right or
left as needed without becoming lost.

Another aspect of the doctrine and practice of the Unity that Comenius
highlighted as useful for the ecumenical church was the idea of three levels of

62. Weeks, *Boehme*, 201–3.

church membership. His version of this was a bit different from the original Brethren's practice, however, because it was based on his educational theory. "Beginners" were to focus on discovering the beauty and goodness of God's creation through their senses. They should learn biblical history, which is more concrete than theology. Those who are "progressing" would then move on to comparison of the Old and New Testaments, while "masters" would "learn about the mystery of Christ reigning in our hearts" and put it into practice. Comenius proposed that a congregation have several pastors, each especially skilled in working with each different ages and types of members (1993:60–61). Recalling the fundamental issue of the Czech Reformation, and advancing a major theme of the Pietist movement, Comenius asserted that reform of the church must begin with the clergy themselves. They must be servants and shepherds who lead by word and example, not lords who rule over their congregations. Clergy should reform "their lives before their doctrine" (1993:84).

As an heir of the Czech Reformation, Comenius urged preachers to rely more heavily on scripture than on their own eloquence. They should preach through the entire Bible rather than rely only on familiar or favorite passages. While the people ought to be prepared for listening to the sermon, it was more important that the preacher be prepared to preach the Word. "We need not therefore wait for this to be infused into us in some extraordinary way as a gift from God; instead, we should prepare for it deliberately, that is, by reading and meditation (I Timothy IV, 13, 15)" (1993:70). Reason and study were tools of faith, and interpreters of God's Word ought to be familiar with the historical context of scripture and progressive revelation.

The quality of sermons would improve, Comenius argued, with the opportunity for questions and discussions. Drawing on the Unity's tradition, he proposed that younger listeners should have the first opportunity to raise questions (1993:73). Most important, sermons should be clear, brief, and connected to the "cardinal points of all Christianity: faith, charity, and hope." Every sermon should be relevant to the lives of the listeners and should not be considered complete until it had been understood (1993:81). Worship should be pleasurable and joyful. Music is particularly important in worship aesthetically, pedagogically, and devotionally. "Let us therefore wrest away from Satan the sweetness of harmony which has been profaned by its use for idle and ungodly purposes, and let us transfer it to this supreme and sacrosanct use, so that the Author of harmony shall be praised in harmonious measures" (1993:92).

Churches needed to teach music to children from an early age and provide music resources that would help adults learn to sing in harmony (1993:92). Since God had created all things to his glory, there was no reason not to use the best musical instruments. "The addition of organ music will bring added sweetness and help to inspire zeal in our hearts. Therefore away with superstition! Away with obstinacy! Rejoice, all ye saints, in glory, and use every art at your disposal to please your God, and His church, and your own souls which overflow with rejoicing" (1993:94). This interest in improving the aesthetics of worship recalls the earlier efforts of Luke of Prague to enrich the Brethren's liturgy by adapting Catholic and Utraquist practices.[63]

HEALING DIVISIONS

Comenius had great hope for religion as a force of good in the world, but he was very critical of the churches of his day. Religion "ought to bring solace in all worldly perplexities and ought not only to show a secure port from the stormy hurricanes of worldly affairs, but also ought to lead into it." But, instead,

> in the whole world scarcely a more intricate labyrinth can be found than the Christian religion (such as it now has become), so multiplex, I say, and varied, and divided into many sects, and cut up into so many thousand questions about faith, and opinions about individual questions, and battles over opinions, that the whole world has nothing similarly intricate. And what is more astonishing, nowhere in the world on account of religious dissentions are there such harsh hatred, such enduring quarrels, such bloody persecutions, such cruel punishments, and such atrocious battles.[64]

In his proposals for dealing with hatred and division among Christians, we can see the Unity's influence on Comenius's thought. He knew that the body

---

63. Crews, "Luke of Prague," 13.
64. *Unum necessarium*, 16.

of Christ was bigger than any small church. Comenius was convinced by his own friendship with Hartlib and Andreae that spiritual bonds could go deeper than a common confession of faith. Reunification of the church was part of the work of Christ, who cannot be divided, and must be a part of the mission of the community of faith. "This is not a matter for discrimination," he wrote. "We have no occasion to differentiate between nations or sects or parties, philosophical or religious or political. Anyone advocating unity must ignore party loyalties. All my proposals are presented to you in the name of Christ alone. You are Christians, sworn to unite and not to separate, to expand and not to contract, to enlighten and not to obscure, to cure anxiety and defend the Kingdom."[65]

Although the different confessions of faith and the many churches might not be reconciled, "yet Christianity will certainly not be irreconcilable, if we have Christ to reconcile us" (1995:125). Comenius was convinced that most of the burning theological and liturgical controversies of his day, some of which had led to armed conflict and even regicide, could be solved through reason and Christian love. As with social reform, he believed that Christians could cooperate with the Lord in practical ways to heal their divisions and prevent further discord. First, though, all Christians needed to become aware of their own sinful tendencies and take reasonable steps to reduce conflict. They should be careful not to oppose "anything which can be confirmed by the evidence of the senses, of reason, and of God's Testimony."

People should also be careful neither to assert nor to deny things in absolute terms unless the truth of the matter was beyond question. Sometimes it would be necessary to suspend judgment until the truth became evident, and some things might have to await Judgment Day, when God would reveal all things. One of Comenius's most intriguing ideas was that "if anything cannot be reconciled in theory, one should begin to try it out in practice, for better practice would follow from the earnest attention given to both aspects." If this failed to yield a clear solution to the conflict, then people should either compromise or agree to disagree (1995:126). In difficult matters, it was also important to remember that faith includes "some element of mystery which is not accessible to reason" (1995:137). Some things are beyond human knowledge but may be revealed in heaven.

---

65. *Panegersia*, vii.

Comenius proposed concrete solutions to many of the theological controversies of his day, and it is not surprising that those solutions usually reflect the doctrine and practice of the Unity of the Brethren. On the question of justification by faith or works, for example, Comenius wrote a very long and erudite proof that this could not be settled by recourse to scripture. Paul and James clearly disagreed on this issue, but the two apostles were addressing different problems. Like Gregory, Luke of Prague, and Blahoslav, Comenius concluded that both faith and works were necessary for salvation (1995:133–34). "Are you inclined to quarrel about the method of Justification?" he asked. "You must rather do everything possible towards your own justification. As Paul praises faith, you must put your trust in our beloved Saviour with all your heart. As James recommends works, you must do everything with a pure heart" (1995:142).

On the vexing question of the Eucharist, Comenius reiterated the Unity's teaching that Christ is truly present in a mysterious way in communion. It would be wrong to try to pin Christ down and control him with human notions. "Since Christ left this unspecified, why should we not also do likewise?" The terms "transubstantiation" and "consubstantiation" did not really matter, so long as it was understood that the true transformation takes place "not in the hand of the priest but in the mouth of him who taketh it worthily" (1995:134–35). Comenius even tolerated use of the words "figure, type, sign, and token" in Holy Communion, so long as it was understood that "signs are not used on their own but in association with the thing which they represent and exemplify" (1995:135). Far more important than the doctrine of the presence of Christ in the Eucharist is the experience that one is truly with Christ though faith.

Comenius believed that doctrinal disagreements should not distract people from the essential nature and purpose of the church. Christ called the church into being to bring people into faith, love, and hope, not to defend controversial doctrines. "What is the good of inquiring how Christ is present to us when we know that he is so? We should rather inquire what we must do to receive him graciously when he is here" (1995:142). In dealing with the perpetually vexing problem of election, Comenius offered advice similar to Luke's: "Are we guilty of probing the question of Predestination too deeply? Rather, we should make our calling and election sure by doing good works (II Peter, I, 10). In short, you must put into practice what others argue about in theory, and you will avoid quarrels and dissensions and never lose the kernels among the shells" (1995:142).

AN UNFULFILLED VISION

Comenius's pansophic reforms might have been too ambitious for the seventeenth century, and perhaps for the twenty-first century as well. Perhaps he placed too much confidence in human reason and the ability of Christians to live according to their faith rather than giving in to their primal fears. Comenius knew that his dream for the restoration of the world was bold and faced many obstacles, but the dream itself could inspire men and women to live better lives and labor for a better world.

> Someone may say here and now that I am indulging in a drunken dream. But I only wish that those who chase after worldly prosperity would sleep off their intoxication, and begin to drink abundantly of this infinitely better sweetness. . . . Let all men indulge in this kind of intoxication and dream the same kind of dream about naught but Christ, heaven, universal salvation, mutual charity and edification and the Sabbath of rest from sorry enslavement to sin! Indeed let us do as men usually do when wine has made them merry and open our mouths in cries of jubilation, and let us sing aloud the hymn of victory to Christ as conqueror and the wedding hymn of the lamb as the bridegroom of the church! (1993:165)

Certainly there were few people in the seventeenth century who answered his call for a general consultation on universal reformation, but his vision for the reform of society remains inspiring.[66]

Comenius's writings are the most eloquent expression of the theological heritage of the Unity of the Brethren. In them we see the union of personal devotion and passion for social justice that characterized the Unity from its inception. We also see the commonsense pragmatism of the Brethren, who understood that theological hairsplitting neither saves souls nor builds the Kingdom of God on earth. True to the teachings of the Brethren, Comenius focused on the essentials of faith, love, and hope rather than on points of division and controversy.

---

66. "The vision disclosed in his writings is one that is intrinsically Christian, by virtue of its consistent and authentic affirmation of the values of love, truth, and freedom. It is a vision that was embodied in the spiritual and cultural traditions of Bohemia from Hus to Havel, but is one which, self-evidently, has a profound and compelling relevance for the whole of humankind." Murphy, *Comenius*, 274.

Fourteen

THE BEQUEST OF THE UNITY

It is appropriate to end this study of the theology of the Brethren with Comenius. Not only was he the last bishop of the Bohemian and Moravian branches of the Unity, he was the best theologian the church produced. His writings sum up two centuries of the Brethren's witness, but in one of Comenius's last works, *Unum necessarium*, we glimpse the frustration of a scholar who has spent his life in study and labor without seeing an improvement in the world. "Books ought to be the antidotes for errors and the directors of human nature, which by itself is topsy-turvy. But as things are now, in truth they are labyrinths. . . . How many questions there are, that come up daily about everything together and about single matters, and once the questions have come up, how many different opinions there are of different things."[1] With all of the confusion in books, one day people may "either read nothing or believe nothing, and unholiness and atheism will overflow everything."[2] Despite this opinion of books, Comenius kept writing until the end of his life in the hope that his words would awaken people to the reality of their earthly lives and the hope for a better world.

Comenius warned his readers that "in truth the world is everywhere full of deceptions and frauds," but he hoped to bring clarity to the true and necessary

---

1. *Unum necessarium*, 64. Hereafter cited parenthetically.
2. It seems fitting to put Comenius's complaint against footnotes and bibliographies in a footnote: "But now almost all the new books that are published are crammed with a copious catalogue of authors, even where there is no need, only to pretend much reading." Ibid., 81.

FIG. 25   Comenius handing *Ratio disciplinae* to the king of England, study by
Valentin Haidt, Moravian Archives, Bethlehem, Pennsylvania.

in life. The "one thing necessary" was, of course, Christ, the guide through the
labyrinth. Christ offered the "thread of simplicity" that could guide people out
of the labyrinth of despair and into eternal happiness. Christ called his followers to embrace simplicity in their worship and their lives, to know and do
their proper duty toward God and their neighbors, and to relinquish their desire for worldly success. To illustrate his point, Christ told his disciples to imitate children, not lords (40). Though Comenius displayed greater learning and
refinement than Gregory the Patriarch or Peter Chelčický, his writings reflect
the Unity's original perspective that both the teachings and the living presence

of Christ are essential in Christianity. By following Christ's teachings and example, believers would find their true happiness even in the midst of frustration and suffering. "Whoever learns this from Christ will not easily stray from his goal of blessedness; he will not easily succumb under the labors he meets; he will not easily be frustrated in his desires (which are tranquility of mind and joy of conscience)" (43).

Comenius was an early advocate of the theology of the heart that placed Christ at the center of the church and its mission in the world. He blamed theologians for whom "to know simply Christ seems too simple a theology" for the disputes and divisions among Christians (97). He reminded his readers that Satan was "a sophist" who was always offering cunning arguments, just as theologians did. The cure for a divided church was the same cure for an individual trapped in the quiet despair of daily living: return to Christ as the center of security. But this return to Christ was not merely an individualist act of personal devotion; it was also a turning toward one's neighbor. "He urges nothing more in all Scripture (after love and obedience due to the Creator himself) than mutual concern for each other, service, and aid" (113).

Central to the Brethren's theology was the conviction that true Christianity is simple, profound, and powerful (64). Rulers, priests, lawyers, and theologians created needless perplexity and complication. Comenius pointed out that the first religion was that of Abraham, and that it was a simple faith: "to believe in one God, to obey one God, to hope for life from God the fount of life." He also quoted Micah 6:8 ("to do justice, love kindness, and walk humbly with God") as a summary of true religion. "See, this was the whole of religion before the law and under the law, to grasp God by faith, to embrace God with love, and to hold God by hope" (88–89).

The Brethren's understanding of the essentials was the foundation of Comenius's theology and of his plans for a reformation of the ecumenical church. The key to the reform of the world lay in "wisdom to discern the distinction between the things fundamental, instrumental, and accidental,"[3] terms parallel to the Brethren's essential, ministerial, and incidental things. The Bible was the chief ministerial, and Comenius held it up as the great fountain of divine truth and guidance, but he cautioned that it had to be studied carefully. Simply

---

3. Comenius, *Bequest of a Dying Mother*, 30.

quoting chapter and verse to support an opinion was not sufficient (70). Like generations of Unity theologians, Comenius urged people to apply reason to the study of scripture and recognize that the Bible did not speak with a single voice. He divided the Bible into "revelation, commands, and promises," which corresponded to faith, obedience (love), and hope. Students began "by learning all the biblical history," but they had to go further to perceive "the true meaning of these three articles: faith, love, hope" (73). The Word of God in scripture, then, was understood as an archetypal message that spoke to each person in his or her own struggle to live authentically amid the competing needs and desires of life.

The ultimate goal of reading the Bible and being part of the community of faith was to become a new kind of being, "created according to God, in justice and holiness of truth" (74). Thus the one thing necessary for health, happiness, and harmony was "to look uniquely at Christ, the image of all perfection, sent to us from heaven: and to adjust all our affairs to this, just as God commanded, and spoke, in person, to Moses" (93). Drawing on Greek patristic thought, Comenius further asserted that "a Christian is a man like Christ, and through that likeness able to be deified" (90). True religion, for Comenius and the Brethren, was about the transformation of the self and the re-creation of true humanity.[4] He concluded his reflections on true religion with the outline of the original catechism of the Unity of the Brethren.

> If anyone questions me further, asking the symbol of my faith, I shall show him the Apostles' Creed, because I know nothing shorter, simpler, or stronger; through its leading I possess the decision of every controversy in summary, and through it I avert the infinite labyrinths of disputes. If he asks what selected forms of prayer I use, I will say the Lord's Prayer, because I believe no better key can be shown for opening the Father's heart than the only begotten Son, who proceeded from the bosom of the Father. If he asks the rule of my life, I will show him the Decalogue,

4. See Ford, *Self and Salvation*. Ford, drawing upon Levinas, Jüngel, and Ricoeur, argues that Christian salvation should be understood as a transformation of the self in terms of hospitality, responsibility, and desire. Though Ford does not cite Comenius, his point is consistent with the main line of Comenius's theology. The encounter with Christ as the other who requires a response from us is transformative when we move out of our isolation and into responsible engagement with other selves. The process of becoming like Christ makes us at once more human and more divine.

because I trust that no one could better express what pleases God than God himself. (117)

Simplicity in doctrine did not mean stupidity; nor did trust in God mean turning away from human responsibility. Faith and reason, service and devotion, love and reconciliation, realism and hope were united in Comenius's thought, just as they were in the teaching of the Brethren from the beginning. Comenius upheld and refined the Unity's theological position that Christianity is not a matter of wrangling over the mysteries of salvation but a discipleship that allows a clear-minded commitment to social justice, personal integrity, interpersonal forgiveness, and sacrificial love. The one thing needful was the Christ who provides a "paradise of the heart" in the midst of confusion and frustration by leading believers out of self-centeredness and greed into universal love and justice.

FEATURES OF THE BRETHREN'S DOCTRINE

The Unity of the Brethren, along with all Czech Protestantism, was destroyed during the Thirty Years' War and the Counter-Reformation, but its legacy survived the seventeenth century. Thanks in large part to the writings of Comenius, the Unity left a bequest for later generations. Comenius's ideas not only influenced modern educational and political theory; his writings were important to the Pietists of the eighteenth century. The Pietist effort to complete the Reformation through reform of Christian living in many ways fulfilled Comenius's vision. The communities established by the Herrnhuters on three continents were laboratories in which Comenius's millennial dream was partially realized.

At first glance it may be hard to see the continuity between Gregory's passionate rejection of feudal corruption and Comenius's ambitious plan for international cooperation and universal salvation. Gregory and the early Brethren were almost classically sectarian and exclusive, while Comenius's universalism remains surprising in its scope. Clearly the Brethren underwent a great deal of development as they adjusted to changing historical circumstances and their own intellectual evolution, but that history is also marked by internal consistency.

Several principles, themes, or ideas remained fundamental features of the Unity's doctrine, and they merit attention today.[5]

1. *The Continual Quest for Truth.* Commitment to continual learning and change is itself one of the consistencies in the Unity's doctrine. The refusal to confuse the relative truths of human doctrinal statements and biblical interpretations with the eternal truths known only to God was one of the Brethren's great contributions to Christian thought. They understood that doctrinal statements can and should change over time. Hus's motto was "truth shall conquer," and the continual quest for truth, rather than a rote regurgitation of received dogma, is an important aspect of the Unity's legacy. The Unity recognized that human understanding of God's creation and human society continues to grow and change.[6] But even while knowledge of the world increases, the fundamental questions of human existence endure. Through changing times and shifting academic fashions, the Brethren never lost sight of the primary task of the church: leading people to deepen in faith, love, and hope. Inherent in this conviction was the awareness that the church must be self-critical. As Comenius noted repeatedly, when a church resorts to deception to defend itself and its doctrine, it ceases to be a church. The purpose of Christian doctrine, for the Brethren, was to bring life, freedom, and a sense of responsibility for the welfare of the world.[7]

2. *Essentials, Ministerials, and Incidentals.* The Unity's most valuable contribution to the history of Christian thought was its distinction between things essential to salvation, things that minister to salvation, and things that are incidental. Though expressed in different terms at different times, this was a consistent feature of the Unity's doctrine, and it played a major role in Comenius's plans for social reform. The tripartite structure allowed for important nuances in formulating church doctrine and rules to live by. It also allowed for

---

5. Some of the material in this section was presented in the 2004 Moses Lectures for the Moravian Theological Seminary, "Faith, Love, and Hope: The Moravian Theological Heritage," which was published in *The Hinge: A Journal of Christian Thought for the Moravian Church* 11, no. 3 (2004): 2–26. My conclusions are similar to those of Jarold Knox Zeman, "Renewal of Church and Society in the Hussite Reformation," Couillard Memorial Lectures, 1980 (Bethlehem, Pa.: Moravian Theological Seminary, 1984).

6. This belief is similar to the position of Friedrich Schleiermacher in *The Christian Faith*, ed. H. R. MacKintosh and J. S. Stewart (London: T. & T. Clark, 1999), 112–17.

7. Dietrich Bonhoeffer echoed the thought of the Brethren when he wrote, "His commandment never seeks to destroy life, but to foster, strengthen and heal it." *The Cost of Discipleship*, trans. R. H. Fuller (New York: Macmillan, 1963), 40.

productive ecumenical dialogue. The doctrine of the essentials defined "Creator, Redeemer, and Sanctifier" as three aspects of the one God, who gives his gifts freely, without compulsion or dependence on human words. The existential response of the Christian in faith, love, and hope was also essential to salvation in this life and the next.[8] Faith, for the Unity, included belief in the Apostles' Creed, but more significantly it meant trust in Christ. This faith conquers fear and brings release to the captive. The Brethren understood love as the heart's desire to serve and please Christ in all things. If there is faith and love, then there must also be hope.

In the Brethren's doctrine, ministerials *communicate* what is sacred but are not sacred in themselves. They are the "means of grace," not grace itself. As such, they are sacred in a relative rather than an absolute sense. The ministerials include church order, the sacraments, the priesthood, and even the scriptures. Christians had died for and killed for these things throughout the centuries, and the Brethren knew from experience that even the most sacred things of Christianity may become idolatrous when they interfere with the knowledge and love of God. Hundreds of years later, the wisdom of the Unity's doctrine on ministerials may be more evident than it was in the sixteenth century. One of the great achievements of twentieth-century ecumenical discussion was the statement *Baptism, Eucharist, and Ministry*, signed in Lima, Peru, in 1982, which is remarkably consistent with the Unity's basic orientation on these controversial issues.

3. *The Voluntary Church.* The Brethren made the separation of church and secular authority a fundamental teaching. Although their conclusion that the Roman Catholic Church had been hopelessly corrupted by Constantine was too extreme, the Brethren's basic suspicion of any alliance between secular and spiritual authority is sound. The Brethren brought this perspective into Protestantism by criticizing both Catholic and Reformation churches for their reliance on the coercive power of the state. Religious faith must be a matter of personal conscience and personal commitment; truth cannot be defended by the sword and stake. Though the Brethren stressed the voluntary principle rather than the state-church model, they did not follow the pattern of the Anabaptist churches

---

8. The twentieth-century Thomist theologian Josef Pieper, quoting Francis de Sales, also makes this point in *Faith, Hope, Love* (San Francisco: Ignatius Press, 1997): "Thus the theological virtues flow back upon themselves in a sacred circle: one who is led to love by hope has thereafter a more perfect hope, just as he also believes now more strongly than before" (104).

in separating completely from other Christian bodies.[9] They defined themselves as a unity, or brotherhood, of people who had voluntarily come together to seek salvation and serve Christ. They were also aware that separation from the Unity did not mean separation from Christ.[10] This contributed to the Unity's persistent efforts to reunite the body of Christ, which may be the greatest and most helpful paradox in the history of the Brethren's theology. The Brethren refused to give up their distinctive organization and voice in the world even as they worked for cooperation among churches with different confessions of faith. Comenius's vision of an ecumenical council of interdependent communities of faith developed out of this fundamental commitment of the Unity of the Brethren, and the World Council of Churches' understanding of itself as "a communion of communions" is a modern version of the Unity's original insight. In the modern world, it is increasingly evident that people need to form intentional communities that give identity and integrity to life without separating themselves from the demands of the world.

4. *Word and Sacrament.* For the Brethren, scripture was the most important thing ministering to salvation and was central to the Christian life, but they were not fundamentalists. They adopted a Christocentric hermeneutic that held that the Bible as a whole should be interpreted through the Gospels. They viewed Christ as the true Word of God in human flesh; therefore Christ was the revelation of the invisible God in human form. The Unity self-consciously applied the principle of "a canon within the canon" and viewed the Old Testament as less authoritative than the New Testament, especially the four Gospels. Christ's law of love, expressed most clearly in the Sermon on the Mount, set forth instructions for believers, and the life of Jesus provided the model for faithful living. Christ was the "one thing necessary" because through Christ humans could know God, be saved from sin and death, and learn the law of love. Scripture pointed beyond itself to God and led people into a faithful relationship with Christ.[11] Since scripture was the touchstone for authentic

---

9. Zeman, in "Renewal of Church and Society," refers to the Unity's evolution from a "proto-Anabaptist sect" to "an equal partner in a new theocratic coalition under a Calvinist king" (24–25). He draws on Troeltsch's typology of sect and church, but in my judgment the Unity charted a distinct path that never fit with Troeltsch's ideal types.

10. Zeman calls this the dimension of *koinonia* in the Unity. Ibid., 12–14.

11. Paul Ricouer discusses the crucial difference between the Bible as an authoritative text and as a sacred object. "Maybe in the case of Christianity there *is* no sacred text, because it is not the text that is

teaching and a guide for Christian living, it was to be read in the language of the people and made available to everyone who professed faith in Christ.

Scripture alone was not a sufficient guide for the church, however. The Czech Reformation began as a reform of the sacraments, particularly the Eucharist, and the chalice became the symbol that united the Hussites. The Brethren offered the other churches an understanding of the Eucharist that respected both the mystery of the sacrament and God-given human reason. They taught consistently that Christ was truly spiritually present in the Eucharist and that believers should therefore take communion in reverence. But they rejected the idea that Jesus was somehow physically present on every altar in the world. Likewise, they taught that infant baptism was good and useful but needed to be completed by an adult profession of faith. The Brethren pioneered the Protestant understanding of confirmation as a rite of passage into adult membership in the church. It was a ritual marking an individual's decision to become a disciple of Christ. The Reformed tradition internalized these teachings of the early Brethren, and they remain a resource for contemporary ecumenical dialogue.

5. *Faith Completed in Love.* One of the hallmarks of the Czech Reformation was the principle that "faith without works is dead" (James 2:17). From Gregory to Comenius, the Unity of the Brethren insisted that it was wrong to separate faith from works, the way some Protestant confessions had done. The Brethren never endorsed the doctrine of justification by faith alone that many people assume is the core of Protestant teaching. Unlike Luther, the founders of the Unity did not separate from the state church because of a crisis of *faith*. They established their community in Kunwald because the dominant church was not *practicing* the faith it preached. Although the Unity rejected the medieval Catholic idea that external acts of piety could ensure salvation, they stood in the mainstream of Catholic teaching that faith must be completed in love. The Unity's ethics was based on the Sermon on the Mount rather than on the

---

sacred but the one about which it is spoken." The Bible has authority because it is the defining text for the community and its life. "Preaching is the permanent reinterpretation of the text that is regarded as grounding the community; therefore, for the community to address itself to another text would be to make a decision concerning its social identity." Ricouer, "The 'Sacred Text' and the Community," in *Figuring the Sacred: Religion, Narrative, and Imagination,* ed. Mark I. Wallace, trans. David Pellauer (Minneapolis: Augsburg Fortress, 1995), 70.

law of Moses. This conviction that ethics is central to Christian theology was reclaimed in modern Protestant thought by theologians like Dietrich Bonhoeffer and Reinhold Niebuhr. We can hear an echo of the teaching of the Brethren in Bonhoeffers's words from *The Cost of Discipleship*: "Cheap grace is the preaching of forgiveness without requiring repentance, baptism without church discipline, Communion without confession, absolution without discipleship, grace without the cross, grace without Jesus Christ, living and incarnate."[12]

6. *Pedagogical View of Faith.* Education was always central to the identity, mission, and theology of the Brethren, and they believed that faith and reason were complementary, not oppositional. The essential goodness of creation and the image of God were not destroyed by the Fall. Salvation in Christ included the renewal of one's mind as well as forgiveness of sins. As a result, the Unity defined teaching as one of the pastoral tasks of the church. As educators, the Brethren preferred clarity to obfuscation, and they recognized that theologians should be able to communicate the fundamental mysteries of life and faith to children. A pedagogical approach to faith assumes that people change and develop in their faith. It also assumes that what is true is true regardless of who says it. Such a pedagogical approach to faith is strong and forthright but also gentle and open. It rejects the use of fear and violence in proclaiming the Gospel because it assumes that God made humans in such a way that they will seek and find him. The Brethren perceived that if church doctrine becomes dogmatic, doctrinaire, and judgmental it ceases to be pedagogical. Religious doctrine is a tool that helps Christians live as followers of Christ, not a weapon to judge and divide them.[13]

7. *Peace and Salvation.* For more than two centuries the Unity of the Brethren was a living witness to a form of Christianity that rejected the institutionalized violence of the state. The Brethren endured persecution and war without abandoning their conviction that the eschatological peaceable kingdom can be realized on earth. Although the Brethren turned away from strict pacifism, they consistently rejected the idea that the church should sanction war and

---

12. Bonhoeffer, *Cost of Discipleship*, 47. See also Bonhoeffer, *Ethics*, trans. Neville Horton Smith (New York: Macmillan, 1965).

13. See Ellen T. Charry, *By the Renewing of Your Minds: The Pastoral Function of Christian Doctrine* (New York: Oxford University Press, 1997), for a modern statement of the relationship between pedagogy, faith, and discipleship.

other forms of oppression and abuse. The Brethren were not naïve about human violence or about the difficulties of achieving justice on earth. Their discussions of Christian life and doctrine were not abstract exercises held in the comfort of the classroom but passionate attempts to live with meaning and purpose in a chaotic and dangerous world. The Unity's theology was forged in the crucible of conflict and persecution. One of the Brethren's greatest insights, as they navigated treacherous waters, is that some things are worth dying for, but few things are worth killing for. There is a world of difference between laying down one's life for Christ and killing someone in Christ's name. Peace begins with toleration and ends with reconciliation through the love of Christ, which surpasses human understanding. By refusing to become partisans in the confessional struggles of their age, the Brethren repeatedly affirmed the teaching that the Creator made all humans in the divine image. This belief was incorporated in their schools, which were models of egalitarian education.

FIG. 26   Modern chalice made from one of the "Brethren's lindens," Moravian Seminary, Bethlehem, Pennsylvania.

CONCLUSION

The Unity of the Brethren was a voice of reason and toleration in a violent age. Certain aspects of their doctrine, such as their prohibition on commerce and their requirement of clerical celibacy, were clearly medieval, but in many ways the Unity charted the course for modern Christianity. The Brethren were a voluntary community of believers who tried to live according to the simple teachings of Christ. They left an inspiring legacy, but the most important lesson they can teach us today may be the simplest of all. The essentials of Christianity are faith, love, and hope. Perhaps the witness of the Unity will help Christians today remember that their faith rests in the Lamb of God, not in Mars or Zeus. The Unity of the Brethren may also help us rediscover that love is not an occasional emotion but a constant attitude of caring for all creation. Most important, perhaps we can learn how to face the future with hope, even in the darkest times. It is hope that allows us to keep watch through the night, knowing that the dawn is coming. It is hope that keeps us working for a better tomorrow in the midst of chaos, fear, and distress.[14] As Paul said, when all else is gone, faith, love, and hope remain (1 Cor. 13:13). And though the greatest of these is still love, what the world needs today is hope.[15]

14. "Hope," according to Václav Havel, "is not the conviction that something will turn out well, but the certainty that something makes sense, regardless of how it turns out." Havel, *Disturbing the Peace* (London: Faber and Faber, 1990), 181, quoted in Murphy, *Comenius*, 273.

15. Jan Lochman identified Comenius as a forerunner of the twentieth-century theologian Jürgen Moltman, who coined the phrase "theology of hope." Lochman, "Chiliasmus versus," 275–82.

Appendix: Timeline of the Unity of the Brethren

✝

1402	Jan Hus becomes preacher at Bethlehem Chapel in Prague
1409	Hus begins promoting the theology of John Wyclif at the University of Prague
1412	Hus writes *On the Church*
1414	Jakobek of Stříbro gives the chalice to the laity
1414–17	The Council of Constance meets to resolve the Great Schism
July 6, 1415	Hus is burned at the stake
1417	Beginning of Utraquist Church
1419	Defenestration of Prague in defense of the chalice; Hussite Wars begin
1420	Táborite Church founded
1420	Four Articles of Prague signed
1421	Chelčicky writes *On Spiritual Combat*, a pacifist tract
1424	Jan Žižka, military leader of Táborite army, dies
1425	Chelčicky writes *Three Estates*, rejecting feudalism and a state church
1433	Utraquists and Catholics at Council of Basel sign the Compacta
1434	Táborites and Orebites defeated by Utraquists and Catholics at battle of Lipany
1435	Jan Rokycana elected Utraquist archbishop of Prague, but is never consecrated
1452	City of Tábor capitulates and Táborite Church is destroyed
1457–58	Brother Gregory establishes Unity of Brethren in Kunwald
1467	Unity elects its first bishop and clergy, creating a separate and illegal church
1474	Gregory dies
1495–1500	Split between Old (Minority) Brethren and New (Majority) Brethren

1501	Publication of Unity's first hymnal
1517	Luther posts his Ninety-five Theses, beginning of the German Reformation
1523	Publication of Luke of Prague's *Children's Questions*
1528	Luke of Prague dies
1532	Jan Augusta elected to Inner Council; Lutheran influence increases in the Unity
1538	Publication of Unity's Confession of Faith, preface by Luther
1547	Renewed persecution following Schmaldkaldic War; Augusta imprisoned
1560s	Unity moves toward Calvinism
1566	Brethren publish a German-language hymnal, work on translating Bible
1575	Signing of the Bohemian Confession of Faith, a joint Protestant confession
1579	Pentateuch published in Czech
1596	Complete Czech Bible published by the Unity
1609	Emperor Rudolf signs letter of toleration for Unity
1613	One-volume Brethren's Bible (Kralice Bible) published
1618	Second defenestration of Prague, beginning of Thirty Years' War
1619	Frederick V of the Palatinate crowned king of Bohemia
1620	Battle of White Mountain, Protestants defeated
June 21, 1621	Day of Blood in Prague
1623	Comenius writes *The Labyrinth of the World*
1627	Czech Protestants forced to emigrate or convert; Unity based in Leszno, Poland
1642	Comenius goes to England to set up pansophic college
1642–48	Comenius works for Sweden on educational reform
1648	Treaty of Westphalia signed
1654	Comenius tries to set up pansophic school in Sárospatek, Hungary
1656	Leszno pillaged and burned
1657	Comenius in Amsterdam, publishes works on pedagogy, reform, and peace

1670	Comenius dies and is buried in the Netherlands
1722	Moravian refugees arrive in Germany claiming to be members of the Unity
1735	Daniel Ernst Jablonsky consecrates David Nitschmann bishop of the Unity

Bibliography

Alighieri, Dante. *The Divine Comedy.* Trans. Mark Musa. New York: Viking Penguin, 1987.

Alt, Robert. "Die Consultatio und ihre Beziehungen zur enzyklopadischen und utopischen Literatur." *Acta Comeniana* 1 (1970): 87–92.

Althusius, Johannes. *Politics.* Trans. Frederick S. Carney. Boston: Beacon Press, 1964.

Andrews, Charles, ed. and trans. *The New Atlantis and the City of the Sun: Two Classic Utopias.* Minneapolis: Dover Publications, 2003.

Antochi, Josif. "Alsted und Comenius in Transylvania." In *Comenius: Erkennen, Glauben, Handeln,* ed. Klaus Schaller, 38–48. Sankt Augustin: Richarz, 1985.

Artress, Lauren. *Walking a Sacred Path: Rediscovering the Labyrinth as a Spiritual Tool.* New York: Riverhead Books, 1996.

Atwood, Craig D. *Always Reforming: A History of Christianity Since 1300.* Macon: Mercer University Press, 2001.

———. "Catechism of the Bohemian Brethren, Translated and Edited from the 1523 Version." *Journal of Moravian History* 2 (spring 2007): 91–118.

———. *Community of the Cross: Moravian Piety in Colonial Bethlehem.* University Park: Pennsylvania State University Press, 2004.

———. "Faith, Love, and Hope: The Moravian Theological Heritage." *The Hinge: A Journal of Christian Thought for the Moravian Church* 11, no. 3 (2004): 2–26.

———. *Jesus Still Lead On: An Introduction to Moravian Belief.* Bethlehem, Pa.: Moravian Church Board of Publications, 2003.

———. "Separatism, Ecumenism, and Pacifism: The Bohemian and Moravian Brethren in the Confessional Age." In *Confessionalism and Pietism: Religious Reform in Early Modern Europe,* ed. Fred van Lieburg, 71–90. Mainz: Verlag Philipp von Zabern, 2006.

———. "Sleeping in the Arms of Christ: Sanctifying Sexuality in the Eighteenth-Century Brüdergemeine." *Journal of the History of Sexuality* 8 (1997): 25–51.

Auba, Jean. "Comenius and the Organization of Education." In *Comenius and Contemporary Education: An International Symposium,* ed. C. H. Dobinson, 52–59. Hamburg: UNESCO, 1970.

Augustine. *City of God.* Garden City, N.J.: Image Books, 1958.

———. *Confessions.* Trans. Henry Chadwick. New York: Oxford University Press, 1991.

Bacon, Francis. *The New Organon.* Ed. Fulton H. Anderson. Indianapolis: Bobbs-Merrill, 1960.

Bainton, Roland H. *Erasmus of Christendom.* New York: Scribner, 1969.

———. *Here I Stand: A Life of Martin Luther.* Nashville: Abingdon Press, 1978.

———. *The Reformation of the Sixteenth Century.* Boston: Beacon Press, 1952.

Barber, Malcolm. *The Cathars: Dualist Heretics in Languedoc in the High Middle Ages.* Aldershot: Ashgate, 2000.

Barstow, Anne Llewellyn. *Witchcraze: A New History of the European Witch Hunts.* San Francisco: HarperSanFrancisco, 1994.

Bartoš, František M. *The Hussite Revolution, 1424–1437.* Trans. and ed. John M. Klassen. New York: Columbia University Press, 1986.

———. "Wenceslas Budovec's Defense of the Brethren and of Freedom of Conscience in 1604." Trans. Howard Kaminsky. *Church History* 28 (1959): 229–39.

Bauer, Walter. *Orthodoxy and Heresy in Earliest Christianity.* Ed. Robert A. Kraft and Gerhard Krodel. Minneapolis: Augsburg, 1971.

Bednář, M. "Comenius's Idea of Pampaedia and Plato's Conception of Paideai." In *Homage to J. A. Comenius,* ed. Jaroslava Pešková, Josef Cach, and Michal Svatoš, trans. Vladimír Kosina, Zdenka Marečková, Paula Novotná-Tipton, and Peter Svobodný, 137–45. Prague: Karolinum, 1991.

Bernard, Paul P. "Jerome of Prague, Austria, and the Hussites." *Church History* 27 (1958): 3–22.

Bettenson, Henry, and Christ Maunder, eds. *Documents of the Christian Church.* 3d ed. New York: Oxford University Press, 1999.

Betts, Reginald Robert. *Essays in Czech History.* London: Athlone Press, 1969.

Beyreuther, Erich. *Studien zur Theologie Zinzendorfs.* Neukirchen-Vluyn: Kreis Moers, 1962.

Biller, Peter. *The Waldenses, 1170–1530: Between a Religious Order and a Church.* Aldershot: Ashgate, 2001.

Blekastad, Milada. *Comenius: Versuch eines Umrisses von Leben, Werk, und Schicksal des Jan Amos Komensky.* Oslo: Universitetsforlaget, 1969.

Bloch, Marc. *Feudal Society.* Trans. L. A. Manyon. 2 vols. Chicago: University of Chicago Press, 1963.

Boehme, Jacob. *The Way to Christ.* Trans. and ed. Peter Erb. New York: Paulist Press, 1978.

Bonhoeffer, Dietrich. *The Cost of Discipleship.* Trans. R. H. Fuller. New York: Macmillan, 1963.

———. *Ethics.* Trans. Neville Horton Smith. New York: Macmillan, 1965.

Bouwsma, William J. *John Calvin: A Sixteenth-Century Portrait.* Oxford: Oxford University Press, 1988.

Bozeman, Theodore Dwight. *To Live Ancient Lives: The Primitivist Dimension in Puritanism.* Chapel Hill: University of North Carolina Press, 1988.

Brady, Thomas A., Jr. "'The Earth Is the Lord's and Our Homeland as Well': Martin Bucer and the Politics of Strasbourg." In *Martin Bucer and Sixteenth-Century Europe, Actes du colloque de Strasbourg (28–31 août 1991),* ed. Christian Krieger and Marc Leinhard, 129–43. Studies in Medieval and Reformation Thought. Leiden: E. J. Brill, 1993.

Brambora, Josef, Josef V. Polišensky, et al. "Research on the Life and Work of J. A. Comenius (1957–1970)." *Acta Comeniana* 3 (1973): 443–94.

Brock, Peter. *The Political and Social Doctrines of the Unity of Czech Brethren in the Fifteenth and Early Sixteenth Centuries.* The Hague: Mouton, 1957.

Bromiley, G. W. *Zwingli and Bullinger.* Philadelphia: Westminster Press, 1953.

Brown, Dale. *Understanding Pietism.* Grand Rapids: William B. Eerdmans, 1978.

Brown, Peter. *Augustine of Hippo.* Berkeley and Los Angeles: University of California Press, 1967.

Buber, Martin. *The Origin and Meaning of Hasidism.* New York: Horizon Press, 1960.

Buchenall, M. S. S. "A Comparative Historical and Philosophical Study of the Educational Theories of John Amos Comenius (1592–1670), Friedrich Froebel (1782–1852), and Maria Montessori (1870–1952)." PhD diss., University of Denver, 1970.

Burnett, Amy Nelson. *The Yoke of Christ: Martin Bucer and Christian Discipline.* Kirksville: Sixteenth-Century Journal and Northeast Missouri State University, 1994.

Busek, Vratislav, ed. *Comenius.* Chicago: Czechoslovak Society of Arts and Sciences, 1972.

Calvin, John. *Institutes of the Christian Religion.* Ed. John T. McNeill. Trans. Ford Lewis Battles. 2 vols. Philadelphia: Westminster Press, 1960.

Cameron, Euan. *The European Reformation.* Oxford: Clarendon Press, 1991.

———. *Waldenses: Rejections of Holy Church in Medieval Europe.* Oxford: Blackwell, 2000.

Campbell, Ted. *Religion of the Heart: A Study of European Religious Life in the Seventeenth and Eighteenth Centuries.* Columbia: University of South Carolina Press, 1991.

Čapék, Jan Blahoslav. "Comenius as Predecessor of the Enlightenment and of Classicism, with Particular Regard to Panaugia." *Acta Comeniana* 1 (1969): 35–45.

Čapková, Dagmar. "The Comenian Group in England and Comenius' Idea of Universal Reform." *Acta Comeniana* 1 (1970): 25–34.

Čapková, Dagmar, J. Dohnalek, and E. Turkova, trans. and eds. *Consultationes de consultatione.* Prague: J. A. Comenius Institute of Education, Czechoslovak Academy of Sciences, 1970.

———. "The Cultural Inheritance of Comenius." In *Johannes Amos Comenius (1592–1670): Exponent of European Culture?* ed. P. van Vliet and A. J. Vanderjagt, 17–23. Amsterdam: North-Holland Press, 1994.

———. "On the New Image of Comenius." *Acta Comeniana* 2 (1970): 470–81.

Caravolas, Jean-Antoine. "Comenius (Komenský) and the Theory of Language Teaching." *Acta Comeniana* 10 (1993): 141–62.

Carpay, J. "Bei Comenius in der Lehre." In *Johannes Amos Comenius (1592–1670): Exponent of European Culture?* ed. P. Van Vliet and A. J. Vanderjagt, 24–40. Amsterdam: North-Holland Press, 1994.

Carroll, James. *Constantine's Sword: The Church and the Jews.* New York: Houghton Mifflin, 2001.

Červenka, Jaromír. "Die Grundlagen der pansophischen Idee des Johann Amos Comenius." *Acta Comeniana* 1 (1969): 77–84.

———. "One Hundred Years of the Views on Comenius' Pansophia." In *Consultationes de consultatione,* trans. and ed. Dagmar Čapková, J. Dohnalek, and E. Turkova, 21–84. Prague: J. A. Comenius Institute of Education, Czechoslovak Academy of Sciences, 1970.

Chadwick, Owen. *The Reformation.* Vol. 3 of *The Penguin History of the Church,* ed. Owen Chadwick. New York: Penguin Books, 1964.

Charry, Ellen T. *By the Renewing of Your Minds: The Pastoral Function of Christian Doctrine.* New York: Oxford University Press, 1997.

Chelčicky, Peter. "On the Holy Church," "Treatises on Christianity and the Social Order," and "On the Triple Division of Society." Trans. and ed. Howard Kaminsky. In *Studies in Medieval and Renaissance History,* ed. William Bowsky, 1:105–79. Lincoln: University of Nebraska Press, 1964.

Cheltschizki, Peter. *Das Netz des Glaubens.* Trans. Carl Vogl. Reprinted in *Quellen und Darstellungen zur Geschichte der böhmischen Brüder-Unität.* Vol. 5 of *Nikolaus Ludwig von Zinzendorf: Materialien und Dokumente,* ed. Erich Beyreuther, Gerhard Meyer, and Amedeo Molnár, 37 vols. Hildesheim: Georg Olms, 1970.

Christianson, Gerald. "Wyclif's Ghost: The Politics of Reunion at the Council of Basel." *Annuarium Historiae Conciliorum* 17 (1985): 193–208.

Čiževsky, Dmitry. "Comenius' *Labyrinth of the World:* Its Themes and Their Sources." *Harvard Slavic Studies* 1 (1953): 83–135.

———. "Comenius und die deutschen Pietisten." In *Aus zwei Welten: Beiträge zur Geschichte der slavisch-westlichen literarischen Beziehungen,* 165–71. The Hague: Mouton, 1956.

Clauser, Jerome K. *Comenian Pedagogy and the Moravian School Curriculum.* University Park: Pennsylvania State University Press, 1961.

Cohn, Norman. *The Pursuit of the Millennium.* 2d ed. New York: Oxford University Press, 1970.

Comenius, John Amos. *The Analytical Didactic of Comenius.* Trans. Vladimir Jelinek. Chicago: University of Chicago Press, 1953.

——. *The Angel of Peace.* Ed. Milos Safranek. Trans. W. A. Morison. New York: Pantheon Books, 1945.

——. *Ausgewahlte Werke.* Ed. Dmitrij Tschizewskij and Klaus Schaller. 4 vols. Hildesheim: George Olm, 1973–83.

——. *The Bequest of the Unity of the Brethren.* Trans. Matthew Spinka. Chicago: National Union of Czechoslovak Protestants in America, 1940.

——. *The Great Didactic of John Amos Comenius translated into English and edited with biographical, historical and critical introductions.* Trans. and ed. M. W. Keatinge. 2 vols. 2d ed. London: Adam and Charles Black, 1923.

——. *Johannes Amos Comenii: Opera Omnia.* Ed. Otalar Chlup. 18 vols. Prague: Academia Scientiarum Bohemoslovakia, 1969.

——. "John Amos Comenius: *Unum necessarium.*" Trans. Vernon Nelson. BD thesis, Moravian Theological Seminary, Bethlehem, Pa., 1958. http://www.moravianarchives.org/images/pdfs/Unum%20Necessarium.pdf.

——. *Kurtzgefa te Kirchenhistorie der böhmischen Brüder.* Schwabach, 1739. Reprinted in *Quellen zur Geschichtsschreibung der böhmischen Brüder.* Vol. 4 of *Nicholas Ludwig von Zinzendorf: Materialien und Dokumente,* ed. Erich Beyreuther, Gerhard Meyer and Amedeo Molnár, 37 vols. Hildesheim: Georg Olms, 1980.

——. *The Labyrinth of the World and the Paradise of the Heart.* Trans. Andrea Sterk and Howard Louthan. New York: Paulist Press, 1998.

——. *Orbis sensualium pictus.* Facsimile of the third London edition of 1672. Ed. James Bowen. Sydney: Sydney University Press, 1967.

——. *Panegersia, or Universal Awakening.* Trans. A. M. O. Dobbie. Warwickshire: Peter I. Drinkwater, 1990.

——. *Panorthosia, or Universal Reform, Chapters 1–18 and 27.* Trans. A. M. O. Dobbie. Sheffield: Sheffield Academic Press, 1995.

——. *Panorthosia, or Universal Reform, Chapters 19–26.* Trans. A. M. O. Dobbie. Sheffield: Sheffield Academic Press, 1993.

——. *A Reformation of the Schooles.* Trans. Samuel Hartlib. Facsimile of the 1642 London edition. Ed. R. C. Alston. Menston, England: Scolar Press, 1969.

——. *The School of Infancy.* Trans. Daniel Benham. Ed. Ernest M. Eller. Chapel Hill: University of North Carolina Press, 1956.

——. *The Way of Light.* Trans. E. T. Campagnac. London: Hodder & Stoughton, 1938.

Cook, William R. "The Eucharist in Hussite Theology." *Archiv für Reformationsgeschichte/Archive for Reformation History* 66 (1975): 23–35.

——. "John Wyclif and Hussite Theology, 1415–1436." *Church History* 42 (1973): 335–49.

——. "Negotiations Between the Hussites, the Holy Roman Empire, and the Roman Church, 1427–36." *East Central Europe* 5 (1978): 90–104.

——. "Peter Payne and the Waldensians." *Bolletino della Societa di Studi Valdesi* 175 (1975): 3–13.

——. "Peter Payne, Theologian and Diplomat of the Hussite Revolution." PhD diss., Cornell University, 1971.

Čornejová, Ivana. "The Jesuit School and John Amos Comenius." In *Homage to J. A. Comenius,* ed. Jaroslava Pešková, Josef Cach, and Michal Svatoš, 82–96. Prague: Karolinum, 1991.

Cranz, David. *The Ancient and Modern History of the Brethren.* Trans. and rev. Benjamin LaTrobe. London, 1780.

Crews, C. Daniel. "Luke of Prague: Theologian of the Unity." *The Hinge: A Journal of Christian Thought for the Moravian Church* 12, no. 3 (2005): 21–54.

———. "The Theology of John Hus, with Special Reference to His Concepts of Salvation." PhD diss., University of Manchester, 1975.

———. "Through the Labyrinth: A Prelude to the Comenius Anniversary of 1992." *Transactions of the Moravian Historical Society* 27 (1992): 27–52.

David, Zdeněk V. "Bohemian Utraquism in the Sixteenth Century: The Distinction and Tribulation of a Religious 'Via Media.'" *Communio Viatorum* 35 (1993): 195–231.

———. *Finding the Middle Way: The Utraquists' Liberal Challenge to Rome and Luther.* Baltimore: Johns Hopkins University Press, 2003.

———. "Utraquists, Lutherans, and the Bohemian Confession of 1575." *Church History* 68 (1999): 294–336.

David, Zdeněk V., and David R. Holeton, eds. *The Bohemian Reformation and Religious Practice.* Prague: Academy of Sciences of the Czech Republic, 1996.

De Schweinitz, Edmund. *The History of the Church Known as the Unitas Fratrum or The Unity of the Brethren, Founded by the followers of John Hus, the Bohemian Reformer and Martyr.* 2d ed. Bethlehem, Pa.: Moravian Publications Office, 1901.

———. *Moravian Manual: Containing an Account of the Protestant Church of the Moravian United Brethren or Unitas Fratrum.* Philadelphia: Lindsay & Blakiston, 1859.

De Vooght, Paul. "Un episode peu connu de la vie d'Erasme: Sa recontre avec les hussites bohemes en 1519–1521." *Irénikon* 47 (1974): 27–47.

———. *L'heresie de Jean Huss.* Louvain: Universitaires de Louvain, 1960.

Dieter, Hans Jörg. "Das Verständnis von Schrift in der Confessio Táboritarium." *Communio Viatorum* 30 (1987): 157–71.

Dobias, F. M. "Aspects of Social Ethics in the Works of J. A. Comenius." *Communio Viatorum* 4 (1961): 72–82, 181–91.

Dobinson, C. H., ed. *Comenius and Contemporary Education: An International Symposium.* Hamburg: UNESCO, 1970.

Duffy, Eamon. *Stripping of the Altars: Traditional Religion in England, 1400–1580.* New Haven: Yale University Press, 1992.

Dunn, Truman. "Facing the Death of the Moravian Church with Courage and Vision." *The Hinge: A Journal of Christian Thought for the Moravian Church* 8, no. 4 (2001): 2–9.

———. "Preserving the Unity: Community and Conflict in Moravian Church History." PhD diss., Union Theological Seminary, 1989.

Ehrmann, Bart D. *The New Testament: A Historical Introduction to the Early Christian Writings,* 2d ed. New York: Oxford University Press, 2000.

Erasmus, Desiderius. *The Essential Erasmus.* Ed. and trans. John P. Dolan. New York: Meridian, 1964.

———. *Ten Colloquies.* Trans. and ed. Craig R. Thompson. Indianapolis: Bobbs-Merrill, 1957.

Erikson, Erik. *Young Man Luther.* New York: W. W. Norton, 1958.

Evans, E. R. W. *Rudolph II and His World.* Oxford: Oxford University Press, 1973.

Fisher, J. D. C. *Christian Initiation: The Reformation Period.* London: Alcuin Club Collections, 1970.

Floss, Pavel. "Komensky's Auseinandersetzung mit dem Cartesianismus in seinen naturwis-senschaftlichen Schriften." In *Comenius: Erkennen, Glauben, Handeln*, ed. Klaus Schaller, 189–96. Sankt Augustin: Richarz, 1985.

Foldes, Eva, and Istvan Meszaros, eds. *Comenius and Hungary*. Budapest: Akademiai Kiado, 1973.

Ford, David F. *Self and Salvation: Being Transformed*. Cambridge: Cambridge University Press, 1999.

Fousek, Marianka S. "The Perfectionism of the Early Unitas Fratrum." *Church History* 30 (1961): 396–413.

———. "The Second-Generation Soteriology of the Unitas Fratrum: A Study in Luke's Directives to Priests, 1527." *Zeitschrift für Kirchengeschichte* 76 (1965): 41–63.

———. "Spiritual Direction and Discipline: A Key to the Flowering and Decay of the Sixteenth-Century Unitas Fratrum." *Archiv für Reformationsgeschichte / Archive for Reformation History* 62 (1971): 207–24.

Fudge, Thomas. "*Ansellus Dei* and the Bethlehem Chapel in Prague." *Communio Viatorum* 35 (1993): 127–61.

———. "The 'Crown' and the 'Red Gown': Hussite Popular Religion." In *Popular Religion in Germany and Central Europe, 1400–1800*, ed. Robert W. Scribner and Trevor Johnson, 38–57. London: Macmillan, 1996.

———. "Hussite Infant Communion." *Lutheran Quarterly* 10 (1996): 179–94.

———. "The Law of God: Reform and Religious Practice in Late Medieval Bohemia." In *The Bohemian Reformation and Religious Practice*, vol. 1, ed. David R. Holeton, 49–72. Prague: Academy of Sciences of the Czech Republic, 1996.

———. *The Magnificent Ride: The First Reformation in Hussite Bohemia*. Aldershot: Ashgate, 1998.

———. "Neither Mine nor Thine: Communist Experiments in Hussite Bohemia." *Canadian Journal of History* 33 (April 1998): 25–48.

———. "The Night of the Antichrist: Popular Culture, Judgment, and Revolution in Fifteenth-Century Bohemia." *Communio Viatorum* 37 (1995): 33–45.

Fuller, Robert. *Naming the Antichrist: The History of an American Obsession*. New York: Oxford University Press, 1995.

Gay, Peter. *The Rise of Modern Paganism*. Vol. 2 of *The Enlightenment*. New York: W. W. Norton, 1966.

Ghosh, Kantik. *The Wycliffite Heresy: Authority and Interpretation of Texts*. Cambridge: Cambridge University Press, 2002.

Gill, Theodor. "Zinzendorf und die Mähren." In *Graf ohne Grenzen: Leben und Werk von Nikolaus Ludwig Graf von Zinzendorf*, ed. Dieter Meyer and Paul Peucker, 37–42. Herrnhut: Unitäts-archiv-Comeniusbuchhandlung, 2000.

Gilmore, Myron P. *The World of Humanism, 1453–1517*. New York: Harper & Row, 1962.

Gonnet, Jean, and Amedeo Molnár. *Les vaudois au moyen âge*. Turin: Claudiana, 1974.

Gontscharow, Nikolai. "The Great Humanist John Amos Comenius." *Acta Comeniana* 1 (1969): 17–24.

Goodrick-Clarke, Clare. "The Rosicrucian Afterglow: The Life and Influence of Comenius." In *The Rosicrucian Enlightenment Revisited*, ed. Ralph White, 193–217. Hudson, N.Y.: Lindisfarne Books, 1999.

Graus, František. "The Crisis of the Middle Ages and the Hussites." Trans. James J. Heaney.

In *The Reformation in Medieval Perspective*, ed. Steven E. Ozment, 76–103. Chicago: University of Chicago Press, 1971.

Green, Richard, ed. *Protestantism and Capitalism: The Weber Thesis*. Boston: D. C. Heath, 1959.

Greschat, Martin. *Martin Bucer: A Reformer and His Times*. Trans. Stephen E. Buckwalter. Louisville: Westminster John Knox Press, 2004.

———. "The Relation Between Church and Civil Community in Bucer's Reforming Work." In *Martin Bucer: Reforming Church and Community*, ed. D. F. Wright, 17–31. Cambridge: Cambridge University Press, 1994.

Groenendijk, Leendert F., and Johan C. Sturm. "Das Exempel Böhmens in den Niederlanden: Comenius' Bedeutung für die familienpädagogische Offensive der pietischen Reformation." *Zeitschrift für Pädagogik* 38 (1992): 163–82.

Hägglund, Bengt. *History of Theology*. Trans. Gene J. Lund. St. Louis: Concordia, 1968.

Hall, Douglas John. *Christian Theology in a North American Context*. 3 vols. Minneapolis: Fortress Press, 1991–98.

Hamilton, J. Taylor. *The Recognition of the Unitas Fratrum as an Old Protestant Episcopal Church by the Parliament of Great Britain in 1749*. Nazareth, Pa.: Moravian Historical Society, 1925.

Hamilton, J. Taylor, and Kenneth G. Hamilton. *History of the Moravian Church: The Renewed Unitas Fratrum, 1722–1957*. Bethlehem, Pa.: Moravian Church in America, 1967.

Hammann, Gottfried. "Ecclesiological Motifs Behind the Creation of the 'Christlichen Gemeinschaften.'" In *Martin Bucer: Reforming Church and Community*, ed. D. F. Wright, 129–43. Cambridge: Cambridge University Press, 1994.

Havel, Václav. *Disturbing the Peace*. London: Faber and Faber, 1990.

Hazlett, Ian. "Eucharistic Communion: Impulses and Directions in Martin Bucer's Thought." In *Martin Bucer: Reforming Church and Community*, ed. D. F. Wright, 72–82. Cambridge: Cambridge University Press, 1994.

Headley, John M. *Tommaso Campanella and the Transformation of the World*. Princeton: Princeton University Press, 1997.

Heim, Mark S., ed. *Faith to Creed: Toward a Common Historical Approach to the Affirmation of the Apostolic Faith in the Fourth Century*. Grand Rapids: William B. Eerdmans, 1991.

Heydorn, Heinz Joachim, ed. *Jan Amos Comenius: Geschichte und Aktualitat, 1670–1970*. 2 vols. Glashutten: Detlev Auvermann, 1971.

Heymann, Frederick G. "The Crusades Against the Hussites." In *The Fourteenth and Fifteenth Centuries*, ed. Harry W. Hazard, 586–648. Vol. 3 of *A History of the Crusades*, ed. Kenneth M. Sutton. Madison: University of Wisconsin Press, 1975.

———. "John Rokycana: Church Reformer Between Hus and Luther." *Church History* 28 (1959): 240–80.

———. *John Žižka and the Hussite Revolution*. Princeton: Princeton University Press, 1955.

———. "Pius Aeneas Among the Taborites." *Church History* 28 (1959): 281–309.

Hill, Christopher. *Intellectual Origins of the English Revolution*. Oxford: Oxford University Press, 1965.

Hillerbrand, Hans J. "Was There a Reformation in the Sixteenth Century?" *Church History* 72 (2003): 525–52.

Hofmann, Franz. "Der enzyklopadische Impuls J. H. Alsteds und sein Gestaltwandel im Werke des J. A. Komensky." In *Comenius: Erkennen, Glauben, Handeln*, ed. Klaus Schaller, 22–29. Sankt Augustin: Richarz, 1985.

Holeton, David R. "The Communion of Infants and Hussitism." *Communio Viatorum* 27 (1984): 207–25.

———. "The Communion of Infants: The Basel Years." *Communio Viatorum* 29 (1986): 15–40.

———. "Revelation and Revolt in Late Medieval Bohemia." *Communio Viatorum* 36 (1994): 29–45.

Hotson, Howard. "Irenicism and Dogmatics in the Confessional Age: Pareus and Comenius in Heidelberg, 1614." *Journal of Ecclesiastical History* 46 (1995): 432–53.

———. *Johann Heinrich Alsted, 1588–1638: Between Renaissance, Reformation, and Universal Reform.* Oxford: Clarendon Press, 2000.

———. *Paradise Postponed: Johann Heinrich and the Birth of Calvinist Millenarianism.* Dordrecht: Kluwer Academic, 2000.

Hřbek, J. "Comenius and His Endeavours to Reform Human Society." *Acta Comeniana* 3 (1973): 17–20.

Hroch, M. "The World as Labyrinth." In *Homage to J. A. Comenius,* ed. Jaroslava Pešková, Josef Cach, and Michal Svatoš, 25–31. Prague: Karolinum, 1991.

Hromadka, J. L., and Amedeo Molnár, eds. and trans. *J. A. Comenius—A Perfect Reformation.* Prague: Comenius Faculty of Theology, 1957.

Hrubes, Jiří. "On the Panegyric of Comenius." *Acta Comeniana* 3 (1973): 247–53.

Hudson, A. *The Premature Reformation: Wycliffite Texts and Lollard History.* Oxford: Clarendon Press, 1988.

Hudson, A., and M. Wilks, eds. *From Ockham to Wycif.* Oxford: Blackwell, 1987.

Huizinga, Johan. *Erasmus and the Age of Reformation.* New York: Harper & Brothers, 1957.

Hus, John. *On Simony.* Trans. and ed. Matthew Spinka. In *Advocates of Reform,* ed. Matthew Spinka, 187–278. Philadelphia: Westminster Press, 1953.

Iwanczat, W. "Between Pacifism and Anarchy—Peter Chelčický Teaching About Society: Hussite Views on the Organisation of Christian Society." *Journal of Medieval History* 23 (1997): 271–83.

Jakubec, Jan. *Johannes Amos Comenius.* 1928. Reprint, New York: Arno Press, 1971.

Johnson, Luke Timothy. *The Creed: What Christians Believe and Why It Matters.* New York: Doubleday, 2003.

Jones, Cheslyn, Geoffrey Wainwright, and Edward Yarnold, eds. *The Study of Liturgy.* New York: Oxford University Press, 1978.

Kalivoda, Robert. "Comenius' Consultatio und Comenius' Philosophie." *Acta Comeniana* 1 (1969): 113–16.

Kaminsky, Howard. "Chiliasm and the Hussite Revolution." *Church History* 26 (1957): 43–71.

———. "The Free Spirit in the Hussite Revolution." In *Millennial Dreams in Action,* ed. Sylvia L. Thrupp, 166–86. The Hague: Mouton, 1962.

———. *A History of the Hussite Revolution.* Berkeley and Los Angeles: University of California Press, 1967.

———. "Hussite Radicalism and the Origins of Tabor, 1415–1418." *Medievalia et Humanistica* 10 (1956): 102–30.

———. "The Religion of Hussite Tabor." In *The Czechoslovak Contribution to World Culture,* ed. Miloslav Rechcigl Jr., 210–23. The Hague: Mouton, 1964.

———. "Wyclifism as Ideology of Revolution." *Church History* 32 (1963): 57–74.

Kaufman, Peter Iver. *Church, Creed, Bishop: Conflict and Authority in Early Latin Christianity.* Boulder, Colo.: Westview Press, 1996.

Kavka, František. "Bohemia." In *The Reformation in National Context*, ed. Robert Scribner, Roy Porter, and Mikuláš Teich, 131–54. Cambridge: Cambridge University Press, 1994.
———. "Politics and Culture Under Charles IV." In *Bohemia in History*, ed. Mikuláš Tiech, 59–77. Cambridge: Cambridge University Press, 1998.
Keen, Maurice. "Wyclif, the Bible, Transubstantiation." In *Wyclif in His Times*, ed. Anthony Kenny, 6–15. Oxford: Clarendon Press, 1986.
Kejř, Jiří. *The Hussite Revolution.* Prague: Orbis, 1988.
Kelley, Donald R. *Renaissance Humanism.* Boston: Twayne, 1991.
Kempis, Thomas á. *The Imitation of Christ.* Trans. Leo Sherley-Price. New York: Viking Penguin, 1952.
Kenny, Anthony, ed. *Wyclif in His Times.* Oxford: Clarendon Press, 1986.
Kienzle, Beverly Mayne, and Pamela J. Walker, eds. *Women Preachers and Prophets Through Two Millennia of Christianity.* Berkeley and Los Angeles: University of California Press, 1998.
Kimball, Charles. *When Religion Becomes Evil.* San Francisco: HarperSanFrancisco, 2002.
Kittelson, James M. "Martin Bucer and the Ministry of the Church." In *Martin Bucer: Reforming Church and Community*, ed. D. F. Wright, 83–94. Cambridge: Cambridge University Press, 1994.
———. *Wolfgang Capito: From Humanist to Reformer.* Leiden: E. J. Brill, 1975.
Klassen, John M. "The Disadvantaged and the Hussite Revolution." *International Review of Social History* 35 (1990): 249–72.
———. *Warring Maidens, Captive Wives, and Hussite Queens: Women and Men at War and Peace in Fifteenth-Century Bohemia.* New York: Columbia University Press, 1999.
Knowles, David. *The Evolution of Medieval Thought.* New York: Vintage Books, 1962.
Kölbing, Friedrich Ludwig. *Nachricht von dem Angange der bishöflichen Ordination in der erneuerten evangelischen Brüderkirche.* Gnadau, 1835.
Kozik, František. *Comenius.* Trans. Stephan Kolar. Prague: Orbis, 1980.
Kramer, Heinrich, and James Sprenger. *Malleus maleficarum.* Trans. Montague Summers. Mineola, N.Y.: Dover Publications, 1971.
Krieger, Christian, and Marc Leinhard, eds. *Martin Bucer and Sixteenth-Century Europe, Actes du colloque de Strasbourg (28–31 août 1991).* Studies in Medieval and Reformation Thought. Leiden: E. J. Brill, 1993.
Kristellar, Paul Oskar. *Renaissance Thought: The Classic, Scholastic, and Humanist Strains.* New York: Harper Torchbooks, 1961.
Kučera, Karel. "An Analysis of the Vocabulary of *The Labyrinth of the World and the Paradise of the Heart,* by J. A. Comenius." *Acta Comeniana* 4 (1979): 339–53.
Kučera, Z. "John Amos Comenius: A Theologian of Universality." In *Homage to J. A. Comenius*, ed. Jaroslava Pešková, Josef Cach, and Michal Svatoš, 190–98. Prague: Karolinum, 1991.
Kyrasesk, J., ed. *J. A. Comenius: Selections from His Works.* Trans. Z. Konecny. Prague: University of the Seventeenth November, 1964.
Lambert, Malcolm. *Medieval Heresy: Popular Movements from the Gregorian Reform to the Reformation.* 2d ed. Oxford: Blackwell, 1992.
Laurie, S. S. *John Amos Comenius: His Life and Educational Work.* London: Cambridge University Press, 1904.
Lee, Sook Jong. "The Relationship of John Amos Comenius' Theology to His Educational Ideas." EdD thesis, Rutgers University, 1987.

Leff, Gordon. *Heresy in the Later Middle Ages: The Relation of Heterodoxy to Dissent, c. 1250–c. 1450.* 2 vols. Manchester: Manchester University Press, 1967.

———. "Wyclif and Hus: A Doctrinal Comparison." In *Wyclif in His Times*, ed. Anthony Kenny, 105–26. Oxford: Clarendon Press, 1986.

Lehar, Jan. "'Labyrint sveta' (The Labyrinth of the World) and Its Characters." *Acta Comeniana* 4 (1979): 225–49.

Lindberg, Carter. *The Third Reformation?* Macon: Mercer University Press, 1983.

Lochman, Jan Milíč. "Chiliasmus versus: Eschatologie und Weltgestaltung in der Perspecktive des Comenius." *Theologische Zeitschrift* 35 (1979): 275–82.

———. *Comenius.* Hamburg: Friedrich Wittig, 1982.

———. *Living Roots of the Reformation.* Minneapolis: Augsburg, 1979.

Luther, Martin. *Luther's Works.* Trans. and ed. Jaroslav Pelikan and Hartmut T. Lehmann. 55 vols. St. Louis: Concordia, 1955–86.

MacCullough, Diarmand. *The Reformation: A History.* New York: Viking Press, 2003.

Macek, Josef. *The Hussite Movement in Bohemia.* Trans. Vilèm Fried and Ian Milner. Prague: Orbis, 1965.

———. "The Monarchy of the Estates." In *Bohemia in History*, ed. Mikuláš Tiech, 98–116. Cambridge: Cambridge University Press, 1998.

MacFarlane, K. B. *John Wycliffe and the Beginnings of English Nonconformity.* London: English Universities Press, 1952.

Martin, David. *Pacifism.* Boston: Routledge, 1998.

McGinn, Bernard. *Antichrist: Two Thousand Years of the Human Fascination with Evil.* San Francisco: HarperSanFrancisco, 1994.

———. *The Calabrian Abbot: Joachim of Fiore in the History of Western Thought.* New York: Macmillan, 1985.

McGrath, Alister E. *Luther's Theology of the Cross.* Cambridge: Blackwell, 1985.

McKee, Elsie. *Katherina Schütz Zell.* Leiden: E. J. Brill, 1998.

———. "Reforming Popular Piety in Sixteenth-Century Strasbourg." *Studies in Reformed Theology and History* 2 (1994): 1–82.

Meszaros, Istvan. "On the History of the Sárospatak School in the Fifteenth–Sixteenth Centuries and on Comenius' 'schola trivialis' There." In *Comenius and Hungary*, ed. Eva Foldes and Istvan Meszaros, 111–32. Budapest: Akademiai Kiado, 1973.

Michel, Gerhard. "Komensky's Studien in Herborn und ihre Nachwirkungen in seinem Gesamtwerk." In *Comenius: Erkennen, Glauben, Handeln*, ed. Klaus Schaller, 11–21. Sankt Augustin: Richarz, 1985.

Milton, John. *Areopagita and Of Education.* Ed. George Holland Sabine. Wheeling, Ill.: Harlan Davidson, 1987.

Miskovska-Kozakova, V. T. "Comenius's Linguistic Theory and Experiment." *Acta Comeniana* 4 (1979): 291–317.

———. "Elements of Syntax in the Constructed Language of Comenius." In *Consultationes de consultatione*, trans. and ed. Dagmar Čapková, J. Dohnalek, and E. Turkova, 119–40. Prague: J. A. Comenius Institute of Education, Czechoslovak Academy of Sciences, 1970.

Molnár, Amedeo. "The Brethren's Theology." In Rudolf Říčan, *The History of the Unity of the Brethren: A Protestant Hussite Church in Bohemia and Moravia.* Trans. C. Daniel Crews. Bethlehem, Pa.: Moravian Church in America, 1992.

———. "Comenius et l'Unité des Freres tchèques." *Communio Viatorum* 1 (1957): 110–15.

———. "Comenius's theologica naturalis." *Communio Viatorum* 8 (1965): 53–64.

———. "Comenius und die Gegenreformation." *Communio Viatorum* 19 (1976): 97–108.

———. "The Czech Confession of 1575." *Communio Viatorum* 16 (1973): 241–47.

———. "Erasmus und das Hussitentum." *Communio Viatorum* 30 (1987): 185–97.

———. "Luc de Prague devant la crise de l'Unité des annees 1490." *Communio Viatorum* 4 (1961): 316–24.

———. "Notes de lecture sur Comenius le theologian." *Acta Comeniana* 2 (1970): 305–11.

———. "Peter Chelčicky's Instructions on the Sacraments." *Communio Viatorum* 19 (1976): 177–93.

———. "Zum Theologieverstandis des Comenius." *Communio Viatorum* 27 (1984): 227–41.

Molnár, Enrico. "The Pious Fraud of Count Zinzendorf." *Iliff Review* 11 (1954): 29–38.

Monroe, Will S. *Comenius.* New York: Scribner's Sons, 1892.

———. *Comenius and the Beginning of Educational Reform.* New York: Scribner and Sons, 1900.

Moravian Church Unity Synod. *Church Order of the Unitas Fratrum (Moravian Church)*, 2002. Bethlehem, Pa.: Moravian Church in America, 2003.

Morée, Peter C. A. *Preaching in Fourteenth-Century Bohemia: The Life and Ideas of Milicius de Chremsir and His Significance in the Historiography of Bohemia.* Slavkov: Eman, 1999.

Mout, Nicolette. "Comenius, Descartes, and Dutch Cartesianism." *Acta Comeniana* 3 (1973): 243–45.

———. "The Contacts of Comenius with the Netherlands Before 1656." *Acta Comeniana* 1 (1969): 221–31.

Müller, Joseph. *Das Bischoftum der Brüder Unität.* Herrnhut, 1899.

———, ed. *Die Deutschen Katechismen der böhmischen Brüder, Kritische Textausgabe mit kirchen- und dogmengeschichtlichen Untersuchungen und einer Abhandlung über das Schulwesen der böhmischen Brüder.* Berlin: Hofman, 1887. Reprinted as vol. 1 of *Nikolaus Ludwig von Zinzendorf: Materialien und Dokumente*, ed. Erich Beyreuther, Gerhard Meyer, and Amedeo Molnár, 37 vols. Hildesheim: Georg Olms, 1982.

———. *Geschichte der böhmischen Brüder.* 3 vols. Herrnhut: Verlag der Missionsbuchhandlung, 1922–31.

———. *Zinzendorf als Erneuerer der alten Brüderkirche.* Leipzig, 1900.

Murphy, Daniel. *Comenius: A Critical Reassessment of His Life and Work.* Dublin: Irish Academic Press, 1995.

Needham, Joseph, ed. *The Teacher of Nations: Addresses and Essays in Commemoration of the Visit to England of the Great Czech Educationalist Jan Amos Komensky (Comenius), 1641–1941.* Cambridge: Cambridge University Press, 1942.

Neuwirth, J. "Comenius and the Plague in Leszno." In *Homage to J. A. Comenius*, ed. Jaroslava Pešková, Josef Cach, and Michal Svatoš, 106–13. Prague: Karolinum, 1991.

Oakley, Francis. *The Political Thought of Pierre d'Ailly: The Voluntarist Tradition.* New Haven: Yale University Press, 1964.

———. "Religious and Ecclesiastical Life on the Eve of the Reformation." In *Reformation Europe: A Guide to Research*, ed. Steven E. Ozment, 5–32. St. Louis: Center for Reformation Research, 1982.

———. *The Western Church in the Later Middle Ages.* Ithaca: Cornell University Press, 1979.

Oberman, Heiko A. *The Harvest of Medieval Theology.* Grand Rapids: Baker Books, 2000.

———. *Luther: Man Between God and the Devil.* Trans. Eileen Walliser-Schwarzbart. New Haven: Yale University Press, 1989.

Obolensky, Dimitri. *Byzantium and the Slavs*. Crestwood, N.Y.: St. Vladimir's Seminary Press, 1994.

Odložilík, Otakar. "A Church in a Hostile State: The Unity of the Czech Brethren." *Central European History* 6 (1973): 111–27.

———. *The Hussite King: Bohemia in European Affairs, 1440–1471*. New Brunswick: Rutgers University Press, 1965.

———. "Two Reformation Leaders of the Unitas Fratrum." *Church History* 9 (1940): 253–63.

Op t'Hof, Willem J. "Protestant Pietism and Medieval Monasticism." In *Confessionalism and Pietism: Religious Reform in Early Modern Europe*, ed. Fred van Lieburg, 31–50. Mainz: Verlag Philipp von Zabern, 2006.

Ozment, Steven E. *The Age of Reform, 1225–1550: An Intellectual and Religious History of Late Medieval and Reformation Europe*. New Haven: Yale University Press, 1980.

———. *Protestants: The Birth of a Revolution*. New York: Doubleday, 1992.

———, ed. *Reformation Europe: A Guide to Research*. St. Louis: Center for Reformation Research, 1982.

———. *The Reformation in Cities: The Appeal of Protestantism in Sixteenth-Century Germany and Switzerland*. New Haven: Yale University Press, 1975.

Palouš, R. "The World of Comenius." In *Homage to J. A. Comenius*, ed. Jaroslava Pešková, Josef Cach, and Michal Svatoš, 11–16. Prague: Karolinum, 1991.

Pánek, Jaroslav. *Comenius: Teacher of Nations*. Prague: Orbis, 1992.

Patapios, Hieromonk. "*Sub utruque specie*: The Arguments of John Hus and Jacoubek of Stříbro in Defence of Giving Communion to the Laity Under Both Kinds." *Journal of Theological Studies* 53 (2002): 503–22.

Pedram, Manouchehr. "A Critical Comparison of the Educational Theories and Practices of John Amos Comenius with John Dewey's Concept of Experience." PhD diss., University of Kansas, 1963.

Pelikan, Jaroslav. *The Christian Tradition: A History of the Development of Doctrine*. 5 vols. Chicago: University of Chicago Press, 1971–89.

Pelikan, Jaroslav, and Valerie Hotchkiss, eds. *Creeds and Confessions of Faith in the Christian Tradition*. 3 vols. New Haven: Yale University Press, 2003.

Peschke, Erhard. *Kirche und Welt in der Theologie der Böhmischen Brüder vom Mittelalter zur Reformation*. Berlin: Evangelische Verlagsanstalt, 1981.

Pešková, Jaroslava, Josef Cach, and Michal Svatoš, eds. *Homage to J. A. Comenius*. Prague: Karolinum, 1991.

Petráň, Josef, and Lydia Petráňová. "The White Mountain as a Symbol in Modern Czech History." In *Bohemia in History*, ed. Mikuláš Teich, 143–63. Cambridge: Cambridge University Press, 1988.

Phillips, M. M. *Erasmus and the Northern Renaissance*. New York: Macmillan, 1949.

Piaget, Jean. "Introduction." In *John Amos Comenius, 1592–1670: Selections in Commemoration of the Third Centenary of the Publication of Opera didactica omnia, 1657–1957*. Lausanne: UNESCO, 1957.

Pieper, Josef. *Faith, Hope, Love*. San Francisco: Ignatius Press, 1997.

Pilz, Kurt. *Die Ausgaben des Orbis sensualium pictus: Eine Bibliographie*. Nurnberg: Selbstverlag der Stadtbibliothek Nurnberg, 1967.

Podmore, Colin. *The Moravian Church in England, 1728–1760*. Oxford: Clarendon Press, 1998.

Polišensky, Josef V., ed. *Addresses and Essays in Commemoration of the Life and Works of the English Hussite Peter Payne-Englis, 1456–1956*. Prague: Charles University, 1957.

———. "Comenius and the Development of European Thought." *Acta Comeniana* 1 (1969): 241–45.

———. "Comenius and the Seventeenth-Century Social and Scientific Revolution." *Acta Comeniana* 2 (1970): 139–46.

———. "Comenius and the So-Called Scientific Revolution of the Seventeenth Century." *Acta Comeniana* 1 (1969): 251–52.

———. "Comenius, Huygens, and Newton, or: The Social and Scientific Revolutions of the Seventeenth Century." In *Jan Amos Comenius: Geschichte und Aktualitat, 1670–1970*, ed. Heinz Joachim Heydorn, 2 vols., 2:187–200. Glashutten: Detlev Auvermann, 1971.

———. "Comenius, the Angel of Peace, and the Netherlands in 1667." *Acta Comeniana* 1 (1970): 59–66.

———. "The Social and Political Premises of the Work of J. A. Comenius." *Acta Comeniana* 4 (1979): 5–26.

Pope, James D. "The Educational Writings of John Amos Comenius and Their Relevance in a Changing Culture." EdD thesis, University of Florida, 1962.

Provincial Elders' Conferences of the Northern and Southern Provinces of the Moravian Church. *Moravian Book of Worship*. Bethlehem, Pa.: Moravian Publication Office, 1995.

Rabb, T. K. "Religion and the Rise of Modern Science." *Past and Present* 31 (1965): 111–26.

Rákos, Petr. "Genti cuique splendorem addit: Comenius Among the Hungarians." In *Homage to J. A. Comenius*, ed. Jaroslava Pešková, Josef Cach, and Michal Svatoš, 270–80. Prague: Karolinum, 1991.

Rawls, John. *A Theory of Justice*. Rev. ed. Cambridge: Belknap Press of Harvard University Press, 1999.

Říčan, Rudolf. *The History of the Unity of the Brethren: A Protestant Hussite Church in Bohemia and Moravia*. Trans. C. Daniel Crews. Bethlehem, Pa.: Moravian Church in America, 1992.

———. "Motifs et modeles de l'Unite des Freres dans la consultation." *Acta Comeniana* 1 (1970): 47–57.

Ricouer, Paul. *Figuring the Sacred: Religion, Narrative, and Imagination*. Ed. Mark I. Wallace. Trans. David Pellauer. Minneapolis: Augsburg Fortress, 1995.

Riemeck, Renate. *Der andere Comenius: Böhmischer Brüderbischof, Humanist, und Pädagoge*. Frankfurt am Main: Stimme-Verlag, 1970.

Rietschel, Georg. *Lehrbuch der Liturgie*. Göttingen: Vandenhoeck Ruprecht, 1951–52.

Roberts, Paul C. "Comenian Philosophy and Moravian Education from 1850 to the Present Day." EdD thesis, Rutgers University, 1979.

Roeber, A. G. *Palatines, Liberty, and Property: German Lutherans in America*. Baltimore: Johns Hopkins University Press, 1993.

Rood, Wilhelmus. *Comenius and the Low Countries: Some Aspects of Life and Work of a Czech Exile in the Seventeenth Century*. New York: Abner Schram, 1970.

Rouse, Ruth, and Stephen Charles Neill, eds. *A History of the Ecumenical Movement, 1517–1948*. Philadelphia: Westminster Press, 1954.

Rubin, Miri. *Corpus Christi: The Eucharist in Late Medieval Culture*. Cambridge: Cambridge University Press, 1991.

Rupp, E. Gordon, and Philip S. Watson, with A. N. Marlow and B. Drewery, eds. and trans. *Luther and Erasmus: Free Will and Salvation*. Philadelphia: Westminster Press, 1969.

Rýdl, Karel. "John Amos Comenius in the Development of European Pedagogical and Philosophical Thinking in the Eighteenth Century." In *Homage to J. A. Comenius*, ed. Jaroslava Pešková, Josef Cach, and Michal Svatoš, 171–80. Prague: Karolinum, 1991.

Sadler, John Edward. *Comenius*. London: Macmillan, 1969.

———. *J. A. Comenius and the Concept of Universal Education*. London: Allen and Unwin, 1966.

Schaff, Phillip. *The Creeds of Christendom*. 3 vols. New York: Harper & Brothers, 1877.

Schaller, Klaus, ed. *Comenius: Erkennen, Glauben, Handeln*. Sankt Augustin: Richarz, 1985.

———. "E revelationum labyrinthis tanden repertus in planum exitus." *Communio Viatorum* 25 (1982): 123–26.

———. *Die Pädagogik des Johann Amos Comenius und die Anfange des pädagogische Realismus im 17. Jahrhundert*. Heidelberg: Quelle, 1967.

———. *Pan: Untersuchungen zur Comenius-Terminologie*. The Hague: Mouton, 1958.

Schattschneider, David. "Three Examples of Comenius' Legacy in America." Paper given at the Czechoslovak Academy of Sciences conference "Comenius' Heritage and the Education of Man for the Twenty-first Century," Prague, March 1992.

———. "The Unitas Fratrum and the 'Renewed' Moravian Church: Continuity and Change." Paper given at conference of the Czechoslovak Society of Arts and Sciences, Bethlehem, Pa., October 1989.

Schleiermacher, Friedrich. *The Christian Faith*. Ed. H. R. MacKintosh and J. S. Stewart. London: T. & T. Clark, 1999.

Schmidt, Martin. *Pietismus als theologische Erscheinung*. Göttingen: Vandenhoeck & Ruprecht, 1984.

Schroer, H. "Reich Gottes bei Comenius." In *Comenius: Erkennen, Glauben, Handeln*, ed. Klaus Schaller, 87–93. Sankt Augustin: Richarz, 1985.

Schulte-Nordholt, G. W. "Comenius and America: Some Remarks on Some Relations." *Acta Comeniana* 2 (1970): 195–200.

Schurr, Johannes. *Comenius: Eine Einfuhrung in die Consultatio Catholica*. Passau: Passavia Universitat Verlag, 1981.

Scribner, R. W. *For the Sake of Simple Folk: Popular Propaganda for the German Reformation*. Cambridge: Cambridge University Press, 1981.

Scribner, Robert, Roy Porter, and Mikulás Teich, eds. *The Reformation in National Context*. Cambridge: University of Cambridge Press, 1994.

Seibt, Ferdinand. "Johannes Hus und der Abzug der deutschen Studenten aus Prag 1409." In *Hussitenstudien: Personen, Ereignisse, Ideen einer frühen Revolution*, ed. Ferdinand Seibt, 1–16. Munich: R. Oldenbourg Verlag, 1987.

———, ed. *Kaiser Karl IV: Staatsmann und Mäzen*. Munich: Adalbert-Stifter-Verein, 1978.

Settari, O. "John Amos Comenius—Musicologist, Pedagogue, and Hymnographer." In *Homage to J. A. Comenius*, ed. Jaroslava Pešková, Josef Cach, and Michal Svatoš, 157–65. Prague: Karolinum, 1991.

Shantz, Douglas H. "Discovering the Key to Reformed Pietist Chiliasm: The Influence of Johannes Coccejus upon Horch, Reitz, and Bröske." *Covenant Quarterly* 61 (2004): 17–37.

Šmahel, František. "The Hussite Movement: An Anomaly of European History?" In *Bohemia in History*, ed. Mikuláš Teich, 79–97. Cambridge: Cambridge University Press, 1988.

———. "Literacy and Heresy in Hussite Bohemia." In *Heresy and Literacy, 1000–1530*, ed. Peter Biller and Anne Hudson, 237–54. Cambridge: Cambridge University Press, 1994.

Smolik, Joseph. "Das Eschatologische Denken des Johan Amos Comenius." *Evangelische The-ologie* 43 (1983): 191–202.

Sobotka, M. "J. A. Comenius and the Philosophy of His Time." In *Homage to J. A. Comenius*, ed. Jaroslava Pešková, Josef Cach, and Michal Svatoš, 125–36. Prague: Karolinum, 1991.

Southern, R. W. *Western Society and the Church in the Middle Ages*. Vol. 2 of *The Penguin History of the Church*, ed. Owen Chadwick. London: Penguin Books, 1970.

Spinka, Matthew, trans. and ed. *Advocates of Reform*. Philadelphia: Westminster Press, 1953.

———, trans. and ed. *John Amos Comenius: A Perfect Reformation*. Prague: Comenius Faculty of Protestant Theology, 1957.

———. *John Amos Comenius: That Incomparable Moravian*. New York: Russell and Russell, 1943.

———. *John Hus: A Biography*. Princeton: Princeton University Press, 1968.

———. *John Hus at the Council of Constance*. New York: Columbia University Press, 1965.

———. *John Hus' Concept of the Church*. Princeton: Princeton University Press, 1966.

———. *The Letters of John Hus*. Manchester: Manchester University Press, 1972.

———. "Peter Chelčický, the Spiritual Father of the Unitas Fratrum." *Church History* 12 (1943): 271–91.

Stephens, W. P. *The Holy Spirit in the Theology of Martin Bucer*. Cambridge: Cambridge University Press, 1970.

Sterik, Edita. "Mährische Brüder, böhmische Brüder, und die Brüdergemeine." *Unitas Fratrum* 48 (2001): 106–14.

Stoeffler, F. Ernest. *German Pietism During the Eighteenth Century*. Leiden: E. J. Brill, 1973.

———. *The Rise of Evangelical Pietism*. Leiden: E. J. Brill, 1965.

Stone, Lawrence. "The Education Revolution in England, 1540–1640." *Past and Present* 28 (1964): 41–80.

Strauss, Gerald. *Luther's House of Learning: Indoctrination of the Young in the German Reformation*. Baltimore: Johns Hopkins University Press, 1979.

Štrupl, Miloš. "Confessional Theology of the Unitas Fratrum." PhD diss., Vanderbilt University, 1964.

———. "Confessional Theology of the Unitas Fratrum." *Church History* 33 (1964): 279–93.

———. "Jan Blahoslav: Father and Charioteer of the Lord's People in the Unitas Fratrum." *Czechoslovakia Past and Present* 2 (1968): 1232–46.

Štverák, V. "The Influence of the Work of J. A. Comenius in the Eighteenth Century." In *Homage to J. A. Comenius*, ed. Jaroslava Pešková, Josef Cach, and Michal Svatoš, 339–47. Prague: Karolinum, 1991.

Sychrova, Hana. "Language as One of the Means of 'the Reform of Human Affairs' and Its Function in the World of the Scientific and Technological Revolution." *Acta Comeniana* 3 (1973): 365–75.

Taves, Ann, ed. *Religion and Domestic Violence in Early New England: The Memoirs of Abigail Abbot Bailey*. Bloomington: University of Indiana Press, 1989.

Teich, Mikuláš, ed. *Bohemia in History*. Cambridge: Cambridge University Press, 1988.

Tillich, Paul. *The Essential Tillich*. Ed. E. Forrester Church. New York: Macmillan, 1987.

Tolstoy, Leo. *The Kingdom of God Is Within You*. Omaha: University of Nebraska Press, 1985.

Tomiak, Janusz. "Comenius and the Notion of a Differentiated Analysis of Education." *Acta Comeniana* 3 (1973): 177–83.

Tourn, Giorgio, Roger Geymonet, et al. *You Are My Witnesses: The Waldensians Across Eight Centuries*. Cincinnati: Claudiana Press, 1989.

Tracy, James D. "Humanism and the Reformation." In *Reformation Europe: A Guide to Research*, ed. Steven E. Ozment, 35–58. St. Louis: Center for Reformation Research, 1982.

Trevor-Roper, H. R. "Three Foreigners: The Philosophers of the Puritan Revolution." In Trevor-Roper, *Religion, the Reformation, and Social Change, and Other Essays*, 2d ed., 237–93. London: Macmillan, 1972.

Troeltsch, Ernst. *The Social Teachings of the Christian Churches*. Trans. Olive Wyon. 2 vols. New York: Macmillan, 1931.

Turnbull, G. H. *Hartlib, Dury, and Comenius: Gleanings from Hartlib's Papers*. London: Hodder & Stoughton, 1947.

———. *Samuel Hartlib: A Sketch of His Life and His Relations to J. A. Comenius*. New York: Oxford University Press, 1920.

Turner, Victor. *The Ritual Process: Structure and Anti-Structure*. Ithaca: Cornell University Press, 1998.

Urfus, Valentin. "Jurisprudence in Comenius's Times." In *Homage to J. A. Comenius*, ed. Jaroslava Pešková, Josef Cach, and Michal Svatoš, 97–105. Prague: Karolinum, 1991.

Uždil, J. "Comenius, a Great Initiator of Esthetic Education." In *Homage to J. A. Comenius*, ed. Jaroslava Pešková, Josef Cach, and Michal Svatoš, 146–55. Prague: Karolinum, 1991.

Vacovský, Adolf. "History of the Hidden Seed." In *Unitas Fratrum*, ed. Mari P. von Buijtenen, Cornelius Dekker, and Huib Leeuwenberg, 35–54. Utrecht: Rijksarchief, 1975.

Válka, Josef. "Rudolfine Cuture." In *Bohemia in History*, ed. Mikuláš Teich, 117–42. Cambridge: Cambridge University Press, 1988.

Van Buijtenen, Mari P., and Cornelis Dekker. *Unitas Fratrum: Moravian Studies—Herrnhuter Studien*. Utrecht: Rijksarchief, 1975.

Van der Linde, Jan Marinus. "Der andere Comenius." *Unitas Fratrum* 8 (1980): 35–48.

Van Vliet, P., and A. J. Vanderjagt, eds. *Johannes Amos Comenius (1592–1670): Exponent of European Culture?* Amsterdam: North-Holland Press, 1994.

Wagner, Murray L. *Petr Chelčický: A Radical Separatist in Hussite Bohemia*. Scottsdale. Pa.: Herald Press, 1983.

Ward, W. R. *The Protestant Evangelical Awakening*. Cambridge: Cambridge University Press, 1992.

———. "The Renewed Unity of the Brethren: Ancient Church, New Sect, or Interconfessional Movement?" *Bulletin of the John Rylands Library* 70 (1988): lxvii–xcii.

Weber, Max. *The Protestant Ethic and the Spirit of Capitalism*. Trans. Talcott Parsons. Los Angeles: Roxbury Publishing, 1996.

———. *The Sociology of Religion*. Trans. Ephraim Fischoff. Boston: Beacon Press, 1991.

Webster, Charles. *From Paracelsus to Newton: Magic and the Making of Modern Science*. Cambridge: Cambridge University Press, 1982.

———. *The Great Instauration: Science, Medicine, and Reform, 1626–1660*. New York: Holmes & Meier, 1975.

———, ed. *Samuel Hartlib and the Advancement of Learning*. Cambridge: University Press, 1970.

Weeks, Andrew. *Boehme: An Intellectual Biography of the Seventeenth-Century Philosopher and Mystic*. Albany: State University of New York Press, 1991.

Wesley, John. *A Plain Account of Christian Perfection*. London: Epworth Press, 1952.

White, Ralph, ed. *The Rosicrucian Enlightenment Revisited*. Hudson, N.Y.: Lindisfarne Books, 1999.

Williams, George H. *The Radical Reformation*. Philadelphia: Westminster Press, 1962.

Williams, George H., and Angel M. Mergal. *Spiritual and Anabaptist Writers*. Philadelphia: Westminster Press, 1957.

Willis, Gladys. *The Penalty of Eve: John Milton and Divorce*. New York: Peter Lang, 1984.

Wilson, Bryan. *The Social Dimensions of Sectarianism*. Oxford: Clarendon Press, 1990.

Wittman, Tibor. "The Image of the New Word in the Didactic Works of Comenius." In *Comenius and Hungary*, ed. Eva Foldes and Istvan Meszaros, 69–78. Budapest: Akademiai Kiado, 1973.

World Council of Churches. *Baptism, Eucharist, and Ministry*. Geneva: World Council of Churches, 1982.

Wright, David F. "Infant Baptism and the Christian Community in Bucer." In *Martin Bucer: Reforming Church and Community*, ed. David F. Wright, 95–106. Cambridge: Cambridge University Press, 1994.

————, ed. *Martin Bucer: Reforming Church and Community*. Cambridge: Cambridge University Press, 1994.

Wyclif, John. *On Universals*. Trans. Anthony Kenny. Oxford: Clarendon Press, 1985.

Yates, Frances A. *The Rosicrucian Enlightenment*. Boston: Routledge & Kegan Paul, 1972.

Young, Robert F. *Comenius in England*. London: Oxford University Press, 1932.

Zeman, Jarold Knox. *The Anabaptists and the Czech Brethren in Moravia, 1526–1628*. The Hague: Mouton, 1969.

————. *The Hussite Movement and the Reformation in Bohemia, Moravia, and Slovakia, 1350–1650: A Bibliographical Study Guide*. Ann Arbor: Center for Reformation Research, 1977.

————. "Renewal of Church and Society in the Hussite Reformation." Couillard Memorial Lectures, 1980. Bethlehem, Pa.: Moravian Theological Seminary, 1984.

————. "Restoration and Dissent in the Late Medieval Renewal Movements: The Waldensians, the Hussites, and the Bohemian Brethren." *Journal of the American Academy of Religion* 44 (1976): 7–27.

————. "The Rise of Religious Liberty in the Czech Reformation." *Central European History* 2 (1973): 128–47.

Index

✝

Page numbers in *italics* refer to illustrations.